Informed Decision-Making through

Forecasting

A Practitioner's Guide to Government Revenue Analysis

Shayne C. Kavanagh
Daniel W. Williams

Government Finance Officers Association

Copyright 2016 by the
Government Finance Officers Association
of the United States and Canada
203 N. LaSalle Street
Suite 2700
Chicago, IL 60601-1210

Library of Congress Control Number: 2016938866

ISBN 978-0-89125-002-9

Printed in the United States of America

Contents

Foreword

Revenue forecasts are the basis on which a government's financial plans and budgets are built because they provide insight to government officials on the resources available to deliver services to the public. However, accuracy alone is insufficient for forecasts to generate the most positive impact on the decisions made by public officials. As the role of the public finance officer continues to expand in terms of leadership, the finance officer becomes responsible for more than just the technical accuracy of the forecast. He or she must also take responsibility for making sure the forecast effectively influences decisions.

This book takes you through a comprehensive approach to forecasting that covers the technical elements necessary to produce accurate forecasts, and the communication and engagement tactics for making the forecast both a compelling message to its intended audience and a vital part of public officials' decision-making.

The Government Finance Officers Association (GFOA) would like to thank the authors— Shayne C. Kavanagh, Senior Manager of Research in the GFOA Research and Consulting Center and Daniel W. Williams, Professor at Baruch College School of Public Affairs at the City University of New York—for writing this publication.

A number of public managers contributed their expertise and experience to the research for this publication. We would like to extend our gratitude for their efforts. Finally, we would like to recognize the other GFOA staff whose efforts and talents were instrumental to the completion of this publication.

Jeffrey L. Esser
Executive Director/CEO
Government Finance Officers Association

.

Acknowledgements

GFOA's greatest strength is the dedication of its membership. A number of practitioners contributed to our research, reviewed draft chapters, and made other contributions that made this book possible. We would like to recognize these individuals below:

Quality Assurance Reviewers

- Dawn Marie Buckland, Director of Administration and Government Affairs Paradise Valley, Arizona
- Erik Colon, Consultant / Analyst, Government Finance Officers Association
- Bob Eichem, Chief Financial Officer, City of Boulder, CO
- Daniel Frockt, CFO, Louisville Metro Government, Louisville, KY
- Cemal Umut Gungor, Director of Finance/City Treasurer, City of Grandview, MO
- Robert Kotchen, Administrative Assistant, Government Finance Officers Association
- Natalie Laudadio, Communications Manager, Government Finance Officers Association
- Larry Lenahan, Budget Analyst, Louisville Metro Government, Louisville, KY
- Walter C. Rossmann, Assistant City Manager, City of Sunnyvale, CA
- Sam L. Savage, Executive Director, ProbabilityManagement.org, Consulting Professor, Stanford University
- Kathleen T. Seay, Director of Finance and Management Services, Hanover County, VA
- Marcia C. Wilds, Revenue and Economic Analysis Coordinator, Fairfax County Government, VA

Research Contributors

- Frank Avera, Senior Management Analyst, City of Reno, NV
- Mike Bailey, Finance Director, City of Redmond, WA
- Joseph Beach, Finance Director, Montgomery County, MD
- Mary Bradley, Director of Finance - retired, City of Sunnyvale, CA
- Ken Brown, Principal, HdL Companies, Diamond Bar, CA

- Gulten Celebi, Senior Operating and Budget Officer, City of Manhattan, KS
- Susan Dodd, Assistant to the Director, City of Sarasota, FL
- Tantri Emo, Deputy Director, City of Houston, TX
- Malisa Files, Deputy Finance Director, City of Redmond, WA
- Steven Gibson, Assistant City Manager, City of Rock Hill, SC
- Robert Hagedoorn, Chief, Division of Fiscal Management, Montgomery County, MD
- Jan Hawn, Finance Director, City of Bellevue, WA
- Stephanie Hettema, Budget & Financial Manager, Kitsap County, WA
- Sue Iverson, Director of Finance and Administrative Services, City of Arden Hills, MN
- Kalesha Kennedy, Budget Officer, City of Irvine, CA
- Thomas Kirn, Economist, City of Seattle, WA
- Andrew Kleine, Budget Director, City of Baltimore, MD
- Glen Lee, City Finance Director, City of Seattle, WA
- Grace K. Leung, Director of Administrative Services, City of Irvine, CA
- Kevin Lorentzen, Fiscal Long-Range Administrator, City of Bellevue, WA
- Diego Martin, Treasury Analyst, City of Santa Barbara, CA
- Amelia C. Merchant, Director, Department of Management and Budget, City of Roanoke, VA
- Charae T. Moore, Budget Manager, City of Colorado Springs, CO
- Michael Nadol, Managing Director, PFM Group
- Jill Olsen, Assistant Finance Director, City of Reno, NV
- Chris Parisot, Management and Budget Analyst, Town of Gilbert, AZ
- Ellie Paulseth, Deputy Director of Accounting and Finance, Washington County, MN
- Michael W. Pease, Budget Manager, City of Santa Barbara, CA
- David Platt, Chief Economist, Montgomery County, MD
- Arif Rasheed, Deputy Director, City of Houston, TX
- Toni Rezab, Assistant Finance Director, City of Bellevue, WA
- David Rodenbach, Finance Director, City of Gig Harbor, WA
- John Ruggini, Finance Director, City of Wauwatosa, WI
- B. Allen Scarbrough, Treasury Management Division Chief, Prince William County, VA
- Diane Shannon, Deputy Director of the Office of Management and Budget, City of Dayton, OH
- Kara Skinner, Chief Financial Officer, City of Colorado Springs, CO
- Penny L. Smith, Finance Director/Treasurer, City of Auburn, AL

- Kelly Strickland, Deputy Finance Director, City of Sarasota, FL
- Chris Swanson, Owner, Government Finance Research Group
- Holly Sun, Budget Administrator, Howard County, MD
- Shelby Teufel, Assistant City Administrator/Finance Director, City of Pleasant Hill, MO
- Katie Thomas, Assistant City Manager, City of Reno, NV
- David Vehaun, City Manager, City of Rock Hill, SC
- Cecilia Velasco-Robles, Municipal Budget Director, City of Tempe, AZ
- Lauri Vickers, Municipal Budget and Finance Analyst II, City of Tempe, AZ
- Mary Vinzant, Assistant to the Town Manager, Town of Gilbert, AZ
- Annie Yaung, Controller, City of Monterey Park, CA

About the Authors

Shayne C. Kavanagh

Shayne Kavanagh is the Senior Manager of Research for GFOA and has been a leader in developing the practice and technique of long-term financial planning and policies for local government. He started GFOA's research and consulting in long-term financial planning and policy development in 2002 and has been working with local governments on financial planning and policies ever since. He is the author of a number of influential publications on financial planning, including the leading book about long-term financial planning in local government, *Financing the Future: Long-Term Financial Planning for Local Government*, and *Financial Policies*, GFOA's flagship publication on the topic. He has written a number of articles on long-term financial planning, financial policies, budget reform, and other related topics for magazines including *Government Finance Review*, *Public Management*, *School Business Affairs*, and *Public CIO*. Prior to joining GFOA, Shayne was the Assistant Village Manager for the Village of Palos Park, Illinois, where he was responsible for managing all aspects of financial management operations, including budgeting, utility billing, payroll, and accounting. He received his MPA degree from Northern Illinois University.

Daniel W. Williams

Professor Daniel Williams has taught at Baruch College for 20 years. Prior to that he was the budget director for the Virginia Medicaid program and held other professional jobs with Medicaid. His research focuses on public-sector forecasting, forecasting methods, budgeting, and performance measurement. In 2006, he and co-author Don Miller received the Outstanding Paper Award from the International Institute of Forecasters for their paper "Shrinkage Estimators of Time Series Seasonal Factors and Their Effects on Forecasting Accuracy," published in 2003 in the *International Journal of Forecasting*. In 2014, he and co-author Joseph Onochie received the Jesse Burkhead Award from the Board of Directors of Public Finance Publications, Inc. for their article "The Rube Goldberg Machine of Budget Implementation, or Is There a Structural Deficit in the New York City Budget?" published in Volume 33 of *Public Budgeting & Finance*.

Chapter 1

Introduction

"Forecasting is very difficult, especially if it is about the future."
   –Niels Bohr, Physicist, Nobel Prize winner 1922

Forecasting revenues is a foundational part of budgeting and financial planning in governments. Revenue forecasts allow public officials to anticipate future resource availability and plan accordingly for things like enhancing services to the community, changing the salaries and benefits of public employees, and changing tax rates. Forecasts that look ahead 12 to 18 months in the future are used to develop budgets that are balanced and affordable. Longer-term forecasts are used to analyze the financial sustainability of existing policies and programs and to provide warning of potential imbalances in a government's financial future. A forecast can be used to create a shared basis for discussion of what the fiscal future might look like and, then, what actions can be taken to change the future. In the absence of a formal forecast, the implicitly held assumption is often that the future will not be much different than the past—an assumption that could be seriously flawed.

However, as Niels Bohr pointed out, forecasting is not without its challenges. With respect to public-sector revenue forecasting, GFOA survey research has found that the biggest challenges are:[1]

- **Ineffective forecasts.** The ultimate goal of a forecast is to improve financial decision-making; however, decision-makers are often much more influenced by factors other than the financial forecast.

- **Administrative burden / staffing capacity.** Forecasting is just one of many tasks that staff must perform, so forecasting competes with those other tasks for time and energy.

- **Lack of confidence in projections for out-years.** As forecasters look further into the future, the forecast becomes more uncertain.

The purpose of this book is to help public officials overcome the challenges of revenue forecasting. Overcoming these challenges will not often be accomplished by adopting more technically sophisticated forecasting techniques. In fact, in some cases, more sophisticated techniques may only exacerbate the problem. This is because more complex techniques may further strain limited staff resources and because they are less accessible and understandable to decision-makers, making the forecast results even less likely to be incorporated into the decision-making process.

Given that more complex forecasting methods are not necessarily the answer, this book is organized around the following basic forecasting principles.

Principle 1 – Simple is often better. Forecasting research has shown that "statistically sophisticated or complex methods do not necessarily produce more accurate forecasts than simpler [statistical methods]."[2] While complex statistical techniques may get more accurate answers in particular cases, simpler statistical techniques tend to perform just as well or better on average. Also, simpler techniques require less data, less statistical expertise on the part of the forecaster, and less overall effort to use. Further, simpler methods are easier to explain to the audience for the forecast. Of course, there are limits to how far a forecasting problem can be simplified. Hence, this book will heed Einstein's advice and make things "as simple as possible, but not simpler."

Principle 2 – An effective forecasting process produces an effective forecast. "Effective" forecasting is not defined by just the accuracy and reliability of the forecasted revenue numbers; it also refers to the extent to which forecasts influence financial planning and decision-making. Hence, effective forecasting is not just a matter of applying technical forecasting tools to a data set. Effective forecasts are a product of a well-designed forecasting process. A well-designed process requires forecasters to think through the interests of their audience and, therefore, ask (and answer) the right questions given their environment and audience. A well-designed process also requires forecasters to test their forecast methods in order to ensure that the most appropriate techniques are being used. Such a process also integrates forecasts into a decision-making system, so that resource allocation decisions are informed by foresight. Finally, in a well-designed process, the forecaster's message to his or her audience is intentionally designed and the lessons learned from one forecast are applied to future forecasts.

Accordingly, this book is largely organized along the steps in the forecasting process. The forecasting process covers the techniques you need for accurate forecasts, and the steps needed for an effective forecast, such as making a compelling presentation and integrating forecasts into planning and budgeting methods.

Principle 3 – Forecaster judgment is an indispensable part of forecasting. Some entries into the forecasting literature emphasize quantitative forecasting methods to the exclusion of the qualitative judgment of the forecaster. While quantitative methods are generally superior to qualitative methods for forecasting,[3] the forecaster's judgment is an indispensable part of making revenue forecasts in the public sector. Just to illustrate a few cases, the forecaster's judgment can and should play an important role when forecasting revenues for which there is little or no historical data available, or changes in the environment, such as a

The Ancient Art of Forecasting[5]

People have been attempting to predict the future for as long as there have been people. Ancient techniques of divination could be considered to fall into one of two categories: artificial (based on observation) or natural (based on dreams or divine inspiration). Artificial techniques included auguring (forecasting based on omens, such as the behavior of animals – think "Groundhog Day"), haruspicy (reading the entrails of sacrificial animals like chickens, goats, or oxen), and, of course, astrology. Natural techniques included interpreting dreams, entering trance states, and consulting the spirit world. Thankfully, particularly for the sake of farm animals, forecasting methods have evolved quite a bit over the years...however, our modern forecasting parallels of statistical observation and expert-intuition forecasts are far from perfect. The record of humanity's continuing but flawed attempts to predict the future counsels the would-be forecaster to maintain a sense of caution and even healthy skepticism.

change in enabling legislation for a tax, call into question the predictive value of historical data.[4]

Notwithstanding, purely judgmental forecasts have many potential weaknesses, so it will usually be a mistake to rely solely on the forecaster's personal judgment to produce revenue projections, or for forecasters to substitute their opinion for the results from a quantitative forecast. Consequently, this book emphasizes hybrid forecasting methods, which bring together the strengths of both quantitative and qualitative forecasting to get the best results.

Principle 4 – Uncertainty is an inescapable part of forecasting. Forecasts are inherently uncertain and the degree of uncertainty typically increases the further the forecaster looks into the future. There is no escape from this ironclad rule of forecasting. The degree of uncertainty can be reduced by using better forecasting techniques, but uncertainty can never be eliminated. Therefore, forecasters must accept that uncertainty exists, assess the level of uncertainty in the forecast, and effectively communicate it to others. In fact, communicating uncertainty may be the most difficult problem forecasters face. In this book, we'll see a variety of ways to manage and express uncertainty in the forecast.

Principle 5 – Size doesn't matter. Regardless of the size of the government agency, the principles of good forecasting remain consistent. While it is true that larger governments often have larger professional staffs and can hire staff with greater professional specialization, our research shows that smaller governments have their own advantages that allow them to achieve forecast accuracy and effectiveness that can match larger governments. For example, small governments have less complex financial and economic environments and the multiple duties typically performed by managers in small governments provide them with an especially well-rounded perspective on forecasting questions.

Organization of the Book

Before moving on to the next chapter and the first step in the forecasting process, we would like to provide you with insight into how the book is organized so that you can make the best use of this publication. First, we will cover our topic roadmap, next we will preview our sources of data, and, last, we will address our assumptions about the role of technology in forecasting and your skill with statistics.

Topic Roadmap

This book has three parts: the forecasting process, case studies, and conclusions. The first part of the book is structured along the seven steps of the forecasting process and comprises the bulk of this publication. The steps are described below, along with the respective chapters in which they are addressed.

Step 1 – Define the Problem. The first step is to define the forecasting problem. This will provide insight into which forecasting methods are most appropriate, what the audience for the forecast wants to know, and the political or other non-technical challenges that might impact the forecasting process. Chapter 2 is devoted to defining the forecasting problem.

Step 2 – Gather Information. Good information is the foundation for good forecasting. Forecasters will need to gather historical information on revenue yields, assess the impact of the financial and economic environment on revenue estimates, and seek out additional information to supplement their judgments. Chapter 3 covers these topics in detail.

Step 3 – Conduct Preliminary / Exploratory Analysis. This step helps the forecaster to understand revenues in more depth before producing a forecast. This improves the quality of the forecast both by giving the forecaster better insight into when and what quantitative techniques might be appropriate and also improves the forecasters' "sense" and "feel" of the data, which may be useful for judgmental forecasting. Chapter 4 addresses preliminary / exploratory analysis.

Step 4 – Select Methods. Depending on the circumstances, some forecasting methods will be more useful than others. The forecaster will need to put thought into selecting the best method and then test his or her choice before producing the forecast. Chapters 5, 6, and 7 describe methods that the forecaster might use: judgmental, extrapolation, and econometric regression. Chapter 8 describes how the forecaster can best select between methods.

Step 5 – Implement Methods. The forecasting methods must be put into practice in a way that produces a useable output and which takes into account and expresses the degree of uncertainty in the forecast. Chapter 9 covers the implementation of forecasting methods and Chapter 10 focuses on dealing with the uncertainty in forecasts.

Step 6 – Use Forecasts. Forecasts must be presented in a way that is compelling and the forecast must be used to impact budget decision-making. A forecast's usability is a product of the link between the forecast and decision-making systems in the organization, the forecaster's credibility, and the presentation approach. Chapters 11 and 12 discuss these issues. After the budget has been adopted, the forecast must be regularly compared against actual revenues and updated when needed. This is the subject of Chapter 13.

Step 7 – Evaluate Forecasts. Comparing forecasts to actual results is the seventh and final step. Chapter 14 addresses not only evaluating accuracy, but also how to evaluate the effectiveness of the forecast in shaping decision-making. Chapter 14 also recaps the most important strategies for improving forecast accuracy and effectiveness from prior chapters.

The second part of the book presents case studies of how governments have used the techniques described in this book to overcome challenges and better fulfill their missions as public-service organizations. Each chapter tells the story of one government and a challenge its public servants faced, the solution that was devised, and how that solution exemplifies the forecasting techniques shown in the first part of this book. Chapter 15 shows how the City of Irvine, California, reinvented its forecasting methods and integrated them into budgeting and planning in the wake of the Great Recession. In Chapter 16, we see how the City of Baltimore, Maryland, used long-term forecasts and scenario analysis to develop a long-term financial plan to reverse decades of economic and demographic decline. The Town of Gilbert, Arizona, and its use of forecasting to support planning for infrastructure maintenance is profiled in Chapter 17. In Chapter 18, the City of Boulder, Colorado, demonstrates how to forecast and budget under conditions of extreme uncertainty.

Chapter 19 is the conclusion. It recaps the essential points made in this book by presenting a checklist of key concepts for each step in the forecasting process.

Finally, *www.gfoa.org/forecastbook* is a companion website to this book that provides supplementary materials. In some places in the book, you will be referenced to the website for additional material.

Our Sources of Data

As you will see throughout, we are strong advocates of making the data underlying forecasts transparent. Applying the same standards to ourselves, we want to make the data underlying this book transparent. Below is an overview of our four primary data sources.

Forecast accuracy survey. GFOA gathered historical budget and actual data from a sample of leading[6] city and county budgeting practitioners across North America. We used this data to identify the most accurate forecasters and then interviewed them to find out how they do it. We also used this data to construct benchmarks for forecast accuracy. Below is a list of the governments that were interviewed. The accuracy benchmarks are discussed primarily in Chapter 9.

Our Highly Accurate Forecasters

- City of Gig Harbor, Washington (pop. 7,800)
- City of Pleasant Hill, Missouri (pop. 8,200)
- City of Grandview, Missouri (pop. 25,000)
- City of Santa Barbara, California (pop. 90,000)
- Hanover County, Virginia (pop. 101,000)
- City of Boulder, Colorado (pop. 103,000)
- Louisville Metro, Kentucky (pop. 760,000)
- Montgomery County, Maryland (pop. 1,017,000)
- Fairfax County, Virginia (pop. 1,131,000)

Forecast effectiveness survey. GFOA surveyed another sample of leading local government budget practitioners to find out which ones were making the most impact on how decisions were made with their forecasts.[7] We conducted interviews with the top scorers and gathered examples of their methods. These governments are listed below.

Our Highly Effective Forecasters

- City of Forest Lake, Minnesota (pop. 19,000)
- City of Sarasota, Florida (pop. 53,000)
- City of Manhattan, Kansas (pop. 56,000)
- City of Auburn, Alabama (pop. 59,000)
- City of Monterey Park, California (pop. 61,000)
- City of Palo Alto, California (pop. 66,000)
- Town of Gilbert, Arizona (pop. 230,000)
- City of Reno, Nevada (pop. 233,000)
- Kitsap County, Washington (pop. 254,000)
- Prince William County, Virginia (pop. 438,580)
- City of Tempe, Arizona (pop. 1,680,000)
- City of Houston, Texas (pop. 2,196,000)

Forecast competition. GFOA gathered historical revenue data from a cross-section of governments of different sizes and locations. For each data series, we applied a set of forecasting techniques to find out which techniques returned the best results. The results of the forecast competition are discussed primarily in Chapter 8.

Secondary research. There is a rich literature on what works for making forecasts as accurate and effective as possible. We have gathered the best thinking from a variety of academic disciplines and industries and applied it to public-sector revenue forecasting. Sources for each chapter are shown in the endnotes.

Our Assumptions about Technology

Microsoft Excel is by far the most commonly used tool for forecasting by local government finance professionals. While more sophisticated tools are available, they are relatively rare in local government finance and often require special training to use. Hence, we will not assume that the reader has access to any technology more sophisticated than Microsoft Excel. At the same time, we will assume that the reader does have access to at least Microsoft Excel and will, therefore, not cover the details of how to manually perform statistical calculations that Microsoft Excel automates. The book is clear on points where we assume that Microsoft Excel will be used to automate a calculation. For the more important calculations, there are endnotes describing some of the critical technical features of Excel. If you need help using functions in Excel, the Internet has a number of good free tutorials for almost any need.

Our Assumptions about Your Statistical Skills

We assume that you have at least some exposure to basic statistics, but we don't assume that statistics was your favorite class in college or that you have picked up this book eagerly anticipating learning the finer points of linear regression models. This is not a statistics textbook—we have omitted detailed descriptions of the statistical techniques underlying certain forecasting methods, especially where Microsoft Excel automates that function. However, some understanding of statistics is necessary to use many forecasting techniques, so we do include formulas and detailed descriptions of how to perform key statistical calculations. To help people with either basic or advanced knowledge of statistics make best use of the book, chapters that feature advanced concepts will provide notice in the introduction of the chapter along with advice on what readers with only basic knowledge of statistics should focus on.

Chapter 2

Step 1 – Define the Problem

"If you don't know where you are going, any road will get you there."
   –Lewis Carroll

Defining the problem a government wants to solve with a forecast defines the forecaster's goal, and the forecaster can then chart a path to reach that goal. Of course, the most immediate goal for most applications of revenue forecasting is to make a projection of what revenues will be 15 to 24 months into the future in order to enable a government to appropriate funds through a legally adopted budget. However, judging from the difficulties that forecasters often face in developing forecasts that have a satisfactory impact on financial decision-making, getting a set of revenue numbers in front of the governing board for adopting a budget is a necessary, but insufficient, goal.

Therefore, the forecaster should start the forecasting process by thinking about what the audience for the forecast wants to know and the political or other non-technical challenges that might impact the forecast. This will guide the forecaster towards providing decision-makers with revenue forecasts of maximum insight for the annual budget and for longer-term financial planning. While each local government will have some distinctive issues to consider, our research suggests that there are three questions that all governments should consider as part of Step 1 of the forecasting process.

Question 1: Where should we focus our forecasting effort?

Decision-makers and budget/finance staff have only so much time to spend on forecasting, so it is wise to focus that time where it will produce the most analytical value. The first consideration in deciding where to focus is the relative size of the revenue sources. Put simply, even a small forecast error in a large revenue could have a big impact on next year's budget and the projected long-term financial outlook. For example, in many governments, property taxes and sales taxes are the largest sources of revenue, so these should get the most attention during the forecast process.

A second consideration is volatility. Some revenues, like property taxes, are fairly stable and predictable from year to year. Other revenues, such as sales taxes on a base of highly discretionary purchases, present much more potential volatility. Wide differences in yield (with all else remaining equal) from one point in a year compared to the same point of the

The Time Horizons of Forecasts

In this book, we assume that most readers will be primarily concerned with making forecasts 15 to 36 months ahead, for the purposes of informing an annual or biennial budget. However, GFOA strongly recommends that governments also create longer-term forecasts. Usually, this book defines long-term forecasts as focusing on about a five-year time horizon, though longer-term forecasts are certainly possible and often can provide great foresight. This book also covers short-term forecasts, which have a time horizon of less than one year. These are used to make sure spending remains firmly within available resources and to make tactical adjustments to the budget where needed.

next year likely indicate volatility. Volatile revenues may require more intensive prediction methods or methods of presenting the forecasts that communicate the level of uncertainty inherent in the forecast. Volatility may also call for policies that guard against volatile revenues causing financial stress. For example, a policy could proscribe volatile revenues from being used to fund regular ongoing expenditures and encourage them to be put towards one-time uses. Conversely, a stable revenue source may merit less attention because it can be depended on to deliver consistent income from year to year. For a stable source, a simple forecasting model may suffice, and the forecaster can focus the bulk of his or her effort elsewhere.

Finally, the forecaster should consider if there are revenues that are too difficult or impossible to forecast. For example, state-shared revenues are often determined by political negotiation and other factors that are not easily modeled by a forecaster in local government. Trying to predict these revenues for an annual budget can be difficult enough, but forecasting them three to five years ahead could be very difficult indeed. So, rather than trying to do the impossible, the forecaster might concentrate on developing more in-depth forecasting models on more knowable revenues like local property taxes and sales taxes, and use a much simpler representation of future state-shared revenues.

Question 2: Is there significant growth on the horizon?

Land uses underpin the fiscal health of local governments. Local development growth (or lack thereof) entails a variety of challenges and opportunities for financial management. Hence, development activity will be important to revenue forecasts, especially longer-term forecasts.

Communities can be at various stages of growth. Some may be in a period of high growth, where large increases in population and construction are expected for many years to come. Some may be experiencing moderate growth, where there is still significant growth occurring, but build-out is within sight. Finally, others may be experiencing little or no growth.[1] Each of these stages raises different questions that a revenue forecast could help answer.

In a high-growth environment, the forecast will primarily be concerned with the impact of new construction in the community. There are two major questions here. First, is deciding when to include new construction in the forecast. Just because a developer has declared intent to build does not mean it is tax-money-in-the-bank for the local government, but there may be substantial political pressure to include the revenue in order to expand spending. The Town of Gilbert, Arizona, and the City of Irvine, California, are among the places in the United States that have grown the most rapidly in past decades, and, in both places, strong revenue forecasts are an important part of their approach to budgeting and planning. For them, the key to developing realistic forecasts that account for the potential for growth is a strong linkage with the community development department, which, in turn, has a solid working relationship with land developers. For example, the community development staff in Irvine survey developers twice each year about their development plans and compile the results into a report that shows anticipated growth up to Irvine's anticipated build-out date (around 2035). This report is then used by revenue forecasters to help create the assumptions behind revenue forecasts.

Of course, some developers are too optimistic about how soon development will happen. Therefore, the Town of Gilbert evaluates developer estimates to see if a different timeline should be used. Sometimes, those alternatives will be based on experiences the Town has had with a developer in the past and the complexity of the development. Other times, those modifications might be based on the Town's experiences with similar kinds of development that have happened in the Town or in neighboring cities. For instance, perhaps developments similar to the one proposed have usually taken longer than the proposed schedule. The Town's budget office works with the planning staff to account for these factors and to determine how the Town's development outlook might impact revenues.

The second major question for high-growth communities is how to estimate the revenue impact of new development once a realistic schedule has been devised for when development will occur. Relying on a developer's estimates is problematic because of some developers' natural propensity for optimistic estimates and the political incentives they may have to over-represent potential new revenues. Instead, the forecaster should seek alternative sources of information. Irvine and Gilbert have developed per-square-foot estimates of revenue, based on factors such as: the actual revenue received from other, similar developments; the experiences of other nearby cities with similar developments; and estimates from specialist consultants. These estimates should also account for the time it takes for revenues from a new development to reach their full potential after the development is completed. For example, not all retail space may be occupied by merchants on the first day.

Especially when locally generated sales taxes are a major part of the revenue impact, the forecaster should also consider the extent to which the revenue generated by a development will truly be new revenue versus just moving economic activity from one location in the community to another. Retail intended to support the local neighborhood, like a grocery store, will often not do much to increase the total sales in the community. Rather, residents will switch their existing shopping to the new, more convenient location. Generally, from 100 percent to 70 percent of revenue generated from taxes on spending by local residents will represent relocation of spending from one merchant to another,[2] depending on factors such as location and how distinct the new shopping opportunity is from existing ones.

Conversely, development that is highly distinctive or that is intended to attract people from neighboring cities or even outside the region may generate new spending and/or draw in new shoppers from outside the community. However, even in these cases the forecaster should consider if all the revenue generated is truly new revenue. For instance, might some people have visited anyway and spent money elsewhere in the community?

A community experiencing high growth may grapple with other issues as well. For example, what are the long-term net benefits associated with potential annexations? Annexations may or may not make financial sense depending on the use of the land and the difficulty of providing the new area with infrastructure and services. There is also the question of the long-term impacts of infrastructure financing. The government may need to incur debt to build new infrastructure. This debt represents a bet that growth will pay off. How sure is the government that growth will pay for itself? Finally, at this stage in the growth cycle, land use decisions are being made that will have major implications for long-range financial health. Are these decisions affordable? For example, an overabundance of low-density residential development may preclude more revenue-positive commercial development and may prove very expensive to serve in the future. Identifying the salient issues facing the community early in the forecasting process allows the forecast to address the issues in the later steps of the process. In Chapter 10 we will see how the technique of scenario analysis can be used to model the impact of highly uncertain future events.

For government in a moderate-growth environment, some of the same issues may arise as in a high-growth environment, but on a smaller scale. However, an important new issue to consider is the decline of temporary "growth revenues" as build-out approaches. Growth may have been at least partially financed by revenues, like building permit fees or impact fees, that might be classified as regular operating revenues in the annual budget, but are really a temporary resource when considered in a multi-year context. The forecast should account for when these revenues might begin to decline and the implications for financial health. For example, the City of Bellevue, Washington, experienced 1.4 percent average growth in the local labor force and about 2.4 percent annual population growth between 2000 and 2014. However, this growth did not occur evenly during this period—it occurred in cycles, leading to spikes in temporary development revenues. The City prepared for this potential source of budgetary instability by recognizing that the spikes in development resulted in short-term revenues. They chose to budget development permit fees in a separate enterprise fund and impact fees (which are one-time in nature and result from the impact of development) in their Capital Investment Plan to support the building of infrastructure.

Also, when a community has reached the moderate-growth stage after a period of high growth, it should place more emphasis on estimates of the long-term operating and maintenance costs of capital infrastructure compared to the revenue streams that support them. In the high-growth phase, the government is likely preoccupied with making infrastructure available. In the moderate growth phase, where build-out is on the horizon, understanding the liabilities associated with operating and maintaining infrastructure and the revenues to support these costs may assume a higher profile than it had in the past. In Chapter 17, we will see how, in the Town of Gilbert, revenue forecasts contributed to a comprehensive long-term asset management strategy as the Town's focus on serving explosive new growth came to include a focus on maintaining what had been built.

In a low or no-growth phase, the major question relates to funding the on-going costs that the community has incurred throughout its development. For instance, the forecast might address how revenues can support maintenance and replacement of infrastructure and other non-current liabilities, such as pension or post-retirement employee health care, while also funding day-to-day services. In some cases, a no-growth community may even face threats to its current revenue base. The continued viability of existing taxpayers may be more questionable than in the past. The forecast might need to account for their potential loss. For example, the City of Palo Alto, California, is built-out. So, there have been on-going discussions about how revenues from different segments of the community, like residents versus businesses, will support the on-going costs of operating the City.

Growth is Good (for Revenues Anyway)

A study of municipalities in the Chicago area demonstrated that high-growth communities enjoyed high rates of revenue increases for all own-source revenue (those not provided directly by the state government), even during periods of economic slowdown.[3] The study showed that municipalities in the highest quintile of population change had appreciably higher revenue growth than the lowest quintile when considering the periods 1994 to 2000 (good fiscal times) and 2000 to 2006 (bad fiscal times). This is true even for sales taxes, which are thought to be highly responsive to economic slowdowns.

Revenue Growth Advantage for High-Growth Cities over Low-Growth Cities		
Tax	Good Times	Bad Times
Property	+ 3.6%	+5.5%
Sales	+ 7.3%	+5.6%
Other	+19.6%	+5.1%

Question 3: What other political issues might impact the forecast?

Budgeting is fundamentally a political activity, so forecasts must account for political issues. Some political/legal issues might have a direct impact on the accuracy of the forecast. For example, a statutory limit on annual increases in property tax revenue would obviously limit what forecasters should project as future revenue. Other political issues might have a less obvious impact on the forecast, but are high-profile issues and, therefore, are of interest to the audience for the forecast. The forecasters should identify these issues and decide how to incorporate them into the forecast. For example, perhaps a community is having a serious political discourse about discontinuing the use of tax increment finance districts. This could have a significant, but uncertain, impact on future revenues, so forecasters would need to show how this policy change could impact the government's financial future.

Sometimes, forecasters might be tempted to leave highly uncertain or speculative issues out of the forecast because they are difficult to model or because they are concerned about the revenues from highly speculative activities being budgeted to fund expenditures. These are valid concerns, but the failure to include these kinds of issues (often the ones of greatest interest to decision-makers) in some fashion can lead to the forecaster losing credibility and the forecast becoming less effective.[4] We will have guidance on how to handle these kinds of special issues throughout the book, particularly in the section on scenario planning in Chapter 10 and the case studies at the end of the book. However, for now the first step is for the forecaster to become aware of those issues. The forecaster should examine strategic plans, records from public meetings, and talk directly with executive managers and/or elected officials to discover which issues are of greatest concern to them.

Conclusion

The first step in the forecasting process is to define the major issues that will impact how the forecast is developed and presented. This examination reveals the known unknowns: issues that have major implications for the forecaster's research, forecast model building, and presentation of the forecast. These issues do not all necessarily need to be readily quantifiable. For example, the forecaster must be aware of political issues that might impact the forecast. How these issues are addressed will have implications for the forecaster's credibility and the forecast's effectiveness.

Chapter 3

Step 2 – Gather Information

"The most reliable way to anticipate the future is to understand the present."
—John Naisbitt, futurist and author of *New York Times* bestseller *Megatrends*

Future revenues are usually, in some way, a product of forces and events that the forecaster can observe right now. Therefore, the purpose of Step 2 is to gather information about revenue sources and the current financial and economic environment. This increases the forecaster's expert knowledge about the general, persistent factors impacting revenue yield, as well as special, unusual events that can cause a disruption in the environment and in prevailing trends. Knowledge of both persistent factors and special events are important because they allow the forecaster to build better quantitative models and to better apply his or her own judgment to the forecast.

Step 2 also includes gathering historical revenue data. Historical revenue data is used to build statistical forecast models, and even where data is not used directly in a statistical model, it provides the forecaster with additional knowledge and insight into revenue behavior. Historical data combined with knowledge of the persistent factors and special events that impact revenue yield give the forecaster the best understanding of the present and the most reliable way to forecast the future.

Know Your Revenues

For local governments that have the most accurate forecasts, a rigorous understanding of how their revenue sources work is a universally critical feature of the forecasting process.[1] It allows them to build stronger quantitative models and exercise more informed and accurate judgement about revenues. A thorough understanding of revenue sources is also important for making forecasts that are effective in influencing decisions.[2] When the forecaster can cite relevant details about revenue streams and the forces that influence them, the forecaster's credibility will be greatly increased and, with it, the chances that the forecast will be heeded.

The first step to better knowing your revenues is to investigate them thoroughly – in fact, the City of Rock Hill, South Carolina, characterizes the investigation of their revenues as "relentless." The goal of this investigation is to develop a mental model of how the revenue works. A "mental model" is a simplified representation of reality that allows the forecaster to conceptualize the economic forces that impact how much income a local government generates from a revenue source.

While the forecaster's own expert knowledge and judgment will be important in developing a mental model, the best forecasters actively seek the knowledge of other experts, including those from other disciplines, to contribute to the model. A single person will only possess a single perspective, and the best answers to complex forecasting problems are generated by bringing multiple perspectives to bear.[3] For example, one of the City of Rock Hill's major revenue sources is water sales from the municipal water utility. The finance staff regularly confers with utility engineers to get their perspective on the factors influencing revenue. The finance staff learned from the engineers that low-flow water technologies were becoming increasingly popular among utility customers, which portended lower sales and, as a result, lower revenues. Rock Hill's experience shows that valuable expertise is located within the forecaster's own organization. Some other examples are:

- Community development staff can contribute insight into land use development trends.
- Economic development staff can give guidance on the performance of local businesses.
- A treasurer can comment on collection rates.
- An assessor can comment on property values.
- Public safety staff can provide insight into changes in enforcement policies that might impact the revenues received from fines.

Forecasters should also strongly consider connecting with their peers in neighboring jurisdictions. Fairfax County, Virginia, and neighboring Loudoun County have similar economic bases, so they regularly discuss local economic trends, share information on special events or other nuances in the local economy, and share their experiences on the usefulness of different kinds of forecasting models.

As forecasters build and refine their mental models, they should document them. Documenting the mental model reveals how a forecaster thinks about revenue, which enables the forecaster to share those thoughts with others, get clear and direct feedback, and update the model based on that feedback. The documented model helps the forecasters ensure they don't overlook any important factors that impact the revenue as the forecasters move through the forecasting process.

Although even a simple checklist is a great way to document the important causal forces impacting revenue, a more powerful way to document a mental model is an influence diagram.[4] An "influence diagram" is a pictorial representation of the causal forces behind revenue yields. An influence diagram can illustrate complex interrelationships between causal forces and can visually represent which forces are most immediately related to revenue yield.

The City of Boulder, Colorado, was one of the most accurate sales tax forecasters in GFOA's survey. Exhibit 3.1 shows Boulder's influence diagram for sales taxes. The diagram shows sales tax yields in the middle. It has two immediate primary influencers – tax rate and total taxable sales. The reader will notice that there are arrows leading from these two influencers to sales tax yield with a plus sign (+) in the arrow. This indicates that Boulder believes these influencers are positively correlated with revenues: an increase in the tax rate or total taxable sales would increase revenues. These two influencers then branch out into multiple paths. The colored boxes are thought to be the most immediately influential items, while the ovals are less influential and/or secondary considerations. A few items have a minus sign (-) in the arrow, indicating a presumed negative correlation. For instance, an increase in non-taxable Internet sales would have a negative influence on total taxable sales for the City, all other things staying the same.

The City has used the diagram to help ensure that the forecasters are placing the most weight on those items that have the greatest impact on sales tax revenue to inform the development of quantitative models. The factors that are most impactful on revenue yield

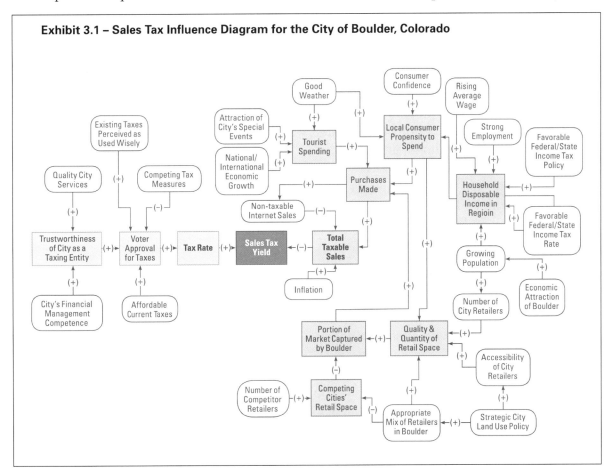

Exhibit 3.1 – Sales Tax Influence Diagram for the City of Boulder, Colorado

should be modeled to help orient new budget staff on how the sales tax works. The diagram is also helpful for explaining how the City's revenues work to people outside of the finance department. Chapter 18 provides a more in-depth look at how Boulder has used influence diagrams alongside other forecasting techniques to solve challenging forecasting problems.

Know the Financial and Economic Environment

Once the forecaster has documented the major forces that influence the revenues in a model of the financial and economic environment, either in an influence diagram or otherwise, the forecaster should further investigate these forces to better understand the major trends and events shaping them. For example, looking at Exhibit 3.1, Boulder might investigate how disposable household income in the region is changing, trends in the local tourism market, whether competing retail shops are being built near Boulder, and how the shopping opportunities for consumers in Boulder are changing.

Before getting into the details of how to assess the financial and economic environment, we should highlight a critical difference in how smaller and larger governments should approach the assessment. This difference is rooted in the *law of large numbers.* The law of large numbers says that as the number of observations increases, the average value of those observations will get closer to the expected average value for the whole population. To illustrate, the chance of flipping a coin and getting heads is 50 percent. Hence, theoretically, after flipping a coin any even number of times you should end up with 50 percent of the flips being heads. However, the chance of getting results much different from a 50/50 split of heads and tails is pretty good with a small number of observations. If you flipped the coin twice, your chance of getting two heads or two tails is not that small – there is a 50 percent chance of getting either 100 percent heads or 100 percent tails. However, if you flipped the coin hundreds of times, your chance of getting results that are drastically different from 50/50 are much smaller. For example, there is a vanishingly small chance of getting 100 percent heads or tails – far less than a 1 percent chance, in fact.

> ### The Chicken vs. the Egg: The Sequence of Knowing Your Revenues
>
> We have chosen to present investigating revenues and documenting the influencing forces in an influence diagram before assessing the trends and special events in the financial and economic environment. In practice, these two steps are part of a cycle, where investigation into trends and special events may cause the forecaster to change his or her mental model of how revenue works, which may then change how the forecaster approaches the assessment of environment. The forecaster should be not just open to changing, but eager to change his or her model in response to new facts.

What are the implications of the law of large numbers for analyzing the financial and economic environment? Imagine a state where municipalities receive a sales tax on automobiles sold in their community. Because cars are a high-priced purchase, the municipal revenue can be significant. As such, it is important that revenue forecasters understand auto sales. Now, imagine that a small municipality has one car dealership within its boundaries and that a much larger municipality has 100 dealerships. It is much more likely that the larger municipality's 100 dealerships, when considered in aggregate, will perform in a manner similar to the expected average performance for dealerships in the region. However, in the smaller municipality, there is higher chance that its single dealership will perform much differently than the regional average. For that reason, the smaller municipality should study issues specific to its dealership – for example, might a certain road construction project keep traffic away from the dealership, or will the dealer be carrying a popular new car model? For the larger municipality, studying each individual dealership would be neither practical nor necessary. It should focus on broader trends and forces that impact auto sales in the region, such as disposable income or fuel prices.

The general guideline we can take from this discussion is that smaller governments should focus their analysis more on the behavior and circumstances of individual tax producers (the micro-level), while larger governments should put more research into the broader trends and forces that most affect their tax base (the macro-level). This is not to say that smaller governments should not examine broader trends or that larger governments should not take steps to understand individual tax producers, but it does provide guidance on where emphasis should be placed.

With those guidelines established, let's turn our attention to macro-level measures of economic activity and how they can be used in the analysis of the financial and economic environment. For smaller governments, regional economic measures like employment, personal income, and housing sales will pertain to a larger geographic region than the jurisdiction's boundaries. This means that the small jurisdiction may not be able to draw a direct relation between regional measures and the performance of local revenues; however, the measures still provide useful general context and background. For example, the Finance Director of the City of Gig Harbor, Washington (population of about 8,000) regularly reads the *Wall Street Journal* and an economic report issued by the State of Washington to stay on top of broader economic trends. For smaller governments where a particular industry dominates the tax base, indicators pertaining to that industry might be helpful as well. For example, the City of Renton, Washington (population 97,000) has a large concentration of airplane manufacturers and an employment head-count tax. Hence, broader trends affecting the demand for airplanes could directly impact employment at the plants and, thus, Renton's revenues.

For larger governments, economic measures are often useful for more than just general background information. The geographic area covered by the indicator is sometimes a close enough match to the jurisdiction's legal boundaries that it could provide more direct insight into future revenues, perhaps even becoming part of a forecast equation or algorithm. Fairfax County, Virginia (population 1.1 million) acquires, from an economic forecasting organization, projections of gross County product and County retail sales, and County employment projections by sector, which then are integrated into the County's forecast models for sales tax and the business, professional, and occupational license tax. National measures might have a direct role in forecasting as well. For instance, Fairfax County learns about trends in car sales from the National Auto Dealers Association, which are relevant to the County's personal property tax.

In Montgomery County, Maryland (population 1 million), the most important revenues are income taxes and property taxes. The County collects data pertaining to these revenues from five different sources. First, the Board of Revenue Estimates, State of Maryland Comptroller, provides state forecasts for payroll jobs, capital gains, and income. The Board's annual December report is most important because it provides the most recent forecast used to derive the state's income tax revenues for the next three fiscal years. Also, it is the only forecast of capital gains available at the state level. The second source of information is property tax assessments, both real property and personal property, from the Maryland State Department of Assessments and Taxation. The third source of data is from a consulting firm that provides data on existing home sales and prices in Montgomery County. This data reveals possible changes to real property assessments. Fourth is another consulting firm that provides a forecast of total personal income, wage and salary income, dividends-interest-rents, existing home sales, and median home prices for the County. Finally, the County uses regional forecasts of housing prices, payroll jobs, and gross regional product from George Mason University.

In addition to gathering these sources of quantitative data, the County also convenes what it refers to as its "business advisory panel" meeting. The panel usually has more than a dozen members in total, including members and staff of the County Council, business executives from various industries that are critical to the regional economy, academics, representatives from the Chamber of Commerce, and the County Executive. It is convened by the County's Director of Finance. The County's forecasting team provides staff support to the panel. The panel meets once a year and receives a presentation of many of the data described in the preceding paragraphs. The panel members provide direct feedback on these economic assumptions, and they also have an open conversation about various economic topics of the day, with discussion questions prepared by the County's forecast team. The panel provides the forecast team with feedback on the veracity of the economic data that the forecast team intends to use as the underpinning for its economic and revenue forecasts, and also provides additional texture that simply isn't available from the County's standard data sets. For example, at one session the County learned that some of the larger property owners were experiencing difficulties getting the sales and rental prices they needed to make their properties sufficiently profitable, so they were planning to appeal the assessed value of their properties. This information had obvious repercussions for the property tax forecast.

Finally, the involvement of the business community in the forecasting process enhances the credibility of both the forecasting process and its outcomes.

A number of lessons can be drawn from Montgomery County's experiences. First, forecasters should know where they can access data that has predictive power for their revenues. Federal and state agencies, local universities, and consulting firms are three leading sources. Data from federal and state agencies often has the advantage of being available free of charge. Other local agencies or even local private businesses may be able to provide useful data as well. For instance, Fairfax County receives vacancy rates from its local economic development authority, which helps provide information on the current state of the commercial real estate market. The City of Grandview, Missouri, conducts quarterly conference calls with utility companies for natural gas and electricity future rates to use in its forecast model for utility taxes.

The second lesson from Montgomery County is that forecasters should know when they can access the data. Data from state agencies and universities is often made available according to a regular schedule. The forecaster should align the forecasting process with these schedules so that important forecasts are made soon after important data becomes available.

The third lesson from Montgomery County is to get multiple perspectives on the same economic phenomena wherever possible. You will notice that there are similarities in the kinds of data collected by Montgomery County across its sources. For example, more than one source provides labor force / personal income data and more than one provides housing statistics. This is because reporting economic statistics is an inexact science, especially when the statistics are projections into the future. Obtaining multiple perspectives allows Montgomery County to triangulate the most likely current and future economic conditions.

Fourth, forecasters should supplement quantitative data with qualitative information on the macro-economic environment, ideally from people who are close to the day-to-day economic activities that generate the revenues. The members of the business advisory panel have perspectives that the County's forecasters would not be able to duplicate. The panel approach should be accessible to almost any local government. For example, the City of Dayton, Ohio, (population 143,000) has its own local expert panel. The panel consists of two university professors, the budget director for the County within which Dayton is located, the Dayton City Manager, the Deputy City Manager, and a number of executives from some of the leading private firms in the area. The format of the panel's discussion and the results are similar to Montgomery County's panel. For both local governments, the panel meeting provides staff with a different and valuable perspective and the participants seem to enjoy the exchange of ideas as well – certainly, something that has proved important to the continued success of the panels.

Finally, it is never too early to think about the credibility of the forecast. Chapter 11, "Step 6 – Using Forecasts: The Foundation," will address the credibility of the forecast in much more detail, but even Step 2 is not too soon to start building credibility, such as how the business community's involvement in the panel does for Montgomery County.

Moving on from Montgomery County and macro-economic analysis, we arrive at micro-level analysis of the revenue base. The forecaster could conduct micro-level analysis at the level of individual tax/rate payers or significant groups of tax/rate payers. Here are some examples of micro-level analysis performed by forecasters:

- The City of Grandview, Missouri (population 25,000) monitors the performance of the top 50 sales tax producers in the community. Grandview's experience has been that the experience of the top 50 is highly indicative of where the rest of the tax base is headed.

- The City of Rock Hill, South Carolina (population 69,000) analyzes historical water-usage patterns over 20 years for detailed segments of its utility customers (e.g., residential, commercial, industrial, and wholesale). These patterns suggest what water use will be in the future.

- The City of Santa Barbara, California (population 90,000) analyzes how well the City captures sales taxes of local residents and visitors in various business sectors based on disposable income of local residents and typical purchasing habits of households in the region.

- The City of Everett, Washington (population 105,000) has a local corporate gross receipts tax (essentially a corporate income tax), and its major local industry is the manufacture of commercial airplanes. Reading press releases and official reports from the manufacturer about sales of new airplanes and making personal visits with the manufacturer's management to talk about how their sales were progressing helped the City better predict revenues.

A couple of lessons can be taken from these examples. First is that Rock Hill's earlier admonition to be "relentless" in investigating the details behind the revenues also applies here. Rock Hill could settle for analyzing usage at a higher level of aggregation or basing their analysis on fewer years of history, but the City feels that it would not achieve the same high level of accuracy with a less rigorous approach. Similarly, Grandview does not just accept the top-50 taxpayer data at face value – it looks for outliers in the data that might not be indicative of the larger trend and adjusts the data accordingly.

The second lesson is to go beyond the spreadsheet and out of the office to better understand the forces acting on the revenue. Everett's example is the most obvious illustration of this, but it applies to the other cities as well. Grandview engages regularly with the local Chamber of Commerce and its events to better understand openings, closings, and expansions of local businesses. We previously discussed how Rock Hill's forecasting staff consults with the engineers in the water department to ensure that revenue analysis models are consistent with the reality that engineers observe in their day-to-day jobs and, thereby, learned that low-flow water technologies had the potential to alter the trajectory of the City's water sales.

Know Special Events and Emerging Trends

The experience of Grandview with its Chamber of Commerce and of Rock Hill with low-flow water technologies illuminates a broader need for forecasters to understand special events and emerging trends, either at the macro- or micro-level. Special events or emerging trends could alter revenue yields from what past experience and current trends might lead the forecaster to expect. By definition, recent or upcoming special events and emerging trends will not be easily discernable from an examination of historical data. Therefore, the forecaster needs to make a special effort to understand events and emerging trends that could impact revenue yields.

Perhaps most important to staying on top of special events and emerging trends is simply to maintain a personal sense of curiosity about what is happening in the financial and economic environment, being observant of relevant details wherever they present themselves, and taking time to think about how what you observe might impact revenues. In the course of this process, the forecaster cannot become fixated on a particular thesis about the trends and events shaping revenues, but should exchange ideas with others and change his or her viewpoint when presented with disconfirming information.[6]

"When I find new information, I change my mind. What do you do?"

–John Maynard Keynes, one of the most influential economists of the 21st century, in response to accusations of inconsistency[5]

For example, in the City of Pleasant Hill, Missouri (population 8,200), the Assistant City Administrator and the Senior Accountant are primarily responsible for the City's revenue forecasting. The Assistant City Manager maintains regular contact with the local business community. For example, she attends Chamber of Commerce meetings and keeps in touch with local banks about trends in loans for new homes and businesses. By being curious and observant about changes in the business community, she learned that a major retailer would no longer be selling one of its most expensive products through its Pleasant Hill location, which portended lower sales tax revenue in the future.

In another example from Pleasant Hill, the City experienced a decline in sales tax revenue over the course of about six months. The City first assumed that a recent change made by the State of Missouri in how the sales tax was administered was the cause. However, data that the City was able to later obtain showed that a majority of the loss of revenue was attributable to businesses that left the City due to more restrictive zoning regulations that the City had started to enforce. Ironically, the data showed that loss of revenue was equal to the salary of the City's Code Enforcement Official. Regardless, the multiple complex forces that influence sales taxes, even in a community of just over 8,000 people, made it difficult to anticipate this loss through personal judgment alone. From this, the Assistant City Manager learned the importance of knowing the City's revenue base and using data to verify and challenge the assumptions that the City's forecasters might hold about how revenue will behave.

Forecasters in a smaller government often have an advantage in recognizing special events and emerging trends because, like the Assistant City Manager in Pleasant Hill, they have a wide range of job responsibilities besides forecasting, so they more naturally gain exposure to a wider variety of information sources. Also, because the tax base is smaller and less complex, it is often easier for forecasters to gain a good understanding of it by simply observing and recording what they learn.

Conversely, some governments, especially larger ones, may need a more structured approach in order to bring together the perspectives of multiple participants and to make sure that relevant forces are not overlooked. The STEEP framework can help organize how the forecaster looks for special events and emerging trends. STEEP asks the analyst to examine events and trends along five categories:

1. **Social.** Demographics, age distributions, consumer trends, etc.
2. **Technological.** Internet, new means of communication, old tax bases disappearing, etc.
3. **Economic.** Inflation, exchange rates, employment, disposable income, tourism, etc.
4. **Ecological.** Oil prices, climate/weather, water levels (e.g., snow pack), etc.
5. **Political.** Changes in federal, state, or local policies, etc.

Analysts should think about events and trends within each category, including the evidence to support the existence of these forces, historical lessons that might provide insight into the impact of these forces, the nature and magnitude of change these forces portend, and, ultimately, the potential impact on the government. Exhibit 3.2 shows examples of forces that might impact a property tax forecast in each of the STEEP categories. It is not necessary to find a force for every element of the STEEP framework. In Exhibit 3.2, there is no force identified for the ecological category for property taxes. Perhaps issues like weather or climate might be relevant to revenues like a utility tax on natural gas usage, though.

Staff in the finance/budget office will usually be the primary analysts of the STEEP framework, but others (e.g., staff in other departments, elected officials) can and should get involved as well. Besides contributing potentially valuable ideas and perspectives, these other participants will likely find the forecast more credible if they can see that their perspectives were taken into account. To illustrate, consider a county government that is developing a property tax forecast. The county finance staff could hold a meeting with representatives from the assessor's office, community development, and economic development departments in order to jointly identify relevant forces in each of the STEEP categories.

Gather Historical Revenue Data

Good historical data on revenue yields is essential to good forecasting for two reasons. First, many quantitative forecasting techniques, which we will discuss in more detail in later chapters, work better when more historical data are part of the forecast. Second, even if historical data will not be used directly in a quantitative forecasting technique, the data can provide a historical analogue that provides insights into the impact of events in the future. For example, what happened to revenues last time there was an increase in the tax rate or the last time there was an economic recession? As Mark Twain said, "History doesn't repeat itself, but it does rhyme."

Forecasters should compile revenue data for as many years back as is practical. The most accurate forecasters in GFOA's survey often maintained and actively used up to ten years of historical data, with some even maintaining much more. Generally, forecasters should make every effort to gather at least five years' worth of data for forecasting. This much data

Exhibit 3.2 – Hypothetical STEEP Analysis for Property Tax

- **Social**
  - **Aging population.** An aging population may have less demand for housing.
- **Technological**
  - **Increasing prevalence of intangible assets.** Intangible assets are becoming a greater share of firms' total assets, thereby reducing personal property tax liability.
- **Economic**
  - **Expected new construction projects.** Large new construction projects could be built during the forecast period.
  - **Housing market.** A depressed market means less demand for new construction.
- **Ecological**
  - None.
- **Political**
  - **Local government's policy towards growth.** The government could adopt policies that encourage or discourage growth – for example, the extent to which the government uses tax increment financing districts.
  - **Tax limitation.** A tax limit could be imposed by the voters.

is required to get a valid result from most statistical forecasting techniques and will give the forecaster a better sense of the historical trends behind the revenues.

Ideally, the data will provide revenues for each month or, if that is not available, for each quarter. This is because monthly data shows trends more precisely, whereas more aggregated data (e.g., annual figures) may obscure how trends changed within the year. Also, monthly data shows seasonal variation. Knowledge of seasonal variation is essential for short-term forecasting and, under some conditions, might improve the accuracy of annual budget forecasts. (We'll address this point in much greater detail later in the book.) For example, the City of Rock Hill compiles 20-year average utility usage rates for each month of the year in order to better understand seasonal-usage patterns. Finally, monthly data is flexible because it can be easily aggregated to a quarterly or annual view, if the forecaster requires.

Though monthly data is ideal, it is possible that circumstances might prevent monthly data from being obtained for all revenues. For example, perhaps the forecaster needs to reconstruct historical data from an old record-keeping system. This can be time-consuming, so how can the forecaster's limited time and energy be best used? Hanover County, Virginia, follows guidelines that should be helpful to all forecasters:

- For small revenues, annual data is sufficient. This follows the dictum that forecasters should spend less effort on smaller revenue sources.

- For larger revenues that the County doesn't receive every month, it maintains quarterly data. For example, property taxes are only received at a few distinct points during the year, so looking at the revenue data from month to month is not very informative.

- For larger revenues that are received monthly, monthly data is retained. For Hanover County, and many other governments, sales taxes are a good example.

Unfortunately, gathering historical revenue data for forecasting will rarely be as easy as hitting a button on the government's computerized accounting system. Usually, the forecaster will have to perform various permutations and manipulations on the data to optimize its predictive power. The following sections offer guidelines to help get good forecasting data from accounting data.

Observe Uniform Accounting Rules

Accounting records are the most common source of data for forecasting. Therefore, governments should establish rules for entering data into accounting records that protect the integrity of the data for forecasting. This will help minimize the number of adjustments needed when the data is downloaded for use in forecasting. The most important types of rules to establish include:

- **Categorizing revenue receipts.** Develop written guidance for the likely contingencies that arise when data is classified into specific records. For example, it would be important to differentiate sales tax revenues received from a tax amnesty program (one-time revenue) versus routine sales tax revenues (ongoing revenue). Each receipt should be clearly assigned to one revenue category; there should be no room for ambiguity.

- **Defining the date of receipt.** If, for any reason, revenue is not recorded on the day it is received into the organization, there should be a field for recording that date and a means of summarizing data by weeks, months, or other periods. If an accounting rule provides a definite alternate date (for example, for funds received in one fiscal period but due for another), the accrual rule should be uniformly applied.

- **Recording the date of receipt.** The procedure for summarizing data, including data received outside its routine fiscal period, should be written and applied uniformly to produce accurate uniform summaries of data for forecasting time periods. In particular, there should be clear standards on how end-of-period data should be recorded – it should not be left to chance if it will be recorded at the end of one period or the beginning of the next, as this creates unnecessary variability in the data. Where it is known that such recording errors have been made in the past, they should be corrected.

If the organization's accounting records do not match these characteristics, ideally, the forecasters should invest the time in scrubbing the data to match the desired formats, to the extent possible. There may be major challenges with modifying the accounting system of record, so the scrubbed data could be stored in a separate system for forecasting. If the data from the accounting system is not useable, annual financial reports can often provide at least annual data that has been thoroughly examined and adjusted for major errors.

Manage Historical Data

Historical data should be carefully maintained for as far back in time as is practical. Even if older data doesn't add much predictive value to the forecast directly, it can often provide useful lessons – for example, what was the impact on revenue the last time there was a rate change? Below are three types of data that can be used to maintain historical revenues for forecasting purposes:

- **Summarized data.** Summarized data aggregates related revenues into larger categories that can be forecasted together. For example, a government might develop a summary category of "licensing fees" that encompasses several different types of licenses and may also involve both revenue and repayment for overcharges. Forecasters only have so much time and energy for forecasting, so the summaries can save time by avoiding the need to forecast the individual components of the category (e.g., each type of license). Data for each summary category should be maintained for every month. (Annual summaries are much less precise.) Summarized data should be retained indefinitely.

- **Component summaries.** Summarized data aggregates multiple revenue types (e.g., many types of licenses) and even multiple types of transactions (e.g., actual revenue as well as repayment for over-charges for the licenses). These aggregations are an important time-saving practice. However, from time to time, it is important to reclassify some aggregated data. Before summarizing data into the classifications for forecasting, the data should be summarized within each specific revenue data category (e.g., type of license) and each specific transaction category (e.g., revenue receipt or another type of transaction). When there are a large number of data categories, judgment can be used to select more specific data categories that are most likely to be needed in the future. These component summaries provide the opportunity to reclassify data long after their original transaction date and, therefore, should also be retained indefinitely.

- **Detailed data.** The opposite of the summarized data are the individual transaction records. Forecasters should discover any need to ask about these within a couple months after first receiving summarized data. Therefore, whatever rules the organization typically follows for retaining detailed data on individual transactions should usually be sufficient for forecasting.

Find and Adjust Outliers

Outliers are extreme values in the data series that do not represent a "typical" data point. Outliers are a problem because the results produced by statistical forecasting techniques will be pulled towards the extreme value. Consequently, forecasters should take steps to find outliers and adjust them to reduce their influence on the forecast.

Finding outliers is the first step. A forecaster can visually inspect the data on a line graph to look for extreme points, but this is an imprecise method and may lead the forecaster to overestimate the number of outliers in the data set. Another method is to find the standard deviation of the data set and consider any data point that lies beyond three standard deviations from the mean to be an outlier. If the reader is not familiar with statistical concepts of standard deviation, it is described in detail in Chapter 4 and can be calculated easily with Microsoft Excel. To illustrate how this would work, if the standard deviation for monthly sales tax revenue were $1.4 million and the mean were $8.3 million, any monthly data point beyond $12.5 million ($8.3 million + $1.4 million x 3) would be considered an outlier. The forecaster would look for outliers on the low side by checking three standard deviations below the mean.

Once the outliers are identified, they should be investigated and adjusted. An investigation into the cause of the outlier data point might suggest the best way to make an adjustment. For example, Fairfax County, Virginia, found an outlier in its sales tax data caused by one-time revenue from a delinquent sales tax amnesty period and was able to identify and remove the amnesty revenues from the data set so that the revenue for that period reflected only the regular sales tax revenue. However, in other cases, such an ideal solution might not be available. Other methods to adjust the data include: [7]

- Reduce the outlier to the most extreme value in which you feel confident. For example, if Fairfax County could not identify the amount of revenue specifically from amnesty, then it might reduce the revenues to an amount equal to the highest revenue from a comparable time period that was not affected by amnesty.

- Replace the outlier with local averages, such as the average of the value immediately before and after the outlier. This might be an appropriate solution if the preceding and succeeding periods are otherwise thought to be substantively similar (e.g., no seasonal effects in the data).

- Reduce the outlier to the value of the third standard deviation. The two preceding methods assume that the forecaster has sufficient familiarity with the revenues to make informed judgments, so this method might be especially appropriate where the forecaster does not have a high level of familiarity with the data.

Finally, it should be noted that in some applications of the social sciences, simply eliminating outliers from the data set is an acceptable practice. This is not an acceptable practice in forecasting because eliminating an entire period would leave a gap in the time series, leading to problems when the series is used to make the forecast.

Adjust for One-Time Revenues

Sometimes a government will receive revenues that cannot reasonably be expected to occur again in future periods. Occasionally, these revenues will not reach the magnitude of an "outlier" as described in the section above, but the forecaster should still take steps to identify them and adjust the data accordingly. For example, the Louisville Metro government has a local occupational tax. A firm that is not based in the community (such as construction contractors) may not be familiar with the City's tax structure, and, as a result, they go without paying the tax for a time and then must pay a large lump sum of missed payments. Louisville adjusts its forecasting data to reflect what the regular ongoing payment from this firm is expected to be in the future, rather than allowing the one-time lump sum payment amount to influence their projections.

Adjust the Data to Optimize Predictive Power

Even when historical data provides a perfect reflection of what happened in the past, the forecasters might find it necessary to make other adjustments in the data in order to maximize its predictive power. Only the data for the most important revenues need be scrubbed in this manner, and the scrubbed data can be kept in a separate system (even just an Excel spreadsheet), as there would be obvious problems with modifying data directly in the general ledger. Below are four common types of adjustment:

- **Policy changes.** If revenue policies or tax rates change, historical data may no longer be a good indicator of the total income a government can expect from a revenue source. The forecaster may be able to adjust the data to simulate what revenue would have been if the new rates or policies had been in force. For example, the tax rates on cigarettes changed in Fairfax County from $0.05 to $0.30 per pack. The County adjusted its historical forecast data by first dividing historical revenues by the $0.05 to arrive at an estimated number of packs sold and then multiplied the result by $0.30 to arrive at an adjusted set of historical data. Making this kind of adjustment allows the data to be included in a forecast model.

- **Number of transaction days in the month.** The number of business days that happen to occur in a month could have a significant impact in recorded revenues. For example, fees collected in offices serving the public will be affected by the number of days the offices are open during the month. Weekdays can range from 20 to 23 days a month, a difference of 15 percent. This range may be further affected by holidays. When a revenue source is affected by the number of transaction days, the data can be corrected by determining the daily average for each month. A similar adjustment may be needed for revenue that is due to the jurisdiction on a single day of the week. If sales tax is due once a week and most businesses pay on Fridays, then about once a quarter they will pay five times; the other two months of that quarter, they will pay four times. In this case, the weekly average for each month should be used.

- **Changes in the tax base.** A government may experience a major change in its tax base. For example, in the City of Roanoke, Virginia, one of the two Wal-Marts in the community closed and moved to a new location outside the city limits, resulting in a sales tax loss for the City. The historical data needed to be adjusted so that it could continue to provide predictive power with just one Wal-Mart.

- **Other local idiosyncrasies.** Each government likely has some of its own idiosyncrasies that can affect the predictive power of its data. The forecaster should identify them and adjust the data accordingly. For example, the City of Boulder has some grocery stores in town that use a 13-month accounting and reporting period, which means that they sometimes remit taxes to the City less than annually. This creates some small peaks and valleys in the City's accounting records that need to be smoothed out for forecasting. Hanover County adjusts for the fact that it doesn't receive its revenues in a timeframe that is consistent with the occurrence of the economic activity underlying the revenue generation. For example, the County receives sales taxes up to two months after a local merchant transacts with a customer, but real property tax revenues are received immediately by the County when the tax is charged. Finally, Fairfax County sometimes erroneously receives revenue from the Commonwealth of Virginia that was intended for the City of Fairfax. The forecasting data needs to be adjusted to disregard this income (because the County does give it back).

Collect Revenue Base Information

Data on the revenue base can be a very helpful piece of information for forecasting. For example, the size of the tax base is useful information for property taxes, and revenue-per-unit produced would be useful for user fees. For example, a town might charge $115 for a marriage license. The per-unit revenue amount is $115. The revenue is the product of $115 times the number of units. Unit information is important to retain for forecasting purposes because a change in total revenues could be a result of a change in the revenue-per-unit or a change in the number of units. Knowing how total revenues have varied with changes in its revenue base is very helpful for estimating the impact of future changes. Revenue base information should be collected and stored with appropriate documentation. Data retention should be the same as with the revenue data. When aggregating data for forecasting purposes, the forecaster should consider the possible loss of future flexibility associated with aggregating unit data across multiple revenues (e.g., merging different rates). Sometimes limited resources, or limited significance to the total forecast will require such aggregating; however, it is still advisable to retain more detail than is needed for the forecast right now, because what doesn't appear important today may become important in the future.

Document Data Management Practices

It is important to document data management and adjustments. This makes the forecasting process more transparent, which helps credibility. It also helps in checking how the forecast performed and then modifying the approach where needed. For all data adjustments (related to transaction days, policy and rate changes, and building initial records from summary reports when necessary), the forecaster should maintain a clear record of the adjustment, exactly how it is calculated and on what information source the calculation is based, for what forecasts and forecast periods it is used, and when it first began to be used. All unit data, rates that relate to unit data, and methods of recomposing total revenue from units and revenue per unit should be recorded in the working papers.

Working with Consultants and Other Departments

Step 2 of the forecasting process is where the forecaster may start to work closely with other departments in the government and with outside consultants. These two relationships can have a big impact on forecast accuracy and effectiveness, so we will go into them in more detail here.

Working with Departments

Involving departments in the forecast is essential to accuracy. Earlier in this chapter, we gave examples of how departments like community development, treasury, utilities, public safety, and more can contribute information that the forecaster would not otherwise have access to. Departments can be engaged informally or formally. For example, Gig Harbor's Finance Director simply talks to his peers in the organization about trends they see in the community, while Fairfax County organizes monthly revenue review meetings and invites representatives from many different departments to attend. As these examples suggest, less formal methods for engaging may suffice for smaller governments, while larger governments may need more structured forums.

The information provided by departments can vary as well. For example, in Gig Harbor, departments only contribute their perspective on relevant events or trends in the financial and economic environment. In Hanover County, departments with relevant expertise provide direct feedback on the accuracy of the budget department's assumptions about the forces underpinning the revenues. In other cases, departments might be able to share specific data about what would drive revenue forecasts, such as the anticipated number of permits that will be issued, the expected number of participants in a recreation program, or the number of citations that will be issued. In some cases, a department might even provide a forecast directly. Which departments to involve most closely and what information to get from them will depend on the nature of the revenue sources and what expertise departments have available to contribute, but forecasters should always make the effort to engage departments in the forecast at some level.

In addition to improved accuracy, engaging departments also improves the effectiveness of the forecast.[8] When departments feel they have made a substantive contribution to the forecast, they are more likely to support it, making the forecast more credible in the eyes of others. Also, the details about the financial and economic environment that other departments contribute may help to create the appearance of a more comprehensive analysis. Finally, when departments feel that they are part of the process, they are far more likely to proactively bring relevant information about the financial and economic environment to the forecaster's attention rather than waiting to be asked.

Working with Consultants

Consultants can provide technical skills or resources that aren't economical to maintain on staff and/or can provide an outside perspective on forecasting issues, bringing different information to bear than staff. Consultants can help with technical skills, such as forecasting techniques, computer programs, or even cleaning and preparation of historical data. Some consultants may have highly specialized expertise in forecasting particular revenues for a certain region. For example, a number of cities in California use consultants to make property tax and sales tax forecasts. Many governments also find that consultants bring additional credibility to the forecast as impartial, outside experts, which can be helpful for raising issues that may not be very easy to talk about, otherwise.

However, there are a number of cautions when it comes to using consultants. First, outside consultants will almost certainly not have as good of an understanding of the local government's unique political and economic circumstances as the staff. This kind of understanding is critical to making the best forecasts. As such, governments should beware of outsourcing all forecasting to consultants. Second, some consultants may specialize in a particular forecasting technique and, therefore, tend to look to apply it to all forecasting problems. As will be discussed later in this book, the best technique depends on the particulars of the situation. Finally, if consultants bring to bear techniques that are more complex than staff can use on their own, there is a very real danger that staff will be unable to update the forecast in a timely manner and/or will not be able to adequately explain how the forecast was produced, harming the credibility of the forecast and reducing the likelihood that it will be used in the future.

Conclusion

Knowing the government's revenues and the financial and economic environment in which they exist is vital to the job of the forecaster. The governments that participated in our research emphasized the efforts they have made to better know their revenues and their financial and economic environments as essential to accurate and effective forecasts.

With respect to accuracy, expert judgment is very commonly used by governments to make forecasts, as we will discuss in more detail later in this book. If this expertise is not honed by the kind of practices described in this chapter, it can very easily be misapplied. The forecasters's expert judgment can also contribute towards building better quantitative models.

With respect to effectiveness, local government revenue forecasts take place in a complex financial and economic environment and the audience for the forecast, such as the governing board, usually does not have expert knowledge of how local government revenues work. If the forecaster can demonstrate a firm command of the facts surrounding the revenue and speak clearly and confidently to the issues in the environment that are of greatest concern to the audience, then the audience will be much more likely to incorporate the forecast into their decisions.

Chapter 4

Step 3 – Exploratory Analysis

After historical data has been gathered, but before it is used to make a forecast, the forecaster should conduct an exploratory analysis of the data in order to build familiarity with the data and to find meaning in the data. This will improve the quality of the forecast both by giving the forecaster better insight into what quantitative techniques might be appropriate and also improving the forecaster's sense and feel of the data. This chapter discusses the tools and techniques that the forecaster can use to find and analyze patterns or trends in the data.

Fundamental Tools of Exploratory Analysis

There are three fundamental tools for conducting the exploratory analysis: visualizing data with graphs to reveal patterns that might not be apparent from an examination of the raw numerical data; using descriptive statistics like measures of central tendency, rate of change, and measures of variation; and disaggregating revenues into smaller, more easily understood component parts.

Data Visualization

The most important part of exploratory analysis is to graph the data for visual inspection.[1] Graphs help forecasters see patterns and trends that would be difficult or impossible to spot with just an inspection of the numbers. For example, Exhibit 4.1 graphs the monthly sales tax data for the City of Colorado Springs. The graph shows that there are repeating seasonal patterns in the sales tax. The red circles denote January revenues, which are always the highest of the year due to holiday shopping. The green circles show revenues from

Advanced Content in This Chapter

The tools and techniques are presented in increasing order of statistical sophistication, so readers without much of a statistical background should focus on the first section, "Fundamental Tools of Exploratory Analysis," and the second section, "Business Cycles." They should also familiarize themselves with the concept of deseasonalization in the third section, because even if the reader is not able to perform the technical steps of this technique, it is good to be aware of the potential impacts of seasonality on forecast accuracy.

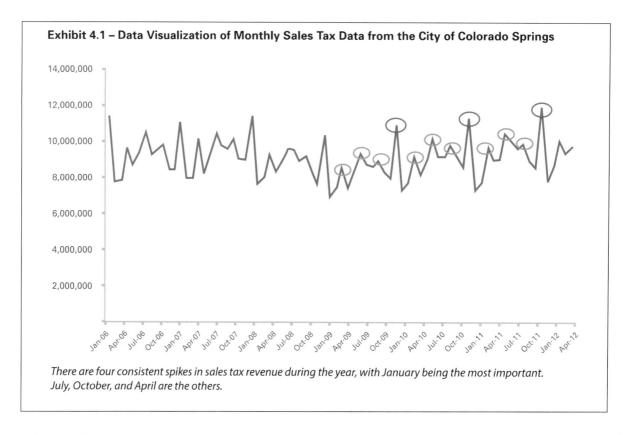

Exhibit 4.1 – Data Visualization of Monthly Sales Tax Data from the City of Colorado Springs

There are four consistent spikes in sales tax revenue during the year, with January being the most important. July, October, and April are the others.

July, October, and April, which all see revenue spikes due to quarterly sales tax filings for smaller vendors. The sales tax is often regarded as a very volatile revenue source. Exhibit 4.1 shows that there are certainly ups and downs in Colorado Springs, but the pattern is very predictable, which makes the forecasting job much different than if the volatility were unpredictable.

Graphical inspection of data is also helpful for discerning long-term trends in the data. Exhibit 4.2 shows monthly sales tax data for Colorado Springs again, this time back to 1996. With all of the seasonal variation present in the monthly data, the long-term trend is not necessarily immediately apparent. In cases like this, it can be helpful to apply a *line of best fit* to the data. A line of best fit is a line through a series of data points that is intended to best represent the overarching trend. A line of best fit does not necessarily have to be straight, but a straight line will be appropriate for most forecasting applications. Exhibit 4.2 includes a line of best fit that shows an increase in the overarching trend in sales tax revenue.

Statistically, the line of best fit minimizes the total difference between the actual revenue data points and corresponding points on the line of best fit – the line goes right through the middle of the data points to the greatest extent possible. The statistical calculations needed to develop a line of best fit are not overly complex, but are tedious to perform. Fortunately,

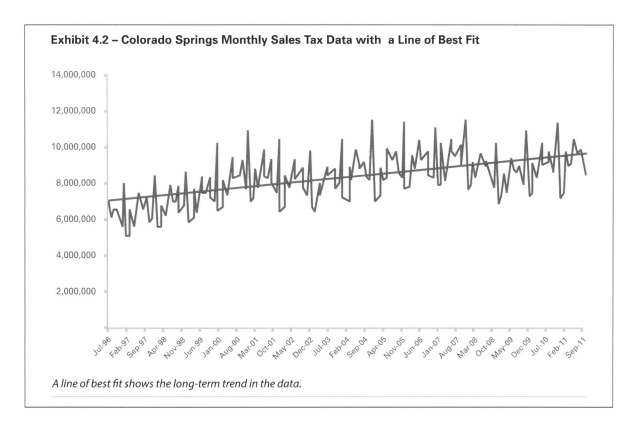

Exhibit 4.2 – Colorado Springs Monthly Sales Tax Data with a Line of Best Fit

A line of best fit shows the long-term trend in the data.

spreadsheet applications like Excel can automatically add a line of best fit to a graph with just a few clicks.

Finally, the forecaster might consider displaying revenue information geospatially. This might help the forecaster (and the audience) better make the connection between revenue yields and the on-the-ground activities that generate revenue in the community. For example, in the City of Arden Hills, Minnesota, traffic-fine revenue had acquired a reputation of being a fundamentally volatile and, therefore, undependable revenue source after fine revenue decreased precipitously and unexpectedly one year. To better understand the situation, City staff used its geographic information system to show the relationship between citation activity and roadway activity. They discovered that a major roadway closure had led to a big drop in the number of citations issued, which led to the decline in revenue. Hence, the decline in revenue was not the result of random forces, but was the result of forces the City could anticipate and plan for in the future.

Descriptive Statistics

Descriptive statistics describe the features of the data set. Common statistics include measures of central tendency, rates of change, and measure of variation.

The most common measures of central tendency for revenue forecasting are the "mean" and the "median." The mean matches the common definition of the "average" (the sum of all observations divided by the number of observations). The median is the middle observation in the data set. To illustrate, "5" is the median for the set of numbers 3, 4, 5, 6, and 50. For this same set of numbers, "13.6"

Exhibit 4.3 – Formula for the Rate of Change

Rate of change = $(Y_t - Y_{t-1}) / Y_{t-1}$

Y = Revenue for a given period

t = A time period (e.g., a month or year)

t-1 = The time period immediate before "t"

is the mean. Hence, each measure gives a different perspective on where the center lies. As our simple illustration shows, the median reduces the influence of extreme values on the measure of central tendency. The mean gives equal weight to all the values. For revenue forecasting, the mean will often be an adequate measure of central tendency, as most revenue data sets will not have the same kind of extreme values as our simple illustration above and because most of the forecaster's audience will have a more intuitive understanding of the definition of the mean, compared to the median. However, it can be helpful to calculate both in order to observe differences between the two.

Rates of change measure the percentage increase or decrease in a revenue from one period to the next and provide a sense of the direction of the revenue. Exhibit 4.3 provides the formula for the rate of change. Exhibit 4.4 shows annual rates of change in annual sales tax revenues for the City of Colorado Springs, including a 5-year average.[2] Though Exhibit 4.4 uses annual figures, rates of change and measures of central tendency might be especially illuminating when analyzing shorter-term data. For example, what is the average change in sales tax data from month to month during the holiday season?

Exhibit 4.4 - Rates of Change in Annual Sales Tax Revenues in Colorado Springs

	5-Year Avg	2011	2010	2009	2008	2007
Revenue	118,194,093	121,044,708	117,036,816	110,166,583	118,035,519	124,686,839
Annual Change	-0.3%	3.4%	6.2%	-6.7%	-5.3%	1.1%

The exhibit shows that, on average, Colorado Springs' sales tax revenues have declined by a miniscule amount during the five-year period. The problem with the average, though, is that it obscures variation. The five-year average of -0.3 percent implies that Colorado Springs' sales tax revenues have been stagnant during the five-year period. However, an examination of the individual data points shows that the City's revenues have been anything but stagnant! It is just that the ups and downs during the five years largely balanced each other out at the end of five years.

Because of this flaw of averages, it is important to get some sense of the degree of variation in the data.[3] The most basic measure of variation is the range. The range is simply the difference between the minimum and maximum values of the data set. So, using the data from Exhibit 4.4, the minimum, in dollars, was $110 million and the maximum was $124.7 million, giving us a range of $14.7 million. Including the minimum, maximum, and/or range of the data set with the average of the data set provides useful context.

You may notice some shortcomings of relying on minimum, maximum, and range as a measure of variability. Foremost, these measures say nothing about the distribution of the data. For example, do most of the data points cluster tightly around the mean or are they spread out and more evenly distributed between the minimum and maximum? These are not trivial questions. They have important implications for planning and budgeting. For example, if data points tend to cluster very tightly around the mean, that tells you that there is little variation and it is safer to budget revenues closer to the mean value. If the data points are more widely distributed, then there is more variation and it is riskier to budget a number closer to the mean (since there is a better chance that the actual revenues could be much further away from the mean).

A visual way to answer these questions is a *histogram*. A histogram is a representation of the distribution of data. A histogram starts by dividing the data into various discrete intervals (sometimes called "bins") along a horizontal axis, where each bin is of an equal size, though the first and last bin could be open-ended in order to capture outliers. For example, if one were to develop a histogram for rolling a six-sided die, it would be logical to have six bins, one for each side of the dice. Then, a column (i.e., vertical bar) extends upwards from the base of the bin, rising to a height equal to the frequency of data points in that bin. So, for our six-sided die, each of the bars would be at roughly the same height, given enough rolls of a fair die (i.e., not loaded). Since there is an equal chance of each side of the die occurring when we roll it, we should get an even distribution of results across all six bins. Exhibit 4.5 shows what this histogram would look like.[4] For data that has a much wider range of potential values than a die (like financial data), each bin could represent a range of possibilities. Perhaps one bin would be revenues less than $1 million, the next between $2 and $3 million, the next between $3 and $4 million, and so on until reaching a point where it is logical to develop a bin for all observations in excess of some amount.

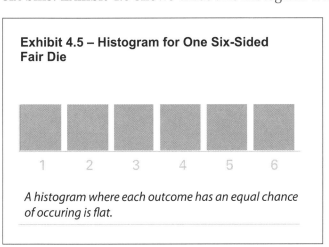

Exhibit 4.5 – Histogram for One Six-Sided Fair Die

1 2 3 4 5 6

A histogram where each outcome has an equal chance of occuring is flat.

The histogram's shape tells you the distribution and probability of different values occurring. For example, Exhibit 4.5 tells us that there is an equal chance of rolling any number, one through six. However, flat histograms are pretty rare in real life outside of a die rolling, because the real-life events that one would want to plot in a histogram are actually the result of many underlying events. For example, sales tax revenue is the result of many retailers selling to many customers. Therefore, real life is more like rolling many six-sided dice at once. For the sake of simplicity, let's take two dice rolled at once, where the possible results are two (two ones) through twelve (two sixes). Hence, snake-eyes might be like a retailer having an all-time worst sales year, while a 12 is like one having a banner year. Both

Why More Data is Better

The histogram for a six-sided die shows why more historical data is better for forecasting and analysis. Imagine if you had only three observations of the die rolling. Your histogram would tell you that at least three of the numbers had no chance of occurring. Even if you have 6 or 12 observations, there is a good chance that your histogram would be inaccurate because it is not that unlikely that you might roll a given number three times or not at all. However, if you have hundreds of observations, it is highly unlikely that you would get great differences between the total number of occurrences of each side of the die, and the histogram would look much like Exhibit 4.5.

are relatively rare because many things would have to go wrong or right, respectively, for either to happen – much like there is only one way to get a two and one way to get a 12 with two dice, yet many ways to get a seven (or have a mediocre sales year). Consequently,

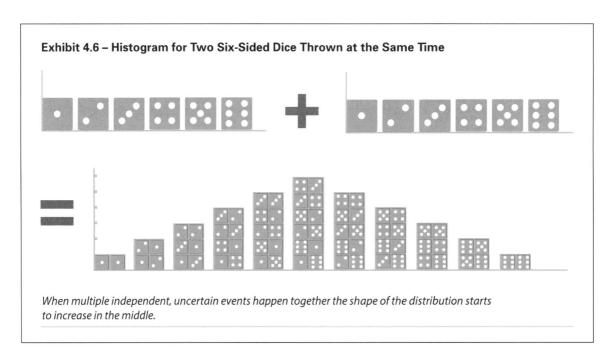

Exhibit 4.6 – Histogram for Two Six-Sided Dice Thrown at the Same Time

When multiple independent, uncertain events happen together the shape of the distribution starts to increase in the middle.

the histogram for two dice being rolled at once does not look like two single die roll histograms being put on top of each other, but rather looks like Exhibit 4.6, where the distribution starts to increase in the middle.[5]

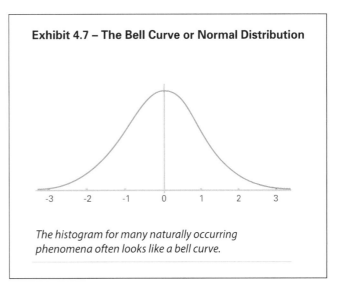

Exhibit 4.7 – The Bell Curve or Normal Distribution

The histogram for many naturally occurring phenomena often looks like a bell curve.

If one were to roll more and more dice together, the resulting histogram would begin to take on the shape of the well-known *bell curve* in Exhibit 4.7. In the bell curve (also known as the "normal distribution"), the ends of the distribution (also known as the "tails") get very small because there is a very low chance of an extreme result (think of the chances of rolling 10 ones or 10 sixes on 10 dice at once). At the same time, the middle gets larger because there are more ways to get more average results. Chapter 10 describes how Colorado Springs used a bell curve to explain to the City Council that while the staff's forecast (the middle of the bell curve) had the best chance of occurring, there was a significant chance that actual revenues could be higher or lower. Staff then invited the Council to discuss the different level of risk they were willing to assume in setting the budget. Would they pick a number above the middle and risk a greater chance of a shortfall? Would they pick a number less than the middle to decrease the odds of shortfall, but also reduce the amount of services they could budget for?

Histograms can be used to analyze volatility in revenues. Exhibit 4.8 shows histograms for a municipality's year-over-year percentage changes in total quarterly sales tax revenues and for changes in taxes from two specific categories of retailers. Looking at quarterly revenues provides more data points than would be available from looking at annual revenues. Looking at year-over-year data eliminates seasonal effects that would show up if we used quarter-to-quarter data.

The vertical axis measures the percent of observations in a given bin. The horizontal axis describes the range of percentage points that comprise each bin. So for example, for total sales taxes, we can see that about 35 percent of the time, the year-over-year quarterly change was between 0 percent and 4 percent. From the taxes from consumer essentials, we see that almost all of the time changes have been between -8 percent and +12 percent. The histogram also resembles a normal distribution. Compare this to taxes from auto sales where there is a much wider range of experiences and not nearly so neat of a shape to the histogram. Consequently, this City would need to be more careful about how it forecasts and budgets revenues from auto sales compared to consumer essentials.

In versions of Excel prior to Excel 2016, static histograms can be created with the Microsoft "Analysis ToolPak" add-in. Starting with Excel 2016, an interactive histogram became available as a native chart feature, similar to Excel's other standard chart functions.

Moving on from histograms, a discussion of measures of variation would be incomplete without a discussion of *standard deviation*. Standard deviation is a descriptive statistic of how dispersed data is from the middle (mean) of the data set. For a given data set that is normally distributed (i.e., where the histogram looks like a bell curve), most of the observations (68 percent) lie within one standard deviation of the mean, while the vast majority (95 percent) lie within two standard deviations of the mean.[6] Exhibit 4.7 provides a visual representation of the standard deviations in a bell curve, where +/- 1 is one standard deviation away from the mean, and so on. As you can see, most of the area of the histogram lies within one standard deviation of the mean and the vast majority within two.

Standard deviation can provide a sense of how much variability there is in the data set. For a given mean, a higher standard deviation would indicate more variation, while a lower number would indicate less variation. For example, if our mean is 100 and the standard deviation is 10, then 68 percent of the observations lie between 90 and 110 and 95 percent lie between 80 and 120. If our mean is 100 and our standard deviation is 15, then 68 percent of the observations lie between 85 and 115.

Standard deviation can be used to help estimate how unusual revenue incomes are for

Exhibit 4.8 – Histograms of Sales Tax Volatility

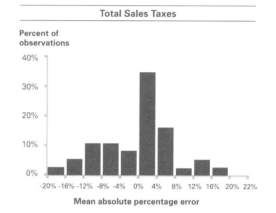

Total Sales Taxes

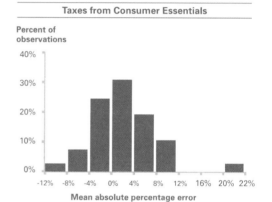

Taxes from Consumer Essentials

Much less volatility

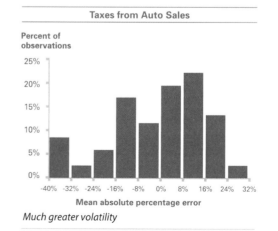

Taxes from Auto Sales

Much greater volatility

a given period. For example, in Chapter 3 we discussed that any observation that is outside of three standard deviations from the mean is an outlier and should be adjusted. Forecasters might also wish to examine observations between two and three standard deviations from the mean, not necessarily to adjust them, but to see what might be learned from these unusual observations for predicting future large deviations from historical patterns.

A detailed explanation of the formula used to calculate standard deviation is beyond the scope of this chapter, but any statistical textbook and many free Internet resources can provide one. At this point, the lessons for the reader to understand about standard deviation are:

- Standard deviation is a statistical measure of variation.

- Standard deviation can be easily calculated using standard Excel formulas.[7]

- Standard deviation is used as part of a number of statistical forecasting techniques, so forecasting technicians will need to be familiar with the concept.

- The formula used to calculate standard deviation is not overly complex, but the explanation of standard deviation is not intuitive to a lay audience. Therefore, the forecaster will be better off using histograms to communicate the level of historical variation in revenue to others.

Disaggregation

Disaggregation is a powerful tool for forecasting because it breaks a potentially daunting forecasting problem down into less demanding tasks. A larger series of data, like "property taxes," may actually contain smaller series of data that will be easier to analyze on their own. For instance, it might be easier to analyze residential property taxes and commercial property taxes separately. Similarly, sales tax revenues may comprise many different types of underlying components, all with very different revenue yield patterns. Rather than attempting to forecast all at once, it might be easier to forecast yields for different sources of sales tax and then aggregate the results. Disaggregation could also be used to break revenues into components such as units and dollars per unit. This might be particularly useful for revenues like water sales (price per thousand gallons), intergovernmental revenues (which are often distributed on a per capita basis), or permits or citations. This kind disaggregation could also be useful for more general tax revenues. For instance, an estimate of municipal revenue per square foot of commercial space could be used to forecast the revenue generated from a new shopping complex.

Exhibit 4.9 shows how sales taxes could be disaggregated in Colorado Springs. In Colorado Springs, "sales taxes" are actually composed of retail sales taxes, a use tax, and revenue from audits of sales tax producers, though all are generally regarded as "sales tax" revenue during budget discussions. Exhibit 4.9 shows that the annual rates of change are much more variable for the use tax and the audit revenues than for the retail sales tax. The bottom rows reproduce the aggregate sales tax data that was originally in Exhibit 4.4, for comparative purposes. The rate of change in the aggregate sales tax number differs, often substantially, from the rate of change for the retail sales tax numbers. Because each of the components of the sales tax behaves very differently, there could be advantages to forecasting each separately and then re-aggregating the results.

Exhibit 4.9 – Disaggregated Sales Tax Revenue in Colorado Springs

	2011	2010	2009	2008	2007
5-Year Trends for Retail Sales Tax Only					
Revenue	111,735,533	108,212,533	101,247,887	107,356,298	113,211,788
Annual Change	3.3%	6.9%	-5.7%	-5.2%	1.7%
5-Year Trends for Use Tax					
Revenue	6,024,785	6,454,560	5,668,451	8,490,105	9,264,952
Annual Change	-6.7%	13.9%	-33.2%	-8.4%	-12.4%
5-Year Trends for Sales Tax Audit Revenue					
Revenue	3,284,390	2,369,723	3,250,245	2,189,116	2,210,099
Annual Change	32.8%	-27.1%	48.5%	-0.9%	51.3%
5-Year Trend for All "Sales Tax" Revenue					
Revenue	121,044,708	117,036,816	110,166,583	118,035,519	124,686,839
Annual Change	3.4%	6.2%	-6.7%	-5.3%	1.1%

The City of Seattle forecasts sales taxes in eight separate categories (i.e., general retailing, other retail, wholesale trade, construction, etc.) or, if the time available for forecasting is short, along three separate categories (i.e., retail trade, construction, all else). Seattle has found that the more disaggregated model is more accurate most, but not all, of the time. In general, the differences were not large, but the more disaggregated model performs better when the economy is headed into recession or is in recession. This could be because the more disaggregated model is more sensitive to industries that are more heavily impacted by recession (e.g., construction) and because it is easier to apply the forecaster's judgment to a disaggregated model. In other words, it is easier for the forecaster to precisely think about and apply factors that might influence individual industries, compared to doing the same for the entire sales tax base at once.

Business Cycles

Beyond the fundamentals of exploratory analysis, the forecaster will potentially want to examine other more complex issues within the data, starting with *business cycles*. Business cycles are fluctuations in economic activity that an economy experiences over a period of time and are typically characterized by recessions or expansions.[9] It can be helpful to understand how sensitive revenue has been to expansions and recessions. Exhibit 4.2 showed a line of best fit for Colorado Springs' sales tax revenue, but was not helpful for showing how the sales tax reacted to the ups and downs of the economy. To address this, Exhibit 4.10 replaces the line of best fit with a *trend-cycle line* for sales tax overlaid on monthly sales tax revenues. As the name implies, a trend-cycle line is intended to show longer-term trends and the impact of cyclical phenomena. It does this by smoothing out seasonal variation, leaving behind the cyclical pattern.

The trend-cycle line is easy to calculate using a "centered moving average" for a 12-month period. To illustrate, a simplified 12-month centered moving average defines the average value for a given month as the mean of that month plus the six months before, and the five months after.[10] So, for example, in Exhibit 4.10, the moving average for January '05 would be an average of the revenues for August '04 through July '05. February '05 would be an average of September '04 through August '05, and so on. The trend-cycle in Exhibit 4.10 more clearly shows the impact of the 2001 "dot.bomb" recession and the 2007 "Great Recession" on the City's revenue than looking at the monthly data alone. The red arrows mark the beginning and end points of the two downturns, providing insight into the depth and length of the downturns for Colorado Springs – potentially useful information for forecasting during downturns or expansions in the future.

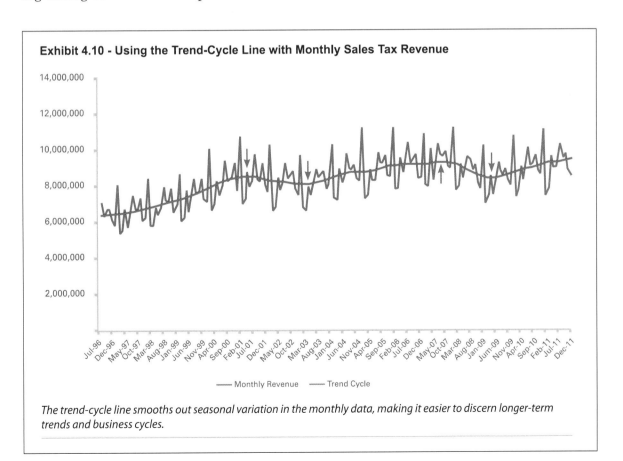

Exhibit 4.10 - Using the Trend-Cycle Line with Monthly Sales Tax Revenue

The trend-cycle line smooths out seasonal variation in the monthly data, making it easier to discern longer-term trends and business cycles.

Seasonality

Using a moving average to reveal the trend-cycle line has the effect of smoothing out seasonal variation. However, seasonal variation is important in its own right. In forecasting, *seasonality* refers to the existence of a data pattern that recurs over a standard time period. Commonly, the standard time period is a year and the data seasons at least partly correspond to the common weather seasons: spring, summer, fall, and winter. However, seasonality in forecasting does not necessarily mean that the period of time is a year or that seasons correspond to weather seasons. For example, a utility billing operation typically sends bills at the same time each month, resulting in an influx of revenue within a certain time period after the billing. In this case, the time period in question is a month and the cause of the seasonality is the timing of the billing cycle. We saw earlier in this chapter how the quarterly filing of sales taxes caused a seasonal pattern in sales tax data in Colorado Springs. If, for the sake of discussion, Colorado had monthly filings instead of quarterly filings, we would likely observe fairly even tax revenues for most of the year, except for the holiday shopping season when we would see a recurring uptick in sales tax revenue – a form of seasonality. Seasonality could even be observed in a shorter time period, such as a week or even days. To illustrate weekly seasonality, perhaps a recreation operation has more walk-ins for its programs on weekends than on weekdays.

When data is recorded in periods of less than one year (e.g., quarters or months), it is important to recognize where seasonal patterns exist, because seasonal patterns could reduce the accuracy of quantitative extrapolation techniques that use monthly or quarterly data. This is because extrapolation techniques seek to forecast forward the underlying trend in the data. Seasonal variations in the data create "noise" that makes it difficult for the forecasting technique to accurately discern and forecast the underlying trend. A study of the accuracy of various statistical techniques showed that seasonal adjustment (i.e., adjusting the data to take out seasonal effects) reduced the size of the forecasting error, on average, by over 25 percent.[11]

That said, under some circumstances seasonal adjustment may not substantially improve an aggregate annual forecast (i.e., a forecast made by adding up 12 monthly results or 4 quarterly results), but there is little evidence that it ever makes the forecast worse when the data exhibits seasonality. Seasonal adjustment is more likely to have a larger positive impact when forecasting a given month or quarter, rather than a whole year. Therefore, forecasters should first examine the data to see if there are important seasonal patterns, which we will demonstrate in the following paragraphs. If there are important seasonal patterns, the forecaster can experiment with deseasonalization techniques to see if accuracy can be significantly improved.

To see whether there is a seasonal pattern, it is helpful to graph the data in overlapping annual periods. Exhibit 4.11 shows the net personal income tax receipts for New York State[12] beginning with Fiscal Year 2007; the data are graphed over calendar years for convenience, so month 1 is January. There is clear peaking in January and April, with less pronounced quarter end peaks except in March. It is perfectly reasonable to conclude that these data are likely seasonal.

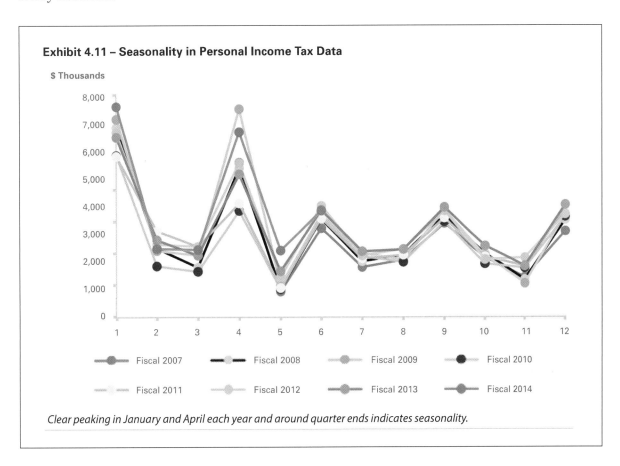

Exhibit 4.11 – Seasonality in Personal Income Tax Data

Clear peaking in January and April each year and around quarter ends indicates seasonality.

Exhibit 4.12 shows a non-seasonal pattern of peaks and troughs for the total revenue other than personal tax receipts. Although there is a pronounced peak in July for one year, June in another year, September in a third, and December in yet another, the only possible consistent uptick is with December, and it is at most very modest. Treating these data as seasonal is likely to introduce more error than it removes.[13]

You can visit *www.gfoa.org/forecastbook* for additional examples of how to inspect for seasonality using graphs. However, you should be aware that all of our examples have rather unambiguously shown seasonal impacts. In real life, visual inspection of the data may not offer quite the same level of certainty.[14]

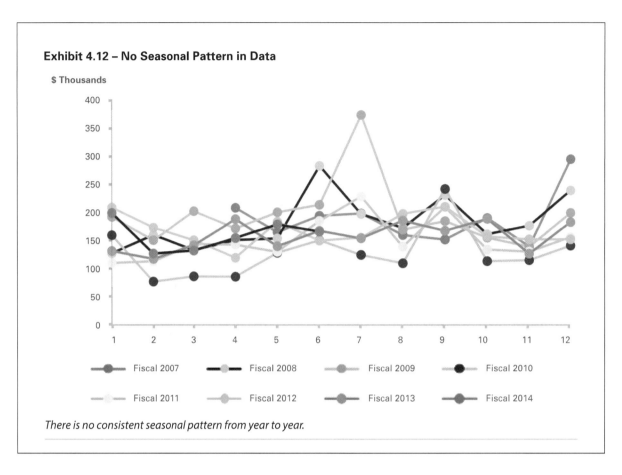

Exhibit 4.12 – No Seasonal Pattern in Data

There is no consistent seasonal pattern from year to year.

Correcting Seasonality with Classical Decomposition

There are many methods of correcting for seasonality (also known as *deseasonalization*), some of which require sophisticated software and extensive effort to model seasonal factors. In this chapter, we cover what is probably the most accessible method for deseasonalization: *classical decomposition*. Classical decomposition is a relatively simple method, but the reader should be cautioned to place emphasis on "relatively." Classical decomposition still requires some mathematical acumen to perform. If it seems to be beyond the capabilities of the forecaster, it may be wise to consider procuring outside assistance with adjusting data for seasonality.

Before getting into the specifics of how to perform classical decomposition, it will be useful to become familiar with a bit of the theory that underlies seasonal adjustment methods. The theory is that the observed revenue can be decomposed into three elements: seasonal, trend, and error. In other words, some portion of the observation is due to the fundamental underlying trend in the revenue, part is caused by seasonal variation, and another portion is caused by random variation (also sometimes referred to as "error" in forecasting science).

- **Seasonal:** Represents variation that regularly occurs during certain points of the year, such as the holiday spending or quarterly filings in Colorado Springs.
- **Trend:** Comprises the fundamental underlying trend in the data. Trend tells us in which direction revenues are headed, independent of seasonal variation. Exhibit 4.10 provides an illustration of a trend.
- **Error:** Accounts for random variation that isn't explained by seasonal or trend effects. Practically speaking, the error component is what is left after taking seasonal and trend effects into account.

Essentially, what we are trying to do with deseasonalization is to separate the seasonal component from trend and error.

It is also important to know that the mathematical relationship between the seasonal component and the trend component could be multiplicative or additive. A *multiplicative relationship* means that the size of the seasonal effect increases proportionately with increases in the trend. For example, imagine that income tax revenues are growing over time because the population is growing (a trend). Proportionately, more people would now be filing income tax returns in April, so the seasonal component would be some multiple larger than before. An *additive relationship* means that the seasonal component is just added on top of the trend and doesn't change proportionally with changes in the trend. A multiplicative relationship is more common in most revenues, so we will focus on that, but we will also show how to handle an additive relationship.

Exhibit 4.13 illustrates multiplicative classical decomposition, with income tax data. Column (2) shows the month and year, while column (1) provides a numeric sequencer to help keep track of the periods in the data set. Note that this data set actually has 87 observations, seven years and a quarter, but Exhibit 4.13 shows only first 24. All 87 are used in the calculations. You may download the entire data set and calculations at *www.gfoa.org/forecastbook*.

In column (3), we show the actual data. These data are somewhat simplified for demonstration purposes, but the full unmodified data should be used for practical purposes (except for removing outliers or other idiosyncrasies that compromise the predictive value of the data, as was discussed in the previous chapter).

The calculation of classical decomposition begins with column (4), labeled Centered MA-12, which calculates a 12-month centered moving average. The concept of a 12-month centered moving average was explained in detail in the earlier section on business cycles in this chapter. In Exhibit 4.13, the 12-month moving average of $2,882 that appears in period 7 is the average of the values of column (3) for periods 1 through 12. The 12-month moving average $3,259 for period 24 is the average of period 18 through 29 (25 through 29 are not pictured). Note that if the seasonal period is of some other length, the moving average

Exhibit 4.13 – Classical Decomposition Method of Seasonal Adjustment, Assuming Multiplicative Seasonal Factors

(1) Period from Start	(2) Month & Year	(3) Revenue Amount	(4) Centered MA-12	(5) MA-2	(6) Raw Seasonal Factors	(7) Average	(8) Adjusted	(9) Damped Seasonal Factors	(10) Use Seasonal Factors	(11) Deseasonalized Data
1	4/1/2006	5,560							1.6926	3,285
2	5/1/2006	918							0.3978	2,308
3	6/1/2006	3,191							1.2099	2,637
4	7/1/2006	1,786							0.7128	2,506
5	8/1/2006	2,049							0.7224	2,836
6	9/1/2006	3,373							1.1963	2,820
7	10/1/2006	2,132	2,882	2,873	0.7421	0.7094	0.7099	0.7128	0.7128	2,991
8	11/1/2006	1,421	2,865	2,868	0.4955	0.5304	0.5308	0.5355	0.5355	2,654
9	12/1/2006	3,083	2,871	2,885	1.0685	1.1751	1.1759	1.1741	1.1741	2,626
10	1/1/2007	6,816	2,899	2,908	2.3438	2.1189	2.1203	2.1091	2.1091	3,232
11	2/1/2007	2,465	2,917	2,925	0.8429	0.8284	0.8290	0.8307	0.8307	2,967
12	3/1/2007	1,785	2,932	2,944	0.6064	0.7026	0.7031	0.7060	0.7060	2,528
13	4/1/2007	5,356	2,955	2,961	1.8092	1.6984	1.6996	1.6926	1.6926	3,164
14	5/1/2007	998	2,966	2,963	0.3368	0.3915	0.3917	0.3978	0.3978	2,509
15	6/1/2007	3,528	2,959	2,975	1.1853	1.2112	1.2120	1.2099	1.2099	2,916
16	7/1/2007	1,995	2,993	3,005	0.6637	0.7094	0.7099	0.7128	0.7128	2,799
17	8/1/2007	2,235	3,019	3,015	0.7413	0.7191	0.7196	0.7224	0.7224	3,094
18	9/1/2007	3,643	3,012	3,029	1.2026	1.1975	1.1983	1.1963	1.1963	3,045
19	10/1/2007	2,270	3,047	3,136	0.7239				0.7128	3,185
20	11/1/2007	1,338	3,224	3,230	0.4142				0.5355	2,499
21	12/1/2007	3,492	3,236	3,243	1.0769				1.1741	2,974
22	1/1/2008	7,118	3,250	3,262	2.1823				2.1091	3,375
23	2/1/2008	2,381	3,274	3,266	0.7290				0.8307	2,866
24	3/1/2008	2,210	3,259	3,267	0.6765				0.7060	3,130

Adjustment Factors

Adjusted Seasonal Factor	Damping Factor	Damped Seasonal Factor
1.0000	0.9900	1.0000

would be of that same length (e.g., a four-quarter moving average for quarterly data, a seven-day moving average for weekly data, etc.).

Note that the 12-month moving average will terminate when the last observation is included in the average, which is six periods before the end of the entire data set in our example (or any data set using a 12-month moving average). Extending the moving average beyond this point leads to incorrect results, as less than a full year of data would be included in the average. For illustrative purposes, let's imagine that the data depicted in Exhibit 4.13 represents our entire data set (though this would be a very small amount of data to use in developing a forecast). In this case, our last 12-month moving average entry would appear in period 19 because calculating a 12-month centered moving average past period 19 would require data from period 25 and beyond. Consequently, the entries for periods 20 through 24 would be blank.

The 12-month centered moving average does remove seasonality from the data, but an additional step is required due to an unfortunate feature of the Gregorian calendar – there are only 12 months! This means that the 12-month centered moving average does not return the average precisely for the month it is centered on, but one half month before. To illustrate, forgetting Exhibit 4.13 temporarily, assume that you have data for January through December, where the value for January is 1, February is 2, and so on, until you get to 12 for December. A twelve-month centered moving average for July will not be "7," but rather "6.5." So, until a national calendar reform gives us 11 or 13 months in a year, we must apply a corrective. This can be done by taking a two-month moving average of the period in question plus one period in the future. Hence, we would average together the July value of 6.5 with the August value of 7.5 to get a value of "7" for July. This is an extra step beyond the simplified approach to moving averages we described earlier, as part of our Colorado Springs exmaple. This extra step brings more precision to the deseasonalization calculation.

Returning to Exhibit 4.13, column (5) applies this technique. For example, the two-month moving average of 2,868 for period 8 is the average of the 12-month moving averages of periods 8 (2,865) and 9 (2,871). This series of averages terminates one period before the end of the 12-period moving average (not pictured). Note that if the seasonal period contains an odd number of observations in the first place, such as seven days in the week, the two-period moving average calculation is unnecessary. The first moving average will be correctly centered at the middle observation.

In column (6), we produce the raw seasonal factors by dividing the actual revenue yields in column (3) by column (5), the refined annual moving average. This begins to tell us the proportional impact of seasonality on the data. For instance, if there were little seasonal impact, we'd expect all of the figures in column (6) to be close to 1.0 because the revenue in any given month should be pretty close to other months and, all in all, close to the 12-month moving average. However, many of the figures in column (6) are not close to 1.0. January and April, for example, are two months we know have much higher income tax revenues than other months. Therefore, they have appreciably higher values in column (6) than the other months.

To generalize from Exhibit 4.13, the formula for the raw seasonal factor is:

$$S = A / MA_{L,C}$$

This can be read as: the raw seasonal factor is found by dividing the actual revenue yield for a given period by the appropriate centered moving average associated with the seasonal length. The L in $MA_{L,C}$ refers to the length of the moving average, which we have assumed will be 12 in our example, and the $_C$ refers to the fact that it is a centered moving average. Remember that where the seasonal period contains an even number of observations, the two-period moving average of the $MA_{L,C}$ should be used, and where the seasonal period contains an odd number of observations, the $MA_{L,C}$ itself should be used.

Column (7) is labeled Average. For each seasonal period – January, February, and through to December – we average all the calculated raw seasonal factors. Recall that our completed data set is 7.25 years, but we lose 13 observations to computing moving averages (i.e., the six blank cells in periods 1 through 6 that are shown on Exhibit 4.13 plus seven blank cells at the end of the data set, which are not pictured). This means that for nine months of the 12 months in the year, there are averages of 6 raw seasonal factors, and for three months, there are averages of 7 raw seasonal factors. These averages are shown in column (7) and they are our initial seasonal factors. To illustrate, the 0.7094 shown in period 7 is the average of all of the raw seasonal factors for all of the October periods in the data set.

If we total the 12 figures in column (7), they should, theoretically, match the count of the seasonal periods, 12 in this instance, but often they do not (11.9919 in this case). To adjust for this, we compute an adjustment factor, which is the expected total, 12, divided by the actual total of 11.9919, which gives us 1.0007. The generalizable formula is:

$$S' = \frac{L}{\sum_{i=1}^{L} S}$$

Here, L is the length of the seasonal period, S is the initial seasonal factor, and S' is the adjusted seasonal factor.

Column (8), Adjusted, shows the adjusted seasonal factors, where the figures shown in column (7) were multiplied by 1.0007. We average the numbers in column (8) to confirm that they average to one, which is equivalent to those numbers totaling 12 (or L). This adjustment is sometimes called normalization.

There is evidence that the use of classic decomposition to adjust seasonality likely overstates the true impact of seasonal factors.[15] Accurate corrective processes are very complex and not demonstrated here. A judgmental method that may somewhat reduce the risk of overstating seasonality uses a *damping factor*. A damping factor reduces the impact of the seasonal factors by drawing all the seasonal factors closer to 1.0. The risk of this method is that it could go too far and excessively damp the seasonal impacts; however, the forecaster should always adjust, but never by very much. A damping factor is a number between zero and one that is multiplied by the adjusted seasonal number and added to a component that draws the seasonal factor closer to 1.0. The formula is as follows:

$$S_d = S' \cdot d + (1 - d)$$

In this formula, S_d is the damped seasonal factor, S' the adjusted seasonal factor, and d is the damping factor.[16] There is little empirical evidence to suggest a correct damping factor, so it is advisable to exercise caution and pick a number very close to 1, which will result in a minimal damping effect. Column (9) shows the results of the formula above applied to the figures in column (8) using a d of 0.99. Again, these figures should be averaged to confirm that they average to 1.0.

In column (10), labeled "Use Seasonal Factors," the final damped seasonal factors are arrayed across the entire series, using the appropriate seasonal factor for each month. To illustrate, period 1 is the month of April, so uses a seasonal factor of 1.6926, which is the seasonal factor for April, as shown in column (9) for period 13. 1.6926 is also used in column (10) for period 13, and would also be used for period 25, if it were shown.

In column (11), we divide column (3), revenue amount, by the seasonal factors in column (10) to get the deseasonalized series. The generalizable formula for this is:

$$A' = \frac{A}{S_d}$$

The formula reads: the deseasonalized value of the actual is the original actual divided by the damped seasonal factor.

Exhibit 4.14 shows the deseasonalized data compared with the original seasonal data. The Exhibit shows that the deseasonalized data would be much more tightly centered around a line of best fit than the original data and it should therefore be easier to extrapolate revenues going forward. The reader might also note that there are still some rather large peaks, especially on the right-hand side of the chart. Seasonal adjustment will not necessarily eliminate all of the variations in the data. This large outlier at the end of the series suggests a possibility that the seasonal pattern is changing, which should be reviewed again with the next year of data; however, it could also reflect unusual activity in the next-to-last period of the data.

The reader will recall that the foregoing discussion of classic decomposition assumed multiplicative seasonal factors, where seasonal variation has a multiplicative relationship

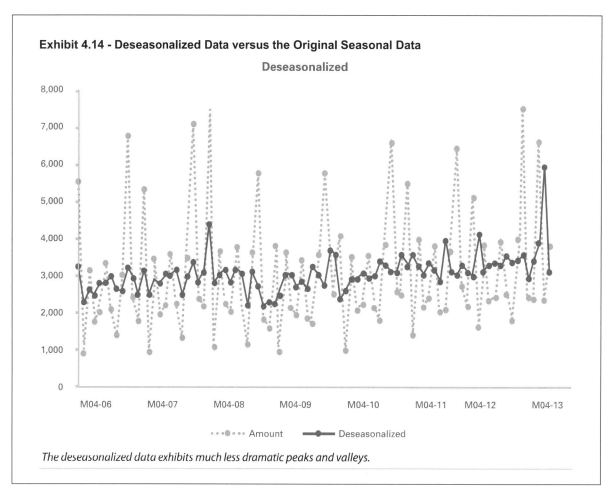

Exhibit 4.14 - Deseasonalized Data versus the Original Seasonal Data

The deseasonalized data exhibits much less dramatic peaks and valleys.

with the trend. The classical decomposition technique can be modified to assume additive seasonal behavior if multiplicative seasonal factors are not appropriate. For example, perhaps the seasonal component stays the same although the series has a trend (moves up or down across time). Exhibit 4.15 illustrates additive decomposition in a manner similar to Exhibit 4.13. You can also download the entire data set and calculations at *www.gfoa.org/forecastbook*.

Let's walk through Exhibit 4.15, starting with the two moving averages, column (4) and column (5), which are found as with the multiplicative decomposition.

The raw seasonal factor, column (6), is found by the formula below:

$$S = A - MA_{L,C}$$

To illustrate, in period 7, we would subtract 2,873 from 2,132 to get -741.1.

Exhibit 4.15 - Classical Decomposition Method of Seasonal Adjustment, Assuming Additive Seasonal Factors

(1) Period from Start	(2) Month & Year	(3) Revenue Amount	(4) Centered MA-12	(5) MA-2	(6) Raw Seasonal Factors	(7) Average	(8) Adjusted	(9) Damped Seasonal Factors	(10) Use Seasonal Factors	(11) Deseasonalized
1	4/1/2006	5,560					NA		2154	3,406
2	5/1/2006	918					NA		-1841	2,759
3	6/1/2006	3,191					NA		633	2,558
4	7/1/2006	1,786					NA		-894	2,680
5	8/1/2006	2,049					NA		-859	2,908
6	9/1/2006	3,373					NA		605	2,768
7	10/1/2006	2,132	2,882	2,873	-741.1	-894	NA	-885	-885	3,017
8	11/1/2006	1,421	2,865	2,868	-1446.9	-1448	NA	-1434	-1434	2,855
9	12/1/2006	3,083	2,871	2,885	197.7	533	NA	528	528	2,555
10	1/1/2007	6,816	2,899	2,908	3908.0	3398	NA	3364	3364	3,452
11	2/1/2007	2,465	2,917	2,925	-459.5	-523	NA	-518	-518	2,983
12	3/1/2007	1,785	2,932	2,944	-1158.5	-903	NA	-894	-894	2,679
13	4/1/2007	5,356	2,955	2,961	2395.5	2176	NA	2154	2154	3,202
14	5/1/2007	998	2,966	2,963	-1964.8	-1860	NA	-1841	-1841	2,839
15	6/1/2007	3,528	2,959	2,976	551.6	639	NA	633	633	2,895
16	7/1/2007	1,995	2,993	3,006	-1011.0	-903	NA	-894	-894	2,889
17	8/1/2007	2,235	3,019	3,015	-780.1	-868	NA	-859	-859	3,094
18	9/1/2007	3,643	3,012	3,029	613.7	611	NA	605	605	3,038
19	10/1/2007	2,270	3,047	3,136	-865.7		NA		-885	3,155
20	11/1/2007	1,338	3,224	3,230	-1892.0		NA		-1434	2,772
21	12/1/2007	3,492	3,236	3,243	249.5		NA		528	2,964
22	1/1/2008	7,118	3,250	3,262	3856.4		NA		3364	3,754
23	2/1/2008	2,381	3,274	3,266	-885.2		NA		-518	2,899
24	3/1/2008	2,210	3,259	3,267	-1056.8		NA		-894	3,104

In column (7), this value is averaged across all units of the same seasonal period as we did with the multiplicative factor. For example, all of the October values in the data set for column (6) average out to -894, as shown in column (7).

Because we cannot check to see if the averaged raw seasonal factors in column (7) average to 1.0 or add up to 12.0 as we can with multiplicative decomposition, the adjustment (normalization) process used in column (8) of Exhibit 4.13 is not applicable here.

For column (9), the damping formula is simplified as below:

$$S_d = S' \cdot d$$

Exhibit 4.15 again assumes a *d* of 0.99 for the same reasons described for multiplicative decomposition.

The seasonal factors to use indicated by column (10) are created as they were in Exhibit 4.13 – the appropriate seasonal factor from column (9) is associated with each period in column (10). The deseasonalized data in column (11) are found by using the following formula:

$$A' = A - S_d$$

The result is, again, a series of data that can be extrapolated forward.

Correlation Analysis

The objective of correlation analysis is to compare revenues to variables that are thought to be predictive of revenue, such as economic or demographic statistics. The forecaster is looking for strong relationships, which then could be used in quantitative forecasting techniques or even simply to provide additional insight for judgmental forecasts. The most important statistic for correlation analysis is the correlation coefficient, often known simply as "r". The correlation coefficient measures the extent to which to two variables move in the same direction or opposite directions and expresses this, respectively, as a positive number or a negative number between +1.0 and -1.0. An "r" value of 1.0 is a perfect positive relationship, and -1.0 represents a perfect inverse relationship. A value of a zero indicates no relationship. Generally, an "r" value closer to 1.0 or -1.0 would indicate a relationship worth exploring further. For example, as we will see later in this chapter, there is a high correlation (0.98, using the raw data) between the total professional business services employment in Fairfax County and the County's annual business professional occupational license tax revenues. Consequently, the direction employment is going could provide a good clue as to where license revenues are going.

Besides providing useful insights into the behavior of revenues, the correlation coefficient is relatively easy to interpret. First, "r" is always a number between +1.0 and -1.0. Second, there are no "units" associated with "r" that must also be interpreted. To illustrate, Fairfax County's "r" is not 0.98 dollars or 0.98 jobs per dollar – it is simply 0.98. These two features make "r" more intuitively understandable than many of the other statistics described in this chapter.

However, much like other statistics described in this chapter, the manual procedures to calculate the correlation coefficient are not complex, but they are tedious. Fortunately, Microsoft Excel can calculate the correlation coefficient for a set of data with a single function.[17]

So far, the reader likely has not found correlation analysis too difficult to grasp. Unfortunately, there is a cloud that goes along with this silver lining. Oftentimes in revenue forecasting, the variables that are correlated may naturally increase (or decrease) over time. A simple and widespread example of a natural increase is inflation. For a correlation analysis where both variables are expressed in dollars, part of the observed relationship of both variables increasing together over time could simply be both variables experiencing inflation. There are many other factors that could lead to natural changes in two variables over time, resulting in an overstated, and potentially misleading, correlation coefficient. Therefore, especially where the correlation coefficient is quite high, the forecaster should consider taking steps to factor out time differences to see if the correlation holds.

To factor out natural increases over time, we can use technique called *differencing*, The term differencing means that we are literally finding the difference between two observations. In order to factor out a natural increase over time, we simply take a given period and subtract that from the immediate preceding period. The formula for this operation appears below:

$$d^{(n)}(t) = x_t - x_{(t-n)}$$

For our purposes, $n=1$ because we are interested in the difference between observations that are a single period apart. The formula says the difference d of the first period ($n=1$) for the time series t is equal to a given period x_t minus a period that is n periods behind in the time series t-n. In statistics, this equation is often called the "first difference of the first period." If n were equal to 12, it would be called the first difference of the 12th period. Both are called the "the first difference" because differenced numbers can be differenced again, producing "second differences," and so forth (this would be done for more advanced techniques than we will show in this book).

When we difference two variables that we believe are correlated, we are able to correlate the differences, as well as the original numbers, and then compare the "r" values for both the original and differenced data.

To understand how and why this techniques works, Exhibit 4.16 provides a computational example for Fairfax County's sales tax revenue. How the technique works is very simple. To illustrate, the difference of the first period for 2003 is 2003's value minus 2002's. A difference of the first period is calculated for every year in the data set except 2002 because we don't have 2001 data. MS Excel's correlation function is then used to find correlation coefficients for the differenced and original data. As Exhibit 4.16 shows, without differencing, there is a very high correlation between sales tax revenue and employment. With differencing, there is still a positive correlation but not nearly so high.

As for why differencing works, a thought experiment can make the point. Imagine that the employment figures in Exhibit 4.16 were largely static such that that difference from period to period was effectively zero (e.g., employment was about 543,000 for every period), yet the revenues were still changing by the same amounts. We know, intuitively, that if employment has not changed, yet revenues are changing materially, then the employment numbers do not tell us much, if anything, about future revenues. Accordingly, we would get a correlation coefficient close to zero on the differenced data. However, we would get a correlation coefficient close to 0.4 on the actual data – certainly less than the 0.89 we got with the original set of actual data, but not an inconsiderable number. This is because with the original data, one large number (revenue) is consistently compared to another large number

Exhibit 4.16 – Differencing for Sales Tax Revenue and Total Employment in Fairfax County, Virginia

Year	Actuals (in thousands)		Differences of the 1st Period (in thousands)	
	Revenue	Employment	Revenue	Employment
FY 2002	125,577	543	NA	NA
FY 2003	126,785	525	1,208	−18
FY 2004	140,070	533	13,285	8
FY 2005	147,782	544	7,712	12
FY 2006	152,476	566	4,694	21
FY 2007	159,224	575	6,748	9
FY 2008	160,855	585	1,631	11
FY 2009	153,853	586	-7,003	0
FY 2010	149,547	571	-4,305	−15
FY 2011	154,757	574	8,082	3
FY 2012	162,840	581	5,210	8
FY 2013	166,894	590	4,054	9
	Correlation = 0.89		Correlation = 0.52	

(employment), and even if the employment number is unchanging, the correlation formula calculation returns a positive relationship. When we correlate the differences, the change in revenues would be compared to numbers close to zero, so the correlation formula returns a relationship closer to zero.

If "r" is the essential statistic for correlation analysis, then the *scatterplot* is the essential graphic. A scatterplot provides a picture of the interrelationship between the two variables. On a scatterplot, one variable is arrayed on the horizontal axis and one on the vertical axis. The intersection of each variable in the series is plotted as a point on the graph. Microsoft Excel can automatically create scatterplots as one of its standard charting graphics.

Exhibits 4.17 and 4.18 illustrate with scatterplots developed from Fairfax County's data. The data has not been differenced in order to make the scatterplots easier to comprehend for the reader, but the forecaster should consider creating scatterplots of differenced data in order to better discern true relationships. Exhibit 4.17 highlights the third data point from the left, where, in 2004, license revenues were $102 million and employment was 167,000. Other points represent the license revenues and employment for others years; however, the data is not arranged chronologically – the position of the points depends purely on the revenue and employment values.

Exhibit 4.17 seems to show a clear linear relationship between license revenue and professional and business service employment in Fairfax County: when employment goes up, revenue also goes up. In fact, the "r" is 0.98 (and 0.76 when differenced).

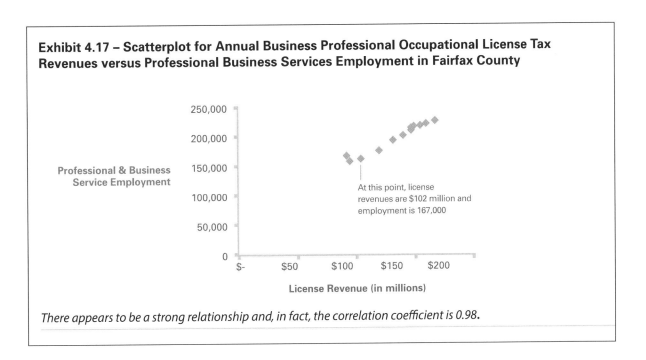

Exhibit 4.17 – Scatterplot for Annual Business Professional Occupational License Tax Revenues versus Professional Business Services Employment in Fairfax County

There appears to be a strong relationship and, in fact, the correlation coefficient is 0.98.

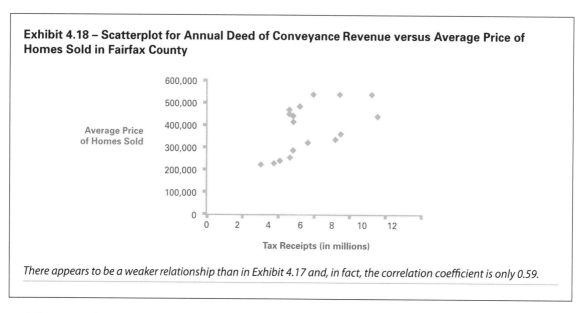

Exhibit 4.18 – Scatterplot for Annual Deed of Conveyance Revenue versus Average Price of Homes Sold in Fairfax County

There appears to be a weaker relationship than in Exhibit 4.17 and, in fact, the correlation coefficient is only 0.59.

Exhibit 4.18 does not show nearly so clear a relationship between annual deed of conveyance revenue and average price of homes sold in Fairfax County. It would be difficult to say what future revenue might be based on a change in home prices. Accordingly, the correlation coefficient is only 0.59 (0.48 when differenced). Negative correlations could also be helpful. Fairfax found a negative correlation between mortgage interest rates and recordation tax revenues, so if mortgage interest rates are on their way up it could portend a decline in recordation tax receipts.

In addition to visually aiding the search for interrelationships between variables, scatterplots also help correct for a limitation of the correlation coefficient that we haven't discussed yet. The statistics used to calculate the correlation coefficient look for a linear relationship between the two variables. A linear relationship is where the two variables in question change together at some constant rate. It is possible for variables to have non-linear relationships, which a correlation coefficient would underemphasize. To illustrate, Exhibit 4.19 shows a scatterplot on the left with a perfect linear relationship and an "r" of 1.0, and a scatterplot on the right with a perfect exponential relationship, but where the "r" is only 0.62. Both relationships are mathematically perfect, but the correlation coefficients vary widely. Public-sector revenue forecasters will probably not encounter too many exponential relationships, but the point remains that a visual inspection of the data can be very illuminating and can help uncover nuances that a single "r" statistic might obscure.[18]

Finally, no discussion of correlation would be complete without addressing the difference between correlation and causation. Simply put, just because two variables are correlated does not mean one causes the other. It could be, for example, that there are one or more additional variables that drive change. The implication of this limitation of correlation analysis is that policy analysts should be cautious about using the results of correlation analysis for policy changes (e.g., taking action to influence a variable in the hopes of in-

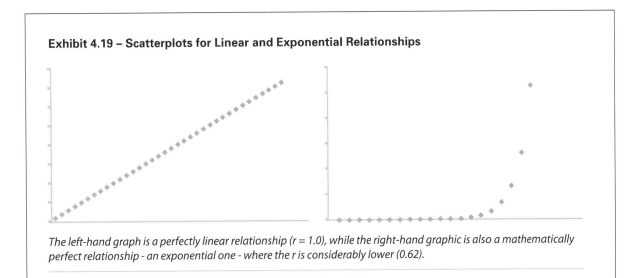

Exhibit 4.19 – Scatterplots for Linear and Exponential Relationships

The left-hand graph is a perfectly linear relationship (r = 1.0), while the right-hand graphic is also a mathematically perfect relationship - an exponential one - where the r is considerably lower (0.62).

creasing revenues), but this should not stop forecasters from using correlations as predictive tools. In fact, forecasters in many fields have successfully used correlation analysis for prediction. For example, the highly successful FICO credit scoring model is based on correlated variables, but not cause and effect. In fact, many of the variables used in credit scoring (e.g., length of credit history) clearly have no direct causal relationship with whether or not a person chooses or is able to pay back a loan. Yet, FICO credit scoring has allowed a vast increase in the number of loan, credit card, and personal finance applications to be processed with little difference in the amount of losses on bad loans.[19] The recommendations Netflix makes to its customers on what films to watch is also a product of correlation analysis, and the Center for Disease control also uses correlation analysis to narrow down the potential source of food-borne illness outbreaks (before employing other methods to determine the precise cause). So revenue forecasters should not be put off by the possibility of a correlation not equating to causation. In many cases, correlations will prove sufficient for predicting the direction of revenues, or can at least point the forecaster in the direction of true causal relationships, if those are necessary for policy decisions. Forecasters should simply exercise appropriate caution when using correlations to forecast, such as continuing to monitor the relationship to ensure ongoing predictive power.

Conclusion

Step 3 of the forecasting process, Exploratory Analysis, serves to deepen the forecaster's familiarity with historical data. This contributes to the forecaster's ability to accurately predict revenues. Just as important, it also helps the forecaster tell the story of the forecast to its audience. When the forecaster can explain why revenues behave as they do, the forecaster's credibility goes up and the audience will be more likely to take heed of the forecast when making financial decisions.

To conduct an exploratory analysis, begin with the basics, like graphing the data for a visual inspection and using descriptive statistics to see big trends and get a handle on the basic features of the data set. Beyond these basic exploratory tools, the forecaster should consider some more advanced techniques. The most important one covered in this chapter is deseasonalization. Some revenues may exhibit consistent seasonal patterns. These patterns could reduce the effectiveness of quantitative forecasting techniques, so it is advisable for forecasters to investigate the data for evidence of these patterns and take steps to reduce their impact on the forecast.

Chapter 5

Judgmental Forecasting

Now that we have covered gathering revenue data and preliminary exploratory analysis in Steps 2 and 3 of the forecasting process, we will soon arrive at Step 4: Select Forecasting Methods. Before we can select between the methods, though, we must know the methods that are available. There are two basic methods of forecasting: *judgmental* and *quantitative*. Judgmental forecasting relies on the expert knowledge of the forecaster. Quantitative forecasting relies primarily on historical data and statistical techniques. Almost all local government revenue forecasting contains at least some element of forecaster judgment. One reason judgmental forecasting is so common is because it is easy to use; however, it is also easy to misuse.

On one hand, human judgment (especially when predicting the future) is inherently flawed and has been shown by forecasting research to be generally inferior to quantitative forecasting methods. On the other hand, forecasting research has also shown that human judgment can make valuable contributions to forecasting, under the right conditions. Further, when historical data is absent or is of limited predictive value, human judgment is the only option left. This chapter will provide an overview of judgmental forecasting, including:

- **Efficacy.** Learn what forecasting science says about the predictive value of judgmental forecasting.

- **Conditions for use**. Learn how to determine when it is appropriate to use judgmental methods in forecasting.

- **Judgmental forecasting.** Learn how to understand judgmental forecasting as a product of human cognition and behavior.

- **Judgmental forecasting methods.** Learn how to use specific techniques for using judgment most effectively.

We will address quantitative statistical forecasting in the next two chapters.

Efficacy of Judgmental Forecasting

Forecasting science generally recommends against purely judgmental forecasting methods for two reasons. First, the process used to construct the forecast exists primarily in the forecaster's head, so it is not transparent and not easily replicated. As a result, it may be difficult to explain the forecast to others and to develop consistent forecasts over time.

Second, a wide body of literature suggests that judgmental forecasts are likely to be of dubious accuracy.[1] One particularly well-known example comes from a landmark study by the political scientist Phillip Tetlock.[2] Tetlock conducted a study over 15 years where he asked 284 experts to assign probabilities to one of three possible future scenarios for various forecast questions germane to their field (e.g., economics, domestic politics, international relations). The three available choices for each scenario covered persistence of the status quo, a change in one direction (e.g., more economic growth in a given country), or a change in the opposite direction (e.g., less economic growth in a given country).

The results did not reflect well on expert judgment. A *New Yorker* review of Tetlock's work put it memorably: "The experts performed worse than they would have if they had simply assigned an equal probability to all three outcomes—if they had given each possible future a thirty-three percent chance of occurring. Human beings who spend their lives studying the state of the world, in other words, are poorer forecasters than dart-throwing monkeys, who would have distributed their picks evenly over the three choices."[3] In all cases, even rudimentary statistical methods would have provided more predictive power.[4] Further, these disappointing results were consistent regardless of area of expertise, experience, or degree of specialization. In other words, greater expertise did not lead to better judgmental forecasts.

Use Any Quantitative Technique

As a rule of thumb, the forecaster should always seek to apply some quantitative technique, any quantitative technique, before relying solely on expert judgment for a forecast.

However, Tetlock's findings do not mean that expert judgment has no role in forecasting. Rather, it can be quite useful under the right conditions.

Conditions for Use of Expert Judgment

Research does not universally pan judgmental forecasting. Some research suggests that judgmental forecasting can be as good as the best statistical techniques under certain conditions:

- The expert has access to information that would not be reflected in the results from a quantitative model.[5] This could be a very common occurrence in government revenue forecasting, where special events in the financial and economic environments reduce the predictive power of historical data. For example, a change in the tax rate, growth in the community, or changes in governing law could all have significant implications for future revenues.

- The expert has a history of making and learning from similar forecasts and the environment is relatively stable (i.e., low impact from seasonal or business cycles). [6]

- There is little or no good historical data available. Non-recurring revenues or new revenues would meet this condition.

Even if a government finds itself in one of the three conditions above, it should exercise judgment carefully because judgments are prone to error.

To Err is Human: Cognition and Behavior in Forecasting

Thinking back to Tetlock's study, you may wonder why people are so poor at forecasting. Much of the answer has to do with what are called *cognitive biases*. A cognitive bias is a deviation in judgment that is inherent to the way the human mind works and that leads people to draw irrational conclusions from their observations. The challenge with cognitive biases is that they operate unconsciously and their influence is often subtle.

Consider, for example, the cognitive bias of *overconfidence*. Cognitive psychology suggests that about 80 percent of people have an inborn tendency to overestimate their chances of experiencing good events and underestimate their chances of experiencing bad events; people are more optimistic than realistic.[7] People also regularly overestimate their own capacities. For example, most people believe they are more attractive, personable, honest (not to mention many other positive traits) than the average person. While an optimistic outlook on life has many benefits, better financial forecasting is not one of them. In fact, of the many cognitive biases that can afflict forecasting, the optimism bias is thought to be one of the most important.[8] Optimism could lead to underestimation of the cost of large projects or overconfidence in the assumptions behind a revenue forecast. Exhibit 5.1 lists common biases in forecasting.[9]

Exhibit 5.1 – Common Biases in Forecasting

Type of Bias	Description of Bias	Example
Overconfidence	Unjustified belief in the accuracy of forecast assumptions	The forecaster is too certain about the potential future behavior of key revenue drivers
Recency	The most recent events dominate those in the less recent past	News headlines about a recent high-profile, but idiosyncratic, event overshadow more important long-term trends
Availability	Relying on specific events easily recalled from memory over more pertinent information	Basing a forecast on a particularly vivid issue that may have received a lot of political attention, but really is not that impactful
Anchoring	Being unduly influenced by initial information, which is given more weight in the forecasting process	Using a historical high or low as the starting point of discussions for a long-term, multi-year forecast
Confirmation	Interpreting data in a way that supports the conclusions one wishes to draw	Drawing conclusions from a third party's economic analysis that support the outcome that the forecaster wants
Underestimating Uncertainty	The need to reduce anxiety results in underestimating future uncertainty	Showing a point forecast or single forecast as the only future outcome and not accounting for possible variance in the forecast.

Source: Modeled on a table that originally appeared in Spyros Makridakis, et al. *Forecasting Methods and Applications,* 3rd ed. (Hoboken, New Jersey: John Wiley and Sons). 1998.

Daniel Kahneman is a psychologist who won the Noble Prize for economics for his work relating to decision-making, including cognitive biases. Kahneman is not optimistic about the possibilities for eliminating these biases, as they are largely hardwired into human cognition.[10] However, Kahneman and other researchers have suggested a number of techniques that forecasters can use to hone their judgmental forecasts in light of these biases.[11]

First, promote discussion of biases and their impact on forecasting. Use Exhibit 5.1 to make participants in the forecasting process aware of potential cognitive biases and then encourage participants in the process to help each other recognize when biases might be at work. Implicit in this recommendation is that it is advisable to have more than one person involved in the forecasting process. This is important because: a) people are better at recognizing biases in others than in themselves; and b) having multiple people involved slows the forecasting process down, which provides more time for rational thinking. (Going too fast invites the human brain to rely on its biased intuition.)

Another good first step is to document the organization's accumulated wisdom about the revenue source. This could be an influence diagram or simply a checklist of key factors that ought to be considered before the forecast is made.[12] This helps forecasters stay focused on the most relevant factors, not overlook key factors, and maintain some consistency in forecasting approach. We saw an example of an influence diagram in Chapter 3.

Keep records of how forecasts are made and review past performance before making new forecasts.[13] Feedback allows the forecaster to learn. Keep and learn from records not only on the forecast itself, but also on judgments of key assumptions behind the forecast. This is because the forecast itself may be a product of too many variables to provide useful feedback. Reviewing how judgment performed on the key assumptions behind the forecast might be more instructive.

When you are ready to make the forecast, start with an algorithm. Judgmental forecasting does not necessarily mean pulling a forecast from the ether. Quantitative data can be used to help develop a starting point for the forecast. A traditional statistical model could fill this role, or, if that is not possible, even a simple non-statistical algorithm would likely represent an improvement on pure expert judgment alone. In fact, forecasters should be able to develop at least a simple algorithm for virtually any revenue source. For instance, property tax revenue would be a product of the assessed value multiplied by the tax rate multiplied by the collection rate. Even a simple algorithm that reflects factors behind the item being forecast can significantly improve decision making.[14] Non-statistical algorithms are such an important technique for improving the use of expert judgment that it will be revisited in greater detail later in this chapter.

Use reference cases or analogous situations to guide your judgmental forecast. For example, if you need to forecast revenues for a new tax or fee, have similar governments implemented this tax/fee before and what was their experience? If a major new retailer is moving into the community, what impact does that retailer have on the sales taxes of other communities where it also has locations? Reference cases could also come from historical experiences. If a tax rate is going to rise, what happened to revenues the last time it rose? If the economy is entering recession, what happened to revenues in the last recession? The point is that your forecasting question is probably not totally unique, so use what has actually happened in similar situations as a basis for your forecast. Chapter 19 shows how the City of Boulder used a historical reference case to make a highly accurate judgmental forecast.

As part of making the forecast, obtain several independent judgments, rather than just relying on one person's forecast. Research suggests that judgmental forecasts can be improved by simply averaging the results of multiple independent forecasts.[15] This averages out unsystematic differences between the forecasters in how they develop the forecasts. However, the use of groups to make judgmental forecasts can be tricky because group interactions do not always support better forecasting and decision-making. Structuring group interactions to support good forecasting will be covered in more detail later in this chapter.

In addition to the abovementioned steps for creating a forecast, an essential part of honing a judgmental forecast is to actively question the assumptions underpinning the forecast. This is because the biases in Exhibit 5.1 can just as easily impact the assumptions underlying the forecast as they can the forecast itself. One simple method is to write down all important forecast assumptions and then two reasons why each assumption might be wrong, thus prompting some introspection of the forecast assumptions. For example, often forecasters might assume that the last actual observation is a good starting point for the forecast. However, further introspection might reveal that the most recent available actual number is not an appropriate starting point because it represents an unusually high or low observation, which would then bias the entire forecast in that direction (this an example of the "anchoring" cognitive bias in Exhibit 5.1). In this case, the forecaster might decide to use an average of recent observations to pick the forecast starting point instead.

As another way to question assumptions, Kahneman recommends a *pre-mortem*.[16] With this approach, once the forecasters have reached a forecast, but before they have publicly committed to it, they should hold a brief meeting of individuals who are knowledgeable about the forecast. The participants imagine that it is a year in the future and that the forecast has been horribly wrong and are to write a brief history of what happened. The pre-mortem helps temper uncritical optimism and forces people to consider the possibilities of why their initial estimates might be wrong.

Just as the forecaster should critically examine his/her assumptions, the forecaster should also scrutinize the forecast itself. One method is similar to what we saw for assumptions. The forecaster should explicitly and rigorously consider why their initial judgmental forecast might be wrong. They next produce a second, revised estimate. They then combine the two estimates. Researchers have found that this method can produce a significant improvement in accuracy.[17]

Finally, always require justification of the forecast, ideally in writing. A justification of the forecast leads to higher forecast consistency – if forecasters know that they must explain their reasoning to others, they are likely to develop a more consistent reasoning.[18] If the justification is written down, it can be used to learn from the forecast results when results become available.

Think Like a Fox

Cognitive biases do much to explain the limitations of judgmental forecasts. However, there may be another part to the explanation that comes from Tetlock's work. While Tetlock did not find that experience or degree of specialization made a difference in an expert's forecast accuracy, he did find another variable that made a difference. Tetlock categorized the forecasters into one of two cognitive styles: hedgehogs and foxes.[19] In short, hedgehogs subscribe to one or more clear overriding ideas or approaches to a question. Foxes take a more multi-disciplinary approach, using many ideas and changing approaches as circumstances suggest. Tetlock demonstrated that foxes outperform hedgehogs on forecasting by a significant margin in his experiments. Foxes are thought to be better forecasters because the way they think is more appropriate to the task of forecasting. In fact, hedgehogs performed worse than random guessing. The best foxes approached the accuracy of some quantitative extrapolation models. Exhibit 5.2 is adapted from the work of noted statistician and forecaster Nate Silver[20] and shows differences in attitudes between the two in more detail.[21] Hence, a government will want to recruit "foxes" to lend their judgment to the forecasting task. In fact, many of the most accurate and most effective forecasters in GFOA research credited a large part of their success to fox-like thinking: they get information from many different sources, including potentially conflicting sources, and bring it together into a coherent picture of what revenues will look like in the future. In order to help you recruit foxes, you can access a spreadsheet version of the cognitive style assessment used by Tetlock (note this test is not the same as Exhibit 5.2) at *www.gfoa.org/forecastbook*. The assessment categorizes the test-taker as a strong to weak fox or hedgehog.[22]

Exhibit 5.2 – Foxes versus Hedgehog Thinking in Forecasting

How Foxes Think	How Hedgehogs Think
Multidisciplinary. Incorporate ideas from different disciplines regardless of their ideological origin.	**Specialized.** Often have spent the bulk of their careers on one or two great problems. May view the opinions of "outsiders" skeptically.
Adaptable. Find a new approach or pursue multiple approaches at the same time if they aren't sure the original one is working.	**Stalwart.** Stick to the same approach. New data is used to refine the original model.
Self-critical. Sometimes willing to acknowledge mistakes in their predictions and accept the blame for them.	**Stubborn.** Mistakes are blamed on bad luck or on idiosyncratic circumstances – a good model had a bad day.
Tolerant of complexity. See the universe as complicated, perhaps to the point of many fundamental problems being irresolvable or inherently unpredictable.	**Order-seeking.** Expect that the world will be found to abide by relatively simple governing relationships once the signal is identified through the noise.
Cautious. Express their predictions in probabilistic terms and qualify their opinions.	**Confident.** Rarely hedge their predictions and are reluctant to change them.
Empirical. Rely more on observation than theory.	**Ideological.** Expect that solutions to many day-to-to-day problems are manifestations of a larger theory or struggle.

Source: Nate Silver. *The Signal and the Noise.* (The Penguin Press: New York, New York). 2012.

Finally, it should be noted that the fox/hedgehog dichotomy is not intended to say that one cognitive style is inherently better than the other—just that foxes are better suited to the forecasting task in particular. Hedgehogs may be better suited for other tasks. For example, noted management science researcher Jim Collins[23] believes that hedgehog thinking is much better suited to achieving success in running and growing a company.[24]

Beware of Telegenic Hedgehogs

An interesting finding of Tetlock's is that the forecasts of hedgehogs tend to get more media exposure because they put their forecasts in certain, unambiguous terms—in other words, a media-friendly format. In fact, the level of media exposure a forecaster received was negatively correlated with forecast accuracy!

The Problem with Group Forecasting, and Its Solution

In this chapter we have extolled the benefits of bringing multiple perspectives into the forecast in order to improve the quality of the judgment that is applied to the forecast. To do this, governments commonly use group deliberation (i.e., a group of people discuss a problem and reach a conclusion through consensus). This is understandable because people generally prefer group deliberation as a way of decision-making over leaving the decision to be made by an individual (especially when the individual is not them). Furthermore, decisions reached by a group enjoy greater support than decisions made by an individual. The trouble is that there is a substantial body of evidence that suggests that the quality of decisions made by group deliberation is often worse than decisions reached by individuals![25] This is especially true when the "correct" answer is unknowable at the time the group makes its decision, which is precisely the case when making forecasts. However, there is also substantial evidence that forecasts improve significantly when they are made using statistical groups – that is, taking individual forecasts from a number of people and averaging them together. So, the evidence from statistical groups proves that more heads are, in fact, better than one, but why then does group deliberation produce lower-quality forecasts than individuals?

First, in deliberative groups, members are susceptible to what is called a *cascade effect*, where those that speak first influence those who speak later, perhaps even discouraging others from offering factual evidence that contradicts the prevailing opinion of the group.[26] This cascade effect is especially pronounced when the first speaker holds a high rank or or is held in high esteem, but it is by no means limited to such a situation. The famous Asch conformity experiments provide a stark illustration of the cascade effect.[27] In short, a subject was placed in a group of people and was told that the experiment was about measuring people's visual acuity. Unbeknownst to the subject, all of the other members of the group were confederates of the experimenter. The experimenter showed the group a line of a certain length and then a group of three other lines of varying length, where one of the three lines was the same length of the first line (See Exhibit 5.3). The group members were asked one by one which of the three lines matched the length of the first line with

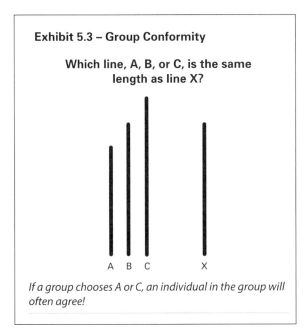

Exhibit 5.3 – Group Conformity

Which line, A, B, or C, is the same length as line X?

A B C   X

If a group chooses A or C, an individual in the group will often agree!

the subject answering last. This process was repeated with the group multiple times for lines of different lengths. On some occasions the experimenter's confederates unanimously picked the wrong line and when it came to the subject's turn to pick, nearly 75 percent of the subjects went along with the incorrect group view at least once during the course of the experiment.

If cascade effects are prevalent in a group with no pre-existing social relationships and where the group has selected an unambiguously wrong answer, like in the Asch experiments, it is not difficult to imagine that cascade effects would occur in forecast groups. Group conformity happens both for social reasons (the individual doesn't want to contradict the group) and for informational reasons (the individual believes the group must know better so changes his or her own view). Now, imagine a forecast meeting starts with the City Manager giving his or her view on future property values in the city, who is then followed by the Community Development Director, who echoes the City Manager's view. It is now the Budget Officer's turn. The Budget Officer has access to solid information that contradicts the views aired by the City Manager and the Community Development Director. Will the budget director share this information? The cascade effect and group conformity tendency suggests that there is a good chance the answer will be "no."

The second reason that group decisions are often of low quality is that even outside of the cascade effect, information that is already commonly known by the group will tend to dominate the discussion and crowd out other perspectives.[28] For example, imagine a county is considering a small increase in its sales tax rate, which has been widely and energetically discussed at public meetings of the county board. This topic would likely dominate group discussions about future revenues, even if everyone is already aware of it. Further discussion of the rate increase is unlikely to provide much additional insight, and could take time away from discussing other, less obvious factors that the group members are not yet widely aware of that are poised to have a material impact on sales tax revenues.

The third and final reason is that group deliberation amplifies the cognitive biases described in Exhibit 5.1.[29] For instance, earlier we described overconfidence as the most dangerous bias for forecasters. Now imagine that the forecaster at a school district is overconfident in an assumption that enrollment will grow by 8 percent over the next three years. The forecaster brings the assumption before the group and the group goes along with it. A few members of the group feel the assumed growth is too high, but they either defer to the perceived expertise of the forecaster or simply don't want to make waves. The forecaster, and much of the rest of the group, comes away from the meeting even more confident in the assumption than they were before because they perceive their assumption to have been confirmed by the group! Group deliberations generally increase the participants' confidence in the conclusions that the group reached, even if the conclusions are wrong.[30]

In another example of how groups can amplify cognitive biases, imagine there is a new economic development project happening in the community that has gotten a lot of positive attention in public meetings and even the press lately. The recency bias already might lead an individual forecaster to overweight this event in the forecast. In a group meeting, this event would likely be brought up and its importance echoed by a number of different people, leading it to be over-weighted even more than it would by an individual alone.

So, how can forecasters gain the benefits of groups while sidestepping the pitfalls? By carefully designing the group processes used for forecasting.

The Delphi method is the most time-honored design for group forecasting. It was invented in the 1950s and is named after the Oracle of Delphi, a character in Greek mythology that could foretell the future.[31] Essentially, the Delphi method makes a group of forecasters into a statistical group, but preserves some limited and highly structured feedback between the group members. This sidesteps many of the pitfalls of group deliberation, while preserving some of the benefits of feedback and information exchange between members. The Delphi method starts by convening a group of forecasters (ideally at least five and as many as 20). The forecasters then supply forecasts over two or three successive rounds. After each round, a facilitator provides all of the participants with an anonymous summary of all of the forecasts made during the previous round, as well as the reasons the forecasters provided for their judgments. Thus, forecasters are encouraged to revise their earlier answers in light of the replies of other members of the panel. It is believed that, during this process, the range of the answers will decrease and the group will converge towards the optimal answer over each successive round of forecasting and revision. The process ends after a pre-defined stop criterion (e.g., number of rounds, achievement of consensus, stability of results). The mean or median score of the final round determines the final forecast. Generally, it is thought that three rounds are sufficient to get good results with Delphi.

Delphi works because: a) the participants' forecasts are anonymous and independent, so the forecasts are not subject to cascade effects or the other problems that can arise with in-person interaction; b) the forecasters have the opportunity to change their opinions over the rounds, so feedback from the other group members is used; and c) the group members' responses are averaged in the end, so the final forecast is the product of a statistical group.

In order to make the best use of Delphi, use forecasters with appropriate expert knowledge of the revenue being forecast. Non-experts might be prone to changing their view to match opinions of others or their estimates may be the product of little more than guessing. Also make sure to use forecasters with different perspectives. This way the combined knowledge of the forecasters should cover a more comprehensive scope of the factors that impact revenue yield. For example, a forecast for the property tax might include people from the finance, assessor, collector, and/or community development departments. Finally, share all results with the group. It is very important that the feedback to the forecasters include a narrative rationale from each of the participants. Otherwise, the participating forecasters are responding to what appears to them to be an assortment of numbers. It is a good idea to supply participants with the rationales for all of the forecasts, not just some.[32]

It is not necessary to adhere strictly to the textbook Delphi approach to improve group forecasts. Any system where multiple experts provide their forecast anonymously and remain anonymous throughout the process should be a major improvement on a typical deliberative group decision-making process.[33] A modified Delphi approach could also include some room for deliberation, for example, before the anonymous forecasts are made or in-between forecast rounds.

The City of Dayton, Ohio, uses a quasi-Delphi method for its local income tax revenues. The City forecaster surveys about a dozen City staff in order to gain a diverse perspective on how the income tax might perform. The participants submit their forecasts to the City forecaster via e-mail, without deliberation with other staff. This way, staff members' forecasts remain independent and anonymous. After a single forecast round, the forecasts are averaged together to get a final forecast.

Forecast from the quasi-Delphi method is then combined with other quantitative methods that the City uses to arrive at a final forecast for income taxes. Exhibit 5.4 shows the mean average percent error (MAPE) of the City's annual budget forecast for an eight-year period, for six different forecasting methods the City uses to forecast its income tax. MAPE is explained more fully in Chapter 6, but, in short, it is the absolute value of the percentage difference between the forecast and what the actual revenue turns later turns out to be. MAPE is a standard statistic used to describe the accuracy of a forecast: a lower percentage error means that the forecast is more accurate. Exhibit 5.4 includes the quasi-Delphi approach, various quantitative methods (these methods are covered in later chapters), and a weighted average of the results from the other five methods (the importance of combined or averaged results is explained in Chapter 9).

As you can see, although the quasi-Delphi forecast is only the fifth most accurate method, it does outperform at least one quantitative technique and its level of accuracy is still respectable relative to the other techniques. Further, the City finds the quasi-Delphi forecast to be a valuable part of its forecasting process because it makes a positive contribution to the average forecast. This is because including more methods in the average reduces the risk of large errors in the adopted budget number; even though the City's single best forecasting technique might be very accurate in most years, it could miss badly in one year.

The City would like to expand its quasi-Delphi forecasting to require explicit rationales for the forecast from the participants and, eventually, to incorporate feedback rounds to make it more like classic Delphi forecasting. The City's experience shows that forecasting in groups can make a positive contribution and that forecasting practices can evolve over time, as resources allow.

Exhibit 5.4 – Dayton's MAPE over an Eight-Year Period

Method	MAPE
Econometric model	1.58%
Time Series Regression	1.69%
Average (Weighted)	1.71%
Exponential Smoothing	1.72%
Quasi-Delphi	1.99%
Trend Forecast with Adjustment	2.14%

Moving on from Delphi, more recent research has discovered teamwork methods that allow participants to deliberate on forecasts productively. Phillip Tetlock and others conducted a multiyear study of judgmental forecasting that showed that, when provided with guidance on proper forecasting teamwork, team forecasts were 23 percent more accurate than individual forecasts. The team forecasts also beat pure statistical groups by about 10 percent. (Delphi groups were not tested.) This same study showed that, when using proper teamwork and when members rigorously follow forecasting best practices like those described in this chapter, teams can do even better – much better, in fact – than the statistics cited above.[34]

Tetlock's study revealed four essential capacities for effective forecasting teamwork and deliberation. The first is the ability to understand the perspectives of other people. For instance, you should not only be able to understand why a team member thinks that tourism will decrease next year, but also be able to restate the argument in your own words in a way in which your teammate would agree.

The next capacity Tetlock's research uncovered is precision questioning. When one person questions another person in precise terms, rather than just posing a broad or vague challenge to the veracity of the other person's views, it helps the team focus on the real differences in viewpoints and explore those differences in a meaningful, productive way. For example, imagine your teammate expresses the opinion that tourism will decline, thereby negatively impacting hotel occupancy taxes. You might ask your teammate precise questions about why he or she holds this belief: which type of tourism will decline, those that attend for special events or those that come for more routine amenities? Or, what time of year will the decline occur? The goal is to understand the thinking behind a prediction so that it can be tested. If it turns out your teammate believes that there will be a decline in the number and/or quality of special events that attract tourists, the team can take steps to investigate, like talking to the convention and visitors bureau to compare the upcoming year's schedule of events with those from prior years.

Teams must also learn how to confront each other constructively. If team members are too deferential, teams can experience the cascade effect described earlier in this chapter. However, if team members are too aggressive, team members might become less willing to collaborate. Precision questioning can help promote constructive confrontation. Teams can also try assigning specific roles to team members. For example, for a property tax forecast, land use planners might be explicitly charged with examining assumptions around growth in property values and providing constructive feedback and challenge, where necessary, to the forecaster.

Finally, team members must also feel free to admit what they don't know and request assistance from their teammates. The team members should also take joint ownership of the results the team produces, so a team member sees it as "our" forecast and not "their" forecast. When this is the case, all team members will be more committed to achieving an accurate forecast and will apply their effort accordingly.

Though Tetlock's results are very encouraging for the role of teams in forecasting, there are a few limitations that must be acknowledged. First, the conditions for Tetlock's experimental study were very different from what would occur inside a real-life organization. The study participants included individual volunteers from across the world, who were grouped into teams at random, and almost all of their interactions took place over the Internet (e.g., e-mail, web conferencing, discussion boards, etc.). It was, therefore, highly unlikely that any team members would have pre-existing social relationships or that they would form strong relationships during the course of the study. It is reasonable to assume that because there were no superior-subordinate relationships on the teams and perhaps not even social relationships of any kind outside of the teams' work, the pressure to conform would be much less than would be experienced on a team made up of co-workers.

The second limitation is that, even under the conditions of Tetlock's study, managing a team so that it uses effective teamwork can be a challenge. Not all the teams in Tetlock's study performed equally well.

The lesson from the research presented in this chapter is that team deliberation, as it is often practiced, is a suboptimal approach to forecasting. The Delphi approach to team forecasting is a straightforward, technical solution to the challenges of group forecasting. However, Delphi might not take full advantage of a group's potential to share and synthesize diverse perspectives. As Tetlock's study suggests, if proper teamwork is used, team deliberation can produce good, and even great, forecasting results. However, forming and managing a high-performing forecasting team is not straightforward, especially in the setting of a government organization. Nor is it a purely technical matter, with step-by-step instructions that can be followed. Consequently, the best approach might be a combined Delphi/deliberation approach. Delphi techniques could be used to preserve a degree of anonymity of the participants and to remove the worst pressures for conformity, while Delphi's rounds of anonymous forecasting could be supplemented with collaborative deliberation on the results of the Delphi forecasts, conducted within the teamwork guidelines recommended by Tetlock.

Non-Statistical Algorithms

When we speak of a forecast made using judgment, the first method that might come to mind is the proverbial finger in the air. However, there is a much better method that brings together expert judgment with quantitative forecasting, and that can sometimes be as good as and maybe even better than some statistical techniques. That method is a non-statistical algorithm, also sometimes called a mathematical model. Forecast algorithms are usually constructed in a spreadsheet like Microsoft Excel, and the forecaster uses his or her knowledge of the factors that drive revenue yield to write formulas to help make the forecast. To provide a simplified illustration, an algorithm to forecast revenue for a water utility might multiply the average gallons of water used per home by the number of homes by the average price per gallon.

When might the forecaster choose to use an algorithm? Foremost, when conditions favor the use of forecaster judgment over statistical methods, the forecaster should try to develop an algorithm rather than relying on pure intuition. This includes situations where historical data is either unavailable or where the historical data is of low predictive value because of factors like significant changes in the legal environment or in the composition of the tax base.

The City of Irvine, California, for instance, uses algorithms for short- and long-term forecasting. The City has grown rapidly since the year 2000—over a 60 percent increase in population between 2000 and 2013. This means historical revenue data is of limited usefulness for forecasting because of the rapid changes in the size and composition of the City's tax base. The City's algorithms use demographic and economic variables to forecast revenues. For instance, the City's algorithm for estimating annual hotel room tax revenues multiplies two basic variables: the available rooms within the city limits and per-room tax revenue. The per-room revenue is arrived at by calculating a 10-year, inflation-adjusted average of per-room revenue. For the number of hotel rooms, the City's finance department works closely with other City staff, such as the community development department, for insight into developers' plans for new hotels, the status of projects under construction, and other significant happenings that could impact the number of available rooms. For example, a large hotel in the City was undergoing extensive remodeling, so its rooms were expected to be unavailable for booking for a long time.

The result produced by the algorithm is not the final forecast, though. It is adjusted by City staff based on their judgment and knowledge of the economic environment. To illustrate one such environmental factor, the City knows that trends in hotel tax revenues tend to closely match trends in the sales taxes produced by the "restaurant and hotel" category of businesses in the community. The City has access to category-by-category sales tax information through the State of California, and contracts with a specialized consultant to help analyze future directions in each category of sales tax. As a result, if the consultant expects the hotel and restaurant category of sales tax to grow or decline, it is a good clue that hotel taxes will go in the same direction and the hotel tax forecast would be adjusted accordingly. The hotel tax is only about 6 percent of the City's total general fund revenue, so the forecast for the hotel tax does not merit the same time and energy that the City puts towards forecasting more important revenues. The algorithm provides a simple and effective method for guiding the City's revenue estimates and has produced accurate results: over the three years since the City has started using this method, the mean absolute percent error (MAPE) has been 2.2 percent.

The City uses more sophisticated algorithms to forecast its most important revenues, sales and property taxes, over the long term (two to 20 years in the future). The City has achieved good results. To illustrate, it started using the model in 2010 to make five-year forecasts for sales taxes. Over each of the five years that the City forecasted (fiscal year '11 through fiscal year '15) the MAPE was about 2.6 percent. The City's sales tax algorithm has three components, each representing a different causal factor of the City's sales tax revenues. The primary component is the number and sizes of taxable businesses in the community. Two other components provide supplementary information: the size of the labor force within the City limits, and residential purchasing power. The results from these two components are used to make adjustments at the margin to the output from the first component.

Within each of these components, the algorithm uses different variables to arrive at an estimate of revenues. The component on the number and size of businesses relies on the projected square footage of various categories of sales-tax-producing businesses and the assumed sales-tax revenue produced per square foot for each category. The labor-force component uses a projection of the size of the labor force in Irvine and then takes into account the average annual per worker spending in Irvine and the proportion who live outside Irvine (to avoid double-counting them in the residential component), as well as other factors to help better reflect how much the work force's purchasing power will incrementally impact the City's sales tax estimate. The residential purchasing power component uses housing prices to estimate changes in residents' level of disposable income, which then incrementally impact the sales tax projection.

For Irvine, algorithms are especially useful because the City lacks predictive historical data. However, even when high-quality historical data is available, an algorithm might be a better choice when the forecaster has access to detailed information about tax/fee rates and the units on which those taxes and fees are paid (e.g., gallons of water sold, number of citations issues, total assessed value of property). For example, the City of Rock Hill, South Carolina, has been able to make accurate forecasts of its property taxes by taking the assessed value of existing property in Rock Hill, adding to that the anticipated assessed value of new properties (using building permit records), and multiplying the total by the City's tax rates for commercial and residential properties. Utilities are another revenue source where algorithms can be useful. To forecast its utility revenues, Rock Hill takes account of historical usage and resulting revenues, changes to the utility rates, and anticipated growth in the number of utility accounts.

As the cases of Irvine and Rock Hill illustrate, a forecasting algorithm can take many forms. Below are some basic principles to observe when building a spreadsheet model to produce forecasts using an algorithm for any situation. While this section was written with non-statistical algorithms and mathematical models in mind, many of the same design principles can apply to statistical models as well.[35]

The purpose of the model is clear. Forecasting models might have multiple purposes. The most obvious purpose is to produce a forecast! However, sometimes a model might be intended primarily to present a forecast rather than to calculate the forecast. It is often better to build separate models to accomplish distinct purposes in order to keep each model as streamlined as possible. For example, one model might be used to develop a forecast and another model might be used to present the forecast, where the output from the forecasting model is input into the presentation model. This is often a useful approach because a forecasting model will often focus on one particularly important and/or complex revenue, while the presentation model will show the forecasts for many revenue sources and also expenditures.

The elements of the model are transparent. A revenue forecast model will comprise a number of component parts. Each of these distinct parts should be obvious to a user. This makes the model more credible and makes it easier to transfer knowledge of how to use the model from one person to another. At a minimum, a forecasting model should make obvious the following elements:

- **Historical data.** All historical data used in the model should be labeled as such. Besides the date of the data, a model should note any important adjustments made to the data for modeling purposes. For example, an Excel "comment" could be used to note where an outlier was removed.

- **Explicit assumptions made.** A model will often make a number of explicit assumptions that have a direct mathematical role in the algorithm. To illustrate, if a water utility billing forecast is made by multiplying an assumed price per gallon by the number of gallons sold, then the assumed price per gallon should be clear. In the Excel spreadsheet, the price per gallon should be contained in a conspicuous area of the worksheet, in its own cell, clearly labeled. Formulas in the workbook would then reference that cell, rather the price being built directly into the formula.

- **The forecast.** The model will, of course, produce a forecast which should be clearly shown as distinct from actual revenues. Further, any adjustments that the forecaster makes to the forecast produced by the algorithm should be clearly shown.

- **Decompositions.** A model may decompose revenue into smaller parts for easier forecasting. For example, a property tax model might have residential and commercial components. We saw how Irvine's sales tax model addressed sales tax yield of different categories of businesses. These decompositions make obvious the knowledge of the forecaster that went into building the model.

Implicitly made assumptions are transparent. Because a model is a simplification of reality, there will always be some assumptions made about the social, technological, environmental, economic, and political forces that could impact the revenue. Most of these assumptions will not be expressed mathematically in the model, so the modeler should include some text that explains the most important assumptions made to simplify reality. For example, sales taxes in most jurisdictions are strongly influenced by business cycles. Regardless, a long-term sales tax forecast model, in most cases, would not attempt to model the impact of future business cycles since these are impossible to predict with any degree of accuracy. Therefore, an implicit assumption in the model is that the economy does not experience any dramatic downturns or expansions. Forecasters should always be forthcoming about such simplifications of reality and be able to explain why the model is still useful.

> *"All models are wrong, but some are useful."*
>
> –George E.P. Box, statistician and member of the American Academy of Arts and Sciences

The model is as simple as possible. Models should avoid over-complexity and should be easy to understand. In addition to the general rule of trying not to accomplish too much in a single model, there are number of Excel practices that should be observed.

- **Separate data from formulas.** Data should never be typed into formulas. Rather data should reside in its own area of the model and be incorporated into formulas via cell references. This makes it possible to clearly label the data and to update the model should the data change.

- **Use cell comments to document the model.** Explain notable features of the model by appending comments to the appropriate cells.

- **Use range names.** Important data is often arrayed in a range of cells. Excel allows plain English names to be assigned to ranges. These "range names" can then be used in formulas, thereby making the formula more transparent.

- **Use consistent conventions for how data is laid out in the model.** For example, lay out all time series data (demographic, economic, financial, operating, etc.) horizontally, where the furthermost left is historic, and the furthermost right is into the future. Lay out descriptive information (lists of funds, departments, accounts, other stat types) vertically. By doing this consistently, it is easier for users to follow how the model works because they don't have to consistently reinterpret the data layout to understand the model.[36]

- **Learn to use the formula auditing tools.** Excel provides tools that allow the user to visually map how a formula draws data from across the worksheet. This can help the modeler verify that the cells are logically arranged and the flow of information is clear.

Test and validate the model. Just like statistical techniques, a non-statistical algorithm/ mathematical model should be tested for accuracy before its results are put to use. Chapter 9 of this book describes testing techniques that can be applied to all forecasting methods, including algorithms.

The model is reusable. The model should be able to evolve. Providing room to add more historical data (without losing older data), using modular designs (rather than monolithic), and adhering to the principles of model simplicity described above all contribute to the reusability of a model. One key Excel practice in this vein is to use formulas that use a cell range as an argument. The "sum" formula is a well-known example of this, wherein a range of cells can be entered into the formula rather than adding each individual cell together in a formula. This allows cells to be easily added and subtracted from the model without having to rewrite the formula. Many Excel formulas have the ability to use range names as an argument.

Provide what-if capabilities. What-if capabilities allow the user of the model to easily (without rewriting formulas) vary key variables and observe the impact on the forecast. What-if capabilities are made possible by separating formulas from the data and key variables (i.e., incorporating them by reference, rather than directly embedding them), and clearly labeling the variables that the user is intended to modify (e.g., by giving those cells a unique color).

Discard bad models early.[37] Developing models is a process of continual learning and refinement. Don't be afraid to completely discard a model that isn't working and start over. In the long run, this will often be more cost-effective than continuing to limp along with the original model.

Conclusion

Forecaster judgment is an indispensable part of forecasting, but also one that is potentially dangerous due to its potential to be misapplied. When used properly, judgmental forecasting can be a very powerful tool, perhaps even surpassing the accuracy of statistical methods in some cases. Judgmental forecasting also requires far less mathematical sophistication than statistical techniques, making it less administratively burdensome to apply. The keys to using judgment to help make accurate forecasts include: breaking down intractable forecasting problems into more tractable ones; using algorithms or mathematical models to guide judgment wherever possible; seeking out and synthesizing diverse sources of information and not becoming wedded to a particular thesis on what drives revenues; working together effectively with others; and, most importantly, continually assessing what works and does not work for making forecasts, discarding the latter and building upon the former.

Chapter 6

Extrapolation Forecasting

Extrapolation forecasting uses statistical techniques to forecast revenues by finding a pattern in a time series of historical data and projecting that pattern forward. Extrapolation techniques are the most common statistical technique found in public-sector revenue forecasting because they are reliable, objective, inexpensive, relatively easy to use, and can be easily automated with Microsoft Excel. Extrapolation techniques can vary widely in their sophistication, from those that can be used with the minimal statistical skills to those that require considerable statistical skills. This chapter will cover the following topics on extrapolation.

- **Efficacy.** Learn about the prediction effectiveness of extrapolation, according to forecasting science research.

- **Conditions for use.** Learn the conditions under which extrapolation will be most useful.

- **Testing forecasting techniques.** This section covers how to test the accuracy of these techniques. Testing procedures are necessary for setting key parameters of the extrapolation techniques.

- **Types of extrapolation.** There are many extrapolation techniques, all of varying sophistication. This chapter will focus

 Advanced Content in This Chapter

Extrapolation is the fundamental statistical forecasting technique, so all readers should familiarize themselves with efficacy, conditions for use, and testing methods for extrapolation. The types of extrapolation techniques are presented in increasing order of statistical sophistication. All readers should become familiar with the basic techniques of moving averages and exponential smoothing. Holt exponential smoothing and damped trend exponential smoothing are more complicated. If you find you are comfortable with single exponential smoothing, strongly consider trying the Holt or the damped trend.

on a limited number of techniques, ranging from relatively simple to moderately sophisticated.

Efficacy

We will start by repeating the good news we introduced in Chapter 1: "statistically sophisticated or complex methods do not necessarily produce more accurate forecasts than simpler [statistical methods]." This was the conclusion drawn from a series of forecasting competitions held from 1982 through 2000 by the esteemed forecasting scientist Spyros Makridakis and his colleagues, called the "M-Competitions."[1] What these studies show is that relatively simple methods, but not the simplest possible methods, produce forecasts that are on average as accurate as relatively sophisticated methods. The simple methods that are likely to be the most effective, on average, are a class of extrapolative techniques that use exponential smoothing methods. These results are consistent with forecasting competitions that GFOA held using local government revenue data, the results of which are described in Chapter 8.

The research is not always clear on why more sophisticated methods fail, but one important reason is that complex extrapolative methods create a very tight statistical "fit" between the forecast and historical data. This tight fit can result in the statistical technique finding patterns that are not legitimate trends. These false trends are then projected forward. Conversely, simple methods ignore such patterns and just extrapolate more generalizable trends.[2] It is also worth noting that not only did relatively simple extrapolation techniques outperform more sophisticated extrapolation techniques in the M-Competitions, but they also outperformed other types of quantitative techniques, such as linear regression, which is the subject of the next chapter.

Beyond the issues raised by the M-Competitions, there are some very practical reasons why relatively simple extrapolative techniques have greater efficacy than more complex forecasting methods. First, government revenue forecasters may have limited training on how to use more complicated methods. This constraint may be offset when specialized software tools are used; however, some level of specialized knowledge and skill is still often required to interpret and adjust the results of complex methods. Second, building and maintaining more complex models may require a considerable commitment of time—time that may be better used in developing a thorough understanding of the data and the financial and economic environments.

Conditions for Use

A data series can be forecast using extrapolation when the underlying data generating process is reasonably stable and when there are an adequate number of observations.

At the risk of circularity, a stable data generating process is one that produces similar results in sequential periods. This does not mean there cannot be change over time, but the change would typically be small and gradual. The values do not have to be perfectly ordered; instead, they can reflect some random noise. Most government revenues have sufficiently stable underlying conditions such that extrapolation techniques will be suitable. For example, underlying conditions of the tax base such as population, tax rates, consumer demand, and so forth do not change radically from one period to the next, especially if monthly data is used for forecasting, as was suggested in Chapter 3. That said, there could be situations in which there are large changes in these conditions, such as might occur in a community experiencing extremely high growth, or if the state were to make a major change to the laws that govern how local governments raise revenue.

There is no perfect rule for how many observations are necessary to use extrapolation. Most extrapolation techniques will produce some useable results with just a handful of observations, but they can be made more accurate with more observations. There is a belief, not well studied, that the length of the historical data series should sharply exceed the forecast horizon (the number of periods to be forecast).

Given everything stated above, most governments will find extrapolation techniques to be of the greatest use for regular, ongoing revenue sources like sales taxes, income taxes, etc.

Testing the Accuracy of Quantitative Forecasting Techniques

Before reviewing the extrapolation techniques available to the forecaster, it is important to understand how to test the accuracy of the techniques. These tests are important for picking amongst different techniques and for adjusting various parameters for a given technique so that it performs optimally. A good way to test the accuracy of any quantitative forecasting technique is to use historical data to produce a forecast for a period that has already occurred and to compare the results to what actually happened. For example, we compare the results that a quantitative forecast technique would have given us for the years 1993 to 2012 for Motor Fuel Tax in Idaho in Exhibit 6.1 (the numbers have been rounded to thousands of dollars to make the demonstration simpler, but in actual forecasting, such rounding should be avoided[3]). The difference between the forecast and the actual result is called an *error* (also sometimes called a *residual*) and can be found with Formula 6.1 below, which reads "error equals actual minus forecast."

Formula 6.1 - Error

$$e_t = A_t - F_t$$

The error, in turn, is then used to calculate various statistics that help evaluate forecast accuracy and bias. These statistics are shown in Exhibit 6.1 and are explained fully in the following pages. You can also download Exhibit 6.1 at *www.gfoa.org/forecastbook* to see the calculations. *Accuracy* refers to how close to the actual result the forecast comes, while *bias* measures the extent to which a forecast will be wrong in a particular direction (i.e., whether a forecast consistently over- or underestimates a revenue). These measures can then be used to optimize extrapolation models by varying certain parameters in the model. When

---

Key to Formula Variables and Symbols

The variables and symbols used in the formulas in this chapter are defined below:

- A = Actual value (as observed and recorded)
- F = Forecast as made by any technique
- e = the difference between A and F, labeled "error" or "residual"
- t = a time index, or its current value in a formula, beginning at 1 for the first observation in the series and continuing 2, 3, ... through the number needed to identify the most distant future forecast
- i = an alternate index subscript
- n = the number of actual observations available
- n' = any number of observations to be excluded from n in a calculation
- n= any modified number of actual observations adjusted to remove any that might not be included in a calculation, such as n= n − n'
- $\sum$ = The Greek letter Sigma, which signifies summation.

---

we explain the extrapolation methods later in this chapter, we will show the parameters that can be varied for each.

As you will see, the error statistics are all various ways of averaging the size of the errors in a forecasting data set. However, the errors will typically be a combination of positive and negative numbers. For example, in Exhibit 6.1 the error for 2008 is +13 and the error for 2009 is −15. This would give us an average error of −1, which would obviously not be an accurate representation of size of the error in these forecasts. Hence, the statistical measures of accuracy take steps to remove negative values from the calculation, either by squaring the error or taking an absolute value.

Exhibit 6.2 summarizes the measures of accuracy and bias that we will discuss in this chapter. However before getting into the details of each measure, it is important to acknowledge that a forecaster does not necessarily need to use all of the measures. As we will see, mean absolute percentage error (MAPE) is the most intuitive of the accuracy measures, so it might be the best option for less sophisticated forecasting needs.

Exhibit 6.1 – Motor Fuel Tax Revenue, Forecasts, and Error Statistics (in Thousands)

Year	Motor Fuel Revenue	Forecast	Error	Squared Error	Absolute Error	Percentage Error	Absolute Percentage Error
1993	141	NA	NA	NA	NA	NA	NA
1994	147	NA	NA	NA	NA	NA	NA
1995	153	NA	NA	NA	NA	NA	NA
1996	159	147.0	12.0	144	12.0	7.5%	7.5%
1997	212	153.0	59.0	3481	59.0	27.8%	27.8%
1998	207	174.7	32.3	1045	32.3	15.6%	15.6%
1999	212	192.7	19.3	374	19.3	9.1%	9.1%
2000	209	210.3	−1.3	2	1.3	−0.6%	0.6%
2001	208	209.3	−1.3	2	1.3	−0.6%	0.6%
2002	214	209.7	4.3	19	4.3	2.0%	2.0%
2003	211	210.3	0.7	0	0.7	0.3%	0.3%
2004	218	211.0	7.0	49	7.0	3.2%	3.2%
2005	220	214.3	5.7	32	5.7	2.6%	2.6%
2006	228	216.3	11.7	136	11.7	5.1%	5.1%
2007	232	222.0	10.0	100	10.0	4.3%	4.3%
2008	240	226.7	13.3	178	13.3	5.6%	5.6%
2009	218	233.3	15.3	235	15.3	−7.0%	7.0%
2010	230	230.0	0.0	0	0.0	0.0%	0.0%
2011	239	229.3	9.7	93	9.7	4.0%	4.0%
2012	237	229.0	8.0	64	8.0	3.4%	3.4%
2013	NA	235.3	NA	NA	NA	NA	NA

MSE=	50	MAE=	12.4	ME=	10.3
RMSE=	19	MAPE=	5.8%	MPE=	4.8%

Exhibit 6.2 – Statistical Measures of Accuracy and Bias

Type	Measures	Key Points
Mean Absolute Error (MAE)	Accuracy	Easier to interpret and explain to others. Does not emphasize large errors as much as RMSE.
Mean Absolute Percentage Error (MAPE)	Accuracy	Turns MAE into a percentage value to make it easier to explain and interpret. Probably the most intuitively understandable of the accuracy measures.
Mean Squared Error (MSE)	Accuracy	Has desirable mathematical properties, so it is used for statistical optimization of forecasts. Not easy to interpret, especially for non-specialists.
Root Mean Squared Error (RMSE)	Accuracy	Takes square root of MSE to make it easier to interpret and explain.
Mean Error (ME)	Bias	Simple measure of bias.
Mean Percentage Error (MPE)	Bias	Turns ME into a percentage value to make it easier to explain and interpret.

We will start our discussion of the measures shown in Exhibit 6.2 with Mean Absolute Error (MAE). For MAE, we drop the negative signs on the errors included in the calculation by taking the absolute value for each value of "e" from the data set that we have elected to include in the calculation, sum those values, and then divide by the number of errors included in the calculation, as shown in the formula below. Exhibit 6.1 shows us that the mean absolute error for all of the errors in the chart is $12,400.

The formula for MAE is shown below. A forecaster might wish to calculate an error statistic for a range of years that is more limited than what is available in the entire data set. For instance, maybe the five most recent forecasts were made with a different forecasting method, so the forecaster wants to check the average error of only those forecasts. For this reason, the sub- and superscripts in the formula denote that the calculation could use only a subset of the available errors to make an MAE calculation.

Formula 6.2– Mean Absolute Error

$$MAE = {\left(\sum_{t=n'+1}^{n} |e_t| \right)}/{n^*}$$

The Mean Absolute Percentage Error (MAPE) makes MAE more intuitive by turning MAE into a percentage value. Many forecasters might find MAPE to be the most useful of the error measures because it is the easiest to understand and communicate. The formula for the percentage error (PE) for a given observation is below:

Formula 6.3 – Percentage Error

$$PE_t = (\frac{A_t - F_t}{A_t}) \times 100$$

The formula tells us to subtract the forecast from the actual value for a given observation and to then divide the difference by the actual. The resulting decimal figure can then be multiplied by 100 to get a percentage figure (or just use Excel percentage formatting).

To then get MAPE, the absolute value of each percentage is taken and the average of all of the absolute values is found. Exhibit 6.1 shows MAPE for the Motor Fuel Revenue, which is 5.8 percent. Many users of the forecast would find a percentage to be a more meaningful measure of accuracy than just a dollar amount, like MAE produces.

Formula 6.4 – Mean Absolute Percent Error

$$MAPE = \frac{(\sum_{t=n'+1}^{n} |PE_t|)}{n^*}$$

Also, unlike errors expressed in just dollar amounts, MAPE statistics are comparable between forecasts for different revenue sources. To say that a property tax forecast has an MAE of $50,000 compared to a sales tax forecast MAE of $35,000, does not provide as much comparative value as saying that the MAPE of property tax is 3 percent versus an MAPE for sales taxes of 6 percent. MAPE tells us clearly that sales tax forecasts are, on average, less accurate. The differences between MAE figures could be due to accuracy or due simply to the size of the revenue (i.e., for a large revenue, even a small percentage error could be a large dollar amount).

We just saw how absolute values can be used to remove negative values from the data set and create error statistics. Another method to remove negative values from the error calculation is to multiply each error by itself or to square each value. Mean Squared Error or MSE is the average of the squared values of each error in the data set. This formula describes the Mean Square Error:

Formula 6.5 – Mean Squared Error

$$MSE = \frac{(\sum_{t=n'+1}^{n} e_i^2)}{n^*}$$

The formula tells us to square each included error from the data set and then sum up each squared error, starting with the first one and, finally, to divide by the number of errors included. Exhibit 6.1 shows MSE calculated for Motor Fuel Taxes at $350,000. While MSE has mathematically desirable properties, ease of interpretation is not one of its advantages – the MSE is $350,000, but the largest actual annual revenue income for Motor Fuel Taxes is $240,000! Root Mean Squared Error (RMSE) can correct for this by simply taking the square root of MSE. In Exhibit 6.1, the RMSE is $19,000. This is far more intuitively understandable as we can say the average forecast error for this data set is $19,000.

The reader might notice an interesting difference between the results of the RMSE and MAE calculations in Exhibit 6.1: the MAE is $12,400 and the RMSE is $19,000! The reason for this is that the RMSE amplifies the impact of large errors. To illustrate, 1997's error of "59" is the largest in the data set and it squares to "3,841." The years 2000 and 2001 each had an error of only "-1.3," which squares to just 1.69, rounded to "2" in the table. When all of the errors are squared and an average is taken, the larger errors have a disproportionately large impact on the result. This means that RMSE has a unique analytic value for the forecaster because big forecasting errors are, of course, a big problem for budgeting! Therefore, RMSE can be helpful for identifying forecasting methods that have a propensity for larger errors. That said, this subtle difference between RMSE and MAE will probably not be expected or understood by the forecaster's audience, so forecasters might wish to stick with MAE (and MAPE) for presenting forecasts to laypeople and should definitely not present RMSE and MAE together.

Moving on to measures of bias, Mean Error (ME) is the standard statistic. The formula (below) is very similar to that for mean squared error, except that the error is not squared. This leaves the negative numbers in place. The formula, then, is the sum of all of the errors in the data set divided by the number of forecast errors in the data set:

Formula 6.6 – Mean Error

$$ME = \left(\sum_{t=n'+1}^{n} e_t \right) \Big/ n^*$$

The formula will produce a negative or positive number, which tells you whether the forecast is more consistently over- or underestimating. In Exhibit 6.1, the ME is +$10,300, which tells us that actual revenue is typically that much more than the forecast (i.e., the forecast regularly underestimates). When using the statistics described in this section to compare different forecasting methods, it is not uncommon for one method to have a lower ME than another, but to also have a higher RMSE/MAE. In these cases, the forecaster must use judgment to decide how much bias to accept in order to improve accuracy. To make this judgment, forecasters should first consider the direction of the bias. If the bias is a negative number (i.e., actual revenue is usually under the forecast), then the forecast might put the government at a greater risk of experiencing a budget deficit during the year. Next, the forecaster should consider the views of the decision-makers who will use the forecast. If they want forecasts to be as accurate as possible, they might be willing to accept greater risk of overestimating revenues. However, if the decision-makers are unwilling to take on this risk, they might prefer the less accurate, but also less risky, forecast.

Finally, Mean Percentage Error (MPE) turns ME into a percentage to make it more understandable. MPE is calculated in the same way as MAPE, except that the percentage errors are not turned into absolute values before finding the average. In Exhibit 6.1, the MPE is 4.8 percent, which tells us the forecast model is biased towards underestimating actuals by that much.

For the sake of simplicity, in this chapter we will primarily use MSE, RMSE, and ME error statistics for the forecast methods we are illustrating. However, in real-life application, a forecaster can use any of the error statistics as he or she might need.

Methods of Extrapolating Time Series Data

In the next sections, five extrapolation methods are discussed in order of increasing sophistication. These are the moving average, moving average of the trend, simple exponential smoothing, Holt exponential smoothing, and damped Holt exponential smoothing. We will discuss how to test the accuracy of extrapolation techniques within the section on moving averages, because moving averages provide an easy-to-understand illustration. The same testing methods can be applied to all extrapolation techniques, though we will not illustrate them. Finally, the spreadsheets used to construct the examples of each method are available at *www.gfoa.org/forecastbook*.

Moving Average

A simple moving average is an average of a group of observations in a time series. It is sometimes labeled MAL where the "L" is replaced with the number of observations included. For example, MA3 refers to a moving average of 3 observations. The reader may recall that in Chapter 4 we introduced the *centered moving average*, which was the average of a given observation plus an equal number of observations before it and observations after it. However, when a moving average is used for forecasting, it is an average of the "L" most recently available observations and the result of the moving average becomes the forecast. When the historical data series reaches the end, the MA is used to forecast all subsequent periods.

The formula for a moving average is illustrated below.[4] While the moving average concept is relatively simple and a formula may seem unnecessary, it is helpful for the reader to understand it because the notations are commonly used in describing forecasting formulas. Hence, grasping the notations for how the formula for a moving average is written will help the reader scaffold up to understanding the formulas for the more sophisticated forecasting methods.

Formula 6.7 – Moving Average

$$MA_L = \left(\sum_{i=1}^{L} X_i \right) \Big/ L$$

- L = Length of the moving average.
- MA_L = A moving average of a given length, such as 3 observations.
- The L superscript tells us that the length of the set of numbers to be summed is L numbers. The subscript "$i=1$" tells us that the initiating point should be the first observation in set.
- X = The numbers to be summed. The subscript i indicates that the summing should start with the first value of X in the data set. The L superscript on Sigma already told us the number of observations to sum.

In order to illustrate the techniques on a scale that is easier to grasp, we have used annual data, but monthly data could be used as well.

Exhibit 6.3 shows how forecasting with a moving average works using a three-period moving average for motor fuel tax in Idaho, in thousands of dollars. For illustrative purposes, two cells in the "MA3 Forecast" column are highlighted along with six cells in the "Motor Fuel Revenue" column. Each highlighted cell in the MA3 Forecast is the average of the three preceding highlighted cells in the Motor Fuel Revenue column. The result of year 2013's MA3 forecast is an average of the actual revenues from 2010, 2011, and 2012.

The MA3 forecast necessarily stops at 2013 because there are not three actual observations available to make a 2014 forecast. If the forecaster wanted a MA3 forecast for 2014, the convention would be to repeat the forecast from 2013 since this is the last available output from the MA3 forecast. However, the obvious practical weakness of this approach is that moving averages are not usually a good choice for long-term forecasting. Forecasts for years 2003 or prior do not exist because we do not have at least

Exhibit 6.3 – Moving Average Forecast

Year	Motor Fuel Revenue	MA3 Forecast
2001	208	NA
2002	214	NA
2003	211	NA
2004	218	211
2005	220	214
2006	228	216
2007	232	222
2008	240	227
2009	218	233
2010	230	230
2011	239	229
2012	237	229
2013	???	235

three historical observations to calculate the moving average.

When considering a forecasting technique, it is wise to review the results in graphical, not just tabular, form. Exhibit 6.4 shows the forecast compared with the actuals. It shows a relatively good match between forecast and actuals, except for the period 1997 through 1999, when a sharp jump in revenues in 1997 caused a large error for a three-year period. The moving average caught up to the new trend that seems to have established itself in the 2000s. Based on his or her judgment, the forecaster might deem that the jump in revenue in 1997 was a highly anomalous event, such that it is no longer relevant for evaluating the potential accuracy of forecasting methods, and it likely would be more effective to omit errors before 2000. In fact, if we omit those errors, the error statistics improve dramatically: RMSE goes from $19,000 to $8,000 and ME from $10,300 to $4,000.

We can also see how the moving average lags behind the drop in revenue associated with the 2009 recession. As a result of the dip in actual revenue in 2009, moving average forecast underestimates revenues after the economy has recovered. This effect lasts until 2009's data is no longer included in the moving average (which we can see in the 2013 forecast).

Monthly vs. Annual Data

In order to illustrate the techniques on a scale that is relatively easy to grasp, we have used annual data, but monthly data could be used as well.

Exhibit 6.4 – MA3 Forecast Compared to Actual Motor Fuel Revenues

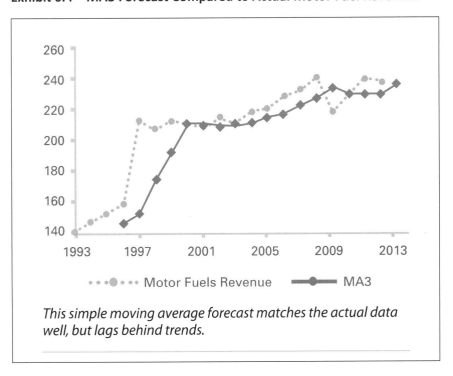

This simple moving average forecast matches the actual data well, but lags behind trends.

Up to this point, we have considered MA3 forecasts. However, it is certainly possible to use moving averages of other lengths to create forecasts, and the forecaster should explore the potential of alternates. To illustrate, Exhibit 6.5 shows the error statistics for MA2, MA3, and MA4 forecasts (moving averages with lengths of 2, 3, and 4 years). The calculations in the chart omit errors before 2000 because, as a general rule, when we compare moving averages of different lengths, we use only errors for those periods that are included in each moving average alternate.

Exhibit 6.5 – Error Statistics for Moving Average Forecasts of Different Lengths

	MA2	MA3	MA4
RMSE	$8,000	$8,000	$9,000
ME	$3,000	$4,000	$6,000

For accuracy, MA3 and MA2 are tied. For bias, MA2 is best. In this instance, the graph in Exhibit 6.4 suggests that, although small, the data had a trend in the mid-2000s. A simple moving average will systematically underestimate a trend like we see in our Idaho data since older, lower values hold down the forecast. Hence, the MA2 moving average forecast produces the least bias since it includes fewer older values. Our next method provides a more sophisticated approach for handling trends in the data.

Moving Average of the Trend

Trend refers to how much a data series arrayed over time (a time series) changes from period to period. Typically, trend refers to a measure, such as an average of trend units that smooths out some of the period-to-period differences found in a time series. This average of trend units is sometimes called *slope*, but in this chapter we will simply use trend to refer to the average of a number of trend units. A trend unit is found by the formula:

Formula 6.8 – A Trend Unit

$$B_t = A_t - A_{t-1}$$

This formula says that the trend (B) at time t is the actual observation (A) at time t minus the actual observation at time t-1 (the immediately preceding actual observation). There will always be one less trend observation (B) than actual observations (A) because we will always be missing one value of A_{t-1}. While B_t measures the trend between the two periods (A_t and A_{t-1}), the value the formula returns for B_t is traditionally associated with the more recent period (the same period as A_t).

When using a moving average to forecast a data series that has a trend, the forecaster will find what we found during the mid-2000s with the Idaho data: the moving average can never quite keep up with the data, and the forecast is always lagging behind the direction of the trend. This is because the result of the moving average calculation is used to forecast the period that comes one period after the data used to calculate the average. However, the moving average actually reflects the middle point of the data included in the average. The middle will always be below the highest (or above the lowest) point.

A common, but suboptimal approach to forecasting forward a trend is to find a rate of growth – taking the percentage change from A_{t-1} to A_t and then applying that percent change to A_t to predict the future period. There are three important weaknesses to this method:

- Applying a percent change to make a forecast is a multiplicative perspective on the trend. For example, compounding interest can quickly turn a little money into a lot of money – it is a multiplicative phenomenon. Perhaps to the disappointment of some budget officers, multiplicative growth does not always occur in government revenues.
- This method relies on a single observation of the trend. It is better to find a moving average of the trend. This will provide a better fit between the forecaster's model and the data.
- When forecasting into the future, we do not want to forecast from a specific prior observation (i.e., A_t). That prior observation necessarily contains some random element. We use averages to remove the random element, so we would not want to reintroduce it by forecasting from a specific observation.

When we use the moving average of the trend forecasting technique, we add a trend component to the moving average forecast that we saw in the preceding section of this chapter. In Exhibit 6.6 we have a computational example of a forecast using West Virginia individual income tax data (which has been inflation adjusted).[5] After the inflation adjusted data, the first column is the trend column, which is calculated using Formula 6.8. We then see a column called "Level MA3," which is just the exact same moving average forecast method we have seen before – it uses Formula 6.7 and is analogous to what was produced for Exhibit 6.3. In Exhibit 6.6, we call it the moving average of the level in order to differentiate it from the moving average of the trend, which we see in the "Trend MA3" column. The moving average of the trend is calculated like the moving average of level except that the variable averaged is the trend units (B_t) (Formula 6.9):

Formula 6.9 – Moving Average of the Trend

$$MA(trend)_L = \left(\sum_{i=1}^{L} B_i\right)\Big/L$$

The formula for making a forecast is below. It says that the forecast is equal to the moving average of the level plus the moving average for the trend, which first must be multiplied by the length of the moving average period plus one, the sum of which is divided by two:

Formula 6.10 – Moving Average Forecast with Trend

$$F = MA(level)_L + MA(trend)_L \times ((L+1)/2)$$

Here is how the formula would look to get the forecast for 1997 in Exhibit 6.6:

$$1{,}143 = 1{,}069 + 37 \times ((3+1)/2)$$

The reader may be wondering what the purpose of $(L+1)/2$ is in the formula. We include this because, in a data series with a trend, the moving average will be most closely associated with the time period in the middle of the average, so, for instance, if there is a three-period moving average and the three periods are 1994 through 1996 (where we want to forecast 1997), the moving average is centered in 1995. We calculate $(3+1)/2$ to get 2 and multiply this by the trend moving average to estimate the change in the trend from 1995 to 1997, the forecast year, two years later.

Once there is no longer actual data available to calculate the formulas for the moving average of the trend, we use the forecast from the prior period as the new level and add the most recently available trend forecast. To illustrate, in Exhibit 6.6 the forecast for 2014 is 1,745 plus the trend of 30, which equals 1,775. The forecast for 2015 would be 1,775 plus 30 and so on for successive years.

Exhibit 6.6 – Moving Average of the Trend Forecast for Income Tax Revenue (in Thousands of 2012 Dollars)

Year	Income Tax Revenue	Trend	Level MA3	Trend MA3	Forecast	e	e^2
1993	987	NA	NA	NA	NA	NA	NA
1994	1,037	50	NA	NA	NA	NA	NA
1995	1,070	33	NA	NA	NA	NA	NA
1996	1,099	29	1,031	NA	NA	NA	NA
1997	1,125	26	1,069	37	1,143	−18	336
1998	1,220	95	1,098	29	1,157	63	4,011
1999	1,268	48	1,148	50	1,248	20	400
2000	1,288	20	1,204	56	1,317	−29	841
2001	1,324	36	1,259	54	1,367	−43	1,878
2002	1,321	−3	1,293	35	1,363	−42	1,736
2003	1,317	−4	1,311	18	1,346	−29	860
2004	1,298	−19	1,321	10	1,340	−42	1,764
2005	1,378	80	1,312	−9	1,295	83	6,944
2006	1,478	100	1,331	19	1,369	109	11,881
2007	1,507	29	1,385	54	1,492	15	225
2008	1,620	113	1,454	70	1,594	26	693
2009	1,667	47	1,535	81	1,696	−29	860
2010	1,602	−65	1,598	63	1,724	−122	14,884
2011	1,700	98	1,630	32	1,693	7	49
2012	1,756	56	1,656	27	1,710	46	2,147
2013	???	NA	1,686	30	1,745	NA	NA
2014	???	NA	NA	30	1,775	NA	NA

L=	3	ME=	1.0
(L+1)/2=	2	RMSE=	55.6

Exhibit 6.7 compares the RMSE and ME for the level-only MA3 forecast, and the trend and level MA2, MA3, and MA4 forecasts.[6] These results suggest that the trend and level MA3 forecast provides the best fit of those options considered. Even the other trend and level forecasts provide a substantial improvement in accuracy and bias over the level-only forecast.

Exhibit 6.7 – Comparative Error Statistics for the Example Income Tax Forecast

	Level	Trend & Level		
	MA3	MA2	MA3	MA4
RMSE	$97,000	$80,000	$57,000	$80,000
ME	$81,000	($13,000)	$1,000	($14,000)

Exhibit 6.8 graphs the MA3 trend and level forecast against West Virginia's actual income tax revenue. As we can see, the model tracks the data quite well. We can also see that the forecast still lags somewhat behind major inflection points in the revenue. For example, in 2005 revenue started a sharp upwards trajectory, but it took a few years for the forecast to catch up.

Exhibit 6.8 – MA3 Trend and Level Forecast vs. Actual Income Tax Revenue

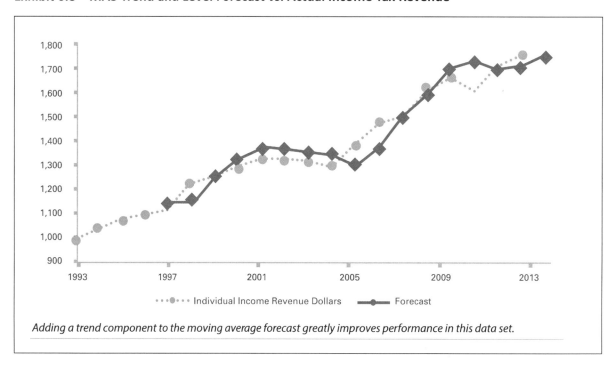

Adding a trend component to the moving average forecast greatly improves performance in this data set.

Simple Exponential Smoothing

Simple Exponential Smoothing (SES) produces an exponentially weighted moving average. It is a way of computing a moving average that provides a specified weight on the most recent observation and decreasing weights on earlier observations. No observation is forgotten, although when the weight for the most recent observation is even slightly large, very old observations receive very little weight. There are several ways to express the formula for SES. The one shown here can be computed in a table with relative ease.[7]

The formulas for the SES are:

Formulas 6.11 – Single Exponential Smoothing

Error $$e_t = A_t - F_t$$

Forecast $$F_t = F_{t-1} + \alpha e_{t-1}$$

The reader will recognize the error formula from earlier in this chapter. The second formula says that the forecast for a given time period is the forecast for the prior period plus error for the prior period multiplied by "alpha" (α). Alpha is a constant between zero and one, which is set by the forecaster in order to determine how much weight to place on prior observations, where a value closer to 1 gives greater weight to the most recent observation than a value closer to zero. (We will cover how to set alpha soon.)

Exhibit 6.9 provides an example of SES forecast using the same Idaho motor fuel tax data from Exhibit 6.1. The first thing to note is that the SES formula will not work so well for the first period in your data set because the formula asks for data derived from the prior period forecast (for which, necessarily, there will be no data). Therefore, the SES formula must be "initialized." It is recommended that forecasters use an average of the first few actual observations to initialize the SES forecast. In Exhibit 6.9, we use an average of the actual revenues from 1993 through 1995, giving us the forecast of 147 for 1993. If you are using monthly or quarterly data for your forecast, you should average all the observations for the first year (since picking just the first few periods could be impacted by seasonality).

With the first forecast in place, we can get the 1994 forecast by taking the 1993 forecast plus error from 1993 multiplied by the alpha value (which we've set at 0.875 for this example). The same approach is repeated for every year in the series until we arrive at the forecast for 2013. To illustrate, the calculation for 1994's forecast is below:

$$142 = 147 + (0.875 \times -6)$$

Again, the permissible values of alpha are from zero to one, although the forecaster would never want to set alpha at exactly zero or one. When selecting an alpha value between zero and one, higher values of alpha imply that the forecast will reflect the most recent observations more heavily and deemphasize the older observations. A higher value also means the forecast will vary more from one year to the next as the SES forecast will change more rapidly to more closely reflect what happened in the prior period. A typical routine for setting the alpha value is to start at 0.5, then move either to 0.25 or 0.75. If the RMSE improves, cut the distance to the limit (i.e., zero or one) in half again (i.e., use 0.125 or 0.875). If the RMSE gets worse, move in the opposite direction (i.e., 0.375 or 0.625). In just a few trials, the RMSE will stabilize near its optimal value. Forecast literature suggests that it is not important to find exactly the right value. In Exhibit 6.9 we have selected an alpha of 0.875.

Some software has specific routines for selecting α, but in our example it must be selected by judgment using the approach described above.

The reader will notice that since the SES formula relies on the error (and hence the actual) for the prior period, there is a problem with getting a forecast for two periods ahead of your last period with an actual value. The convention is to simply repeat the forecast for one period ahead for all other future periods. This approach obviously limits the usefulness of single exponential smoothing for long-term revenue forecasting, so SES will usually be employed for short- or immediate-term forecasting.

Exhibit 6.9 – Single Exponential Smoothing Forecast for Motor Fuel Tax Revenue (in Thousands of 2012 Dollars)

Year	Motor Fuels Revenue	Forecast	e	e²
1993	141	147	−6	36
1994	147	142	5	28
1995	153	146	7	44
1996	159	152	7	47
1997	212	158	54	2900
1998	207	205	2	3
1999	212	207	5	27
2000	209	211	−2	6
2001	208	209	−1	2
2002	214	208	6	34
2003	211	213	−2	5
2004	218	211	7	45
2005	220	217	3	8
2006	228	220	8	70
2007	232	227	5	25
2008	240	231	9	74
2009	218	239	−21	438
2010	230	221	9	88
2011	239	229	10	103
2012	237	238	−1	1
2013	???	237	NA	NA
2014	???	237	NA	NA

α = 0.875

ME=2
RMSE= 8

In Exhibit 6.9, the two error statistics are calculated in the same way as the prior examples in this chapter. To facilitate comparison with the moving average examples we showed earlier, observations prior to 2000 are not included in the error measure statistics. Exhibit 6.10 compares the SES forecast with the moving average forecasts and finds that the accuracy is about the same, but the mean error is improved.

Exhibit 6.10 – Error Statistics for Simple Moving Average versus Single Exponential Smoothing, Using Motor Fuel Tax Data Set

	Moving Average			SES
	MA2	**MA3**	**MA4**	$\alpha = .875$
RMSE	$8,000	$8,000	$9,000	$8,000
ME	$3,000	$4,000	$6,000	$2,000

Finally, the reader may have noticed that our discussion of SES has not mentioned trends. This is because, much like moving averages of the level, SES forecasts will lag behind trends. Hence, if there is a trend in the data, SES should be supplemented with other techniques to account for the trend, which is the subject of the next section.

Holt Exponential Smoothing

Holt exponential smoothing (Holt ES) builds on single exponential smoothing to include a trend component. Below are the formulas used in Holt ES:

Formulas 6.12 – Holt Exponential Smoothing

Error
$$e_t = A_t - F_t$$

Level
$$S_t = F_t - 1 + \alpha e_t$$

Trend
$$B_t = B_{t-1} + \alpha\beta e_t$$

Forecast
$$F_t = S_{t-1} + B_{t-1}$$

The error formula is the same one we have been using. The level formula, when combined with the forecast formula, has the same effect as the formula for SES (since L has already been used to denote the length of a moving average, we use S to denote level in this formula). However, the level is now just one component of the forecast. The trend is the new component. The formula bears little resemblance to the trend formula we used for moving averages with a trend, and looks much more like the level formula for SES. Accordingly, the reader will notice that alpha (α) returns in the formula for the trend and there is now a new Greek letter, beta (β) in the trend formula. Like with SES, both of these represent constants between zero and one that are used to decide how heavily to weight older data in the forecast.

Another important difference between Holt ES and SES is that Holt ES has a more complex process to find the initial value of the forecast (often called "initialization") because we must initialize both the level and the trend. The initialization formulas are shown below. The A in both of these formulas refers to actuals. B_0 is the initial trend and S_0 is the initial level:

Formulas 6.13 – Initializing Holt ES

Initial Trend

$$B_0 = \frac{\frac{\sum_{n+1}^{2n} A}{n} - \frac{\sum_{i=1}^{n} A}{n}}{n}$$

Initial Level

$$S_0 = \frac{\sum_{i=1}^{n} A}{n} - B_0 * \frac{n+1}{2}$$

For the initial trend, the formula tells us to find the average of two equal periods near the beginning of the data. For illustration, we will use the same West Virginia income tax data set that we used earlier in this chapter. Exhibit 6.11 shows the forecast using this data. For our initialization, we selected a three-year period of 1993 through 1995 and a second three-year period of 1996 through 1998. The forecaster could also choose to use a two-year period. For non-annual data, the forecaster can use judgment to select a period, possibly partly advised by moving average results. For our approach with three years, the calculation looks as follows:

$$B_0 = \frac{\frac{(1099 + 1125 + 1220)}{3} - \frac{(987 + 1037 + 1070)}{3}}{3} = \frac{117}{3} = 38.89$$

The average of the first three periods is 1,031, and of the second three periods is 1,148. We subtract the average of the first period from the average of the second period, obtaining 117, and divide that by the number of observations in a period, 3, to find an initial trend of 38.89.

The initial level calculation looks as follows:

$$S_0 = \frac{(987 + 1037 + 1070)}{3} - 38.89 * \frac{3+1}{2} = 1031.3 - 77.8 = 953.5$$

We subtract from the average of our first three actual observations the initial trend multiplied by $(n+1)/2$ (in this case, 2). The reason for including $(n + 1)/2$ as part of the formula is the same as was provided for the moving average with trends.

With our initial trend and level values identified, we can produce an initialization forecast. The forecast in Holt ES is the trend plus the level, which means our 1993 forecast is equal to 953.56 plus 38.89 or 992.5. This allows us to enter our first value in the error column, which is -5.5. This error is the difference between our forecast of 992.5 and 987, the actual revenue received in 1993.

Before we can go beyond the initialization forecast, we must set values for alpha and beta. To get started, you can plug in any values of alpha and beta, as with SES, and then optimize the values of alpha and beta. In order to optimize the values of alpha and beta in the absence of specialized software, the forecaster should systematically test out a series of alpha and beta values. This can be done by simply listing out pairs of likely values in a grid, such as: $\alpha = 0.05, 0.1, 0.15 \ldots 0.95$; and $\beta = 0.001, 0.002, \ldots, 0.01, 0.02, \ldots, 0.1, 0.15, 0.2$ and manually going through the grid to try out each combination to see how different combinations of the alpha and beta statistics impact the error.[8]

Hence, you can start your forecast with the first values of alpha and beta from the grid. The reader will notice that the potential β values are lower than α values in our grid. This is because some forecasting researchers believe that lower β values generally produce better results, although there is some disagreement on this point. Eventually, each potential pair of alpha and beta values should be tried in the formula and the optimal RMSE and ME found. For Exhibit 6.11 we settled on an alpha of 0.65 and a beta of 0.01.

To get the forecast for 1994, we must first identify the level and trend in 1993, using the equations from Formulas 6.12. The results are illustrated below:

$$1993 \; Level = 992.5 + 0.65 \times \text{-}5.5 = 988.91$$

$$1993 \; Trend = 38.89 + 0.65 \times 0.01 \times \text{-}5.5 = 38.85$$

We then add 988.91 to 38.85 to get the 1994 forecast of 1027.8. The forecaster then follows the same approach for each subsequent year until a forecast is obtained for 2013. Much like the other techniques we've described in this chapter, if you want to forecast for periods beyond one period ahead of the last period for which you have actual revenue data (e.g., 2014 in Exhibit 6.11), you must modify the approach. In this case, the approach is exactly like the one described for moving average of the trend – the most recently available trend value is simply added to the forecast for the immediately available prior period.

Exhibit 6.11 – Holt Exponential Smoothing for West Virginia Income Tax Revenue (in Thousands of 2012 Dollars)

Year	Income Tax Revenue	Level	Trend	Forecast	e	e^2
Initialize	NA	953.56	38.89	NA	NA	NA
1993	987	988.91	38.85	992.5	5.4	29.7
1994	1,037	1033.77	38.91	1027.8	9.2	85.3
1995	1,070	1070.94	38.90	1072.7	−2.7	7.2
1996	1,099	1102.79	38.83	1109.8	−10.8	117.4
1997	1,125	1130.82	38.72	1141.6	−16.6	276.2
1998	1,220	1202.34	39.05	1169.5	50.5	2546.7
1999	1,268	1258.68	39.22	1241.4	26.6	708.4
2000	1,288	1291.47	39.16	1297.9	−9.9	98.1
2001	1,324	1326.32	39.11	1330.6	−6.6	43.8
2002	1,321	1336.55	38.82	1365.4	−44.4	1974.0
2003	1,317	1337.43	38.44	1375.4	−58.4	3407.5
2004	1,298	1325.26	37.94	1375.9	−77.9	6064.5
2005	1,378	1372.82	38.03	1363.2	14.8	219.2
2006	1,478	1454.50	38.47	1410.9	67.1	4508.8
2007	1,507	1502.09	38.56	1493.0	14.0	196.9
2008	1,620	1592.23	39.08	1540.7	79.3	6296.3
2009	1,667	1654.51	39.31	1631.3	35.7	1274.1
2010	1,602	1634.14	38.71	1693.8	−91.8	8430.3
2011	1,700	1690.50	38.89	1672.8	27.2	737.2
2012	1,756	1746.69	39.06	1729.4	26.6	708.3
2013	???	NA	39.06	1785.7	NA	NA
2014	???	NA	39.06	1824.8	NA	NA

Exhibit 6.12 shows that Holt ES is more effective than any of the previous methods we have used with the West Virginia data. Exhibit 6.13 compares the Holt forecast with the data.

Exhibit 6.12 – Error Statistics for Holt ES versus other methods

| | MA3 | Trend & Level Moving Averages | | | Holt-ES |
		MA2	MA3	MA4	
RMSE	$97,000	$80,000	$57,000	$80,000	$47,000
ME	$81,000	($13,000)	$2,000	($14,000)	$ 1,000

Exhibit 6.13 – Holt ES Forecast versus West Virginia Actual Income Tax Revenues (in Thousands of 2012 Dollars)

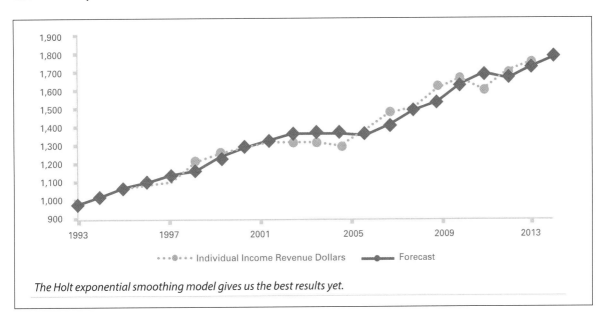

The Holt exponential smoothing model gives us the best results yet.

Damped Trend Exponential Smoothing

A variation of Holt is *damped trend exponential smoothing*. The choice to use a damped trend reflects the belief that any trend will eventually fade away. However, trends can quite frequently be very stable, so the damped trend has the potential to produce inaccuracies even over short forecast horizons. Therefore, should the forecaster choose to use damped trends, he or she should be very cautious and should use a very limited damping factor.

The formulas for damped trend are shown below:[9]

Formula 6.14 - Damped Trend Exponential Smoothing

Error $e_t = A_t - F_t$

Level $S_t = F_t - 1 + \alpha e_t$

Trend $B_t = \phi\ B_{t-1} + \beta e_t$

Forecast $F_t = S_{t-1} + \phi\ B_{t-1}$

The formulas above are very similar to Formulas 6.12 for Holt ES. The most obvious differ-ence is the addition of a third Greek letter, phi (ϕ). Like alpha and beta, phi is a constant from 1.0 to 0, which is used to damp the trend. Hence, phi appears in the formula for the trend and in the trend portion of the forecast equation. The reader may also notice that alpha has been removed from the trend formula and now only appears in the level formula.

Just like Holt ES, the Damped Trend ES must be initialized. The formulas and procedures are exactly the same as with Holt ES (see Formulas 6.13). Exhibit 6.14 shows a computa-tional example of Damped Trend ES using the familiar West Virginia income tax data. The reader will notice that the initialization figures are identical to Exhibit 6.11.

Also, like Holt ES, values must be set for our Greek letter constants before we can generate the forecasts past the initialization period. For alpha and beta, the forecaster can follow the same procedure described for Holt ES (e.g., manually trying out different pairs of values by going through a grid search). For phi, it is very inadvisable for non-experts to stray far from 1. In Exhibit 6.14, phi is equal to 0.999 and most forecasters would want to select a very similar value.[10] The reader will notice that beta has been set lower than in Exhibit 6.11 be-cause alpha has been removed from the trend formula (without alpha the error has a larger impact since it now only is multiplied by one fractional amount: beta).

The constants set, the forecasts can be made. Like Holt ES, we must first get the level and trend for the preceding year. So, to get the forecast for 1994, we must get the level and trend for 1993, using the equations from Formulas 6.14. The results are illustrated below:

$$1993\ Level = 992.5\ + 0.65 \times\ {}^-5.4 = 988.9$$

$$1993\ Trend = 0.999 \times\ 38.9 + 0.001 \times\ {}^-5.4 = 38.8$$

The trend and the level are added together to get the 1994 forecast of 1027.8 and the pro-cess is repeated until arriving at a forecast for 2013. For forecast values beyond 2013, there is a slight change from Holt. We do not simply continue to add the trend since the trend is assumed to be fading over time. Rather, we apply the damping factor (ϕ) to the trend and then add the trend to the level. For each succeeding year the damping factor would be applied again to the trend used for the immediately preceding forecast so that the trend gets smaller and smaller over time.

Exhibit 6.14 – Damped Trend Exponential Smoothing for West Virginia Income Tax (in Thousands of 2012 Dollars)

Year	Income Tax Revenue	Level	Trend	Forecast	e	e²
Initialize	NA	953.6	38.9	NA	NA	NA
1993	987	988.9	38.8	992.5	−5.4	29.7
1994	1,037	1033.8	38.8	1027.8	9.2	85.5
1995	1,070	1070.9	38.8	1072.6	−2.6	6.7
1996	1,099	1102.7	38.7	1109.7	−10.7	114.0
1997	1,125	1130.8	38.7	1141.5	−16.5	271.0
1998	1,220	1202.3	38.7	1169.4	50.6	2557.1
1999	1,268	1258.5	38.7	1241.0	27.0	729.9
2000	1,288	1291.2	38.6	1297.2	−9.2	84.9
2001	1,324	1326.0	38.6	1329.8	−5.8	34.2
2002	1,321	1336.3	38.5	1364.6	−43.6	1903.1
2003	1,317	1337.2	38.4	1374.8	−57.8	3336.7
2004	1,298	1325.2	38.3	1375.6	−77.6	6024.4
2005	1,378	1372.9	38.3	1363.4	14.6	211.7
2006	1,478	1454.6	38.3	1411.2	66.8	4466.7
2007	1,507	1502.1	38.3	1492.9	14.1	198.9
2008	1,620	1592.1	38.3	1540.3	79.7	6347.6
2009	1,667	1654.2	38.3	1630.4	36.6	1338.1
2010	1,602	1633.7	38.2	1692.5	−90.5	8190.4
2011	1,700	1690.1	38.2	1671.9	28.1	792.4
2012	1,756	1746.3	38.2	1728.3	27.7	766.6
2013	???	NA	38.1	1784.6	NA	NA
2014	???	NA	NA	1822.5	NA	NA

$\alpha = 0.65$ RMSE= 43.3
$\beta = 0.001$ ME= 1.7
$\phi = 0.999$

Exhibit 6.15 shows the error statistics for the damped trend ES versus the other methods we have used for the West Virginia income tax data. It shows that the short-term effect is roughly the same as Holt ES (a plot of the forecasts and actuals for damped trend ES would look very similar to Exhibit 6.13). However, we would see a greater difference in the long-term, as the damping of the trend starts to be become more noticeable.

Exhibit 6.15 - Error Statistics for Damped Trend ES versus Other Methods

		Trend & Level Moving Averages			Exponential Smoothing	
	MA3	MA2	MA3	MA4	Holt-ES	Dampened Trend
RMSE	97,000	80,000	57,000	80,000	47,000	47,000
ME	81,000	(13,000)	2,000	(14,000)	1,000	2,000

Conclusion

Extrapolation techniques are the most commonly used statistical techniques in public-sector revenue forecasting and have been proven effective by forecasting research. They use historical data to project forward patterns in the future. This chapter has described these patterns from two perspectives:

- Level: The "level" is how far a given revenue observation is from zero at a point of time. Seasonal, trend, and random forces cause the level to change.

- Trend: "Trend" refers to how much a data series arrayed over time (a time series) changes from period to period.

Simpler extrapolation techniques account only for the level. This creates a risk of the forecast lagging behind the direction of the trend. Below is a summary of each of the techniques from the simplest one we present to the most complex. The forecaster can use the results of tests for accuracy and bias to optimize the selected forecast method.

Moving Average	
Complex?	Not at all. Minimal statistical abilities required.
Accounts for trends?	No, moving averages underestimate a trend.
Full use of historical data?	No, only accounts for data within the length of the moving average.
Use for long-term forecasting?	One-period ahead forecast is repeated for all future periods.

Moving Average with Trend	
Complex?	A little more complex than simple moving average, but should be well within the capabilities of most public finance professionals.
Accounts for trends?	Yes, adds a trending component to the standard moving average.
Full use of historical data?	No, only accounts for data within the length of the moving average.
Use for long-term forecasting?	Better than simple moving average as a trend component is added.
Single Exponential Smoothing (SES)	
Complex?	While the mathematical operations are not complex, the concept behind SES is not as intuitive as with moving averages.
Accounts for trends?	No, SES underestimates the trend.
Full use of historical data?	Yes, all historical data influences the forecast. A weighting factor is used to decide how much influence it has.
Use for long-term forecasting?	One-period ahead forecast is repeated for all future periods.
Holt Exponential Smoothing	
Complex?	Adds trend calculation to SES, so adds another level of complexity.
Accounts for trends?	Yes, adds a trending component to SES.
Full use of historical data?	Yes, all historical data influences the forecast. Two weighting factors are used to decide how much influence it has.
Use for long-term forecasting?	Better than SES because trend component is added.
Damped Trend Exponential Smoothing	
Complex?	Adds a third weighting factor to Holt, so adds more complexity.
Accounts for trends?	Yes. This method damps the strength of the trend over time, using a weighting factor.
Full use of historical data?	Yes, all historical data influences the forecast. Two weighting factors are used to decide how much influence it has.
Use for long-term forecasting?	Similar to Holt, but the trend will be deemphasized.

Chapter 7

Regression Forecasting

In this chapter we examine simple regression forecasting. Regression forecasting of econom-ic data is often labeled *econometrics*. Although econometrics can also refer to many other types of economic modeling, this chapter does not examine the broad range of economic modeling; it is focused on regression modeling of economic data.

At its essence, regression modeling uses one or more economic variables (e.g., employment, population, interest rates) to predict revenues. The reader may recall the concepts of a line-of-best-fit and a scatterplot from earlier in this book. A regression analysis essentially

Exhibit 7.1 – The Essence of Regression Analysis

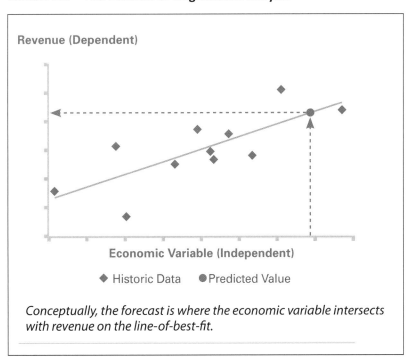

Revenue (Dependent)

Economic Variable (Independent)

◆ Historic Data   ● Predicted Value

Conceptually, the forecast is where the economic variable intersects with revenue on the line-of-best-fit.

finds a line-of-best-fit through a scatterplot of revenue and the economic variables by minimizing the average distance between the line and each historical observation. In conceptual terms, Exhibit 7.1 shows how revenues can then be forecasted by locating a value of the economic variable along the line and seeing the corresponding revenue amount. The chart shows, as diamonds, the intersection of various historical revenue figures (called the "dependent variable" in statistics parlance) with the economic variable (the "independent variable"), through which a line-of-best-fit is drawn. A given value of the independent variable is selected and where that value intersects the line-of-best-fit (the red circle in 7.1), we find the corresponding value on the vertical axis, which tells us how much revenue to expect.

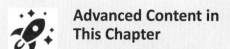

Advanced Content in This Chapter

Regression forecasting is an advanced method. Readers without a strong statistical background may wish to read the introduction and the sections "Efficacy" and "Conditions for Use" to learn what regression forecasting is, but are otherwise advised to skip this chapter and focus on the other techniques presented in this book.

A forecaster will not actually plot values on a graph in order to project revenues, but he or she will perform the mathematical equivalent. This mathematical equivalent starts with an equation that the reader may recognize from high school geometry: the equation for a straight line. In Formula 7.1, Y is the dependent variable, x is the independent variable, b is the slope of the line-of-best-fit (i.e., its direction and steepness), and α is the y-axis intercept (i.e., where the line-of-best-fit intersects the y-axis). Essentially, the forecaster finds the slope and intercept for the line-of-best-fit and inserts a value of x in order to predict Y, or future revenue. Finally, note that while Formula 7.1 includes only one independent variable, regression equations can, and often do, have multiple independent variables represented (this will be covered in detail later in the chapter).

Formula 7.1 – Equation for a Straight Line

$$Y = \alpha + b(x)$$

While the essential concepts behind regression forecasting are not too complex, regression analysis is, in fact, an advanced forecasting technique. The forecaster must validate the relationship between the independent variable and the revenue and must use statistical techniques more advanced than we have covered so far in this book to validate the forecasting model's performance, just to name a couple of the more complex aspects of regression forecasting. While the content of this chapter will describe these issues and more, readers should be aware that regression forecasting is not advisable for novice forecasters.

Efficacy

A review of the available experimental research on the effectiveness of regression forecasting versus other common types of forecasting methods (i.e., judgmental and extrapolation) does not prove a decisive, large difference in accuracy between regression and the other forecasting methods studied.[1] The research shows that regression does have an edge over judgmental and extrapolative methods, but that regression does not outperform the other methods in all cases (in fact, in one study, regression outperformed extrapolation only 51 percent of the time). So, while regression is a potentially useful forecasting tool, it is not necessarily superior to other revenue forecasting methods.

Two other points about the efficacy of regression forecasting are salient:

- Some forecasting literature suggests that regression methods are riskier than extrapolation methods because, although regression techniques are likely to be more accurate for most periods, extrapolation methods make fewer severe errors. The potential for larger errors is a serious consideration when using a forecast for budgeting and financial planning.

- Some forecasting scientists believe the regression forecasting is better suited to long-term forecasting than extrapolation methods (while extrapolative methods are better for short term).[2] The reasoning is that in the short term, changes in the financial and economic environment are likely to be smaller, so extrapolating past revenues forward could work well, while in the longer term the changes could be much larger, so forecasting according to the underlying causal variables of revenue yield would produce better results.

In conclusion, regression could be a useful tool in the forecaster's kit, but will usually be a supplement to, rather than a substitute for, other methods. Further, the forecaster's ability to use regression is limited by his or her ability to meet the conditions described in the next section, which are more rigorous than the conditions for using extrapolation. Accordingly, we found that regression methods were used almost exclusively by larger governments who have specialized forecasting staff.

The City of Dayton's experience, shown in Chapter 5's Exhibit 5.4, is illustrative of the role of regression forecasting in local governments. Dayton uses econometric regression along with other techniques to predict income tax. Though accuracy of regression compares favorably to the other techniques the City uses, it doesn't rely on it entirely. Fairfax County has a similar experience for its sales taxes. It uses econometric regression along with other techniques, though its econometric forecasts are of about the same accuracy as its extrapolation forecasts.

Conditions for Use

The first and most basic condition for the use of regression forecasting is that the forecaster has identified one or more independent variables that are correlated with the revenue. Ideally, there will also be a causal relationship between the independent variable and revenue, in addition to just correlation. This is because variables can be correlated for accidental reasons.[3] For example, with time series data, the mere passage of time may cause both variables to change such that they appear correlated. While we can take steps to remove time as an accidental source of correlation, forecasters should also observe three general rules for accepting causality of the independent variable:

1. **The causal direction goes the right way.** There is no reason why the dependent variable (revenues) should influence the behavior of the independent variable, at least in the short run. For example, expenditures cannot be used to predict revenue because there is a good chance that revenues constrain expenditures in most localities.

2. **There is a correct temporal relationship.** The independent variable is temporally independent and prior to—or, for long lasting observations, concurrent with—the dependent variable. For example, sales transactions precede later receipt of sales tax revenue.

3. **There is a reasonable explanation.** The best support for causality comes in the form of published peer-reviewed academic research that shows that the variables are causally related. Absent this, the forecaster should provide an understandable explanation for the independent variable to influence the dependent variable. Ideally, the influence should be direct, rather than indirect, through one or more intermediary variables. For instance, the technique of *influence diagramming* shown in Chapter 3 could be helpful for thinking through the causality of relationships.

The second condition for the use of regression forecasting is that both the independent and dependent variable information reflect stable underlying conditions, and are therefore highly *autocorrelated* from one period to the next. Autocorrelation means there is a basic similarity in a data set from one observation to the next, due to the stable underlying features of the data. The reader may recall that a similar condition was required for the use of extrapolation techniques and that in most cases the populations, tax rates, consumer demand, and other features that underlie public-sector revenue forecasts will not change radically over the short term. This means public-sector revenue data sets are often autocorrelated.

Regression will usually work better when the forecaster uses *lagged variables*, that is, independent variables from an earlier period that predict a dependent variable from a future period. Use of lagged variables is ideal because the forecaster is using actual values of the independent variable to predict future revenues. However, a practical limit on this approach is that the actual values of an independent variable will only provide predictive value for a short distance into the future. Though we might be able to predict revenues one year into the future using the current value of a given independent variable, the predictive power will quite likely become considerably less as the forecast time horizon moves outward.

Where a useful lagged independent variable is not available, the alternative is to predict the independent variable into the future and then use it to forecast the revenue. In this case, a condition for use of regression forecasting is that reliable predictions can be obtained for the independent variable. For instance, reliable population projections looking many years into the future for a jurisdiction are usually available, which might be useful for projecting sales tax revenue. Weather patterns and consumer confidence might also be useful for predicting utility and sales tax revenues, but projections of these independent variables are far less reliable! Less reliable predictions of the independent variable introduce more uncertainty into the forecast.

As a final condition, the forecaster must have a sufficient number of historical observations available to conduct regression forecasting. As a general rule, somewhere around 20 observations should be available, and preferably many more. Also, the number of independent variables in a regression model should be small in comparison to the number of observations. In other words, if you have few observations, you should have substantially fewer independent variables.

Using Regression Forecasting

We begin our discussion of using regression forecasting by introducing the formula for *multiple regression*—a type of regression where multiple independent variables are used to forecast revenue. Formula 7.2 shows the equation for a multiple regression. The first formula represents the actual relationship between the independent and dependent variables. It says that we predict the dependent variable Y using an *intercept*, labeled β, and a series of independent variables labeled x_1, x_2, etc., each of which is multiplied by its coefficient β_1, β_2, etc. There is also an error component (ϵ) that represents the random variation in the model. This model is called linear regression because the formula is a linear combination of a series of independent variables multiplied by their coefficients plus the intercept.

The second formula is used to estimate the relationship between the independent and dependent variables, and is the formula that will be directly used by forecasters. The formula says that we predict the dependent variable $\hat{Y}$ (pronounced "Y-hat" and traditionally used to denote the prediction coming from a line-of-best-fit) using a y-axis intercept (usually just called "intercept") labeled α, and a series of independent variables labeled x_1, x_2, etc., each multiplied by its coefficient β_1, β_2, etc.

Formula 7.2 – Multiple Regression

$$Y = \alpha + \beta_1 x_1 + \beta_2 x_2 + \dots \beta_n x_n + \varepsilon$$
$$\hat{Y} = \alpha + b_1 x_1 + b_2 x_2 + \dots b_n x_n$$

The mathematics behind calculating Formula 7.2 can be performed automatically by software, and are beyond the scope of this book. However, before calculating anything, we need data and to think about the form of the data.

Preparing Data for Regression Forecasting

Exhibit 7.2 shows population, per capita income, and personal income taxes for West Virginia for 1993 through 2012.[4] (This exhibit and other tables that illustrate how to perform a regression are available at *www.gfoa.org/forecastbook*.) It shows the Consumer Price Index (CPI) for the same period.[5] The CPI is used to adjust per capita income and income taxes in West Virginia from nominal to constant dollars. A state GDP deflator may be better, but none is available for the period. The two columns from this table that are carried forward for forecasting are the population and the per capita income in constant dollars.

Exhibit 7.2 – West Virginia Population, Per Capita Income, and Income Taxes

Year	Independent Variables				Dependent Variable
	Population	Per Capita Income	CPI	Per Capita Income Adjusted*	Personal Income Tax Revenue*
1993	1,817,539	16,549	144.5	26,300	987,188
1994	1,820,421	17,269	148.2	26,750	1,037,372
1995	1,823,700	17,817	152.4	26,846	1,069,681
1996	1,822,808	18,567	156.9	27,178	1,099,129
1997	1,819,113	19,373	160.5	27,710	1,124,512
1998	1,815,609	20,472	163.0	28,836	1,219,950
1999	1,811,799	21,049	166.6	29,012	1,267,884
2000	1,806,962	22,173	172.2	29,566	1,287,710
2001	1,798,582	23,573	177.0	30,572	1,323,723
2002	1,799,411	24,302	179.9	31,022	1,320,772
2003	1,802,238	24,773	184.0	30,913	1,317,132
2004	1,803,302	25,599	188.9	31,114	1,298,334
2005	1,803,920	26,443	195.3	31,093	1,378,077
2006	1,807,237	28,372	201.6	32,320	1,478,293
2007	1,811,198	29,497	207.3	32,664	1,506,572
2008	1,814,873	31,286	215.3	33,372	1,619,994
2009	1,819,777	30,968	214.6	33,138	1,666,547
2010	1,854,368	31,806	218.1	33,486	1,602,280
2011	1,855,364	33,403	224.9	34,096	1,700,464
2012	1,857,296	34,477	229.6	34,477	1,755,746

*Expressed in 2012 dollars

These two variables are our independent x variables for the forecast of personal income tax. The theory is that the tax revenue is produced by the number of people available to pay taxes and the amount of money they have to be taxed. These are the principal ingredients of this tax. Undoubtedly there are more ingredients, such as the number of individuals with very high income and the number who have insufficient income to pay any taxes at all. The model we make here is only a first approximation of the model an experienced forecaster would want to use.

These variables are not yet ready for forecasting. First, we should also use an inflation adjusted dollar value of the dependent variable, income taxes, and the independent variable per capital income.

However, we also need to address the potential for *trending* and *nonlinearity* in the data. A forecaster can check for trending by graphing out the data series, but with most monetary and population data sets it is safe to assume that there is some form of trending occurring.

Trending means that the data changes in the same direction across sequential observations, although the direction of the trending does not have to be consistent across the whole series (e.g., the data could exhibit an upward trend to a point, and then a downward trend). When both an independent variable and the dependent variables exhibit trending, the forecast can reflect spurious correlation, because the correlation reflects a natural change over time rather than an actual relationship between the two variables.[6]

Nonlinearity means that the size of the (trending) change steadily increases with each period. In other words, the trend is not best represented by a straight line, but by a line that curves up or down. This is a problem because we are using "linear" regression to forecast, which assumes the relationship between the variables is best represented as a straight line.[7] The population data, the per capita income data, and the tax revenue data may very likely exhibit trending and nonlinearity.

The solution is to find the logarithm (called *log* for short) for all of our variables and make a regression model of the logged variables. For those readers who do not recall their high school calculus classes well, the *common log* of a number is the exponent to which the base number, ten, must be raised to produce that number. For example, the common log of 1,000 is 3 because 10^3 is equal to 1,000. Logarithms can have base numbers other than ten. Another common type of logarithm is called the *natural log*, which uses 2.718... as its base because this number has mathematically desirable properties.[8] For our purposes of forecasting revenues, the type of logarithm does not matter much, but the reader should be aware of the difference because Excel offers multiple logarithm functions to cover logarithms of different base numbers. In this chapter, we have chosen to use the natural log.

Exhibit 7.3 – Log Transformation and Lagging of Variables

| Year | Independent Variables | | Dependent Variable |
	Log Population, Lag 1 Year	Log 2012 Per Capita Income, Lag 1 Year	Log 2012 Personal Income Tax Revenue
1994	14.413	10.177	13.852
1995	14.415	10.194	13.883
1996	14.416	10.198	13.910
1997	14.416	10.210	13.933
1998	14.414	10.230	14.014
1999	14.412	10.269	14.053
2000	14.410	10.275	14.068
2001	14.407	10.294	14.096
2002	14.403	10.328	14.094
2003	14.403	10.342	14.091
2004	14.405	10.339	14.077
2005	14.405	10.345	14.136
2006	14.405	10.345	14.206
2007	14.407	10.383	14.225
2008	14.409	10.394	14.298
2009	14.412	10.415	14.326
2010	14.414	10.408	14.287
2011	14.433	10.419	14.346
2012	14.434	10.437	14.378
2013	14.435	10.448	???

Logarithms have the effect of "straightening out" non-linear relationships in the data. Excel can find the log of numbers using a simple function command. However, the reader should note that a logarithm will not work on negative numbers, so if the data set includes negative numbers, this transformation does not apply. While there are adjustments that can be made if there are negative numbers in the data set, these adjustments are very complex and are beyond the scope of this book. Thankfully, negative numbers in forecasting data sets are rare.

Using Excel's logarithm function, we take the log of our variables, including our dependent variable, resulting in the variables shown in Exhibit 7.3.[9] The table also lists the two independent variables as "Lag 1 Year." This means that the values of the independent variables for a given year are used to make the forecast of the dependent for one year ahead, as opposed to using independent variables for a given year to make the forecast for the same year. So, to illustrate, the 1994 log of population in Exhibit 7.3 is 14.413. This is the log of 1,817,539 in 1993 from Exhibit 7.2. The log is moved to 1994 in Exhibit 7.3 to show that it has been lagged one year and that it is used to predict revenues in 1994. Therefore, the personal income tax data in Exhibit 7.3 is the only data that is actually from the year indicated on the table. The other two columns are lagged one year. At the bottom of Exhibit 7.3 we have observations for the independent variables, but not the dependent variable. We will later use these to make a prediction.

To make a regression in Excel, we use the Data Analysis tool. This is an add-in that ships with Excel, but the forecaster may have to specifically enable it in order to use it. (Visit the Microsoft website for instructions for enabling the Data Analysis Tool.) Once enabled, the data analysis tools are found on the right-hand side of the "ribbon" on the data tab. When the Data Analysis tool is selected, the forecaster will see Exhibit 7.4, which provides a number of options, including regression. The forecaster selects regression and sees Exhibit 7.5.

The field "Input Y Range" near the top of Exhibit 7.5 is used to select the dependent data, including the label at the top of the range. Do not allow for any empty space between the label and the first observation. The "Input X Range" field is used to select the independent variables. They also must be contiguous with each other and with their labels. Both ranges should have the same number of rows, and you should not have any empty cells in either the Y range or the X range. Having included the labels, the "Labels" box should be checked.

The user can select a cell in the current worksheet to put the output or allow Excel to create a new sheet. If selecting a new worksheet, the new sheet will be in the same workbook unless specified otherwise. If selecting an output range, the entire range does not have to be specified, only the cell at the top left corner of the range. If using this option, the forecaster should be careful not to specify a range that already contains data because pre-existing data will be overwritten.

In the "Residuals" section of the pop-up window, the forecaster should select the top two boxes: "Residuals" and "Residual Plots." The residuals are used for calculating an important

Exhibit 7.4 - Excel Data Analysis Tools Pop-Up Window

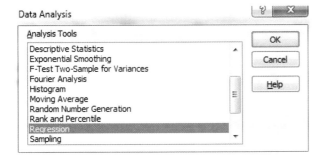

Exhibit 7.5 – Excel Regression Pop-Up Window

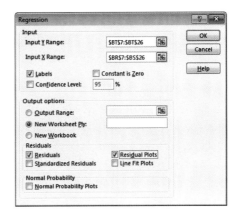

statistic not computed by Excel, and the residuals plot is used for a visual examination of randomness.

Exhibit 7.6 shows the first part of the regression output from Excel using the data from Exhibit 7.3. Note that when Excel produces the output, it is unformatted and the forecaster must add formatting to have it look like Exhibit 7.6 and be readable, primarily by sizing columns properly and selecting the number of decimal places to display. Additionally, we have bolded some portions of the table to help you more easily find sections referenced in the main text. The numbers of most interest are the adjusted R-squared, the F-statistic and its significance, the t-statistics, and p-values for the independent variables. In the interest of brevity, we have chosen not to explain every element of the Excel output – but the ones that we have bolded are explained and are the ones you need to know to complete the regression forecast.

The first statistic of interest is R-squared, otherwise known as the *coefficient of determination*. R-squared values will range from 0 to 1.0 and describe the proportion of total variation in revenues that is explained by the independent variables. For example, an R-squared value of 0.85 would tell us that 85 percent of the observed variation in the revenues is attributable to the independent variables. Accordingly, a higher R-squared value is generally better for the forecaster. However, sometimes in life when something seems too good to be true, it probably is, and that might be the case in Exhibit 7.6, where we see the R-squared values are quite high. Hence, we will focus on *adjusted R-squared*, which is a variation on standard R-squared that accounts for a common phenomenon wherein unwarranted increases in R-squared occur simply by adding additional independent variables to the model, even if those variables don't actually provide any additional explanatory benefit.

Relationship Amongst r, r², and R²

The reader may remember "r" as the correlation coefficient from Chapter 4. A value of "r" can be squared to give us "r²", which is the coefficient of determination of a given variable. R^2 is the coefficient of determination for an entire model. Hence, we cannot take the square root of the R^2 figures from Exhibit 7.6 to get "r" values for the independent variables. Notwithstanding, the "r" values for the individual independent variables are very helpful, and we will cover their use later in this chapter.

Consequently, adjusted R-squared will always be equal to or less than R-squared, and could even be negative.

The fact that the adjusted R-squared is still extremely high leads us to be suspicious that the data may contain spurious correlation due to autocorrelation. This point may require elaboration. While autocorrelation in the independent variables themselves helps with predicting the next future period dependent variable, autocorrelation in the errors of the forecast model undermines its use. Later in this chapter, we will return to the issue of finding autocorrelation in the errors and, if it is present, correcting it, using tools such as the Durbin-Watson statistic.

The next statistic of interest is the F-statistic. The F-statistic is used to test whether or not the relationship observed in the data (the slope of the line) is attributable to pure chance. Unfortunately, the F-statistic taken in isolation is difficult to interpret. Generally, a larger F-statistic means that the relationship is less likely attributable to chance. However, in order to really discern the significance of the F-statistic, we must consult the *significance F* number, which tells us the likelihood of getting the given F-statistic by chance. In Exhibit 7.6 we have an F-statistic of 191 and the corresponding significance is .000. This tells us that there is essentially no chance of obtaining an F score that large simply by luck. If there were a weak relationship, such that the observed relationship could have just as easily been produced by random variation in the data set, then we would expect to see a much higher significance F. Generally, a significance F above 0.05 is undesirable and above 0.10 is very undesirable.

While the foregoing statistics concern the regression model on the whole, the t-statistics and p-values for the two independent variables are used to verify that the independent variables are each reasonably correlated with the dependent variable. The t-statistic is a measure of how far the observed relationship is from what we would expect if a relationship did not exist. However, like the F-statistic, the t-statistic is not easy to interpret in isolation. The p-value plays a similar role for the t-statistic as F-significance does for the F-statistic. We look for a p-value that is less than or equal to 0.05. We find that both variables meet the condition, with t-statistics of 18.7 and 2.7 and p-values of 0.000 and 0.016. Sometimes, a t-statistic above 2 is used as a rule-of-thumb for finding statistical significance, but it is important to always consult the p-value because the it tells you the likelihood of obtaining a given t-value purely by chance. In other words, even if the t-statistic is above 2, a p-value that is above 0.05 should give the forecaster pause before relying on the findings. That said, generally, a t-statistic above 2 will be sufficient when there are at least 15 observations in the data set. If there are less than 15 observations, this rule-of-thumb is not reliable.

The regression function in Excel will output more information than what is shown in Exhibit 7.6. The rest of the output is shown in the first three columns of Exhibit 7.7. The first column is just a sequencer of the observations. The second column shows the predicted values of the log of personal income tax revenue for the period covered in the data set (i.e., 1994 through 2012 for our example). The third column appears as a result of selecting residuals in the regression dialog box (see Exhibit 7.5). The reader may recall from earlier chapters that "residuals" are the same thing as errors and are calculated by subtracting the forecast from the actual for each period. The residuals are used to calculate the Durbin-Watson statistic (DW) and a measure of autocorrelation of the errors, ρ (the Greek letter rho), which are shown in the remaining columns of Exhibit 7.7 (the last column shows r = ρ, which is to say we are estimating ρ). DW, rho, and their importance are explained after the table.

Exhibit 7.6 – Output of Excel Regression Statistics Using the Data in Exhibit 7.3

SUMMARY OUTPUT

Regression Statistics

Multiple R	0.9797
R Square	0.9599
Adjusted R Square	0.9549
Standard Error	0.0343
Observations	19

ANOVA

	df	SS	MS	F	Significance F
Regression	2	0.4495	0.2248	191	0.000
Residual	16	0.0188	0.0012		
Total	18	0.4683			

	Coefficients	Standard Error	t Stat	P-value	Lower 95%	Upper 95%	Lower 95.0%	Upper 95.0%
Intercept	-41.661	13.588	-3.066	0.007	-70.466	-12.856	-70.466	-12.856
Log Per Capita Income	1.810	0.097	18.664	0.000	1.605	2.016	1.605	2.016
Log Population	2.575	0.952	2.705	0.016	0.557	4.592	0.557	4.592

Exhibit 7.7 – Output of Excel Regression Statistics, Plus Durbin-Watson Statistic

RESIDUAL OUTPUT			Durbin Watson = 1.143		r= ρ = 0.4133
Observation	Predicted Log PIT	Residuals	Numerator	Denominator	Numerator
1	13.871	-0.018	NA	0.0003	NA
2	13.905	-0.022	0.0000	0.0005	0.0004
3	13.916	-0.006	0.0003	0.0000	0.0001
4	13.937	-0.005	0.0000	0.0000	0.0000
5	13.967	0.047	0.0027	0.0022	-0.0002
6	14.034	0.018	0.0008	0.0003	0.0009
7	14.040	0.028	0.0001	0.0008	0.0005
8	14.067	0.029	0.0000	0.0008	0.0008
9	14.116	-0.022	0.0026	0.0005	-0.0006
10	14.144	-0.053	0.0009	0.0028	0.0012
11	14.141	-0.065	0.0001	0.0042	0.0034
12	14.155	-0.018	0.0021	0.0003	0.0012
13	14.154	0.052	0.0050	0.0027	-0.0010
14	14.229	-0.004	0.0031	0.0000	-0.0002
15	14.254	0.044	0.0023	0.0019	-0.0002
16	14.298	0.028	0.0002	0.0008	0.0013
17	14.292	-0.005	0.0011	0.0000	-0.0001
18	14.359	-0.013	0.0001	0.0002	0.0001
19	14.394	-0.015	0.0000	0.0002	0.0002
		TOTALS	0.0215	0.0188	0.0078

The DW statistic is used to help examine the errors or residuals of the regression equation for autocorrelation. Autocorrrelation means that the direction of the error in one period (either a positive or negative error) is predictive of the direction of the error in the next period. For example, positive autocorrelation means that if the regression equation over-predicts in one period, it is likely to over-predict in the next period. If the residuals are autocorrelated, the value of the regression equation could be compromised. The formula for DW is shown in Formula 7.3.

Formula 7.3 – Durbin Watson Statistic

$$DW = \frac{\sum_{t=2}^{n}(e_t - e_{t-1})^2}{\sum_{t=1}^{n} e_t^2}$$

The numerator says starting with the second observation, for each residual, subtract the residual on the row before, then square that value, then add up those squared values. In Exhibit 7.7 that gives us 0.0215. The denominator says square each residual and add those squared values, giving us 0.0188 in our example. The last step is to divide the numerator by the denominator, which produces 1.143 in our example. Precise interpretation of the Durbin-Watson statistic can be complex, but can be done using statistical tables easily available on the Internet. However, the general interpretation is, if the number is substantially below 2, the residuals are positively autocorrelated. Our sample DW statistic is 1.143, which implies positively autocorrelated residuals. If a DW statistic is substantially above 2, it is negatively autocorrelated. Values near 2 are random (not autocorrelated).

We can verify the presence of autocorrelation by visually inspecting the data with a scatterplot. When graphed on a scatterplot, positive autocorrelation of time ordered residuals will show an "n" or "u" shape. Exhibit 7.8 shows the outputs from checking the "residual plots" option on the regression dialog box, with some added refinements.[10] The plots show that, as illustrated with the dotted line, the middle of the data is found above the zero line, implying an "n" shape. If the residuals were negatively autocorrelated, the data points would shift back and forth, between positive and negative numbers, evoking a "w" shape on the graph. If the residuals were not autocorrelated, the data points would appear randomly plotted.

Exhibit 7.8 – Residual Plots from Data in Exhibit 7.3

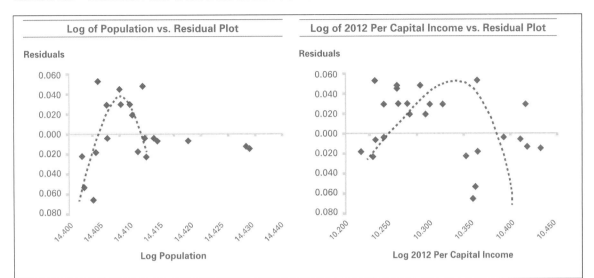

Ideally, there will not be autocorrelation of the residuals, but if there is, there are steps that can be taken. In our example, we found autocorrelation using the DW statistic and we confirmed it with a visual inspection of the data. Hence, we need to further transform the data. To do this we calculate an estimator, $r = \rho$. The formula for r is:

$$r = \frac{\sum_{t=2}^{n}(e_t * e_{t-1})}{\sum_{t=1}^{n} e_t^2}$$

The denominator of this formula is identical to that of the DW statistic. In the numerator, instead of subtracting and squaring, we simply multiply the residual by the one in the preceding row. Exhibit 7.7 shows the results of the calculation of the numerator as well as the final r value, 0.4133.

We use r to adjust all the previous variables, using the formula below (where V refers to any variable and V' refers to the adjusted value of the variable):

$$V'_t = V_t - r * V_{t-1}$$

This adjustment reduces our number of available observations by one, eliminating our oldest observation. Exhibit 7.9 applies this adjustment to the variables from Exhibit 7.3 (1994 is taken out because there is no 1993 data to supply a value for V_{t-1} for a 1994 adjustment).

Exhibit 7.9 – Autocorrelation Corrected Data

Year	Adj. Log Population, Lag 1 Year	Adj. Log 2012 Per Capita Income, Lag 1 Year	Adj. Log Personal Income Tax Revenue
1995	8.458	5.988	8.158
1996	8.459	5.985	8.172
1997	8.458	5.995	8.184
1998	8.456	6.010	8.256
1999	8.455	6.042	8.261
2000	8.453	6.031	8.260
2001	8.452	6.048	8.281
2002	8.448	6.073	8.268
2003	8.450	6.074	8.266
2004	8.452	6.064	8.253
2005	8.452	6.072	8.318
2006	8.452	6.069	8.364
2007	8.454	6.108	8.354
2008	8.455	6.103	8.419
2009	8.456	6.120	8.417
2010	8.458	6.104	8.366
2011	8.476	6.117	8.442
2012	8.468	6.131	8.449
2013	8.469	6.134	NA

We can use the data in Exhibit 7.9 to re-run the regression, just as we did for the data in Exhibit 7.3. Exhibit 7.10 shows the new regression output. The DW statistic has been added, by the authors, to the regression output table as well. We can see that the DW statistic is much closer to 2 than it was. We can also see that the adjusted-R squared is lower than it was in Exhibit 7.6, but is still quite high. The F- and t-statistics continue to indicate that a solid relationship exists.

Exhibit 7.10 – Output of Excel Regression Statistics Using the Data in Exhibit 7.9

SUMMARY OUTPUT

Regression Statistics	
Multiple R	0.9460
R Square	0.8949
Adjusted R Square	0.8808
Standard Error	0.0315
Observations	18

DW
1.817

ANOVA

	df	SS	MS	F	Significance F
Regression	2	0.1263	0.0631	63.8	0.000
Residual	15	0.0148	0.0010		
Total	17	0.1411			

	Coefficients	Standard Error	t Stat	P-value	Lower 95%	Upper 95%	Lower 95.0%	Upper 95.0%
Intercept	-24.207	9.900	-2.445	0.027	-45.309	-3.104	-45.309	-3.104
Adj. Lag 1 LN 2012 PCI	1.711	0.169	10.142	0.000	1.352	2.071	1.352	2.071
Adj. Lag 1 LN Pop	2.618	1.196	2.188	0.045	0.068	5.167	0.068	5.167

The sample regression model that we presented in this chapter is a basic one that can be improved. For instance, one might examine the unusual distribution of residuals on the population scatterplot (e.g., on population vs. residuals, most observations fall between 8.450 and 8.460, and two are well beyond those parameters) and determine whether there is missing information to be considered. While answering this question may improve this model, the model is still workable for forecasting purposes. Nevertheless, the competent forecaster will commit time for examining issues not resolved in the first round of model building.

Before accepting the model, however, we should examine the input variables to see if they are correlated.

Exhibit 7.11 – Dialog Box for Excel's Data Analysis Tool

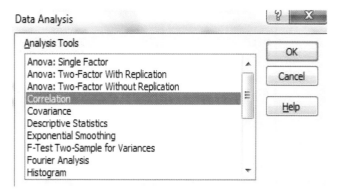

In Exhibit 7.11, we see that in the Data Analysis tool window, we select "Correlation." In Exhibit 7.12, we select the range where the data are found and an output range (be sure there is nothing in this output range or nearby cells). If we include the labels, we check the labels box. The output of the correlation function is "r" (i.e., correlation), but we are interested in r^2, which is easily computed from "r" by squaring it.

Exhibit 7.12 – Selecting the Input Range

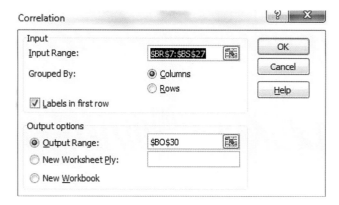

To illustrate, we use four versions of our independent variables in Exhibit 7.13. First is the correlation of the original data. However, we adjusted the per capita income (PCI) to remove inflation, the correlation of which is shown on the second row. We then took the log of those variables, and the resultant correlation is shown on the third row. These are the independent variables that we use for the first regression calculation shown in this chapter. Finally, we adjusted the data for autocorrelation. The correlations for these independent variables are on the fourth row.

While the correlation, "r," in the first row may be slightly concerning (the r^2 value is still less than 0.20, or 20 percent), the correlations in the third row (r^2 of less than 0.10, or 10 percent) or the fourth row (r^2 of less than 0.07, or 7 percent) reflect substantial independence.

Exhibit 7.13 – Correlations of Independent Variables from the Sample Regression

Original Data		Population	Per Capita Income
	Population	1	
	Per Capita Income	0.438106	1
Inflation Adjusted		Population	2012 PCI
	Population	1	
	2012 PCI	0.3382	1
Log of Inflation Adjusted		Lag 1 LN 2012 PCI	Lag 1 LN Population
	Lag 1 LN 2012 PCI	1	
	Lag 1 LN Population	0.3074	1
Adjusted for Autocorrelation		Adj. Lag 1 LN 2012 PCI	Adj. Lag 1 LN Pop
	Adj. Lag 1 LN 2012 PCI	1	
	Adj. Lag 1 LN Pop	0.2587	1

Making the Regression Forecast

The first step of making the forecast is relatively straightforward. We will start from the formula for a regression equation shown earlier in this chapter and repeated here for your convenience. As a refresher α is the intercept and β is the coefficient for each independent variable.

$$\hat{Y} = \alpha + \beta_1 x_1 + \beta_2 x_2 + \cdots \beta_n x_n$$

We start by taking the values for the coefficients α and β_n from the Excel regression output (i.e., Exhibit 7.10) and inserting them into the formula. Using the data under the column labeled "coefficients" in the lower left-hand portion of Exhibit 7.10, yield the formula below.

$$\hat{Y} = -24.207 + 1.711 x_1 + 2.618 x_2$$

Next, we designate the actual variables by replacing x_1 and x_2 with the titles of the actual independent variables:

$$\hat{Y} = -24.207 + 1.711 * (Adj\ Lag\ 1\ LN\ 2012\ PCI) + 2.618 * (ADJ\ Lag\ 1\ LN\ Pop)$$

In Exhibit 7.14, we make this calculation in the first step to developing our forecast. The results are shown under the heading "Predicted." The input data are shown in three preceding columns, and in the two columns before that we show the original tax data and its transformation to constant dollars.

Before going further, the reader should note that had we not transformed the variables (i.e., taking the log, adjusting for autocorrelation), the forecast would be finished at this point – instead of using the values from Exhibit 7.10 for the coefficients, we would have used figures from an Excel regression output based on the original data (Exhibit 7.2). The resulting equivalent of the "Predicted" column in Exhibit 7.14 would have been the actual forecast.

However, since we did apply the adjustments, after computing the regression model, we need to reverse the transformation. This reversal will put the predicted data in the same form as our actual data, so that it can be used in an actual budget forecast. There are three steps to reverse the transformations we made, which are performed in the opposite order that we used to create the transformations. First, we reverse the autocorrelation of error transformation. The formula for this is:

$$Predicted' = Predicted/(1 - r)$$

This is the same r that we used in making the original transformation, 0.4133. The result is shown in the column labeled "Predicted'".

Next, we take the antilog of this value. When we use the natural log, we find the antilog with the Excel expression below. We show the result of this transformation in the column labeled "Antilog".

$$= EXP([Cell\ Address])$$

Finally, we re-inflate the data by reversing the calculation of constant dollars. The formula is:

$$PN_t = PC_t * I_t/I_b$$

The above can be read: the predicted nominal dollars for period t (PN_t) is equal to predicted constant dollars for period t (PC_t) times the index for period t (I_t) divided by the index for the base year (I_b).

Exhibit 7.14 – Forecasts for Regression Equation

Year	W. VA Personal Income Tax (PIT)	W.VA PIT 2012 Dollars	Adj. Log 2012 PCI, Lag 1 Year	Adj. Log Population, Lag 1 Year	Adj. Log PIT Revenue	Predicted	Predicted'	Antilog	Income Tax Forecast (re-inflated)
1995	709,923	1,069,681	5.988	8.458	8.158	8.18	13.94	1,136,820	754,482
1996	750,889	1,099,129	5.985	8.459	8.172	8.18	13.94	1,131,246	772,831
1997	786,190	1,124,512	5.995	8.458	8.184	8.19	13.96	1,161,083	811,758
1998	866,107	1,219,950	6.010	8.456	8.256	8.21	14.00	1,200,733	852,464
1999	919,879	1,267,884	6.042	8.455	8.261	8.26	14.09	1,311,108	951,239
2000	965,721	1,287,710	6.031	8.453	8.260	8.24	14.05	1,264,701	948,465
2001	1,020,690	1,323,723	6.048	8.452	8.282	8.27	14.09	1,315,968	1,014,710
2002	1,034,665	1,320,772	6.073	8.448	8.268	8.30	14.15	1,395,897	1,093,516
2003	1,055,523	1,317,132	6.074	8.450	8.266	8.31	14.16	1,414,112	1,133,241
2004	1,068,212	1,298,334	6.064	8.452	8.253	8.30	14.14	1,383,686	1,138,435
2005	1,171,987	1,378,077	6.072	8.452	8.318	8.31	14.16	1,415,695	1,203,979
2006	1,297,720	1,478,293	6.069	8.452	8.364	8.30	14.15	1,402,565	1,231,243
2007	1,360,511	1,506,572	6.108	8.454	8.354	8.38	14.28	1,583,378	1,429,870
2008	1,518,746	1,619,994	6.103	8.455	8.419	8.37	14.27	1,568,557	1,470,524
2009	1,557,403	1,666,547	6.120	8.456	8.417	8.40	14.32	1,656,900	1,548,388
2010	1,521,895	1,602,280	6.104	8.458	8.366	8.38	14.28	1,595,084	1,515,060
2011	1,665,885	1,700,464	6.117	8.476	8.442	8.45	14.40	1,794,762	1,758,266
2012	1,755,746	1,755,746	6.131	8.468	8.449	8.45	14.41	1,808,778	1,808,778
2013	???	???	6.134	8.469	NA	8.46	14.42	1,834,755	NA*

*CPI Forecast required to re-inflate antilog column

For the year 2013 we already have the lagged 2012 independent variables for the regression model, so we can make a forecast, which we see in the predicted, predicted', and antilog columns. To take the final step of getting the nominal (current) dollar value of the forecast, we would need a predicted value for CPI.[11] A forecast of CPI can be obtained from specialist vendors, or the forecaster may create his or her own forecast of CPI.

If the forecaster wanted a forecast for the year 2014, he or she would need a predicted per capita income level and a predicted population for 2013 (since the variables are lagged by 1 year), which would then be transformed and put into the regression equation just like we did to get the forecast for 2014. The forecaster would also need a predicted CPI for 2014 to make the final transformation. Forecasts for beyond 2014 could be obtained in the same way by obtaining predicted values for the independent variables and CPI for the appropriate periods. Of course, the uncertain nature of the predictions of these variables introduces additional uncertainty into the forecast over when these variables are defined by actual, not predicted, values. Chapter 10 will discuss strategies for dealing with uncertainties in forecasts generally, including regression.

Forecast Model Performance

In this section, we compare this model with forecasts of the West Virginia income tax data made using extrapolation techniques. Exhibit 7.15 shows the RMSE and ME of the retransformed dollar data (in thousands of dollars). It is necessary to use the error statistics for the retransformed dollar data since we would use this to make our budget decisions.

You can see that the results are not as good as the Holt or Damped Trend methods (i.e., the values are further away from zero). Also, the ME of regression is only better than one other technique, MA3. However, this should not be taken to mean that regression will not produce an equal or better outcome. What it means is that the forecaster should continue exploring meaningful information and find other possible independent variables that may improve the model.

Exhibit 7.15 – Comparison of Error Statistics for Extrapolation vs. Regression

		Trend & Level Moving Averages					
	MA3	MA2	MA3	MA4	Holt-ES	D-Trend	Regression
RMSE	97	80	57	80	47	47	59
ME	81	(13)	2	(14)	1	2	(25)

Exhibit 7.16 shows the forecast compared with actuals (in thousands of dollars). What is interesting about this forecast is that while it misses some periods more severely than the extrapolation methods, it is much more accurate for other periods.

Exhibit 7.16 – Forecast vs. Actual for Regression of West Virginia Income Tax Revenue

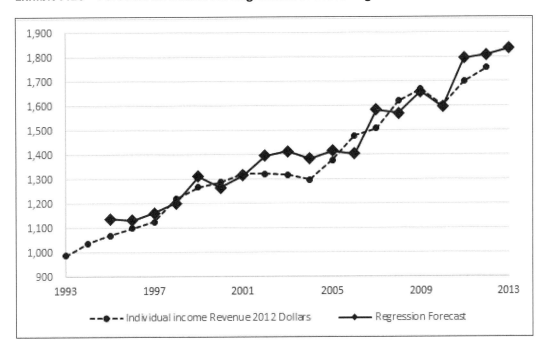

Conclusion

Regression forecasting uses one or more independent (explanatory) variables to forecast revenue. While the basic idea behind regression is not that complicated, it is, in fact, a sophisticated forecasting technique, and one that can be challenging to use correctly. The forecaster must, foremost, find independent variables that have legitimate explanatory power. Then, it is necessary to find sufficient data to build a model that can be adequately tested. Consideration must also be given to whether a lagging relationship between the independent and dependent variables is available so that historical data for the independent variables can be used to forecast future revenues, or, if not, whether reasonably accurate future values of the independent variables are obtainable.

Though complex, regression forecasting has been shown by forecasting researchers to produce accurate results. Some researchers believe it is particularly useful for long-term forecasting because its use of the causal forces behind the revenues may be better at predicting the large changes in revenues that can occur over long periods of time, compared to extrapolative methods which project forward historical patterns.

Chapter 8

Step 4 – Select Forecasting Methods

In prior chapters we have examined a variety of forecasting methods, including judgmental methods, extrapolation techniques, and econometric regression. So how does a forecaster choose amongst these methods? To help determine which forecasting method(s) are most accurate and, therefore, which should be among forecasters' first choice, we conducted a forecasting competition.

Which Method is Best? A Forecasting Competition

Forecast competitions compare the relative accuracy of different forecast approaches, whereby a number of diverse data series are forecasted by different techniques and where each technique is used under similar conditions.[1] The intent is to eliminate the statistical skill of the forecaster or the forecaster's familiarity with the financial and economic environment as a factor in forecast accuracy and thereby find out which technique offers the most predictive power, all other things remaining equal.

For our competition, we used 55 data series of the General Fund, sales tax, property tax, and other taxes from 18 different local governments across the United States.[2] The participating governments ranged in size from 4,000 to 1.4 million residents, with half the governments having between 25,000 and 200,000 residents. You can download the data series and the rules of the competition at *www.gfoa.org/forecastbook*. You can also access a paper that describes the contest in more detail than is provided in this chapter.[3]

We used these data series to conduct hypothetical forecasts, where the last 18 months to two years of actual revenue data was held out from the forecast formula and then compared to what the forecast formula predicted would happen for the held-out time period. Our intent was to emulate the time horizons governments face when forecasting revenues as part of the annual budgeting process.

Fourteen methods were included in the competition. Most of the methods are discussed in this book, including exponential smoothing, moving averages, and naïve methods. We excluded two methods that are described in this book. First, we excluded econometric regression due to the practical challenges of identifying predictive variables and obtaining data for 55 data series. Second, we excluded non-statistical judgmental techniques because the design and execution of these techniques is highly dependent on the judgment of forecasters who are very familiar with the financial and economic environment where the data originates. We did not have such familiarity.

For the techniques that were included in the competition, we used Microsoft Excel to produce forecasts for the 55 data series. We excluded local government involvement to make sure that different levels of forecaster skill in these governments did not affect the results.[4]

We also included a forecasting method that has not been described in this book yet: the use of automatic forecasting software. Automatic forecasting software allows non-experts to use more sophisticated forecasting techniques by automating virtually the entire process of creating a forecast. The software vendors invited to the competition were Autobox and ForecastPro.[5] The vendors were given the data sets, except the holdout data, and asked to provide the forecasts produced automatically by their software (see Exhibit 8.1 for more information on forecasting software and how it works).

> ### What Are Naïve Forecast Methods?
>
> Naïve forecasts make minimal use of historical data to produce a forecast. Examples of naïve methods include: taking the last period's actual value as the forecast for the subsequent period; applying a historical growth rate to the last observed actual value; and averaging all observed values to get a forecast.

During the course of the entire competition, it was our intent to limit the forecasting methods used to those that could be performed by a moderately skilled forecaster, either by using standard Microsoft Excel, or by using a specialized software package that produces forecasts out-of-the-box and that does not require the user to have any special expertise in the methods the software uses to produce the forecast.

For the Excel-based forecasts, three kinds of data preparation methods were performed before the forecasts were made, using techniques described earlier in this book. First, outliers were adjusted. Second, data was deseasonalized. Third, data was deflated to arrive at real dollars, though both real dollars and nominal dollars were used in the competition in order to compare the results from both. ForecastPro and Autobox were only given the raw data and we specified that their software was expected to automatically perform any needed preparation.[6]

The highest performing techniques are shown in Exhibit 8.2. The results are first divided by periodic data (monthly or quarterly) and annual data. The periodic and annual tables then are each divided into three different perspectives on the results. The "All Series" row shows the highest performing techniques across every series. The seasonality rows show the highest performing techniques for different kinds of seasonality in the data. Note that the data was not deseasonalized when the data was forecasted using historical data in annualized form, so those rows show how accurate the forecasts were when the data with the

Exhibit 8.1 - What Is Automatic Forecast Software and How Does It Work?

Automatic forecast software is designed to automate the process of making a forecast. Its greatest advantages are that it eliminates the time and effort that would be required to perform forecasts in Excel. It also makes more sophisticated statistical techniques accessible to the forecaster. Different forecast software packages might have somewhat different approaches to forecasting, though.

For example, ForecastPro features an expert selection system. Here is how it works:

1. Data is entered into the software from spreadsheets, text files, ODBC, etc.

2. The user directs the software to perform a forecast. The user has the option to change some of the default settings for how the forecast will be performed, but this is often not necessary. ForecastPro did not change the default settings for their submission to the forecast competition.

3. The software's expert selection system picks the best forecasting method to use. The software uses a combination of rule-based logic and out-of-sample testing to pick the method. The forecasting methods that the software chooses from include many of those described in this book, such as exponential smoothing methods and econometric regression, plus others that are not described in the book due to their high complexity. ForecastPro also performs data preparation steps as the software judges necessary, such as deseasonalization. The software can optimize the use of simpler forecast methods much more efficiently than can be done in Excel.

4. The software calculates the forecast using the method it has selected. No user intervention is required to produce the forecast, and ForecastPro did not intervene when producing their submission to the forecast competition. The user could intervene, though, in order to dictate that the software use a particular method.

5. The user is provided with the output and could choose to apply a judgmental adjustment. The software provides the ability to track and document any such adjustments.

Autobox does not use an expert selection system, but rather is designed to optimize the use of a sophisticated forecasting method called Box-Jenkins (after its originators) or ARIMA (auto-regressive integrated moving average). ARIMA is a much more sophisticated technique than those we have described in this book. Autobox automates the complex mathematical calculations that underlie ARIMA, adjusts and prepares the historical data to achieve the best results with ARIMA, and mathematically optimizes the parameters of the model (which would be subjectively set if the method were to be performed manually). For example, Autobox has rigorous automated procedures for scanning for and adjusting outliers and also examines the data for trends or patterns and changes in those trends or patterns over the course of the data series. Autobox also can include causal variables in its analysis in order to give a perspective on the forecast beyond that provided by extrapolation. Like ForecastPro, Autobox performs most of its functions automatically, by default. If needed, users can change default settings. The results provided by Autobox to our forecasting competition were based on Autobox's default settings, with no additional user intervention.

indicated seasonal properties was forecasted forward by aggregating the historical revenue to annual totals. The last four rows in Exhibit 8.2 show which techniques performed best for different kinds of revenue.

Overall, the results show that one approach does not produce the most accurate forecasts in all cases. We can say, however, that the best results appear to be available when using monthly or quarterly data with single exponential smoothing, damped trend exponential smoothing,[7] and forecasting software like ForecastPro and Autobox. In fact, ForecastPro had the most accurate overall results of all the methods included in the competition.[8] AutoBox also consistently performed well.

Exhibit 8.2 – Results of the Forecasting Competition

Using Quarterly or Monthly (Periodic) Data				
Type of Series	**Best Technique**	**MAPE**	**Second Best Technique**	**MAPE**
All Series	Forecast Software	6.12%	Damped trend exponential smoothing, nominal dollars	6.78%
Additive Seasonality	Single exponential smoothing, nominal dollars	7.41%	Forecast software	7.71%
Multiplicative Seasonality	Forecast software	5.48%	Damped trend exponential smoothing, nominal dollars	5.58%
Sales Tax	Forecast software	3.98%	Single exponential smoothing, real dollars	4.05%
Property Tax*	Damped trend exponential smoothing, nominal dollars	5.39%	Damped trend exponential smoothing, nominal dollars	6.09%
Other Revenue	Forecast software	7.36%	Forecast software	7.63%
Total General Fund	Damped trend exponential smoothing, nominal dollars	4.62%	Damped trend exponential smoothing, real dollars	4.90%
Using Annual Data				
Type of Series	**Best Technique**	**MAPE**	**Second Best Technique**	**MAPE**
All Series	Last observation, real dollars	6.82%	Last observation, nominal	6.98%
Additive Seasonality	Damped trend exponential smoothing, nominal dollars	6.30%	Damped trend exponential smoothing, real dollars	6.71%
Multiplicative Seasonality	Single exponential smoothing, real dollars	6.71%	Last observation, real dollars	7.03%
Sales Tax	Single exponential smoothing, real dollars	6.24%	Single exponential smoothing, nominal dollars	6.98%
Property Tax*	Damped trend exponential smoothing, nominal dollars	5.90%	Damped trend exponential smoothing, nominal dollars	5.94%
Other Revenue	Last observation, real dollars	6.95%	Last observation, nominal dollars	7.14%
Total General Fund	Last observation, real dollars	3.79%	Damped trend exponential smoothing, nominal dollars	4.17%

* The competition featured a variation of damped trend exponential smoothing that also performed well for property taxes.[9]

While the methods described above were the most accurate, the competition also showed that even simpler methods can perform well. To illustrate, the MAPEs for the forecast software and damped trend exponential smoothing with nominal dollars were, respectively, 6.12 percent and 6.78 percent, the best and second-best MAPEs across all series. By way of comparison, using the previous year's revenue, adjusted for inflation, as the forecast for the subsequent year produced a MAPE of 6.82 percent. This is only 11 percent less accurate than the best techniques. This is good news for local government forecasters because using quarterly or monthly data often requires that forecasters deseasonalize the data. Consequently, forecasting with annual data will be less complex, but could still produce a reasonably accurate result. The most promising forecasting methods for annual data appear to be damped trend, single exponential smoothing, and using the previous year's actual revenue, adjusted for inflation, as the forecast for the subsequent year.

Overall, the competition results suggest that forecasters should seek a quantitative method that produces a MAPE no greater than 7.5 percent on average. It is important to understand a limitation of this MAPE figure, though. The forecasts in the competition were performed by forecasters who did not have any knowledge of the forecasting environment, so this MAPE threshold refers only to the results provided by the quantitative technique. It does not necessarily reflect a desirable level of accuracy in the final forecast because a final forecast should take account of information that was not available to the forecasters in the competition, but that would be available to the forecaster in a local government, such as local economic conditions, legislative changes, etc. That said, a MAPE of 7.5 percent is still useful for judging the relative accuracy of different quantitative techniques that the forecaster might choose. The next chapter provides benchmarks of accuracy levels achieved by actual government forecasters that can be used to judge the accuracy of the final revenue forecast. Another limitation of the 7.5 percent figure is that the average MAPE may not be achievable with every forecast.

In addition to providing insight into which methods to use, the forecasting competition provided insight into the methods to avoid. Most notably, using simple trending or period-to-period growth rates to forecast revenue produced poor results – a MAPE of around 10 percent for annual data and much higher for quarterly and monthly data. An explanation might be that using growth rates assumes that revenues increase in a multiplicative fashion (like compounding interest), but they rarely do. Using the previous year's actual revenue, adjusted for inflation, produced a much more accurate result, perhaps because it assumes no such growth – rather it assumes the current year will be essentially the same as the last, except for inflation. This said, simple trending or period-to-period growth rates can occasionally produce accurate forecasts – and in some cases they did in our competition – but these results were not consistent.

Picking the Method to Use for Annual Budget Forecasting

As our competition showed, no single technique will be best in all circumstances. In fact, in some cases the difference in accuracy between different techniques was so small as to be inconsequential. Therefore, it is wise to consider multiple methods and then test them for their potential predictive power by simulating the conditions the forecaster would face when making an actual forecast. Because the properties of each government's revenue portfolio are at least somewhat different than other governments', a given forecasting technique will perform at least somewhat differently from government to government.

The forecaster should start his or her search for a forecasting method with those that had the best performance in our competition. For periodic data, forecasting software was the best method. If forecasting software is not available, damped trend exponential smoothing or single exponential smoothing are good alternatives. For annual data, the best overall method was using inflation adjusted data and taking the previous year's revenue as the forecast. Although forecasts made from periodic data are usually slightly more accurate than forecasts made from annual data, the great ease of calculating inflation adjusted last-observation forecasts means that there is very little cost to considering it. If forecasting software is available, the forecaster might also try using annual data with the forecasting software. Although this combination was not included in our competition, the strong performance of forecasting software with periodic data suggests that it would be worth considering using the software with annual data as well.

The results of the forecast competition suggest that other methods might be useful in particular circumstances. The forecaster can pick other methods from Exhibit 8.2 that did well for the kinds of data series the forecaster wishes to forecast.

Additionally, the forecaster might consider a few other possibilities. First, if the method currently being used to forecast revenues has proven successful, it should continue to be considered. Second, though it wasn't included in the competition, the forecaster might consider econometric regression if he or she has access to data for useful predictive variables and the statistical skills to use the technique successfully. Third, a non-statistical algorithm (e.g., a mathematical model, as discussed in Chapter 5) might also be considered, especially if there is a low quantity or quality of historical data available. Finally, if the forecaster is uncomfortable with statistical methods like Holt exponential smoothing or damped trend, consider including the moving average method of forecasting. Though this method did not do as well as the others in the competition, it did perform respectably.

After taking into account all of the possibilities described above, the forecaster will have a number of candidate methods. The predictive potential of these methods can then be estimated using a process similar to what we used for the forecast competition. In Chapters 6 and 7, we demonstrated the use of hold-out data tests (also called out-of-sample tests) wherein some of the data for some periods are held out of the forecast and the model is used to predict the periods that were held out. The predictions are then compared to the actual results from those periods to determine accuracy (how close the forecast is to actual) and bias (the extent to which a forecast generally over- or underestimates). A number of common error statistics to measure accuracy and bias were described in Chapter 6. Hold-out testing can be used for any statistical forecasting method and could even be used for non-statistical algorithms, so the forecaster can use hold-out testing to determine which of the candidate forecasting methods has the most potential.

Why Not Use Just Real Last Observation?

Some readers might be wondering: with a MAPE that is only 11 percent higher than the best forecasting method using periodic data, why not just use last year's revenue, adjusted for inflation, as the primary forecasting method? Given the radical simplicity of the last real observation method, this is a reasonable question to ask. However, there are four reasons why forecasters would not want to limit themselves to this method. First, the best forecasts come from using a combination of methods, so limiting the forecast to just one method is always suboptimal. Second, because the last observation approach uses only one data point to make a forecast, it will be prone to larger errors than other methods. To illustrate, the largest error produced by this method in our competition was 33 percent, while the largest produced by the best periodic method, automatic forecasting using software, was 20 percent. Third, there are methods that can be used to minimize the errors in more sophisticated techniques. For example, in Chapter 6 we showed how the parameters in exponential smoothing models can be optimized. Such opportunities do not occur with last observation. Finally, periodic forecasts will provide more insight into how revenues might be expected to behave during the year, which is potentially useful information for managing budgets. The last observation method does not provide such insights.

That said, forecasters might think about how they could take advantage of the last real observation method. For example, perhaps the method could be quite useful for minor revenue sources where the improvement in accuracy available from more sophisticated methods may not be worth the effort, given the small dollar amounts at stake.

To conduct a hold-out test, exclude from the historical data set the most recent 18 months, six quarters, two years, or whatever other period would result in the best simulation of length of time into the future that the forecaster would have to predict when making a budget forecast. Then, use the forecast methods to make a projection for the periods that were held out and compare the results to what actually happened. Those methods that are most accurate under the simulated conditions will presumably be most accurate when used to make real forecasts as well.

An optional part of the hold-out test is to account for changes in the financial and economic environment (e.g., a change in the tax rate). Accounting for changes in the environment will give the most accurate estimation of how the forecast technique will perform in real life. To do so, the forecaster must gather information about the forecasting environment that is not reflected in historical data, such as a policy change (e.g., a change in the tax rate) and record its impact. However, only information the forecaster would have had before the start of the hold-out period should be recorded for the test. The intent is to simulate the information the forecaster would have had at the time so that the forecast can be adjusted to reflect that information. This kind of adjustment will allow the forecaster to most accurately simulate the performance of the forecast models.

However, the forecaster could exclude adjustments for changes in the environment from the hold-out test. This would streamline the testing procedure, but would only allow the forecaster to observe the relative performance of the different methods. This would not provide as much insight into how the methods would perform in real life but would at least tell the forecaster which method would be most promising for making real forecasts.

> ### What Techniques Do the Best Government Forecasters Use?
>
> Just as our competition showed that many different techniques can work, our research found that the best government forecasters used many different techniques. This is true within a government and across governments. It was common for a single government to use a number of different techniques to forecast the same revenue source, because one single technique will not always return the best results. Unsurprisingly, complex methods were less common than simpler methods. Some forecasters used econometric regression and even ARIMA techniques, but many others used non-statistical algorithms, moving averages, and even simpler extrapolation techniques.

Picking the Method to Use for Long-Term Forecasting

Our competition did not cover long-term forecasting, but research suggests that three different methods have the most potential. First are extrapolation techniques with a trending component, such as Holt exponential smoothing. We found in the competition that a trending component often did not add to the accuracy for an annual budget forecast, but over a multi-year period a trend has a more important impact on revenues.

Second, econometric regression techniques incorporate information on underlying causal forces (e.g., economic data) into the forecast, so should be better able to predict the effect on revenues of the larger changes in these variables that could occur over a longer-term time horizon. To use econometric regression for long-term forecasting, the forecaster must have access to reliable estimates of future values of independent or predictive variables and quality historical data. The characteristics of predictive variables that are necessary for regression forecasting were discussed in detail in Chapter 7, but to summarize, the forecaster must first identify one or more variables that are correlated with the revenue, the variables must reflect stable underlying conditions (i.e., it is safe to assume the variable will continue to have a similar relationship with revenues in the future), and the predictive variable must have a lagging relationship with revenue yield or at least credible future values of the predictive variable must be available to use in the forecast. If these conditions are met, regression forecasting is an option.

Finally, a non-statistical algorithm (mathematical model) could be used. An algorithm could provide a less complex way to use causal forces to predict long-term changes in revenues. For example, the City of Irvine, California, uses total square feet of retail space, among other variables, to predict its sales tax revenue over the long term with a good degree of accuracy. (See Chapter 15 for details on Irvine's experience with developing its algorithm.) While there is not a broad base of research on the accuracy of these algorithms for long-term forecasting, Irvine's experience suggests that an algorithm will work best when it incorporates variables that are directly related to revenue yield. Irvine knows how much sales tax revenue is typically generated per square foot of retail space and can make reasonably accurate predictions of how much retail space will be in the community in future years. It would be inadvisable to develop a non-statistical algorithm using variables with a causal, but less direct, relationship. For example, regional employment and disposable income levels could also be related to revenues, but it would be much more difficult to estimate the precise sales tax revenue impact of any given level of employment or disposable income using just a non-statistical algorithm. These variables could help with the prediction, but might be best in a secondary role.

The predictive power of long-term forecasting techniques could be estimated using hold-out testing, though the hold-out period would need to be longer than we used for annual budget forecasts. We did not perform a long-term forecasting competition, but we did gather historical long-term forecasts and actual revenue from five of the local governments that participated in our research. Exhibit 8.3 shows the MAPE for general fund revenue forecasts two to five years into the future. Each figure in the table is based on all of the forecasts made by a government for the indicated time period. For example, the MAPE of 2.9 percent in the lower left corner means that one of the local governments achieved a MAPE of 2.9 percent for every two-year ahead forecast it made. The row labeled "average" is the average MAPE achieved by all five governments. Unsurprisingly, the average MAPE grows larger the further out into the future the forecast goes. What is, perhaps, surprising is that the minimum MAPE stays around 5 percent for three- to five-year forecasts. Maybe even more surprising is that two of the five local governments were able to maintain MAPEs pretty close to the minimum for all of their forecasts. One government was in a very high growth environment and the other was in a low growth environment. This shows that consistently accurate long-term forecasts are possible, even within different financial and economic environments. Forecasters could use the average MAPEs in Exhibit 8.3 as rough benchmarks for selecting and testing their own long-term forecasting methods, and use the minimums as an attainable goal.

Exhibit 8.3 – MAPEs for Long-Term Revenue Forecasts

	Number of Years Ahead Forecasting			
	2 Years	**3 Years**	**4 Years**	**5 Years**
Maximum	7.4%	14.3%	16.9%	26.3%
Average	5.4%	9.5%	13.0%	17.3%
Minimum	2.9%	4.2%	5.5%	5.0%

Conclusion

A forecasting competition we conducted suggests that a single best forecasting technique does not exist for all situations. Therefore, the forecaster will need to examine the potential of different techniques. The type of revenue being forecasted, the periodicity of the historical data, and seasonality patterns can all influence which technique will work best. After identifying a number of techniques with potential, the forecaster should conduct hold-out tests of the forecasting methods to see which ones perform best. This will help the forecaster produce the most accurate forecasts possible, while demonstrating rigor to the audience of the forecast. Testing the methods also helps ensure that the forecaster does not misspend energy on implementing ineffective methods.

Chapter 9

Step 5a – Implement Forecasting Methods: The Basics

Once the methods have been selected, they can be used to make a forecast. Prior chapters discussed how to use individual forecasting methods. This chapter describes additional steps that forecasters should consider after they have obtained results from the individual forecasting techniques, but before the results are inducted into decision-making processes like budgeting and long-term financial planning. We will discuss: averaging the results of different forecasting methods to get a more accurate combined forecast; making judgmental adjustments to a statistical forecast before presenting the forecast to decision-makers; and testing forecasts to verify their predictive power before inducting the results into decision-making processes.

However, before we get into these topics, let's briefly review the importance of the relationship between the forecast and the budget calendar. In short, the forecaster should time the implementation of the forecast with key events in the economic and financial environments and the budgetary decision-making process. To illustrate, forecasters in the State of Maine formerly prepared a forecast in December, with a revision in early March, for the biennium budget that began on July 1. Income taxes were an important part of Maine's revenue. In mid-March many corporate income tax filers would make their final payments for the last calendar year, and in early to mid-April, many individuals would file their income taxes. Hence, in many years, the State's forecast made in March would be rendered largely obsolete within a month if either the corporate or individual income taxes differed much from what was expected. As result, Maine changed the date of the revised forecast from early March to early May, after the income taxes had come in, but still far enough in advance of the fiscal year start that the forecast could inform budget decision-making.[1]

Averaging Forecasting Methods

In the last chapter, we saw that after selecting forecasting methods, the forecaster may have more than one viable candidate. There is evidence that when there are multiple forecasts for a single revenue source, with each made from substantially different methods, a better forecast for that revenue can be obtained by averaging the multiple forecasts together.[2] There are two reasons why averaging is thought to improve forecasts. First, different techniques use data differently and, therefore, averaging may obtain more total information out of a data series. Second, different techniques fail more severely under different conditions, so averaging mitigates against the most severe forecast errors. One oft-cited study tested averages of different combinations of 14 quantitative forecast techniques, including varying the number of forecasts included in the average.[3] The results showed large and consistent reductions in mean absolute percentage error (MAPE) across a variety of combinations, some of which are displayed in Exhibit 9.1. Note that the figures in Exhibit 9.1 describe the percent reduction in MAPE, not MAPE itself. Also note that the data the researchers used for their experiment was not necessarily public-sector revenue data.

Exhibit 9.1 – Percent Reduction in MAPE from Averaging Forecasts, Experimental Results

# of Forecasts in Average	Monthly Data	Yearly Data	All Data
5	16.4%	9.1%	16.3%
4	14.3%	8.5%	14.3%
3	11.4%	7.6%	11.5%
2	6.9%	5.7%	7.2%

Many researchers cite between four and five models as the number necessary to gain the benefits from averaging. However, even a two- or three-forecast average could reduce noise and better reveal the underlying pattern, as Exhibit 9.1 shows. In fact, these researchers found that even the best performing technique in isolation could be improved (albeit slightly) by averaging with just two to three other high performing techniques.

We can demonstrate the power of averaging using the forecasts we have developed for West Virginia income tax revenues in previous chapters. To do so, we will compare the average of the regression model from Chapter 7 and the Holt Exponential Smoothing model from Chapter 6 with all other forecasting methods for the West Virginia data that this book has presented. We have not included any of the other techniques in the average because the remaining techniques have too much of an underlying similarity to Holt Exponential Smoothing; that is, they are either other varieties of exponential smoothing or moving averages, which are closely related to exponential smoothing methods. The computation for getting an average forecast is very simple: add the forecasts for a given period together and divide by the number of forecasts. For past periods, the result can then be compared to the actual value for that period in order to compute error statistics, just as we have done in prior chapters. Exhibit 9.2 compares the RMSE and the ME from the Holt/regression average with all the other methods. The RMSE is reduced below the RMSE for either Holt or regression, and is the lowest RMSE of any method considered. However, the ME for the averaged methods is substantially more than Holt Exponential Smoothing, but substantially less than regression.

Exhibit 9.2 – Error Statistics for Holt/Regression Average vs. Other Methods

		Trend & Level Moving Averages			Exponential Smoothing			Average Holt / Re-gression
	MA3	MA2	MA3	MA4	Holt-ES	D-Trend	Regres-sion	
RMSE	97,000	80,000	57,000	80,000	47,000	47,000	59,000	46,000
ME	81,000	(13,000)	2,000	(14,000)	1,000	2,000	(25,000)	(11,000)

Exhibit 9.3 shows the Holt/regression average compared with actual data. Except for two periods in the mid-2000s, it reflects a very nice fit. This graph, plus what we see in Exhibit 9.3, strongly supports the selection of the average as the forecasting method of choice for this data set.

Exhibit 9.3 – Holt/Regression Forecast vs. Actual Data

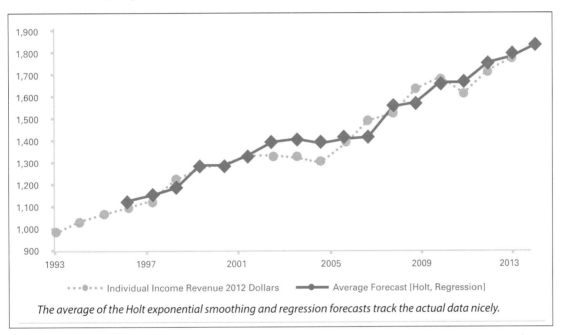

The average of the Holt exponential smoothing and regression forecasts track the actual data nicely.

Averaging can also work with purely judgmental forecasts. The errors associated with purely judgmental forecasts have not been studied in nearly as much depth as quantitative forecasts, so the guidance on how many forecasts to average is not as definitive. However, leading forecast scientist Spyros Makridakis suggests five or so contributors as a minimum to aim for, if using purely judgmental forecasts.[4] Makridakis suggests fewer contributors are necessary if using a hybrid of quantitative and judgmental techniques.

Regardless of whether the techniques are quantitative or judgmental, the forecaster should usually use a simple average, where each technique is given the same weight. Besides being easier to calculate, research has shown that, generally, simple averaging delivers better results than more elaborate methods of statistical weighting.[5] That said, weighting could be introduced if one method has been shown to consistently provide a significant accuracy benefit over others, but weighting should be the exception, not the rule.

Making Adjustments to Forecasts

Forecasters often make adjustments, based on their own judgment, to a forecast derived from quantitative methods in order to correct for a perceived deficiency in the forecast. The good news is that there is substantial evidence in forecasting research that it is possible for quantitative forecasts to be made more accurate when forecasters judgmentally adjust forecasts to account for the effects of special events and changes in the environment that were not incorporated into the quantitative model.[6] In fact, these adjustments can lead to substantial increases in accuracy[7] and GFOA's research indicates that governments with the most accurate forecasts often adjust the results of their quantitative models.

The bad news is that forecasters often go too far – making unnecessary adjustments and even making adjustments when they are not in possession of useful information about special events or changes in the environment.[8] The forecaster might erroneously choose to adjust the forecast because the forecaster believes the statistical technique is missing a pattern in the data (when, in fact, it is the forecaster who sees a pattern that is not there), or because it gives the forecaster a greater sense of confidence in the forecast to make some small adjustment based on personal opinion.

Given this double-edged sword of judgmental adjustments to the forecasts, caution is warranted when applying judgments. Below are a series of guidelines for most safely applying judgments:[9]

- Make judgmental adjustments only in cases where the forecaster is in possession of important information that would affect the forecast and where that information is not reflected in the quantitative model. For example, suppose a city develops a statistical sales tax forecast using its historical data, but the forecaster knows that a very large new shopping complex is set to open in the near future. Here, an adjustment to the statistical forecast is clearly warranted.

- Adjustments will usually be more successful when historical data has lower predictive power. Prior chapters in this book have described methods for testing the predictive power of quantitative forecasting techniques. For techniques with low predictive power, judgmental adjustments would be more useful. For example, if a forecasting technique cannot perform within the forecaster's desired accuracy range, it is a good candidate for adjustment.

- Adjustments to shorter-term forecasts will usually be more useful. As forecasts extend further out into the future and become more uncertain, any special knowledge or insight the forecaster may have about environmental change becomes increasingly speculative.

- Document adjustments. Keep records of adjustments made to see if they increase the predictive power of the forecast.

- Use a structured method to apply judgments. Rather than apply adjustments in an ad hoc fashion, develop a process to apply judgments in a more orderly fashion. For example, perhaps the forecasters must agree on the adjustment to make before performing a statistical forecast. The idea is that the forecaster should already know of any important information not included in the quantitative model so he or she can identify the adjustment beforehand. Waiting until after the statistical forecast is done might bias the forecaster towards making adjustments for other reasons. Another approach is to require that amounts of the adjustment come from an independent source or at least from an analysis performed independent of the forecast (e.g., perhaps a financial impact analysis was performed for new development long before the forecast was made). The idea is to avoid the pressure to use adjustments to "back into" a preferred forecast number.

> **Stick to the Facts**
>
> Adjustments should be based on known events that are certain to occur or at least highly likely to occur. Making adjustments based on more speculative information may call into question the credibility of the entire forecast if the audience does not agree that a given adjustment should have been made.

In public-sector revenue forecasting, the need to adjust commonly stems from some change in the policy environment on the horizon that could result in significant changes to revenue yields. Often, this adjustment is made by simply adding or subtracting a lump sum from the forecast in the amount anticipated to be gained or lost as result of the policy change.

Sometimes, though, the policy can be integrated directly into the forecast. For example, when the forecast consists of an algorithm using a fixed tax rate and variable tax units, the tax units are the forecast and are multiplied by the tax rate. If the tax rate changes on a specific date, the change can be included directly within this multiplication, taking effect on the date of the changed rate, leading to a more direct estimate of the resulting revenue. For more complex integration with exponential smoothing models, the forecaster may want to consult work by Williams & Miller.[10] With regression modeling, sometimes the effect of the policy change would be reflected in the independent variable. The process used to arrive at the value of the independent variable that is used in the regression model could also be used to estimate the change that would occur in the independent variable with the policy change.

Testing the Forecast

Before asking anyone to base decisions on the forecast, the forecaster should test the forecast to ensure it will produce reasonably accurate results. GFOA found that the most common way that local governments test their forecast is the *smell test* – showing the forecast and the underlying assumptions to a group of qualified peers to find out if the forecast smells right. Because the testers are using their judgment to assess the quality of the forecast, many of the same guidelines apply here as were offered earlier in this book for using judgment to make the forecast (see Chapter 5). Most importantly, the testers should have some kind of relevant expertise in the financial and economic environment that the revenue exists within, and the testers should provide perspectives that are different from that of the forecaster. In many cases, the group used to help develop the forecast and to test the forecast might be composed of the same people, so selecting group members carefully will benefit both forecast development and testing.

In Chapter 5, we discussed the weaknesses of group deliberation for making forecasts. Unfortunately, for many of the same reasons discussed there, deliberative groups may also be flawed smell testers of forecasts. However, forecasters can structure the test in a way to gain the benefit of the group members' multiple perspectives while avoiding the pitfalls associated with group deliberation.[11]

First, establish the criteria to evaluate the forecast against as soon as possible – for example, the criteria for a successful forecast might be established when the group starts work on the forecast. Examples of criteria to use might include: Was the method used to reach the forecast clear? Are the assumptions consistent with your understanding of what is happening in the financial and economic environment? All things considered, would you be willing to recommend this forecast as a decision-making tool to other staff or board members?

Second, have group members provide feedback anonymously to avoid the social pressures that can warp decision-making. For example, perhaps the testers provide their assessment of the forecast over a simple, but anonymous, electronic survey tool or by sending an e-mail to a neutral third party who compiles the results. This does not necessarily preclude group discussion. The group could discuss the result of the survey afterwards. Finally, it might be helpful to adopt a transparent and simple mechanism for translating the feedback into a decision. For example, perhaps the team agrees to move forward with the forecast only once a super-majority of reviewers say (anonymously) that they would be willing to recommend the forecast as a decision-making tool to others.

Even with the steps above, human judgment is a potentially flawed test of the forecast, so the forecaster should also use statistical tests. In fact, statistical testing should be done as the forecasting model is being constructed and selected, just as we did in Chapters 6, 7, and 8. Even after a forecasting method passes its initial tests, testing should be repeated regularly; though a particular forecast model may have performed well in the past, a change in the environment may degrade the model's effectiveness.

A very quick and easy way to mathematically test any forecasting technique is to compare it against a *naïve forecast*. There are two basic types of naïve forecasts. A "naïve 1" forecast takes the most recently available prior period's actual result and uses it as the forecast for the next period. "Naïve 2" adds a trending component by taking the most recently available prior period's actual result and adding the change from the period before, which then becomes the forecast. Because you need to know what the actual revenue was to find out if your technique or the naïve technique performs better, you can only perform this test retroactively. However, if the naïve approach consistently outperforms the forecasting method in question, a refinement or replacement of the method may be in order. In fact, as we saw from the results of the forecasting competition, using the previous year's actual revenues to forecast for the subsequent year, when adjusted for inflation, can produce reasonably accurate estimates. As a result, a naïve forecast can provide a stiff test of forecast accuracy, especially when using real dollars.

Exhibit 9.4 shows how this test would work for the single exponential smoothing (SES) forecast of motor fuel taxes that originally appeared in Chapter 6. As we see by the error statistics at the bottom of the table, the naïve 1 method actually performs slightly better, which implies that the single exponential smoothing method is a sub-optimal forecasting method for this data (see Chapter 6 for an explanation of the error statistics). In this case, perhaps the data has a trend that should be accounted for using a technique such as Holt exponential smoothing.

Another potentially helpful testing method is to make a forecast of the entire fund's revenues using the extrapolation techniques described in Chapter 6. These forecasts could then be compared to the forecast made by projecting individual revenue sources. In theory, the forecasts of the individual sources should be more accurate because it will be easier for the forecaster to apply his or her expert judgment to individual revenue sources, rather than all the fund's revenues at once. However, our forecasting competition showed that extrapolative forecasts of general fund total revenues can be reasonably accurate. If the forecaster's best estimate for a fund's revenue is not more accurate than extrapolating revenue for the entire fund at once based on historical data, then the forecasting method should be reconsidered.

Finally, the forecaster could compare the accuracy of his or her forecast to the accuracy achieved by other governments. To help, GFOA conducted a survey of winners of the GFOA Distinguished Budget Presentation Award in order to collect historical records of local governments' general fund revenue forecasts versus the revenues they actually received. We asked for annual forecast and actual data for a ten-year period. Because the fiscal years and data archiving capabilities of the respondents varied, not all governments submitted data for the same period of time, but most of the data points we received fell between 2004 to

Exhibit 9.4 – The Naïve Forecast Test

Year	Motor Fuels Revenue	SES Forecast	Naïve 1 Forecast	Naïve 2 Forecast	SES Error	Naïve 1 Error	Naïve 2 Error
1993	141	147	NA	NA	-6	NA	NA
1994	147	142	141	NA	5	6	NA
1995	153	146	147	153	7	6	0
1996	159	152	153	159	7	6	0
1997	212	158	159	165	54	53	47
1998	207	205	212	265	2	-5	-58
1999	212	207	207	202	5	5	10
2000	209	211	212	217	-2	-3	-8
2001	208	209	209	206	-1	-1	2
2002	214	208	208	207	6	6	7
2003	211	213	214	220	-2	-3	-9
2004	218	211	211	208	7	7	10
2005	220	217	218	225	3	2	-5
2006	228	220	220	222	8	8	6
2007	232	227	228	236	5	4	-4
2008	240	231	232	236	9	8	4
2009	218	239	240	248	-21	-22	-30
2010	230	221	218	196	9	12	34
2011	239	229	230	242	10	9	-3
2012	237	238	239	248	-1	-2	-11
2013	???	237	237	235	NA	NA	NA

SES ME: 5.76   Naïve 1 ME: 5.00   Naïve 2 ME: -0.44
SES RMSE: 14.76   Naïve 1 RMSE: 14.71   Naïve 2 RMSE: 21.41

2013. In total, we had just over 650 data points for total general fund revenues, from cities and counties of all sizes. The vast majority of respondents were in the United States and a few were in Canada. We also received hundreds of observations for specific revenue sources, but chose to focus only on property and sales taxes because they were, by far, the most common major revenue sources.

We used this data to develop benchmarks of forecast accuracy for total general fund, property tax, and sales tax revenue for all governments and for governments in different population size bands. We first converted the data into absolute errors so that we could focus on the distance of forecasts from actual revenue, disregarding whether the forecast was under or over. We then developed the benchmarks in the form of histograms in order better show the variation in accuracy across our data set, and we also calculated the mean absolute percentage error for each histogram.

Before we arrive at the discussion of the results, it is important to note that our respondents do not represent the average local government. First, because the participants in our survey were winners of GFOA's budget award, it is reasonable to assume that their forecasts are generally more accurate than a typical government. Second, we received a response rate of about 33 percent to our survey. It would not be unreasonable to assume that respondents to a survey about forecasting are more interested in forecasting, so they probably place more emphasis on it than non-responders. Hence, our results are better thought of as benchmarks based on governments that likely represent some of the best revenue forecasters, rather than typical forecasters.

We will start our review of the benchmarks with those for all general fund revenues, in Exhibit 9.5. One of the most striking findings is that the largest governments have significantly more accurate forecasts than everyone else, with about 75 percent of the errors coming in below 4 percent. This is probably a product of the more sophisticated methods these governments can bring to bear, and because their large tax bases mean that the law of large numbers and the forces of diversification help prevent very large swings in revenue from one year to the next.

Another interesting feature of Exhibit 9.5 is that all of the graphs peak near the left-hand side of the histogram and then slope downward to the right. This is interesting because one might expect the histogram to peak near the MAPE and then slope downward on each side. Rather, these governments are often quite accurate, but occasional large errors cause the MAPE to rise. One cause could be unexpected economic conditions. For example, the MAPE for all governments was 6.6 percent in 2007, a time when many forecasters were caught unaware by the Great Recession. Other times, the forecaster could be caught off guard by some unique event that causes revenues to diverge significantly from expectations, like the closure of a major retailer for a smaller community. The lesson here is that forecasts can often be quite accurate, but the forecaster should be prepared for uncertainty in the forecast and the attendant risk (the subject of the next chapter).

Errors for State Governments

The Nelson A. Rockefeller Institute of Government conducted a review of the accuracy of state government revenue forecasts from 1987 to 2013.[12] They found that the MAPEs were as follows:[13]

- Sales taxes: 3.2%
- Personal income taxes: 5.8%
- Corporate income taxes: 16.1%
- Sum of the three taxes: 5.0%

Exhibit 9.5 – Distribution of Forecast Errors for All General Fund Revenue

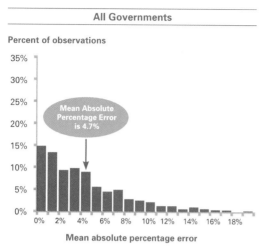

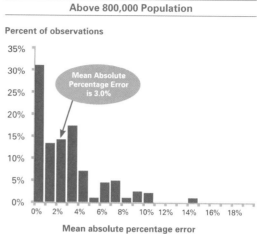

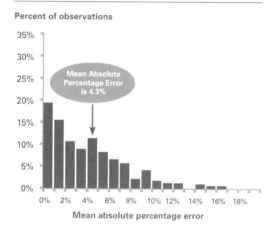

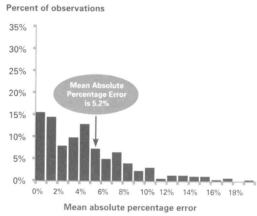

The largest governments have signiﬁcantly more accurate forecasts than everyone else, with about 75 percent of the errors coming in below 4 percent. All of the graphs peak near the left-hand side of the histogram and then slope downward to the right.

Exhibit 9.6 shows property tax errors. Again, the largest governments have a big accuracy advantage, though all governments are more accurate than for general fund revenues in total.

Exhibit 9.6 – Distribution of Forecast Errors for Property Tax Revenue (General Fund)

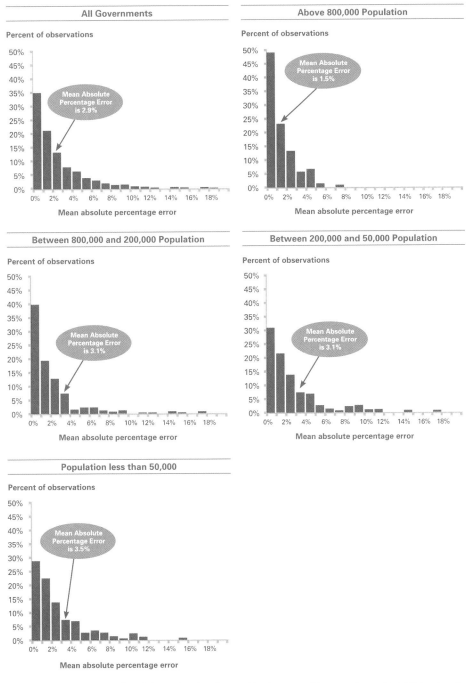

Property tax errors are significantly lower than for all general fund revenues. The curves have a high left-hand peak.

Finally we have Exhibit 9.7, which shows sales tax errors. Perhaps unsurprisingly, the sales tax MAPEs are generally larger than total general fund revenues and the shape of the histograms are generally flatter.

Exhibit 9.7 – Distribution of Forecast Errors for Sales Tax Revenue (General Fund)

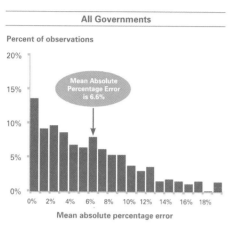

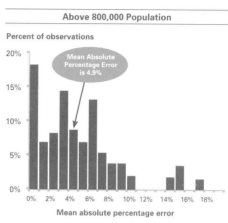

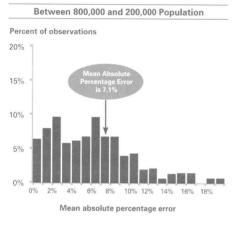

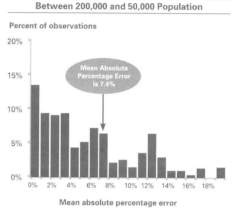

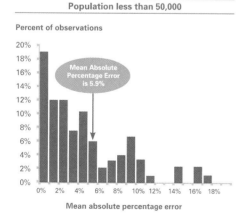

Sales tax errors are higher and the shape of the histogram is flatter.

Conclusion

After results have been obtained from individual forecast models, but before those results are inducted into decision-making, the forecaster should look for opportunities to produce multiple forecasts and average together the results. If forecast models are based on sufficiently different methodologies, research strongly supports the idea that averaging their results can lead to substantial gains in forecast accuracy.

Before the results from a quantitative forecast are published, forecasters often wish to make manual adjustments to the numbers. In some cases, these judgments can increase the accuracy of the forecast, but it is also common for adjustments to actually reduce accuracy. Therefore, judgment should be applied selectively, when circumstances merit it. For example, if the forecaster is aware of important changes in the financial environment that wouldn't be reflected in the data used to make the forecast, then an adjustment would be warranted.

Finally, forecasters should take steps to test the accuracy of the forecast before using it to make decisions. Testing the forecast helps ensure that the forecast will be as accurate as possible. Also, if the accuracy of prior forecasts compare favorably to the tests described in this chapter, it could help improve the credibility of the forecaster with his or her audience.

Chapter 10

Step 5b – Implement Forecasting Methods: Dealing with Uncertainty

"In these matters the only certainty is that nothing is certain."
—Pliny the Elder

While Pliny the Elder wasn't referring to revenue forecasting when he coined the phrase above, he might as well have been. Even short-term revenue forecasts are subject to some degree of uncertainty, and the degree only increases as the time-horizon of the forecast gets longer. Nevertheless, forecasts are typically presented as *point forecasts*, which means that the forecast is represented as a single data point (see Exhibit 10.1). However, presenting a forecast as a single point implies a much greater degree of certainty in the forecast than is actually available. Of course, the actual revenues very rarely match the forecast on the dot and can occasionally miss by a large margin.

Therefore, as part of implementing the forecasting methods, forecasters should take steps to communicate uncertainty in the forecast. Besides being more honest about the degree of accuracy decision-makers can expect, communicating uncertainty offers real potential for improving decision-making. First, recall that in Chapter 5 we discussed the problem of overconfidence in forecasting: research has shown that people are too optimistic about their ability to predict the future. Also, consider that research has shown that people tend to focus entirely on the information that is placed in front of them, to the exclusion of other possibilities.[1] The implication of this research for point forecasting is that people will likely be unjustifiably confident about the point forecast, and will focus their attention on the

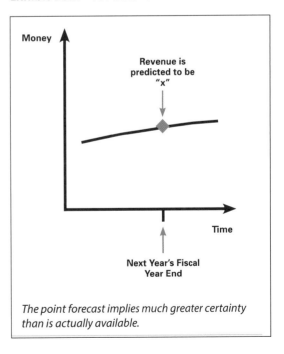

Exhibit 10.1 – A Point Forecast

The point forecast implies much greater certainty than is actually available.

point forecast and not give adequate consideration to other possible outcomes. Hence, they are unlikely to plan sufficiently for futures that differ from the point forecast.[2] By illustrating that the future is a range of possibilities, not just a single point, forecasters can better encourage decision-makers to consider how to respond if revenues come in over or under the forecast.

While a point forecast provides a false sense of certainty, it also provides a sense of comfort. Conversely, presenting a range of possible future revenues heightens the uncertainty of the forecast and may make some decision-makers uncomfortable. The allure of a point forecast is further accentuated by the fact that, ultimately, a single number is needed for budgeting. As a result, the forecaster needs to gain the permission of his or her audience to present and discuss the uncertainty in the forecast.

Getting Permission to Be Uncertain

People like certainty. Getting permission to bring uncertainty into the forecasting conversation begins with establishing that budgeting, by its very nature, is about planning for an uncertain future. Unlike the revenue figures in backwards-looking documents, such as a comprehensive financial report, it is not just possible that the forward-looking numbers published in a budget will be at least somewhat different from what eventually comes to pass; it is probable. A famous quote from military science captures the idea that plans usually don't usually work out as envisioned: "No plan survives contact with the enemy."[3] However, the point is not that planning is pointless. As another military scientist, General Dwight D. Eisenhower, said: "Plans are nothing; planning is everything." Though plans may be rendered obsolete by reality, the act of planning prepares the organization for the future, no matter what ultimately happens.

Those Who Don't Learn From History...

The differences between prior forecasts and actual revenues can be used to demonstrate the inherent uncertainty in forecasting and the need to plan accordingly.

A good planning process considers a range of options.
When you have more options, you actually require less knowledge about the future because you have more courses of action you can choose from once the future unfolds. The author of a number of acclaimed books on uncertainty, Nassim Taleb, uses the metaphor of planning a vacation at one of two resorts.[4] The first resort provides a wide array of options for things to do. The second resort has a narrow range of options. You would need to take the time to learn more about the second resort before booking a trip in order to make sure the resort offers an activity you would like, whereas you could more safely book a trip to the first resort without knowing as much about it because the resort is likely to have at least something that will satisfy your tastes once you arrive. Put another way, options help you stay flexible and adaptable to new realities.

Of course, the amenities of resorts can be known with absolute certainty before booking a trip. Future revenue yields are usually not known with absolute certainty before building a budget or a financial plan. The point forecast can imply that they are completely knowable. This can decrease the perceived need for options. Discussing uncertainty in the forecast promotes the need to consider options – both for how to handle setbacks and good fortune. Options create flexibility and adaptability, leading to a more resilient financial strategy for your organization. One last quote, this time from a chemist and microbiologist, Louis Pasteur, provides the closing argument for recognizing and discussing uncertainty and options: "Chance favors the prepared mind."

So, how can this general argument for acknowledging and planning for uncertainty be translated into specific tactics for getting permission from decision-makers to be uncertain? It starts with the language that forecasters use to describe and present the forecast. Most fundamentally, describe the forecast as an "estimate" and use other terms that convey that there is some degree of uncertainty in the forecast.

> **Advanced Content in This Chapter**
>
> All readers should go through the sections on prediction intervals, scenario analysis, and risk-mitigating strategies. After prediction intervals but before the latter two topics are sections on using bell curves and simulation to model uncertainty. These two techniques require more comfort with statistics. The sections on scenario analysis and risk mitigation should be accessible to all readers.

Next, a particularly powerful way to highlight uncertainty is to focus on the uncertainty in the forecast assumptions. The forecast numbers themselves, for many members of the audience, are inherently abstract and difficult to understand. By comparison, the forecast assumptions, like how much the population will grow or whether local businesses will expand or contract, are relatively concrete. If the audience can appreciate that the future behavior of key features of the financial and economic environment is uncertain, then it will be easier for them to appreciate that the forecast that is based on these features must also be uncertain. For example, in the City of Manhattan, Kansas, the forecaster refers to particularly uncertain key assumptions as "wild cards" in her forecast presentation, thereby highlighting their potential to change the City's revenue outlook.

Prior experiences can also be used to help the audience to accept that uncertainty and risk are inherent parts of forecasting. For example, the 2007/2008 housing bubble deflation is a widely-recognized instance of assumptions about the direction of housing prices being wrong and local government revenue forecast accuracy suffering as a result. The State of Utah even develops formal reports that disclose the level of historical volatility in state revenues in order to help state policymakers understand the impact of volatility on the State's prospective budgetary plans.

Finally, the finance officer should provide decision-makers with a financial planning and budgeting process where the uncertainty expressed around the forecast is used to make better decisions. Decision-makers will be more comfortable with discussing uncertainty when they see how the information can actually be used. Later in this chapter, we will see more about how the municipalities of Boulder and Colorado Springs have used information on uncertainty to make better decisions.

Once the audience has accepted the basic premise that forecasts are uncertain, the forecaster can help them assess the level of uncertainty that they face and prepare for it.

Two Kinds of Uncertainty

Once the forecaster's audience has accepted that forecasts are uncertain, the forecaster should depict that uncertainty for them and help them work through how to use this information in decision-making. Before we delve into the techniques for doing this, we should understand the two basic kinds of uncertainty that a forecaster will encounter.[5] The first kind is routine uncertainty that occurs in every forecast. To illustrate, the forecaster might know that the tax base generates between about $20 million to $25 million in sales taxes each year, but doesn't know where exactly on this spectrum revenue yield will fall in any given year. The second kind of uncertainty involves special, unexpected, impactful events. A good example is when a major employer in the community is considering ceasing its operations, thereby significantly altering the tax base. There may be uncertainty around when and if the employer will close down and how much revenues will decrease as a result. Other examples of special, impactful events might include state legislation that changes local government resources or a large new land development in the community.

> **By Acknowledging Uncertainty, Can You Increase the Risk of Overspending?**
>
> Some finance officers might be concerned that acknowledging that revenues could be higher than what a point forecast suggests could lead decision-makers to spend more. However, seeing that revenues could also be less than the point forecast should more than balance out any such effect. In fact, a preponderance of psychological research shows that people tend to be loss averse – the prospect of a loss weighs more heavily than the prospect of an equally sized gain (about twice as heavily, in fact). Later in this chapter, we will show how the Council of the City of Colorado Springs selected a conservative budgeting strategy when shown an objective forecast along with a representation of the uncertainty inherent in the forecast.

Assessing and Presenting Routine Uncertainty in the Forecast

We will see three different methods that are intended to address the routine uncertainties that every forecaster must contend with. The first method will be prediction intervals.

Prediction intervals are the easiest to create of the methods we review, but also have the most limitations. Placing the forecast on a bell curve distribution is the second method. It is provides a more nuanced view of uncertainty than prediction intervals, but requires greater statistical skill to develop and use. Finally is simulation, which is the most sophisticated and potentially powerful method, but also the most challenging to develop. With any of these methods, the forecaster does not necessarily have to apply them to the revenue forecast for the entire budget. Rather, the forecaster can apply these tools to situations where the government has the greatest chance of experiencing revenue yield much different from the point forecast, and encourage discussion of uncertainty and options around those particular instances.

Before we delve into these three methods, we should point out that all of them involve expressing uncertainty in precise probabilistic terms, such as: "The forecaster is 90 percent certain that actual revenues will be between $20 million and $25 million." While expressing uncertainty in probabilities may, at first, feel a bit unnatural for some people, it is a vital forecasting skill. In fact, research has shown that forecasters that use this kind of probabilistic thinking are significantly more accurate than those who don't.[6]

Prediction Intervals

The most basic way of presenting uncertainty is called a *prediction interval*.[7] A prediction interval sets an upper and lower limit on the range of most likely outcomes. The prediction interval is assigned a percentage level of confidence. So, for example, we might say that we are 90 percent confident that next year's sales tax revenues will be between $15 million and $20 million.

As the level of confidence goes up (i.e., moves closer to 100 percent), the size of the range necessarily expands, because in order to be more confident that the actual revenue will fall within our interval, we must include a wider range of possibilities in the interval's prediction. Also, as we predict further out into the future, the size of the range necessarily increases even as the confidence level remains the same. This is because the further we get from the present, the more uncertain things become, so we must include a wider range of possibilities in the prediction interval in order to maintain the same level of confidence.

Exhibit 10.2 – Prediction intervals

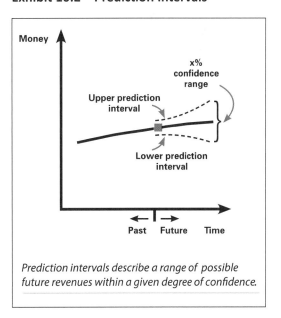

Prediction intervals describe a range of possible future revenues within a given degree of confidence.

A prediction interval can be set using the forecaster's judgment or using a statistical formula. First, let's consider the statistical approach. Formula 10.1 is used to calculate a prediction interval for a *one-step-ahead forecast*, which is a forecast for the period following the last available actual period. For instance, the immediately forthcoming year would be one step ahead from the current year when making annual forecasts. The prediction interval is equal to the forecast plus-and-minus a constant multiplied by the square root of the mean squared error (RMSE). The constant in this formula is known as a "z-score." A z-score indicates how many standard deviations a measurement is from the mean in a normal distribution. To illustrate, a z-score of 1.0 indicates it is 1 standard deviation above the mean. There is a different z-score for each level of confidence a forecast might like to model, though forecasters would typically choose a confidence level between 80 percent and 90 percent. Much higher than 90 percent and the range becomes so large as to cease to provide actionable information, and below 80 percent decision-makers may be uncomfortable using the range. Formula 10.1 shows three commonly used z-scores, and additional z-scores can be easily obtained from the Internet and most statistical texts.[8] The mean squared error is simply the average of the squared difference between the actual and forecasted value for every point in the data set. Squaring the error removes any negative signs. A square root is then taken to return the number to a magnitude relevant to the data set.

Formula 10.1 – Prediction Interval (PI), One-Step-Ahead Forecast

PI = (The forecasted revenue) +/- (z-score x square root of mean squared error of historical data)
90% confident z-score = 1.65   85% confident z-score = 1.44   80% confident z-score = 1.28

To illustrate how the formula for a one step ahead prediction interval works, Exhibit 10.3 provides a set of hypothetical prediction intervals for Fairfax County, Virginia's general fund fiscal year 2013 forecast. The right-hand side of the table provides the intervals for various levels of confidence. Notice that the intervals get narrower as the confidence level drops. The left-hand side shows a sample of the data used to calculate the intervals, plus the FY 13 actual (gray cell) to show how the actual compares to the forecast prediction interval. Notice how the actual of $3.5 billion falls within all of the prediction intervals. Second, notice that Fairfax County has a record of pretty accurate forecasts. In fact, for the 20-year history used to construct the interval, the County's MAPE was only 1.7 percent. This means that intervals will be narrower than for a government with a history of less accurate forecasts; since the County has a history of accurate forecasts, we can be more confident in a narrow prediction interval. For comparison, we have included the data for a midsized city that has a history of less accurate forecasts than Fairfax County. Here the 10-year historical MAPE is 7 percent. You can see that the intervals tend to be relatively larger because the historical accuracy of forecasts is less. In fact, all of the intervals shown for Fairfax County vary only from about 2 percent to 3 percent from the FY 13 forecast. Conversely, the midsized city's intervals range from 8 percent to 12 percent different from the forecast.

Exhibit 10.3 – Examples of Prediction Intervals for Forecast Data

Fairfax County, Virginia, General Fund, Billions of Dollars

	Forecast vs. Actual						Prediction Intervals for FY 2013 Forecast				
	FY 08	**FY 09**	**FY 10**	**FY 11**	**FY 12**	**FY 13**		**95% PI**	**90% PI**	**85% PI**	**80% PI**
Forecast	3.29	3.32	3.31	3.24	3.31	3.47	Upper	3.58	3.56	3.55	3.54
Actual	3.30	3.33	3.35	3.32	3.38	3.50	Lower	3.37	3.39	3.40	3.41

A Mid-Sized City, General Fund, Millions of Dollars

	Forecast vs. Actual					Prediction Intervals for FY 2014 Forecast				
	FY 10	**FY 11**	**FY 12**	**FY 13**	**FY 14**		**95% PI**	**90% PI**	**85% PI**	**80% PI**
Forecast	46.46	52.15	47.08	48.88	51.06	Upper	57.56	56.53	55.83	55.30
Actual	52.05	55.19	49.91	49.54	50.16	Lower	44.56	45.58	46.28	46.81

While the formula for one-step-ahead forecast intervals is simple enough, a statistical calculation becomes more complex for multiple steps ahead. This is because the root of the mean square error statistic from Formula 10.1 is based on one-step-ahead forecasts, which must be modified to reflect the average error in making the n-step-ahead forecast (and this must be repeated for every value of n of interest). So, for example, if the forecaster wanted a statistically derived prediction interval for a three-year-ahead forecast, he or she would need to calculate an RMSE for all the prior three-year-ahead forecasts in the historical data set. Besides being tedious to perform and more complex than Formula 10.1, many governments do not have access to a rich enough historical record of multiyear forecasts to be able to calculate a useful RMSE.

Fortunately, there are non-statistical, judgmental methods for calculating prediction intervals, including for the one-step-ahead forecast (if it is not possible to use Formula 10.1). However, research has shown that judgmentally set prediction intervals are usually too narrow compared to what a statistical formula would have produced – by a factor of around 50 percent![9] It could be that the forecaster is overconfident and therefore underestimates the size of the interval, or it could be that the point forecast establishes a mental "anchor" from which the forecaster is subconsciously hesitant to stray. [10]

Below, we will examine a number of judgmental approaches for setting prediction intervals that are designed to combat the problem of excessively narrow ranges. Note that it is still necessary to set a percentage confidence level, such that the forecaster is being asked to judge an interval for which they are x percent confident. Also, as a general rule, it is advisable to obtain individual estimates from multiple people and then average them together to reach a judgmentally set prediction interval.

The first judgmental approach to setting prediction intervals is to think about the top and bottom of the interval as two separate questions, rather than to think about the total size of the interval as one question.[11] This causes the forecaster to systematically access different pools of knowledge: knowledge about what might cause the revenue to be higher than forecasted, and knowledge that might cause it to be lower. However, be aware that when considering only one end of the interval at a time, you must adjust your percentage confidence level to reflect that you are only considering the one end. For example, if you want to be 90 percent certain that actual revenue falls within your interval, then that means there is a 10 percent chance that it will fall on either of the two sides of your interval. Therefore, when considering just one end of the interval there would be a 5 percent chance that actual revenue would fall outside of just that end of the interval. To illustrate, for a 90 percent confident prediction interval, the forecaster would think about the upper limit that he or she is 95 percent confident revenues won't exceed and the lower limit that he or she is 95 percent confident that revenues won't fall below. This will total up to the 90 percent prediction interval.

Research shows that if the high and low ends of interval are considered separately, then people are able to estimate an interval that is about 70 percent as wide as a statistical formula would suggest is appropriate – a big improvement over 50 percent.[12] Interestingly, even further improvement is possible. If the forecaster also thinks about their best estimate for the middle of the range as part of this exercise, then they access a third pool of knowledge. This can lead to even greater accuracy – in fact, one study showed that people were able to develop ranges that were only about 5 percent narrower than statistically derived prediction intervals.[13]

Because the middle of the range is, essentially, the point forecast, forecasters should have plenty of tools and techniques, which have been described in other chapters, to think critically about the middle of the range. To help forecasters set the top and bottom of the middle range, they should think through the two statements below. The time periods referenced in the statements can be changed from 18 months to what is appropriate given the time horizon of the forecast and when the estimate is being produced:

- Imagine that it is 18 months into the future and revenues have come in way over the forecast. Think about all the reasons this happened.

- Imagine that it is 18 months into the future and revenues have come in way under the forecast. Think about all the reasons this happened.

This style of thinking is called *prospective hindsight* because it invites the forecaster to work backward from a certain (though hypothetical) future, rather than asking the forecaster to speculate on an uncertain future. This method of thinking has been shown to generate about a 25 percent improvement in the number of insights generated over pure speculation. This is because the concrete way in which the statement is phrased makes it easier for the forecaster to imagine themselves in that scenario.[14] A greater number of insights about how the future could be different from what is expected will lead the forecaster to widen his or her prediction interval.

A second purely judgmental approach for setting prediction intervals relies on the research finding that judgmentally set intervals are typically around 50 percent too narrow compared to what a statistical formula would suggest is adequate. First, decide the interval probability (e.g., 90 percent, 80 percent, etc.), and then ask a series of knowledgeable judges to estimate the range of upper and lower values that would include 90 percent (or 80 percent, or whatever probability you selected) of all possible outcomes. Average all the results to get an interval. This interval will likely be too narrow – so double it![15]

This approach might be particularly useful if the forecaster obtains estimates from a large number of people or where it might otherwise be difficult to ensure that the participants use, with rigor, the techniques for separately estimating the top, bottom, and middle of the range. Note that it would be inadvisable to set the top and bottom of the range separately and then double the ranges because that would likely result in an excessively wide range.

A third way to set a prediction interval is to use the one-step-ahead statistical interval as an anchor. Though Formula 10.1 is not overly complex and will be within the capabilities of many governments, statistically derived multi-period prediction intervals would be more challenging. A one-step-ahead statistically derived interval could be calculated and used as a starting point for judgmentally developing prediction intervals for additional future periods. In other words, the forecasters know that the interval for future periods must be at least as wide as the one-step-ahead interval and should probably be wider, especially as they look further into the future. The techniques that were described earlier for estimating the different points of the interval separately could be used for estimating the size of the interval beyond one step ahead.

Once a prediction interval has been set, the forecaster can use it to facilitate a conversation about the range of likely revenues and how the government's service strategy can be designed accordingly. Chapter 18 provides a case study of how the City of Boulder used a prediction interval to help design a series of prioritized service expenditure tranches, where the highest priority services were aligned with the most likely amounts of future revenue and lower priority expenditures were to be covered by the less likely amounts of revenue.

Placing the Forecast on the Bell Curve

Prediction intervals define a range of possible revenues and an estimated chance that actual revenue will fall somewhere within that range (e.g., the forecaster is 90 percent confident the revenues will be between $11 million and $15 million). An important weakness of prediction intervals is that they don't speak to the relative likelihood of different revenue yields within the interval. In most cases, it is more likely that actual revenues will be somewhere near the midpoint of the interval than near the ends of the interval. In other words, continuing with our example above, it is probably more likely that revenues would come in at $13 million than $11 million. However, nothing in the presentation of a prediction interval would lead the audience to this conclusion; in fact, it might mislead the audience to think that all numbers within the interval are equally likely or, worse, to focus on the ends of the interval. This characteristic of prediction intervals means there is still a fair amount of ambiguity within an interval.

The City of Colorado Springs, Colorado, has been an innovator in identifying and mitigating risk in financial planning and forecasting.[16] Their forecasting story is intertwined with the City's general fund reserves strategy. In the early 2000s, the City had a long-time, informal reserve target equal to 10 percent of expenditures. However, the Great Recession depleted the reserve to an all-time low of 5.3 percent of general fund expenditures. (GFOA Best Practices call for a minimum of 16.6 percent.) In 2011, a new mayor, Steve Bach, was elected. Mayor Bach believed that a higher reserve going into the Great Recession would have allowed the City government to avoid making the draconian cuts that were necessary to weather the downturn. In order to determine the right level of reserves, the City catalogued the various risk factors it was subject to, such as volatility in sales tax revenue and exposure to natural disasters, and then assessed the need to hold reserves as a risk mitigation device. As a result, the City determined that it should have a general fund balance equal to 25 percent of its general fund revenues as a reserve for risk mitigation. The City made progress building toward its goal, reaching about 23 percent. Unfortunately for the City, though, a number of the risks it was exposed to came to pass, including the largest wildfire in Colorado history, so the City's fund balances were reduced to around 18 percent of general fund revenue.[17] Because the Mayor was aware of the risks that necessitated the reserves in the first place, he was very focused on replenishing the reserves so that the City would continue to be protected.

Given this history of depletion and rebuilding of the reserves, the City staff has been required to think carefully about the relationship between revenue forecasts and the City's ability to replenish its reserves. The biggest challenge with replenishing reserves is making the tough decision to forego current services in order to put money aside for reserves. To help the elected officials balance the need to support ongoing services with rebuilding the reserves, City finance staff decided to use the inherent uncertainty in the revenue forecast as a decision-making tool.

First, City finance staff made clear that the forecasts of City's sales and use tax (the City's largest revenue source) were not best understood as precise point-forecasts, but rather as a range of possible future revenues. Therefore, elected officials could determine which value within the range they would like to use for budgeting: a higher value in the range would allow for more planned expenditures on services, but had an accompanying higher risk that the forecast would not be met, thereby potentially depleting fund balance; a lower value in the range would restrain additional planned expenditures on services, but had an accompanying higher probability that the forecast would be met or exceeded, thereby potentially adding to fund balance.

Because a simple prediction interval would leave the relative probability of meeting a higher versus lower forecast within the range unclear, the finance staff felt they need to provide more precise information to the elected officials. As such, the finance staff assumed that the probability of different revenue outcomes takes the shape of the "normal distribution." The normal distribution is where data points are distributed symmetrically around the mean in the shape of a bell (the normal distribution is also known as the "bell curve"). Many phenomena take the shape of a bell curve such as the heights of American men, standardized test scores, and even how close people park to the entrance at shopping malls![18] Exhibit 10.4 illustrates the City's forecast for its revenues as a normal distribution. The middle of the distribution is a single number that the staff believes will be closest to the actual revenues, which is referred by the staff as "the expected value." The expected value is in the middle because there is an equal (50 percent) chance that actual revenues will be above the expected value and a 50 percent chance revenues will be over it. The highest probability outcomes cluster around the expected value (i.e., the middle of the distribution).

The great advantage of a normal distribution is that the percent of observations that fall above or below a given point on the distribution can be measured using widely available and commonly understood standards. Exhibit 10.5 shows, on the right-hand side, the point of the distribution considered to be one standard deviation above the middle of the distribution. By definition, one standard deviation above the median of a normal distribution is the point at which 16 percent of the observations are above and the rest are below.

Exhibit 10.4 – City of Colorado Springs Uses Normal Distribution with Revenue Forecasts

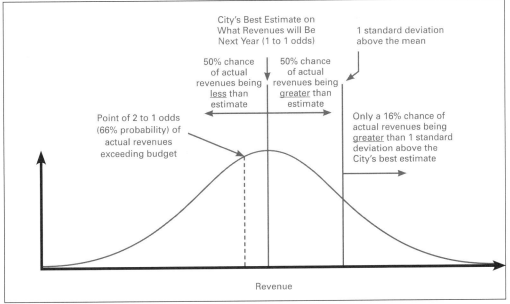

The City used this property of the normal distribution to calculate the odds of actual revenue being greater than the City's budgeted revenue. For example, at the peak of the normal distribution, the odds are 1 to 1 because there is an equal chance of budgeted revenue being greater than or less than actual revenue. At the end of the Great Recession, knowing that end-of-year surpluses could be used to replenish the City's partially depleted reserves, elected officials were invited to select the odds that they would be comfortable with for the budget. After some discussion, the elected officials settled on a budgeted revenue figure that provided 2 to 1 odds, or a 66 percent chance, that there would be a surplus (see Exhibit 10.4 for where this falls on the bell curve). Put another way, elected officials deliberately lowered the amount they would budget in exchange for a greater chance of realizing an end-of-year surplus. As the City gradually built its reserves back up, elected officials reduced the odds of a surplus (to 1.5 to 1 or 60 percent), thereby increasing the amount of money available for current services while still providing a good chance revenue would exceed budget and reserves could slowly be replenished.

While Colorado Springs' method does require more statistical acumen than developing a prediction interval, the assumption of a normal distribution does greatly simplify the process of describing the relative likelihood of different revenue outcomes. Hence, this technique should fall within the capabilities of many, if not most, revenue forecasters. The steps to developing this kind of presentation are as follows:

1. **Develop an objective forecast of future revenues.** Using techniques such as those described in this book, the forecaster develops an objective estimate of future revenues (what Colorado Springs refers to as the "expected value"). This becomes the median of the normal distribution. It is important that this estimate not contain a built-in conservative bias for two reasons. First, the normal distribution assumes there is a 50 percent chance of actual revenue being either above or below the estimate. A conservative estimate presumably would have greater than a 50 percent chance of being less than actual revenues. Second, decision-makers will later be invited to select the odds of actual revenue being greater than budgeted revenue. If they select a conservative approach (a greater than 50 percent chance of a surplus), then the presence of a built-in conservative bias would result in a more conservative forecast than decision-makers intended.

2. **Determine the standard deviation of the residuals.** You may recall that the "residual" is the difference between the forecasted and the actual revenues. We use the residuals of historical forecasts to determine how much variance there is likely to be in the current forecast. Finding the standard deviation allows us to estimate revenue incomes at different odds or probabilities along the normal distribution. To provide a simple example, if Colorado Springs's forecast (the assumed mean of the normal distribution or expected value) is $145.5 million and the standard deviation of its residuals is $2.6 million, then we can estimate that actual revenues are 68 percent likely to be between $148.1 million and $142.9 million ($145.5 million +/- 1 standard deviation, or $2.6 million). Building

on this basic method in the next steps, we can calculate odds or probability for any potential future revenue income.

Before we move on, though, it should be noted that calculating the standard deviation requires at least 15 observations of the residual. Calculating a standard deviation using the residuals from only a few observations is possible, but would be inadvisable for two reasons. First, if there are any unusually large residuals, it will inordinately skew the results, because there would be fewer, more typical results to average it out. Second, when there are few observations, the formula for standard deviation will automatically produce a number larger than what the forecaster might otherwise expect the data set to produce. (i.e., indicate a larger variation). The size of this effect increases as the data set gets smaller. Colorado Springs used the residuals from its monthly forecasts to estimate the standard deviation for its forecast model in order to get more data points than would be available from just annual forecasts.

3. **Develop a normal distribution of the data.** With the standard deviation in hand, we can develop a normal distribution. Fortunately, Excel makes this task very easy with built-in formulas that produce a normal distribution using the mean (the objective

> **How to Make Up Residuals**
>
> Residuals do not necessarily have to come just from forecasts made in the past. Historical data can be used to simulate what a forecast model would have forecasted for a prior period and this simulated forecast can be compared to what actually happened in order get a residual. While this method would necessarily exclude the effect of any judgment-based adjustments to the forecast, it is a good way to generate an objective set of residuals retrospectively.

forecast / expected value), the standard deviation, and, finally, the hypothetical revenue target (i.e., the number that would actually be budgeted). The website for this book (*www.gfoa.org/forecastbook*) provides an example of such a model in Excel. Exhibit 10.5 shows how the output might look from such a model. For Exhibit 10.5, the objective forecast was $145 million (the forecast number is an input, not an output, so it is not pictured in the exhibit). Consequently, when we look under the first column, potential budgeted revenues, and find $145 million, we see that the odds of actual revenue meeting or exceeding the budget are 1:1 and the probability is 50 percent. We also see that $145 million is where there is the greatest chance of actual revenue equaling the forecast exactly, though the probability is still relatively small (15.3 percent). If a more conservative approach was desired, elected officials might pick a budget like $143 million, where there is a 77.5 percent chance of actual revenues meeting exceeding the budgeted target and the odds are 3.5:1.

Exhibit 10.5 – Normal Distribution of the Sales and Use Tax Forecast Possibilities

Array of Potential Budgeted Revenue (Millions of Dollars)	Probability of Budget Equaling Actual	Probability of Actual Revenue Meeting or Exceeding Budgeted Revenue	Odds of Actual Meeting or Exceeding Budget
137	0.1%	99.9%	800.3:1
138	0.4%	99.6%	246.5:1
139	1.1%	98.8%	85.4:1
140	2.4%	97.1%	33.2:1
141	4.7%	93.5%	14.4:1
142	7.9%	87.2%	6.8:1
143	11.4%	77.5%	3.5:1
144	14.2%	64.7%	1.8:1
145	15.3%	50.0%	1.0:1
146	14.2%	35.3%	0.5:1
147	11.4%	22.5%	0.3:1
148	7.9%	12.8%	0.1:1
149	4.7%	6.5%	0.1:1
150	2.4%	2.9%	0.0:1
151	1.1%	1.2%	0.0:1
152	0.4%	0.4%	0.0:1
153	0.1%	0.1%	0.0:1
154	0.0%	0.0%	0.0:1
155	0.0%	0.0%	0.0:1
Total ->	99.9%		

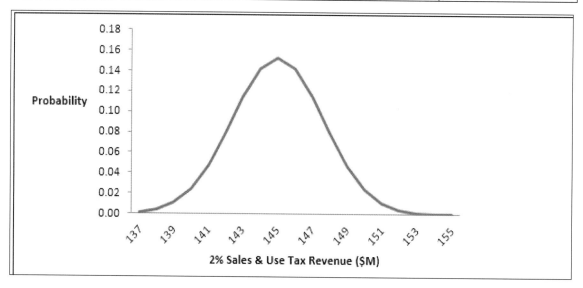

4. **Present the odds.** Colorado Springs develops a histogram similar to Exhibit 10.4 to show where different potential revenue budgets might fall on the spectrum of probabilities. The City does not provide the details of the model to the City Council and generally has found that the histogram is sufficient (though, if Council members wanted to see the details, those details could easily be provided to them). Further, the finance staff pick out a few specific points on the histogram (e.g., points where the odds are 1 to 1, 2 to 1, 1.5 to 1) to highlight with the Mayor and Council. This focuses the discussion. If the audience were asked to consider all the points on the curve, it would be more difficult to come to a decision. Given this information, the Mayor and Council then discuss the odds of surplus or deficit they are willing to live with as they set the budget.

In summary, the City of Colorado Springs has found that this method enables the Mayor and the Council to have an informed discussion about the level of risk they are willing to assume in setting the budget. The method is not too difficult to perform, though it does require access to enough residual observations to develop a meaningful standard deviation of forecasts versus actual residuals. Thus, this technique might be a good option for forecasters with at least some basic statistical training and the ability to generate sufficient residuals.

Simulation

A weakness that is common to both prediction intervals and the bell-curve method is that both rely on descriptions and static illustrations to get across ideas about uncertainty and probability that the audience passively views. Thinking probabilistically can be difficult to grasp. The very use of the term "grasp" to connote understanding suggests that true comprehension is best achieved through hands-on experience, which static descriptions and illustrations fail to provide. Not surprisingly then, researchers have found that simulated experiences can be a highly effective communication tool for statistical information and uncertainty in particular.[19] Interactive simulation helps people better appreciate the role of uncertainty and chance in complex situations by allowing them to directly manipulate key variables and observe the result. It provides them with an awareness of uncertainty and the capacity to account for it that leads to better decisions. Research has shown that simulation has led to better decision-making for financial problems, such as individual retirement planning and accurately perceiving the risk-return profile of investments.[20] It stands to reason that simulation could lead to better budgeting and planning and decisions for public finance as well.

Simulation is based on an underlying statistical technique called Monte Carlo analysis (also known as "stochastic analysis"). According to the author of *The Flaw of Averages*, Sam Savage, Monte Carlo analysis is the mathematical equivalent of shaking a ladder before you climb it. Like bombarding a ladder with random physical forces to test its stability before you climb it, a mathematical model is bombarded with random inputs in order to observe what might happen before decisions are carried out.[21] To illustrate, imagine you have a model where forecasted revenues minus planned expenditures equal a budget surplus or deficit. A Monte Carlo analysis could show the probabilities of ending up with surpluses or deficits by randomly varying the amount of revenue received, where the range of variation is based on historical experiences or even expert judgment. If your planned expenditures show that there is an unacceptably high probability of a deficit, it might lead you to different revenue or expenditure budgeting decisions.

Monte Carlo analysis is not new – it was invented in 1946 as part of the Manhattan Project. Up until recently, Monte Carlo analysis was limited to specialized software. However, the increasing power of personal computing and office productivity applications, particularly spreadsheet software, means that Monte Carlo analysis is now within reach for anyone with a copy of Microsoft Excel. Furthermore, a new data structure, the Stochastic Information Packet (SIP), has recently been developed for the sole purpose of communicating uncertainty in an actionable manner, when using Monte Carlo analysis.[22] The SIPmath 2.0 Standard, promulgated by nonprofit ProbabilityManagement.org, allows the uncertainty generated by forecasts to be used directly in Excel worksheets to calculate the chances of meeting a proposed budget.[23] The SIPmath standard simultaneously helps to simplify the design and execution of the Monte Carlo simulation in Excel (and other software applications) and to transfer the results of the simulation between models. The SIPmath standard does not require the user to understand such concepts as standard deviation and z-scores, and even allows the design and results of simulations to be audited.

In a forecasting application, simulation can be used to generate a large number of possible forecasts to demonstrate the range of possible revenues the organization faces. Typically, a simulation would generate between 1,000 and 10,000 different forecasts. In Monte Carlo analysis, each of these forecasts is called a trial. These trials are generated by starting with the forecaster's best estimate of future revenues, which is created using any of the forecast methods described previously in this book. From this estimate, thousands of random variations of that estimate are generated, where the range of variation is determined by the historical level of volatility in revenues. With so many trials of what the future might look like, we can calculate the probability of different actual revenue incomes.

To illustrate how simulation could be used to make better budgeting decisions, imagine that a government has four basic spending areas, arranged from highest to lowest priority: paying debt service, paying for ongoing operating costs, special projects, and a small contingency amount. This government forecasts that revenues will be $400 million next year. Given this, the budget on the left-hand side of Exhibit 10.6 would be considered balanced. In fact, the City Council might decide that it would like to hire more police officers, thereby increasing ongoing operating expenditures, and spend less on non-recurring special projects, as per the right-hand side of Exhibit 10.6. With a traditional view of the budget, this would not show an impact on the risk the government is faced with; the budget is still balanced.

Exhibit 10.6 – A Budget Based on Point Forecast of $400 Million in Revenue

When the budget goes from this…			…to this, it is still balanced and perceived risk is essentially unchanged		
Expenditures (in 100 millions):		Shortfall?	**Expenditures (in 100 millions):**		Shortfall?
$1.0	Debt Service	**No**	$1.0	Debt Service	**No**
$2.2	On-Going Operating	**No**	$2.7	On-Going Operating	**No**
$0.7	Non-Recurring Projects	**No**	$0.2	Non-Recurring Special Projects	**No**
$0.1	Budget Contingency	**No**	$0.1	Budget Contingency	**No**
$4.0	*TOTAL EXPENDITURES*		**$4.0**	*TOTAL EXPENDITURES*	

However, we know that actual revenues almost never come in exactly as they were forecast. There are often differences—sometimes big ones. To simulate this uncertainty, we can take differences between forecasts and actual revenues in the government's prior fiscal years and use those differences to model the potential variability in next year's forecast. This would tell us the chance of having a shortfall, as shown in Exhibit 10.7.

Exhibit 10.7 – A Budget Based on a Simulated Forecast of $400 Million

When the budget goes from this…			To this, we now see there is a risk of shortfall in the on-going operating costs		
Expenditures (in 100,000,000s):		Shortfall?	Expenditures (in 100,000,000s):		Shortfall?
$1.0	Debt Service	0%	$1.0	Debt Service	0%
$2.2	On-Going Operating	0%	$2.7	On-Going Operating	18%
$0.7	Non-Recurring Special Projects	38%	$0.2	Non-Recurring Projects	38%
$0.1	Budget Contingency	50%	$0.1	Budget Contingency	50%
$4.0	*TOTAL EXPENDITURES*		**$4.0**	*TOTAL EXPENDITURES*	

We now see that budgeting $400 million in expenditures is not a risk-free proposition. There is more than a 1/3 chance that this city will not be able to fund all of the special projects that it budgeted. If the city hires more police officers and increases its ongoing operating expenditures, it creates an 18 percent chance for shortfall in ongoing operating costs during the year, where there was none before. City officials could change allocations in the model and observe the effects on the probability of shortfalls occurring and, in the process, gain a more intuitive understanding of the risks and uncertainties involved in forecasting and budgeting. This might cause the officials to reconsider the wisdom of making such a large increase in ongoing operating costs or at least adopt risk-mitigating strategies along with the change in spending strategy. For example, perhaps the officials might select an approach to reaching its service objectives where there is more flexibility to adjust costs if the city doesn't receive as much revenue as it anticipates.

While simulation is a potentially powerful learning tool, there are some important limitations. First, and most obviously, it does take some mathematical and spreadsheet skills to build a simulation. GFOA has worked with a number of local governments on these methods, so the skills required are by no means out of reach, but they are required. Second, simulations are different from some other analytical tools that public managers may be accustomed to in that they do not lead the user to an answer.[24] Rather, they impart experience and build intuition that allow public managers to identify options and make decisions that are informed by an awareness of the uncertainties and risks that are inherent in forecasting and budgeting, but which are often obscured by point forecasts and static graphics. Finally, although simulation techniques have been in use for decades in a variety of industries, they are not common in public finance. Consequently, there is not a great deal of experience or knowledge to draw upon when it comes to designing and building simulation models for public finance. However, some people are trying simulation methods in public finance. You can visit *www.gfoa.org/forecastbook* to see the results we have collected and to learn more about how to use and build simulations, using the SIPmath standard.

Dealing with Uncertainties Arising from Special Events

Apart from routine uncertainties, a forecast has the potential to be impacted by events that could fundamentally alter the government's resource base. This can include new land developments, annexations, changes in the legal environment, declining population and tax base, and more. These events can complicate the forecaster's job in two ways. First, the audience might not give the potential impact of these kinds of events enough consideration – they might be too focused on status quo conditions to the exclusion of other possibilities. In this case, the forecaster needs to broaden the audience's perspective. The second is almost the opposite problem: the audience might be very interested in some highly uncertain, impactful event. In this case, the forecaster needs to address the audience's concern, but it might be irresponsible to model the impacts from a highly uncertain event into the primary budget forecast lest decision-makers build their budget plans around the assumption that the event comes to pass. Fortunately, there is a single tool that addresses both of these challenges: *scenario analysis*.[25]

Scenario analysis was invented Royal Dutch Shell in the 1970s as a response to the increasing political and economic uncertainties facing the oil industry. Because of the successes it has enjoyed at Shell, the practice of scenario planning has become widespread in the oil industry and many other fields as well. In essence, scenario analysis presents decision-makers with three to four scenarios that describe markedly different, yet plausible, versions of the future. The intent of scenario analysis is to help decision-makers broaden their thinking about how the future might turn out and, thereby, develop plans and strategies that are more adaptable to conditions that are different from what they expect to occur. Scenario analysis in its fully realized form is more akin to a comprehensive strategic planning process. However, in this book we will focus on a more limited version of scenario analysis that can help decision-makers broaden their thinking about financial forecasts, and that can be developed, presented, and discussed in a limited amount of time.

The first step in scenario analysis is to gather information to be used in developing scenarios. Typically, scenarios will be much more interesting to the audience if they account for both revenues and expenditures. For revenues, the work that the forecaster has done in the third step of the forecasting process should be helpful (i.e., gathering information about the financial and economic environments – see Chapter 4). In particular, analyzing social, technological, ecological, economic, and political (STEEP) forces and drawing influence diagrams serve to identify the issues that scenarios might be built around. It might also be that there is a specific issue that has already piqued the interest of the audience. In this case, the results of the STEEP analysis and influence diagramming can be used to provide additional supporting detail for the scenarios. The forecaster should also identify forces behind increasing expenditures that audience will have a particular interest in. Examples might include pension costs, employee health care costs, or the costs of servicing a growing population.

From this, the forecaster should then identify a small number of the most important forecast assumptions in order to highlight them in the scenarios. Generally, those assumptions that have both the greatest potential impact and the greatest amount of uncertainty around them are the best candidates for scenarios. For instance, the City of Baltimore chose to highlight population growth, inflation, gross domestic product, and housing growth in scenarios it developed for its long-term financial forecast.

A Case in Point

Chapter 16 provides a detailed case study of the City of Baltimore's use of scenario analysis. The case illustrates many of the concepts described in this chapter.

The next step is to identify three or four scenarios to present. Three or four is enough to get the audience thinking more broadly without overwhelming them. Though scenario analysis is not yet a widespread practice in governments, GFOA found that governments that use scenarios for revenue forecasting often develop three scenarios: a *baseline scenario* that represents the assumptions behind the forecaster's best estimate of future revenues; an *optimistic scenario* that sets the values of key assumptions at a more favorable level, while still remaining within the bounds of what is considered reasonable; and a *pessimistic scenario* that sets the values of key assumptions at a less favorable level, while still remaining within the bounds of what is considered reasonable. Governments that have used this approach report that it is helpful for broadening the audience's perspectives beyond the baseline forecast. In order to select the values of the assumptions for the optimistic and pessimistic scenarios, the forecaster should use a historical analogue or reference case wherever possible. For example, Baltimore, for its fiscal year 2013 to 2022 long-term financial plan, based its pessimistic scenario on the actual conditions it experienced during the Great Recession. Using a historical analogue helps make the scenario appear more plausible to the audience and thereby avoids disputes over whether the assumptions are sufficiently realistic.

However, a lesson from scenario planning specialists in industries outside government is that scenarios can be made more effective by avoiding the "best case versus worst case" construct. The audience may learn more from scenarios if they are designed to elicit thinking about a future that is significantly different from what the baseline forecast assumptions presume, rather than one that is significantly better/worse. This is because the conclusion from a pessimistic scenario can be that the government should rein in its service goals and retrench. A scenario that is presented as being different from the baseline, rather than worse, might still suppose less revenue, but might challenge decision-makers to think about how they could make the most of the resources that are available and adopt strategies to cover downside risk.

In any case, the goal is to develop scenarios that are plausible, but not necessarily probable. Put another way, if the baseline forecast represents the forecaster's best estimate of how the financial and economic environment will go, scenarios do not represent a second-best estimate. Rather, scenarios should cause the audience to consider new possibilities that perhaps it had not previously considered. To do so, the situation envisioned by a scenario can't be so extreme that the audience becomes distracted by concerns about its implausibility. For instance, the assumptions Baltimore used for its pessimistic scenario were actually somewhat less severe than what the City had actually experienced during the Great Recession. As a result, the scenario provided insight into how another recession might impact Baltimore's finances, and was widely seen as plausible, since the City had recently experienced conditions even worse than the scenario proposed.

Once the scenarios have been developed, they can be presented using techniques similar to other forecasts. Interactive what-if analysis might be particularly effective for demonstrating the effects of changing key variables live in front of an audience.

Know Your Options: Risk-Mitigating Strategies

When uncertainty in the forecast is acknowledged, using any of the tools we have covered in this chapter, risks to the government's budget that might have been obscured by a single point forecast are uncovered. Of course, the biggest risk is that revenues turn out to be insufficient to cover planned expenditures. The way to mitigate this risk is to develop options that can be exercised should actual revenues turn out lower than expenditure budgets had assumed. Forecasters can help decision-makers become more comfortable talking about uncertainty by helping them develop risk-mitigating strategies.

The most important risk-mitigating strategy is a budgetary reserve policy, which can establish a reserve that provides a pool of resources that can be used to soften the blow when revenues don't meet expectations. At the core of this policy is a statement on the amount of reserves the government wishes to maintain. The amount the policy calls for will, ideally, be based on a quantitative analysis of the level of revenue volatility risk a government faces. For example, a government with stable revenues would need fewer reserves than a government with volatile revenues, and a government with a less diverse tax base might be more vulnerable than a government with a more diverse base.[26] Besides helping the government be better prepared, a risk analysis makes the reserve amount more credible, and therefore more likely to be maintained, than if the reserve amount is seen as an arbitrary number.[27] The policy should also be clear about the role of reserves in stabilizing the budget if revenues drop unexpectedly. For instance, a policy might prohibit the use of reserve funds on ongoing expenditures unless the government has produced a multiyear plan to show how the budget can be brought into structural balance within a year or two.

Not far behind a reserve policy in importance as risk-mitigating strategies are short-term forecasts and monitoring actual revenues against the forecasts during the year. Comparing actual revenues to monthly or quarterly forecasts provides early warning of impending shortfalls. Adjustments can then be made to spending plans before a crisis emerges. Chapter 13 provides more detail on short-term forecasts and forecast monitoring.

Making adjustments to the budget will be easier if the government already has formal budgetary contingency plans in place at the beginning of the year. Earlier in this chapter, we gave some basic examples of how different types of spending could be grouped into tranches of different priorities. Governments could develop more specific plans as well. For instance, perhaps the special projects the government will undertake are prioritized and the start dates staggered through the year, with lower priority projects starting later. This way, lower priority projects could be cancelled or deferred to the following year if short-term forecasts suggest that the revenues to pay for them won't materialize. The same basic technique could apply to regular operating programs as well. For example, if the budget provides for expanding the police force by ten officers, then perhaps five are authorized to be hired at the beginning of the year and the remaining five in the middle of the year, when it has become clear whether or not the revenue to fund the second five positions will be received. Governments can also look for strategies that turn fixed costs into variable costs so that costs can be more easily reduced if revenues demand it. For example, perhaps a government can contract out a service to a vendor where the terms of the contract allow the government to lower the level of service and the cost paid out, as needed.

Conclusion

When shown a single point forecast, elected officials naturally want to budget services up to the amount of the forecast. However, the finance officer often faces blame if revenues are less than forecast and cuts are then required mid-year. Therefore, finance officers often tend to forecast conservatively. However, persistent and significant surpluses can undermine the finance officer's credibility and damage working relationships. Acknowledging the uncertainty in the forecast is a way to escape this trap. By showing the range of possible revenues, forecasters can lead budget decision-makers through a discussion of how to build a budget that is resilient under different possible futures and develop strategies to cushion the organization against the risk of revenues coming in lower than anticipated.

Chapter 11

Step 6a – Use Forecasts: The Foundation

The purpose of a forecast is to inform financial decision-making. However, public finance managers often find that decision-makers don't give forecasts the weight in decision-making that they should.[1] Public officials will never base their financial planning decisions entirely on a technical forecast, but what steps can public finance managers take to make it more likely that the forecast will have a meaningful influence? To help answer this question, we found a cadre of local governments that have been highly effective in integrating their forecasts into financial decision-making (see Exhibit 11.1).[2] With the insight provided by their experiences and other research from the field of behavioral psychology, we have identified two parts of the foundation for highly effective use of forecasts in decision-making: 1) an environment that encourages decision-makers to induct forecasts into their deliberations; and 2) the personal credibility of the forecaster.

Exhibit 11.1 - Our Highly Effective Forecasters

- City of Forest Lake, Minnesota (pop. 19,000)
- City of Sarasota, Florida (pop. 53,000)
- City of Manhattan, Kansas (pop. 58,400)
- City of Auburn, Alabama (pop. 59,000)
- City of Monterey Park, California (pop. 61,000)
- City of Palo Alto, California (pop. 66,000)
- City of Tempe, Arizona (pop. 163,300)
- City of Reno, Nevada (pop. 233,000)
- Town of Gilbert, Arizona (pop. 240,000)
- Kitsap County, Washington (pop. 254,000)
- Prince William County, Virginia (pop. 430,600)
- City of Houston, Texas (pop. 2,196,000)

An Environment that Favors the Use of Forecasts

To illustrate the power of the environment in shaping the decisions that people make, best-selling authors and researchers on organizational development, Chip Heath and Dan

Heath, describe a university experiment conducted at a movie theater in suburban Chicago in the year 2000.[3] Moviegoers were given a free bucket of popcorn, some getting a large bucket and some getting a medium-sized bucket. Unfortunately for the moviegoers, the popcorn was stale – so stale that it squeaked and one recipient compared it to Styrofoam packing peanuts. However, this is just what the experimenters wanted. They wanted to see if the size of the bucket influenced the amount of popcorn people ate and wanted to be sure that the delectability of the popcorn was not the cause (which it clearly wasn't). They found, by weighing the buckets before and after, that people who were given the large buckets ate 53 percent more popcorn! The experiment was repeated to control for other variables and the results stood: the environment (a larger bucket) clearly influenced how much people ate.

The effect of the environment on individuals' decisions is not limited to gastronomy, but extends to people's work lives as well. For example, W. Edwards Deming was an engineer, author, lecturer, and management consultant whose ideas helped found total quality management, Six Sigma, and Lean, and who is known as "the father of quality."[4] Deming firmly believed that the environment (e.g., organizational culture, work processes) that managers create in an organization is the most important determinant to the quality of work that the organization produces. Deming was also well known for his aphorisms, including, "A bad system will beat a good person every time."

However, it is more common for people to attribute another person's decisions and behaviors to that person's character traits, discounting the importance of environmental factors. In fact, so common was this phenomenon across a large number of psychological studies, that it earned a name: the fundamental attribution error.[5]

Unfortunately, there are no equivalents to the popcorn experiment in public financial management to prove the power of the environment in shaping financial choices in governments. However, a simple thought experiment should suffice. Exhibit 11.2 invites you to consider two hypothetical cities, imaginatively named "A" and "B." Assuming both cities face similar socioeconomic conditions and have public officials of similar abilities, which one do you think will make better use of forecast information and make consistently better choices?

How then, can public managers create an environment that is supportive of using financial forecasts to make decisions? A good place to start is to develop budgetary principles. Principles provide a guiding framework for decision-making to everyone, from elected officials to appointed managers and finance officers. Decision-makers can test their choices against the principles to ensure that short-term pressures are not getting the best of the government's long-term interests.[6] The City of Reno, Nevada, has developed such a set of "Budget Guiding Principles." The principles were adopted by the City Council via resolution and the staff has reproduced them in a number of more accessible formats, including posters that adorn council and staff work areas. The City has found that the principles provide a touchstone during the budget process, helping the City Council and staff to maintain focus

Exhibit 11.2 – A Tale of Two Hypothetical Cities

City "A"	City "B"
Has adopted a written set of financial policies so that everyone knows the standards of good financial management and guidelines for decision-making.	No written financial policies exist. Responses to issues have to be regularly reinvented.
Officials are regularly provided with survey data and other objective indicators of citizen views.	Officials' only form of citizen input is hearing from those that come to public meetings and talk the most and/or loudest.
Staff systematically helps officials recall good decisions (for example, by embedding them in stories that become part of the culture).	Good decisions are not memorialized or used as learning devices.
Have taken steps to gain broad, explicit agreement to a set of formal goals for the city.	No formal goals exist. Everyone has their own idea about what the goals are.
The budget process asks officials to consider how all available revenues can be used to best achieve the community's goals and priorities.	The budget process starts with last year's expenditures and officials focus on making changes at the margins according to incremental differences in revenues from last year.
A strategic long-term financial planning process asks officials to think about how their service priorities can be pursued over a multi-year period in a way that will result in a legacy of financially sustainability.	Budgeting is done year to year. The process does not ask officials to consider the long-term service or financial implications of their decisions.

Exhibit 11.3 – Some of the City of Reno's Budget Guiding Principles

- **Structural Budget Deficit Elimination:** Eliminate the General Fund structural budget deficit through a balanced approach of ongoing expenditure reductions and optimization of revenues, including identification of new revenue sources.
- **Budget Forecasting:** Annually develop and prepare a minimum two-year budget forecast to be utilized by the City Manager in preparation of budget recommendations to the City Council.
- **Use of One-Time Resources:** One-time resources will be matched to one-time expenditures.
- **General Fund Reserves:** When conditions permit, maintain a General Fund reserve between 7 and 8.3 percent.
- **Allocation of New Revenue Sources:** After the General Fund Reserve level is reached, allocation of new revenue sources is to be used to fund an additional reserve for extreme events and/or to pay down contingent liabilities.[7]

---

on the long-term financial health of the City. Exhibit 11.3 provides an illustration of some of Reno's Principles.

Budgetary principles provide a context for and transition to financial policies. Financial policies establish local standards for acceptable and unacceptable courses of financial action, guidelines in which the government can operate, and a standard against which the government's fiscal performance can be judged. Financial policies provide details to back up the principles, without crossing the line into administrative procedure. The GFOA book, *Financial Policies*, provides in-depth guidance on the different kinds of policies a government could adopt, how to develop and adopt them, and the technical details a policy should address. However, here are a few types of financial policies that are especially important for creating a good environment for using forecasts in decision-making:

- **Reserves.** A reserve is the portion of fund balance (or working capital, in an enterprise fund) that is put aside as a hedge against risk. A reserve policy establishes the desired level of fund balance to maintain as a hedge: for example, the policy might require the government to maintain reserves equal to at least 17 percent of its regular operating revenue. A reserve policy implies the need for good forecasting to see if reserve levels will remain at desired levels given future revenues and spending.

- **Structurally balanced budget.** Many local governments are subject to state laws that require a *balanced budget*, where sources of funds equal uses of funds. However, if non-recurring or one-time sources, such as asset sales or use of fund balance, are used to pay for recurring or ongoing uses of funds, such as employee salaries, then the budget is not truly balanced because the government will eventually run out of non-recurring sources and be left with a deficit. A policy on maintaining true structural balance requires that recurring expenditures are covered by recurring revenues. A forecast is required to tell if true structural balance will occur into the future.

- **Non-recurring and volatile revenue policies.** This policy commits the government to using non-recurring revenues for non-recurring expenditures in order to avoid creating structural imbalance. This policy can be extended to include volatile revenues. A volatile revenue is a

Address "Why" with Policies

When adopting policies it is important that decision-makers understand *why* a policy exists, not just *what* it commits the government to doing.[8] For example, *what* a reserve policy commits the government to doing is to hold back some of the government's available funding capacity from the current budget; instead of funding new services or lowering taxes, money is put aside for problems that might occur in the future. This might not be a compelling proposition for some public officials. However, *why* a reserve policy exists is that governments face a host of risks that have the potential to unexpectedly draw down financial resources, and a government needs to be able to continue its essential services even under these conditions – a concept that all public officials should be able to appreciate.

recurring revenue, the yield of which varies significantly from year to year. If a government were to budget recurring expenditures equal to the income from a volatile revenue during a peak in the revenue's performance, the government could find itself in a structural deficit when the revenue comes down from its peak. A policy commits the government to treating extraordinary income from a volatile revenue as a one-time source. Revenue forecasting and analysis is needed to identify which revenue sources qualify as "volatile" and when revenue yields are within normal ranges (versus when they are extraordinary).

- **Long-term financial planning.** This policy commits officials to considering the long-term implications of decisions made today in order to ensure that the short-term benefits of a decision are not outweighed by long-term disadvantages. Naturally, long-term forecasting is required to gain insight into the implications of these decisions.

Though principles and policies help to create the mindset to use forecasts in decision-making, the most important financial decisions are actually made during the budget process. The budget process, then, must be designed to encourage the use of forecasting information. The foremost design principle is that non-traditional budgeting formats tend to encourage better use of forecasting.[9] Traditional budgeting formats are characterized by an emphasis on: control of spending through detailed line items; the inputs into public services (i.e., staffing, materials, etc.) rather than the outcomes; and incremental decision-making wherein the government starts the budget with last year's expenditures and adjusts them up or down at the margins as may be required, given assumed revenue growth or contraction. Conversely, governments whose budgets incorporate a planning orientation, take program performance into account when allocating resources, and take an explicit, structured approach to weighing competing potential uses of resources against each other are more likely to get value out of revenue forecasts.[10]

A good place to start exploring how a less traditional approach to budgeting can encourage better use for forecasting information is the beginning of the budget process. The traditional, incremental budget process tends to emphasize expenditures because budget discussions begin with the question: What did we spend last year? An alternative approach to budgeting starts by asking what resources are available and may even engage public officials in a discussion on whether tax and fee levels are appropriate given the service demands of the public. This difference in approach, although subtle, emphasizes revenue forecasts as a tool to reveal the level of resources available as the starting point for budget discussions. The City of Auburn, Alabama, describes this as a "live within our means" philosophy that has been important for focusing their decision-makers on the forecast.[11]

---

*Targets could also be set for any other decision unit a government uses for budgeting, such as divisions, programs, etc.

Budgeting methods have been developed that place greater emphasis on revenue forecasts at the beginning of the process.[12] One of the more popular is *target-based budgeting* (TBB).[13] TBB gained popularity in the 1980s, perhaps as a simplifying response to the perceived complexity of its forerunner, zero-base budgeting.[14] Under TBB, each department* is given a target spending amount and is asked to submit a budget for that amount. For example, a department may be asked to develop a budget proposal that is 90 percent of the size of what it spent last year. The total target for all of the departments together is necessarily less than what the revenue forecasts say is available because the difference between the targets and the total available is used to fund additional activities beyond what the departments proposed within their target budgets. Departments submit proposals in competition with other departments to use this additional funding, and central decision-makers select from the proposals, up to the amount of revenue available. Thus, revenue forecasts are important in TBB both for setting a viable target for base spending upfront and for determining how much additional funding is available for proposed activities beyond the base amount. TBB continues to be a popular method of budgeting, especially in environments of financial austerity. For example, about one-third of leading local government budget practitioners reported using some form of TBB in the immediate aftermath of the 2008 Great Recession.[15]

A more recent budgeting method is priority-based budgeting.[16] Under this method, the government first determines how much revenue it has available. It then identifies the community's most important priorities or service goals. Next, resources are allocated to the specific programs or activities that are judged to have the most potential for achieving these goals or priorities. Departments are not the primary budgeting unit. The implication is that money will be allocated to programs or activities according to how much revenue is available, not according to how spending was organized in prior years. Priority-based budgeting is not as popular as TBB, but has been gaining rapidly. Just over 20 percent of leading local government budget practitioners reported using priority-based budgeting methods in the immediate aftermath of the Great Recession, which was an increase of about 90 percent over the number using it before.[17]

The effect of either TBB or priority-based budgeting is to allow decision-makers to "go shopping" for programs or services that will do the most to further the organization's objectives. The forecast defines how much is available to use when going shopping.

Beyond annual budgeting is long-term strategic planning and visioning. Strategic planning and visioning is sometimes criticized by participants for being a "blue sky" exercise, where goals are set without respect to the organization's ability to achieve them. However, a strategic plan and vision for the community are actually a powerful opportunity to create an environment that is supportive of forecasting.

To understand how to take full advantage of this opportunity, we need to understand a little about how the human mind works. Cognitive scientists have determined that we each have two mental processes for making decisions, called System 1 and System 2.[18] System

1 works intuitively, reflexively, and quickly. System 2 works rationally, deliberatively, and more slowly. Humans inherently use System 1 far more often than System 2 to make decisions because System 1 requires less biological energy to use. So, what are the implications of System 1 and System 2 for forecasting?

First, we will consider the rational System 2 argument for connecting forecasting with long-term strategic plans and visions. The argument is that long-term forecasting can inject reality into long-term planning by highlighting resource constraints. This encourages decision-makers to weigh the relative importance of long-term goals and identify those which are most important and to see the forecast as essential information for achieving their strategy and vision.

Accordingly, GFOA has long advocated for local governments to undertake strategic, long-term financial planning.[19] Long-term financial planning combines financial forecasting with financial strategizing to identify future challenges and opportunities, causes of financial imbalances, and strategies to secure financial sustainability.

Long-term financial planning has become increasingly common among leading local government budget practitioners: a GFOA survey of leading budget practitioners found that 59 percent of survey respondents have implemented a comprehensive planning process, with many of those starting the practice since 2008.[20] Critically, the vast majority of these (90 percent) believe that multiyear financial planning and projections have improved fiscal discipline and long-term financial sustainability in their governments—and two-thirds of those described the improvement as "significant." The survey revealed three features of long-term financial planning that were strongly correlated with its perceived effectiveness. First was a comprehensive presentation of the forecast, including making assumptions transparent, modeling the impact of different issues impacting the forecast, and showing the implication of the revenue projections for the government's financial condition. Second, was the breadth of the audience for the forecasts. When more people see the forecast, there are a greater number of people who have the potential to act on it. Third, is involving a broad range of stakeholders in developing the forecast. This increases the credibility and support for the forecast. Consequently, when high-quality, collaborative forecasts are part of a long-term financial planning process, it increases the perceived effectiveness of long-term financial planning, thereby supporting future demand for high-quality forecasts.

As we just saw, there is a rational case for decision-makers to use forecasts in support of strategic long-term planning and visioning, and our survey has shown that this practice has made a positive contribution to decision-making. However, this same survey also showed that practitioners are still experiencing significant challenges, overall, with integrating forecasts fully into decision-making, especially long-term decision-making. What is the reason for this apparent contradiction? For the answer we turn back to System 1 and System 2. Though the rational reasons for inducting forecasting into decision-making are very appealing to the rational System 2, the problem is that people do not rely on System 2 most of the time; they rely on the intuitive System 1.

So, how can System 1 be enlisted in support of using forecasts to support decision-making? Political science research has found an answer in the identity model of decision-making.[21] The identity model posits that as an alternative to time-intensive rational decision-making, people take a shortcut based on who they perceive themselves to be (their identity), making a decision consistent with what they believe someone like themselves would do in a similar situation. This explains why voters sometimes vote against their rational self-interest: for example, a millionaire who sees themselves as a progressive person votes for a candidate who might raise their taxes to pay for social services.[22]

A decision-maker's identity can impact their inclination to use and support forecasts in decision-making. For example, in the City of Boulder, Colorado, the community has a strong interest in the sustainability of the natural environment. As such, the City government has a vision for making Boulder more environmentally sustainable and develops strategies and plans accordingly. Decisions are made through the lens of *sustainability*, and the City's leaders have expanded this sustainability identity to include financial sustainability. Hence, decision-makers in Boulder reflexively and intuitively inquire about what forecasts say about the long-term financial sustainability of the City's decisions. In another example, the City of Irvine, California, was founded as a planned community and has a long and very successful history of rigorously planned urban growth. Developing and following long-term plans is part of the City's identity, which has extended to a reflexive reliance on long-term financial plans and forecasts as part of achieving the City's goals.

While Boulder and Irvine are fortunate to have distinctive aspects to their organizational history that readily lend themselves to an identity that supports forecasting, such a history is not necessarily a requirement. The Town of Gilbert, Arizona, for example, has adopted a strategic vision of being "The Best-in-Class: All Lines of Service." This kind of aspiration is not necessarily unique to Gilbert, but it is widely and strongly supported by staff and Town Council. They know that if they want to be the best, they need a coherent, long-term financial strategy to get there. Consequently, any compelling strategic vision and plan to provide better services to the community, along with realization that money is needed to achieve that vision, can form the basis for an identity that supports forecasting. Exhibit 11.4 recaps the identities of the three cities profiled here and the implications for their use of forecasts, and the case studies in the later chapters of this book provide more detail on how a strong identity has helped these cities make better financial decisions.

Once the financial decision-making environment has been designed to support using forecasts, the next step is to institutionalize these new ways of making decisions. This way, the use of forecasts is ingrained into the organization and is less reliant on the leadership of particularly outstanding managers or elected officials. The City of Tempe, Arizona, for example, supports its use of forecasts through the following habitual activities:

Exhibit 11.4 – How Identity Affects Use of Forecasts

City of Boulder, Colorado
- **Who are we?** A sustainable community.
- **So, what do we do?** Use forecasts to make sure today's decisions are sustainable into the future.

City of Irvine, California
- **Who are we?** A city that makes and follows long-term plans to improve the community.
- **So, what do we do?** Use short- and long-term forecasts to make, monitor, and adjust our plans.

Town of Gilbert, Arizona
- **Who are we?** A municipality that strives to be the best-in-class in all lines of service.
- **So, what do we do?** Use forecasts to align our financial resources to become and stay the best.

- One of the City's five official strategic priorities is fiscal sustainability and vitality. This helps keep long-range financial thinking, and thus financial forecasts, on the mind of the City's decision-makers.

- There is regular review of the City's financial policies. The City Council actively uses the policies to guide decisions. The policies require the use of forecasts to make decisions.

- Staff present the forecast twice per year, timed to coincide with points in the budget process where the information is most immediately relevant. For example, the forecast is published in February at the early stages of the budget development process to determine how much the City can spend on services without violating its financial policy of maintaining a fund balance of at least 20 percent of annual revenues during the next five years.

- Quarterly reviews, with the City management team, of actual revenues against the forecast are led by the City's budget staff.

- Staff compile a monthly report of leading indicators of the City's most important tax revenues.

Finally, we'll close with a powerful habit that Kitsap County, Washington, has developed: Elected officials regularly ask if the revenues forecasted by staff are one-time revenues or ongoing revenues. The officials know that one-time revenues are better suited to non-recurring expenditures and ongoing revenues to recurring expenditures. The forecast is designed to differentiate between these two kinds of revenues, which makes the forecast more useful to elected officials.

Credibility of the Forecasters

The credibility of the forecaster is essential because decision-makers are less likely to use a forecast from a disreputable source and more likely to use a forecast from a trustworthy source. To illustrate the importance of credibility, consider that advertisers spend millions of dollars on celebrity endorsements because famous people lend their credibility to the messages the advertisers want to get across.[23] While getting a local sports star to present the forecast is likely not a viable option for most public finance professionals, we can take steps to maximize our own personal credibility and trustworthiness in the eyes of the audience for the forecast. Optimizing our own personal credibility and trustworthiness is important because we often overestimate how trustworthy others perceive us to be.[24]

The fundamental attribution error, described earlier in this chapter, is evidence that people do not usually give enough consideration to the circumstances faced by others. A good place to start building personal credibility, therefore, is to carefully consider the circumstances faced by the audience: What are their concerns? What do they need to know to do their jobs? The early steps of the forecasting process, defining the forecasting problem and gathering information (see Chapters 2 and 3), should help reveal some of the most fundamental issues that the forecast must address.

While having an understanding of the fundamental issues impacting an organization's finances is necessary, it is not sufficient. Members of the audience will have political questions and concerns that must be addressed. While the forecaster will need to use his or her own judgment to decide which particular questions are most important, here are some general questions that are often raised, which forecasters should be prepared to address:

- What are the implications for constituents' tax bills? Can we lower taxes?
- What is the impact on high priority (often capital) projects?
- Can we afford improvements or augmentations to a high-priority service?
- Are our current services and obligations affordable into the future?

Beyond these general guidelines, a forecaster can do more to learn about the audience's specific concerns and respond to them. For example, the City of Sunnyvale, California, was one of the first municipal governments to institutionalize a process of long-term, strategic financial planning in North America. By 1990, the City was doing a ten-year forecast and has continued and refined the practice since. In fact, so well received has long-term planning and forecasting been that the citizens of Sunnyvale passed a grassroots initiative to build a requirement for a ten-year financial plan into the City's charter so that the practice would not end with a change in administrations. The City's financial managers obviously have maintained consistent credibility, and one of their means for doing so was to meet with elected officials to review the long-term forecasts outside of the regular council meetings (e.g., study sessions). This allowed the elected officials to ask questions and exchange ideas with staff about key forecast assumptions before the forecast was presented at the City's council meetings. This allowed staff to fine-tune the forecast presentation, which: a) better aligned the forecast presentation to the informational needs of elected officials; and b) demonstrated to elected officials that staff took their questions and concerns seriously. For example, elected officials were often very curious about how new growth and development projects would impact the City's tax revenues. The informal meetings gave the council and staff the opportunity to discuss the point at which new development would be included in the forecasts versus when it was too speculative to be included. Because there were differences of opinion on this question, the less formal meetings allowed for a more relaxed discussion than might have been possible under the glare of the lights of regular council meetings.

The experience of financial managers in Sunnyvale foreshadows our second step to increasing personal credibility: ensuring that we are seen as someone who produces valuable results, who is honest, and who is dependable.[25] Exhibit 11.5 describes behaviors directly related to forecasting that could enhance or detract from perceptions of the finance officer's credibility.

Whether or not the forecaster has a credibility problem, more credibility is never a bad thing. The following are some suggestions for improving forecast credibility.

Know Your Facts

Having a substantive command of the issues impacting the financial and economic environment was the top piece of advice for increasing credibility from our group of highly effective forecasters. (See Chapter 9.) The forecaster should have knowledge of macro-economic trends that are relevant to the nation or region as well as micro-economic issues that affect the yield of particular tax revenues.

The details a forecaster should know will depend on the community. For example, the City of Palo Alto, California, has a population of about 66,000 and is located at the epicenter of Silicon Valley. Palo Alto's staff remains abreast of the health in the Silicon Valley economy, in general, and growth in venture capital activity, in particular, because this has proven a reliable indicator of the future of the kind of economic activities that impact Palo Alto's revenue sources. Palo Alto also pays close attention to micro-economic statistics. For instance, one of Palo Alto's revenue sources is a tax on hotel occupancy. Hence, Palo Alto monitors room rates, occupancy rates, and the construction of new rooms.

Exhibit 11.5 – Behaviors and Perceptions that Impact Forecaster Credibility[26]

Is the Forecaster Perceived to Produce Valuable Results?		
This characteristic...	**Enhances** credibility when...	**Reduces** credibility when...
Knows the environment	The forecaster shows awareness of details about the financial and economic environment.	The forecaster does not understand critical details.
Alignment with needs of audience	Forecaster answers questions of greatest relevance to the audience	Forecaster answers questions relevant only to the forecaster
Accuracy	Forecast is within accepted tolerances for accuracy	Forecast is outside of tolerances
Technical expertise	Methods are perceived as valid and are consistent with best practices.	Methods appear suspect with no backing by accepted best practices.
Is the Forecaster Perceived to be Honest?		
This characteristic...	**Enhances** credibility when...	**Reduces** credibility when...
Honesty	Forecaster uses clear data and reports findings objectively	Forecaster games facts, focuses on data supporting preferred outcomes
Lack of bias	Forecast rests on assumptions with clear support in reality	Forecast favors a particular slant or way of interpreting data that has clear policy implications
Transparency	Forecaster is able to communicate technical processes and assumptions in lay terms	Forecaster seen as covert or unwilling to explain technical issues. Uses complex jargon.
Acknowledges uncertainty	Forecaster does not make unrealistic promises and plans for contingencies.	Forecaster claims control over uncertainty, makes unrealistic promises, tells audience what it wants to hear
Is the Forecaster Perceived to be Dependable?		
This characteristic...	**Enhances** credibility when...	**Reduces** credibility when...
On schedule	Forecasts are presented when expected and follow-up questions are answered when promised.	Forecasts are presented irregularly. Follow-up questions may go unanswered.
Consistency in practice	There are clear goals. Forecasts are made at regular intervals.	Goals are vague. Forecasts are made when convenient to the forecaster.

The City of Houston, Texas, is the fourth largest city in the United States, so it would not be practical for Houston's forecasters to get to the level of granularity that a smaller government like Palo Alto might. However, Houston does conduct detailed examinations of key industries in the Houston economy, like oil and gas, and other indicators of economic performance that foreshadow revenue yields. As a result, even though Houston's staff may not have the same kinds of details as a smaller city, they still are able to make a credible demonstration of their knowledge of the environment.

Provide a Solid and Clear Set of Forecast Assumptions

The forecaster should translate a strong knowledge of the environment into a set of assumptions about the financial and economic environment that underpin the forecast. The assumptions should rely on objective information that is relevant to the factors that drive revenue yield. To the extent possible, the assumptions should also be compared to forecasts or analysis performed by credible third-party experts such as consultants or universities. Similarities can increase credibility because it shows that the forecaster does not have biases that cause him or her to deviate from what other analysts examining a similar question have found. Differences may also increase credibility if there are clear local circumstances that merit a difference compared to regional trends, which shows the forecaster's knowledge of the environment.

Besides being transparent about the individual assumptions underlying the forecast, the forecaster must also present assumptions together as a coherent set. They must make sense on their face individually and as a collective whole. The audience does not need to know all of the details behind how the assumptions were arrived at, but the audience should be able to understand information used, any major caveats, and especially which, if any, particular forecast assumptions imply that revenues might deviate significantly from past trends.

The Forecaster Who Cried "Wolf"

Be careful about using forecasts to raise an alarm about potential financial crisis. Of course, if trouble is on the horizon, public officials must be made aware of it – however, raising false alarms or even exaggerating the potential for future financial distress in a well-meaning attempt to spur elected officials into action could detract from how people perceive your levels of honesty and objectivity.

Think like a Fox

In Chapter 5, we discussed the fox versus the hedgehog mindset in forecasting, where a hedgehog is committed to one big idea or model and the fox considers many different ideas or models. Our highly effective forecaster governments emphasized the importance of fox-thinking not only for the technical development of forecasts, but also for credibility. A hedgehog mindset can lead the forecaster to stick to a faulty forecast model even when reality is proving it wrong, with the predictable negative consequences for credibility.

Fox-thinking allows the forecaster to change the model and the forecast when circumstances suggest it is necessary.

That said, the forecaster should be cautious about how changes to the forecast model or strategy are presented. If changes are perceived as capricious, reactive, or otherwise unstable, then the forecaster's credibility could be hurt. Be sure to highlight what has worked well in the past and how those practices are being continued alongside, or as the foundation for, new practices. Also, when the need for change first becomes apparent, take it slow when possible. Introduce change in small, but frequent, bite-sized pieces, rather than asking the audience to swallow a large amount of change all at once.

Be Clearly Objective or Conservative

An organization can adopt one of two basic policies on how forecasting will be conducted: "conservative" or "objective." Some public officials exhibit a preference for conservative forecasts, where revenues are systematically underestimated in order to reduce the danger of budgeting more spending than actual revenues prove able to support. An objective approach, conversely, seeks to estimate revenues as accurately as possible with the goal of making optimal use of all available resources.

We asked our highly effective forecaster governments whether their forecasting approach could best be described as objective or conservative. They were almost evenly split, with a slight tilt towards "objective" on the whole. Those who favored the objective approach emphasized the need to provide decision-makers with the full range of options for providing services, to make the best use of resources, and to not overtax constituents. Those who favored the conservative approach stated that their governing board preferred to have a year-end surplus to build fund balances, pay for capital projects, or otherwise direct towards special uses. While there were two rather different philosophies among these governments, there was one important commonality: the decision to be objective or conservative was an explicit one that was consistent with the goals and expectations of the governing board.

In the case of the conservative forecasters, the governing boards had a clear preference for end-of-year surpluses that could be put towards building reserves or paying for capital projects. There is an expectation, then, that actual revenues will exceed what was budgeted, so when they do, no one is shocked or disappointed and the forecaster maintains credibility. However, for governments where the board does not have this same preference, a conservative forecast could lead to credibility problems. If actual revenues consistently exceed forecasts, decision-makers may come to feel that the forecaster is unreliable or, at worst, that they are being manipulated. One government from our research that has been working towards more effective forecasts experienced this challenge. In recent years, this government has moved towards more objective forecasts to be in line with the preferences of the governing board. Before that, when the finance staff produced conservative forecasts, there were feelings among the board members that the finance office was "playing games" with the budget.[27] Clearly, this does not help perceptions of the forecaster's honesty or lack of bias.

However, objective forecasts are not without risk to credibility. Objective forecasts come with a higher risk of actual revenue shortfalls. If these shortfalls then require painful cuts to the budget, the reputation of the finance officer will suffer. Our highly effective forecasters had a variety of strategies for mitigating this risk:

- Conducting rigorous ongoing monitoring of actual revenues versus forecasts during the year so that any shortfalls can be recognized early and preventative action taken before a funding crisis develops.

- Maintaining a dedicated pool of contingency funds to make up for minor shortfalls.

- Identifying the most volatile and unpredictable revenue sources and using those to fund expenditures than can safely be deferred or cancelled if revenues underperform.

- Using flexible expenditure budgeting strategies that allow the organization to more easily adapt to revenue shortfalls. For example, perhaps a new program is only authorized to begin after the midpoint of the year when it has become clear whether or not revenues will reach their anticipated levels.

This approach is nicely summarized by the Town of Gilbert's philosophy: objective forecasting, conservative budgeting.

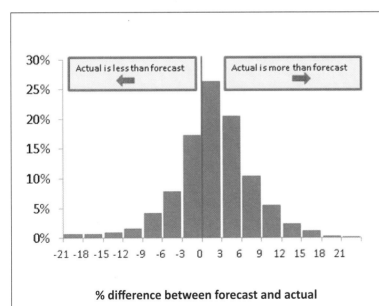

How Widespread is Conservative Forecasting?

The data we collected on forecast errors from local governments suggests most forecasters have a conservative bias. If forecasters were completely objective, we'd expect the histogram to be evenly distributed on both sides of the red line, but the histogram is heavily weighted to the right. This highlights what might be an important divergence in the approaches or our most effective forecasters and other governments.

Actual is less than forecast

Actual is more than forecast

% difference between forecast and actual

Be Accurate

A more accurate forecaster will obviously be more credible than a less accurate one. The good news for those that want to achieve effective forecasts is that there is still a margin for error. In fact, the mean absolute percentage error (MAPE) of the forecasts made by our highly effective forecasters over an average ten-year period was 4.6 percent, which is barely different from the 4.7 percent MAPE achieved by all of the respondents to our forecast accuracy survey. As we discussed in Chapter 9, our respondents likely represent governments that are some of the most committed to progressive budgeting and forecasting techniques in North America, so just matching the average accuracy of this group is a solid level of accuracy.

Establishing tolerances for forecast accuracy and a successful track record of staying within them can build forecast credibility. For example, the City of Tempe aims to stay within ±3 percent of actual revenues with its forecast and has been able to remain within those tolerances about 75 percent of the time since 2010. The need to be accurate applies even to conservative forecasters; if the forecasts are too far under actuals, then credibility problems could develop.

An important practice for developing a reputation for accuracy is not to overpromise and underdeliver on accuracy. Foremost, avoid a large number of significant digits in a forecast. This implies a greater level of accuracy than is possible. To illustrate, present a forecast number as $3.45 million instead of $3,451,752. Going further, acknowledge uncertainty in the forecast and use techniques like those described in Chapter 10 to emphasize the uncertainty and help people visualize it. In fact, if the forecaster can establish a range or interval within which actual revenues are most likely to fall, it gives the forecaster a bigger target to hit.

Even if the forecaster has established a reputation for accuracy, forecasts will still occasionally be off, sometimes even by a wide margin. Large forecast errors don't necessarily destroy the forecaster's credibility, though. In the case of larger errors, honesty is the best policy. Own the error, explain why the error occurred, and, importantly, describe how forecasting procedures will be changed to better guard against similar errors in the future. Having a clear set of assumptions can help in explaining the difference between forecasted and actual revenues: if the assumptions tell a clear story about how the forecaster expected revenues to behave, it is easier to explain how reality came to differ from the story than it is to explain why forecasts were off with no clear story on how revenues were expected to go. This ability to more precisely explain why the forecasts were wrong not only makes it easier for the forecaster to explain how similar errors can be avoided in the future, but it also makes it easier for the forecaster to take steps to fix the problem so that future forecasts will be more accurate.

Help the Decision-Makers Solve Their Problems

If the forecast is framed solely as a limit on what is possible for the government to achieve, the forecaster's perceived value to the decision-making process will be limited. Instead, if the forecast is framed as part of a discussion about how the government can achieve its service goals in a responsible manner, it will be much better received. This requires, as was discussed earlier, making the forecast part of a budgeting process that: a) has a planning orientation; b) takes program performance into account when allocating resources; and c) takes an explicit, structured approach to weighing competing potential uses of resources against each other. However, it also requires that the personal approach of the forecaster be attuned to understanding the choices that decision-makers face in weighing limited resources against community service goals and working with them to get the most out the money available.

Acknowledge and Address Perceptions of Political Bias

Forecasts have an inescapable political aspect to them because of their implications for spending decisions and tax rates. Some audience members might suspect that a forecast has been slanted to serve a particular political agenda. Even if the forecast is completely objective, it is important to address perceptions of political bias so that all policy-makers will be comfortable making decisions based on the forecast. The need to address political bias can vary with the type of government.

Consider, for example, a professional manager form of government, where the manager acts as a chief executive who serves at the pleasure of the whole governing board and where the financial forecasting function falls within the manager's purview. In this case, the forecast might not be perceived to be aligned with one political faction on the board, resulting in little need to address perceptions of political bias.

Conversely, imagine a government with a separate elected legislative and executive branch, as is found in state governments. Here, a forecast produced by a forecaster within the elected executive's span of control might be perceived as biased in favor of the policy objectives of the executive branch. If so, steps might need to be taken to counteract this perception. In some cases, following the credibility-enhancing steps described earlier in this chapter might be sufficient, especially in smaller governments where the forecaster can have personal contact with the audience members and demonstrate his or her personal trustworthiness. In other cases, where it is not practical to develop a reputation of personal trustworthiness sufficient to overcome perceptions of bias, a more systematic solution might be needed. For example, in state governments, *consensus forecasting* is a widely recognized best practice for enabling the governor, lawmakers, and other parties to agree on a single revenue estimate for budgeting.[28] Essentially, a consensus forecast asks representatives from both branches of government to work together to come to a single forecast that both can agree upon. Sometimes other non-partisan participants, such as academics from a state university or business leaders, will be invited to be part of the consensus forecasting process. Typically, each party will come to the table with a separate forecast and, through consensus-building, the parties will arrive at a single forecast. The method for reaching consensus can vary. For example, GFOA examined the consensus forecasting process used by three states and found that each used a different method for reaching consensus. One used simple deliberation and discussion, another used a modified Delphi approach (see Chapter 5), and one relied on averaging together the forecasts of all of the participants (see Chapter 9). It should be noted that research has not found that consensus forecasting improves the accuracy of the forecast – it is only valuable for increasing acceptance of the forecast.

Local governments might be able to borrow some of the ideas behind consensus forecasting. While the legislative branches of most local governments do not have the professional staff support necessary to produce their own forecasts, it might be possible to include representatives of the legislative branch in the forecasting process to the degree necessary to forge agreement on an estimate that everyone can support. It might also be possible to closely integrate credible, non-partisan third-party experts into the forecasting process in order to give legislative branch members the confidence that the forecast is not biased.

Conclusion

Even the most accurate forecast cannot be truly effective if it does not impact real decisions. In this chapter, we covered how finance and budget officers can build the foundation for effective forecasts by creating an environment that supports the use of good forecasting and by building their own credibility as forecasters. We will close with an insight from one of the highly effective forecasters from our research, who observed that the financial management practices that support the use of forecasts to make better decisions can take a while to catch on. Change doesn't happen overnight and the persistence of the finance and budget officer is essential to making a positive change.

Chapter 12

Step 6b – Use Forecasts: Presentation

In the last chapter, we discussed creating an environment that supports the use of forecasts in decision-making, and establishing the personal credibility of the forecaster as the foundation for effective forecasting. The presentation of the forecast is what brings the message home and catalyzes action. So, what makes a good presentation? The forecaster needs a focused and concise message that the audience can understand and remember. The ability to develop such a message is an art and a science that is every bit as vital to the forecaster's job as the technical forecasting procedures we have covered in earlier chapters.

Getting the Message Across

In their book *Made to Stick: Why Some Ideas Survive and Others Die*, Chip Heath and Dan Heath identify the primary obstacle to getting a message across: the Curse of Knowledge.[1] A 1990 Stanford psychological experiment demonstrates the Curse of Knowledge beautifully. A group of people are asked to play a game, where half of the participants are assigned to be *tappers* and half are assigned to be *listeners*. The job of the tapper was to tap out the rhythm of a well-known song to the listener (such as "Happy Birthday" or "The Star Spangled Banner") by knocking on a table, while the listener's job was to guess the song without any prior knowledge of which song the tapper was "playing." Out of the 120 trials, the listeners were only able to guess 3 songs correctly, a success rate of 2.5 percent. The truly astonishing finding was that when asked to project what the success rate of the listeners would be, the tappers estimated 50 percent! In other words, because the tappers knew the song and could hear it play in their heads, they assumed that listeners would have a reasonable chance of guessing the song. Meanwhile, what the listeners really heard was a series of bizarre, disconnected knocks. The lesson from this experiment is that the purveyor of an idea often has a difficult time communicating it because the purveyor can't appreciate how the audience's lack of knowledge impedes their ability to understand the idea.

The implications for forecasters are profound: the complexity of information they are trying to get across to the audience often is more akin to Beethoven or Mozart than "Happy Birthday," so the Curse of Knowledge is a potentially severe problem.

Getting the forecasting message across successfully starts with a clear understanding of what the audience needs and wants to know. Step 1 of the forecasting process, problem definition, should be helpful for identifying these issues. It is important not to leave out issues in which the audience has a strong interest but are "messy," and thus difficult to incorporate into the forecast. Consider using scenario analyses (see Chapter 10) to provide insight on special issues that might not fit neatly into the main forecast presentation.

Besides taking account of special issues, here are some fundamental issues the forecaster's audience will generally need to know:

- The estimate of future revenues and the implications for the government's financial condition, including the key assumptions underlying the forecast and the important causal relationships between the assumptions and the government's revenue. Wherever possible, the assumptions should be linked with supporting evidence from reputable sources, such as state agencies, well-known regional economists, specialized consultants, etc. This shows that the forecaster has done his or her homework.

- The relevance of the forecaster's analysis to the service goals that the audience feels are important.

- A short list of the essential choices that need to be made based on the findings from the two points above, along with the boundaries that the solution must stay within.

- That the forecast is part of a financial-planning process. Its role in the process is to provide the boundaries within which the plan should be developed.

- That the key assumptions underpinning the forecasts are subject to change. If and when they change, the government should be prepared to adapt by updating its financial plans.

The first three points relate to the forecast itself, while the last two address the context for the forecast and helping the audience to understand that uncertainty and adaptability are an integral part of forecasting and financial planning. Governing boards usually have a full agenda so the forecaster often has a limited window of time to get the message across. Limiting the presentation to the essential, high priority issues is important for keeping the audience's attention.

Even if the message is focused on the essentials, a problem is that local government revenues are very often measured in sums that the audience for the forecast has no practical, real-life experience with. They do not have access to millions of dollars in their personal lives, so the forecast numbers are an abstraction to them. Therefore, the forecaster needs to make the numbers more fathomable.[2] The most basic way to do this is to compare revenues to expenditures and reserve levels. This makes the connection between the revenue forecast and the prospects for achieving and maintaining structural balance in the budget. It also suggests, for example, the implications for tax rates, a city's ability to put the same number of police officers on the streets, or a school district's ability to put the same number of teachers in classrooms. See the special appendix at the end of this chapter for the essentials of expenditure forecasting.

Another powerful way to make forecast numbers more tangible is to reduce numbers to a personal scale, such as showing revenues per capita (e.g., per resident or per student) or showing the impact of revenue changes on individual tax bills. Fairfax County, Virginia, shows a five-year history of the property tax on a typical homeowner, using the average assessed value of a home in the County. This shows the impact of any changes in revenue on the taxes paid by a homeowner. The City of Redmond, Washington, has used a method called "the price of government" with good success.[3] The price of government compares the City's revenues against the total personal income of all Redmond residents.[4] This reveals how much of citizens' resources are being consumed by the City and provides a good context for the City Council to discuss what increasing or decreasing revenues mean for the constituents of Redmond.

Exhibit 12.1 – The Price of Government Presentation for the City of Redmond

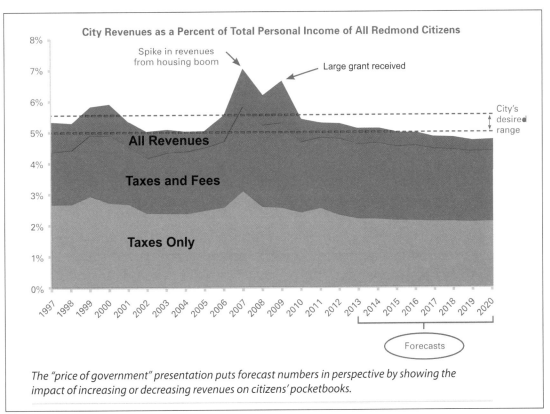

The "price of government" presentation puts forecast numbers in perspective by showing the impact of increasing or decreasing revenues on citizens' pocketbooks.

Exhibit 12.1 shows historical trends in Redmond's price of government as well as the presumed effect of the forecasted revenue on the price of government. The chart contains three layers. The first is all of the taxes the City receives, such as property, sales, utility, hotel, admission, etc. The second layer adds on user fees, including utility user fees, recreation fees, and development fees. The last layer reaches a total for the entire city by adding the City's remaining revenue sources, such as licensing charges, fines, interest income, and grants. These three layers provide three different perspectives that the audience finds important. The first layer, taxes, are paid by Redmond's citizens and are usually the least popular form of revenue among the public, so it is helpful to show taxes' share of the price of Redmond municipal government. The second layer, fees, represents revenues that citizens give to the City, usually voluntarily, in exchange for a valued product or service. The last layer represents revenue sources that perhaps don't come directly out of the pockets of Redmond's citizens (e.g., grants, interest income) or are a direct byproduct of the City's efforts to maintain order in the community (e.g., licenses, fines). However, since this still is money that the City takes out of the private economy, it is considered part of the price of government.

The chart also shows the City of Redmond's desired range of the price of government: 5 to 5.5 percent of personal income, as set by City Council policy. And it shows the reasons why the City has gone above that range. The range was arrived at by debate among the City Council members about the minimum level of revenue necessary to provide the level of service that Redmond residents expect and the maximum level of financial burden that Redmond municipal government should place on its citizens. While agreeing on a target range is not a prerequisite for using the price of government as a presentation technique, it does provide a useful context for discussing the meaning of changes in the price of government that the forecast signals.

Another suggestion for making the abstract tangible is to provide street-level examples of the phenomena that underlie revenue performance. For instance, one city was beginning to run out of developable land, which would lead to a leveling off of the city's revenue growth. In addition to describing the broader trend, the forecaster highlighted, using pictures and maps, specific examples of prominent, valuable, and, until recently, vacant parcels that had been developed and then pointed out how these parcels were the last of their kind. The audience was better able to understand the broad trend by connecting it to parcels they had personally witnessed develop. This technique of describing, in vivid detail, the experience of a particular tax producer that exemplifies a broader trend can be used for any revenue source.

Forecasts can also be related to key variables in a presentation, such as real estate assessments, collection rates, or seasonal fluctuations in order to help the audience relate the forecast to other concepts that they might understand and appreciate. Exhibit 12.8, later in this chapter, shows how property tax revenues could be presented along with property values.

A final way to make forecast numbers more concrete is to use interactive forecasts to simulate changes in key variables or forecast assumptions. Excel (and other software packages) can be used for graphical what-if analyses, where the variables are changed, live, in front of the audience, allowing them to see the effects of the change for themselves. Research shows that such interactivity enhances the audience's understanding and retention of numbers because the audience is able to engage with the presentation, rather than sit as passive observers.[5] The research is supported by the experiences of highly effective forecaster governments – interactive, what-if analysis was cited by many of them as a key to their success. Kitsap County, Washington, elected Commissioner Robert Gelder stated: "I cannot imagine making budgetary decisions with a snapshot-in-time approach" in reference to using a dynamic what-if analysis versus a static presentation.

Even when you follow the steps above, the audience can lose focus – after all, they've likely seen many financial presentations before and forecasting might not be their favorite topic. Including an element of surprise in the presentation can get their attention back.[6] We are not advocating for giving your audience a shock (like telling them revenues will drop off by 10 percent just to get their attention), but piquing curiosity with interesting pieces of information.

One way to do this is to show something surprising about a high profile issue. For instance, financial planning deliberations in local government often come to be dominated by issues that are hot politically but not of great consequence financially. Because of their political prominence, these issues can come to take on imagined financial importance out of proportion to reality. This provides an opportunity: the forecaster can surprise the audience by demonstrating the actual impact of the issue. To illustrate, a small city was working on a strategic, long-term financial plan. The city council had a long-standing goal of bringing a small hotel to the city's downtown area, and had come to believe that the hotel taxes generated would have an overwhelming positively effect on the city's budget. However, in a city of around 35,000, a two-story downtown hotel of less than 150 rooms cannot change revenue trajectories by itself. The city staff, with the help of consultants, developed an Excel model that allowed the staff to conduct what-if analyses on key variables, with the results displayed on a line graph that forecast revenues out five years into the future. One of those variables was building the hotel. At a city council meeting, when the option was selected to assume that the hotel was built, the blue line used to show revenue in the model moved upwards by a barely perceptible amount. After a moment of silence while the facts sunk in, the mayor slammed his fist on the desk and said, "We need to do whatever it takes to move that blue line up!" The city council came to a greater appreciation for the necessity of a more comprehensive strategy to strengthen the city's revenue base than just a downtown hotel.[7]

This same basic approach can be used with any high-profile issue or budgetary item. The forecaster can demonstrate how even large changes to items of small financial consequence do not have much of an impact on the big picture, or how even a small change to large items can have very great consequences. This effect can be enhanced showing long-term projected trends of the item. For example, the City of Redmond, Washington, is limited to an optional one-percent annual property tax increase. Sometimes, people in the City government take the position that a one-percent change is not worth the political difficulties of increasing taxes. However, the City's forecasts are used to show that, at over a third of the City's revenues, even a small change to property taxes makes a big difference, especially over many years.

In order to pique the interest of the audience, staff in the City of Bellevue, Washington, feature a surprising and highly relevant fact in the forecast presentation (they call it a *learning moment*). For example, in one presentation, staff illustrated how long it takes from when ground is broken on a new building to when the new tax and fee revenues hit the City's books. The question and answer was directly relevant to development the City was experiencing, and the concerns Council had about when the revenue would be reflected in the forecasts. The number of steps that need to happen between ground breaking and municipal revenue income was surprising and memorable to the Council.

A presentation pitfall forecasters face is that they may assume that others are equally as quantitatively inclined. Emotions, though, resonate more with most people than dispassionate analysis. Bringing emotion into the forecast doesn't mean making your audience laugh or cry. For example, a great joke might actually backfire if the audience remembers the joke, but not the core message of the forecast. Rather, the goal is to cause the audience to engage with the forecast on an emotional level.[8] One good way to do this is to appeal to an identity that the audience holds. Chapter 11 provided examples of how three different cities established distinct identities that support the use of forecasts. The emotional appeal does not necessarily need to be as deep as an identity. For instance, the City of Tempe uses its AAA bond rating and the pride that instills in public officials as a way to give its forecasts an emotional appeal – the forecasts are seen as critical to maintaining the rating. Any organization probably has something in its inventory of experiences that can make forecasts appealing on an emotional level.

An emotional appeal can be made to an individual's self-interest as well. Psychological research shows that we perceive others to be more motivated by baser interests (money, status) and less motivated by higher-order interests (doing the best thing possible for the community) than they are in reality.[9] So, for example, the forecaster could appeal to elected officials' interest in being good stewards of the public trust and delivering good value to citizens for their tax money, or their interest in leaving the government in better condition than when they first took office.

Finally, we come to confidence. A speaker's confidence has been shown to have a powerful impact on the believability of his or her message.[10] In fact, the term "con man" is a modern shortening of the older term "confidence man" – a powerful, if disturbing, demonstration of the power of confidence to make a message believable! While a forecaster should certainly not seek to "con" the audience, the forecaster must be aware of how his or her perceived confidence will impact how the message is received. For example, earlier in this book we advocated the benefit of "fox" thinking for forecasting: being flexible, adaptable, and changing models when the situation calls for it. We contrasted this to "hedgehog" thinking, which is characterized by certainty, commitment to a model, and, often, confidence in the forecast. Hence, a pure fox may be at a disadvantage when it comes to presenting a forecast, so a balance must be struck between presenting the forecast, along with its inescapable uncertainties, and projecting the confidence that comes from having performed a thorough technical analysis and having designed strategies to mitigate the downside risks.

Telling a Story with Data Graphics

When used well, charts and graphs are a great complement to the forecaster's message because they can communicate a large volume of information quickly and intuitively. They also can help reveal trends and patterns in that data that would not be readily apparent from a visual inspection of the raw data. In short, they tell a compelling story about the data.[11] However, when done poorly, charts and graphs are, at best, a distraction from the forecaster's message and, at worst, confusing, frustrating, and credibility-damaging. The finest graphics are where substance, statistics, and design meet in a coherent whole.[12] The sections below provide guidelines for effective design of data graphics, inspired by the work of Edward Tufte, a political scientist and author of multiple best-selling books on the design of data graphics. Similar to a great graph, the ideas in the section below should be taken together as a whole. Some concepts complement each other and others must be balanced against one another as the forecaster works toward a graphic of optimal communicative power.

> *"If the statistics are boring, then you've got the wrong numbers."*
>
> –Edward R. Tufte, *The Visual Display of Quantitative Information*

Use graphs judiciously. If a picture is worth a thousand words, then an unnecessary graph is a lot of extra reading for the forecaster's audience. Though software like Microsoft Excel makes developing graphs easier than ever before, the downside is that it is too easy to create unnecessary graphs. Before starting a graph, the forecaster should ask him- or herself: What is the essential idea the audience should get from seeing the graph? What will the audience learn that is germane to their questions and concerns? If the forecaster can't come to a good answer to these questions, a graph is probably not needed.

Make the graph interesting and accessible. If a graph is warranted, make sure the presentation is interesting enough to grab the reader's attention and that the message it contains is easy to understand. Of course, a message that is relevant to the audience's concerns is a good start, but there are other good graphic design practices that should be observed. First, a graph will usually tell a more interesting story if there are multiple variables involved.[13] Most good stories have more than one character, after all. Typically, revenue forecasting graphs will include at least the variables of time and money. Additional possibilities include revenues versus expenditures, forecast versus actual, and one revenue source versus another. Further, the variables should exhibit some meaningful variation in the data.[14] Like the characters in a good story, the data in a graph needs to experience change. Though stagnation in the data could be interesting in some cases, it will often not be helpful to capturing the attention of the audience.

After you have identified multiple variables with interesting variations in the data to show, the next step is to select a graph format that can display potentially complex data in an accessible way. Graphics commonly used in financial presentations include column, bar, line, and pie charts. Later in this chapter, we will show how these common types of charts can be designed for optimal communicative power.

A very powerful strategy for making graphics more accessible that has become possible with the increasing power of office productivity technology is to make a graphic interactive. A number of the governments in our research use "what-if" capabilities to provide a live demonstration of the effect on the forecast of changing one or more key variables.

Finally, regardless of which type of graph the forecaster is using, the graph should be attractive to the eye. This attraction should stem from the clarity, precision, and efficiency with which the message of the graph is communicated.[15] How can the forecaster do this? We take up that topic next.

Maximize the Essential, Minimize the Rest. Great writers undergo a process of rigorously reviewing their manuscripts and cutting that which doesn't add to the strength of the story, including unnecessary scenes, characters, and words – anything that distracts from the focus on the story the author is trying to tell.[16] The same applies to telling a story with data and graphs. Edward Tufte has developed a useful concept to maximize what is essential in graphs: the data-ink ratio.[17] Data-ink is the ink on a graph, when it is printed out, that cannot be erased without removing data from the graph. The data-ink ratio is equal to the amount of data-ink divided by the total ink used to print the graph (i.e., a graph consisting of more data ink would have a ratio closer to 1.0). Forecasters should seek to maximize the data-ink ratio, within reason. How can you remove potentially distracting non-data ink from graphics?

First, eliminate or mute grid lines. Many graphs, especially time-series graphs, feature horizontal lines across the graph area that are intended to help the user relate the plotted data points back to values on the vertical axis. However, the core message of a graph rarely requires the audience to know the precise values of the data points. If it is necessary for the audience to know these values, it is usually better to provide a table or to label values for the specific data points that the audience needs know. More commonly, the graph asks the audience to understand the relationship between the data points on the graph rather than the values of individual points. The audience can almost always see these relationships without the grid lines. Therefore, the gridlines are, at best, of limited utility and, at worst, could make interpretation of the graph more difficult if they converge with and obscure the lines the audience should pay attention to. Where gridlines are important to getting a point across, the necessary lines can be added to the graph and the other lines foregone. For instance, in Exhibit 12.1, only the gridlines that bound Redmond's desired price of government are shown.

Second, avoid decorations, especially three-dimensional (3D) graphs. Office productivity software provides a variety of ways to enhance the visual flare of graphs. Most notable among these is the ability to produce graphs that simulate a three-dimensional perspective for line, pie, bar, and other kinds of charts. Some forecasters might be tempted to use 3D graphics in an effort to make the presentation more interesting. However, three-dimensionality might initially draw the eye, but does not add to the communicative power of the graph. In fact, as will be covered later, 3D graphics are more easily misinterpreted than two-dimensional (2D) graphics, so 3D graphics might actually reduce the communicative power of the graph.

Carefully consider borders and axis units. Microsoft Excel adds borders to the graph and provides default values for units of measurement displayed on the axis. Consider if these are truly necessary. A border may just add extraneous lines. Too many units of measurement displayed on the axis might clutter the graph and invite the audience to focus on relating the values on the axis to data points rather than comparing the data points.

Next, question the need for a legend. Microsoft Excel often adds a legend to graphs as a default feature. Instead, consider if the labels can be placed directly on the graph itself. A legend requires the audience to move their attention back and forth between the legend and the graphic in order to interpret the graph. Further, legends are not always easy to interpret. For instance, graphs often use different colors to distinguish different data series on the graph. For graphs that show many series, the colors might start to become too similar (e.g., one shade of blue versus another), making it difficult to translate from the legend to the graph itself. Exhibit 12.1 shows how labels can be applied directly to the graph, and the other graphic examples we'll see later in this chapter provide other alternatives to the conventional legend.

Finally, be careful with colors. With the greater accessibility to color printing and electronic displays, use of color has largely superseded the use of patterns to distinguish graphical elements. However, color brings its own challenges. In addition to the fact that nearly 10 percent of the population in North America is affected by some form of color blindness,[18] it can sometimes be difficult for readers without such challenges to distinguish between colors of similar hue. Therefore, forecasters should be careful to select colors that can be easily distinguished by a diverse audience. The most easily distinguishable colors are: red, green, yellow, blue, black, and white. Pink, cyan, gray, orange, brown, and purple are also good choices, though not as good as the first group of colors.[19]

Avoid misleading graphics. Some graphical techniques have the effect of unintentionally misleading the audience by representing the data with graphics that are out of proportion with the numerical quantities actually in the data. Any technique that distorts proportional relationship between the size of the graphics and the underlying quantities they represent should be avoided. A common example is truncating the vertical axis. For instance, imagine that a forecaster wants to illustrate the difference in actual revenues each year since the 2008 Great Recession (revenues have averaged about $18 million per year since this time). Growth has been slow, so if the forecaster were to do a bar chart of the revenues with the origin set at zero, then the differences between the heights of the bars would be barely perceptible, making for an uninteresting graphic. Therefore, the forecaster elects to start the origin at $16.8 million to produce the effect of "zooming in" on the tops of the bars. The result is shown in Exhibit 12.2. The fundamental problem with this presentation is that while revenues have actually only grown about 7 percent from 2011 to 2014 (or about 2.3 percent per year), the bar shown for 2014 is 179 percent taller than the 2011 bar! It is unlikely that many consumers of this graphic would come away thinking that revenues have experienced explosive growth over the last four years, but it is likely that many would come away with the impression that revenue growth has been more robust than than it actually was. In this example, the forecaster should look for an approach to getting the message across other than a bar chart of actual revenues (e.g., a table or a chart of percent change from year to year).

Exhibit 12.2 – Disproportionate Relationship between Graphics and Data

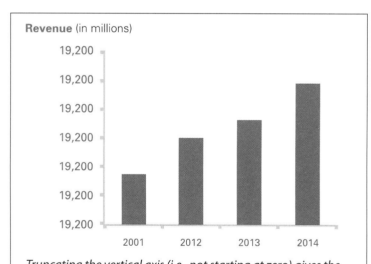

Truncating the vertical axis (i.e., not starting at zero) gives the impression of a much bigger difference in the revenues for each year on the graph than actually exists. There is only about a 7% difference in revenues from 2011 to 2014, but the 2014 bar is 179% taller than 2011's.

Though less common of a problem, forecasters should also beware of truncating the horizontal axis (typically representing time). For example, when showing month-to-month revenue trends, only showing monthly revenue income for the most recent months could be misleading for revenue with significant seasonality effects.

While truncating the axis is an example of an actual disproportional relationship between the size of the graphics and the numerical quantities they are supposed to represent, three-dimensional (3D) graphics can create the illusion of disproportionality. To begin to understand how 3D graphs can have this effect, look at Exhibit 12.3. The exhibit shows two lines, each one with a pair of arrowheads on the end.[20] Now decide which of the arrow "shafts" (excluding the heads) is longer, "A" or "B."

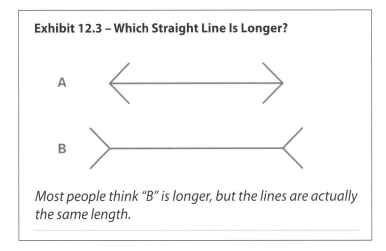

Exhibit 12.3 – Which Straight Line Is Longer?

A

B

Most people think "B" is longer, but the lines are actually the same length.

The right answer is that neither is longer – each shaft is the same length. If you thought "B" was longer, you are in good company: around 90 percent of North Americans perceive "B" to be longer.[21] It is thought that the reason this illusion occurs is that it simulates perspective in the mind of the viewer. The outward pointing "fins" on line "B" evoke an image of an object in the distance, while the inward pointing fins on "A" evoke a closer object.[22] Hence, like a real object that is further away, the mind concludes that "B" is longer than just what the eye perceives. The same misperception can occur in 3D graphs, where the artificial perspective provided by the graphic leads the viewer to see some graphics as larger or smaller than they actually are, thereby distorting the viewer's sense of proportion.

Exhibit 12.4 – Which Slice Represents the Largest Quantity?

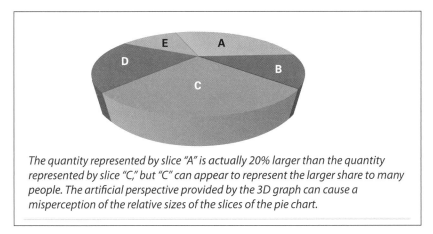

The quantity represented by slice "A" is actually 20% larger than the quantity represented by slice "C," but "C" can appear to represent the larger share to many people. The artificial perspective provided by the 3D graph can cause a misperception of the relative sizes of the slices of the pie chart.

Exhibit 12.4 provides an example of this perspective problem in a 3D pie chart. Can you pick the slice that represents the largest quantity? You could be forgiven for picking "C." Because "C" is intended to appear closer in space, it also has the effect of appearing larger to some people. However, the quantity represented by "A" is larger than that represented by "C" by 20 percent! You might also think that "B" represents a larger quantity than "E," when, in fact, they represent the exact same quantity.[23]

Consider if nominal or real dollars are the appropriate unit of measurement. "Real dollars" have been inflation-adjusted so they are standardized to the value of money in a given year. "Nominal dollars" represent the actual dollars at the time in question. Tufte argues that in time-series displays of money, real dollars are almost always better than nominal dollars because real dollars provide a more honest assessment of the value of money and are the basis for a more accurate comparison of the time periods displayed in the data set. However, in many cases, the forecaster's audience will be thoroughly conditioned to expect nominal dollars, such that to display real dollars would confuse the audience more than enlighten. Further, budget decisions ultimately have to be made in nominal dollars, so nominal dollars might be more immediately relevant to the interests of the audience, in some cases.

Given the arguments for both, the forecaster will need to decide on a case-by-case basis whether real or nominal dollars are best. How to choose? First, when the objective is to give the audience a sense of the change in the resources available to the government across a large time span, give stronger consideration to real dollars. This is because the effect of inflation will be larger across a larger time span, due to the same mechanics behind the miracle of compounding interest. While annual inflation in the United States has traditionally been around 1.5 percent to 4 percent for the last 30 years,[24] the effects can add up over time. To illustrate, 1 US dollar in 2000 was worth over 25 percent less in 2010.

However, be careful about using real dollars when the objective is to compare revenues to expenditures. The inflation numbers used to calculate real dollars typically come from a *consumer price index* (CPI), which represents the price change in a basket of goods and services purchased by the typical consumer. CPI is generally acceptable for inflation-adjusting revenues because, like CPI, revenues are a product of a broad range of economic activities in the economy. However, using CPI to inflation-adjust nominal expenditures may not provide an accurate view of real expenditures, because the types of goods and services purchased by governments are very different than those purchased by the typical consumer. For example, the largest service purchased by governments is typically the labor of public employees. The cost of labor increases each year according to cost increases in labor contracts, health-care plans, and pensions, to name the most important factors. As public finance managers know, these increases are often materially greater than increases in CPI (to state it mildly). Consequently, a CPI-adjusted comparison of revenue and expenditures would not provide an accurate view of the real level of resources received and used by the government. For the purposes of constructing the most insightful graphic, the forecaster may be better with nominal figures. Much of the time, the intention will be to focus the audience on the difference between revenues and expenditures within the same year and then comparing the relative annual revenue-versus-expenditure differences between years, in which case real dollars are largely irrelevant. If the objective of the graph is such that the real value of expenditures is important to communicate, then the forecaster could identify and use alternative inflation indices that better reflect the price changes faced by the government.[25]

In the end, the forecaster should choose nominal or real dollars based on which will better support decision-making. For example, if the governing board is being asked to adopt a budget estimate, nominal dollars would be better because numbers are needed that are relevant to the current year. However, if the forecaster needs to convey a sense of total resources available, real dollars might be better. For instance, if the governing board is considering raising the tax rate, real dollars could provide real insight into how the total resources available have changed over the years. If inflation has eroded the purchasing power of the revenue the government receives from the tax such that real revenues have declined, there would be a stronger case for raising the tax. The forecaster should always avoid using nominal and real dollars in the same graphic.

Use text as an integral part of the presentation. Text on graphics is not only acceptable, it is advisable as a way to point out key features of the graphic.[26] All graphs should include a clear title and labels for the axes, and notate, where applicable, if the dollars presented are in units of millions, thousands, etc. Beyond these basics, messages can be included on the graph to call attention to important events in the data. It may also be advisable to include a caption that explains the main idea of the graphic. The goal is for the graphic to be as self-explanatory as possible, because consumers of the forecast may see the graph on a slide without hearing the forecaster's explanation or might skip over accompanying block text if the graph appears in a written document.

To help make the text that appears with a graphic understandable and as readable as possible, words should be spelled out and abbreviations that non-expert readers would not readily understand should be avoided. Words should also run left to right as much as possible, avoiding vertically-run words and, especially, words running in multiple directions. Avoid all-capital letter typography – consensus among researchers is that all-capital letter typography is significantly more difficult to read for most people.[27]

Finally, forecasters can consider presenting a summary table along with the graph in order to provide the audience with access to the exact figures. This might be helpful when the audience needs to know the trends and relationships shown by the graph as well as the precise values of the variables.

Using Common Data Presentation Formats

Now that we have seen general principles for creating effective data graphics, let's turn our attention to how these principles can be applied to common graphical formats. Column (i.e., vertical bars), line, and pie charts are especially common. Area charts, horizontal bar charts, and combinations of any of the foregoing also often make appearances in forecasting presentations. Tables should not be overlooked in this discussion because they sometimes communicate better than graphics. Finally, the Excel files used to create the graphs that appear in the following pages can be downloaded at *www.gfoa.org/forecastbook.*

Column

A column graph, also sometimes called a vertical bar chart, consists of rectangles stemming from the x-axis, where the height of the rectangle represents a given quantity. Column graphs are useful for showing change over a time series. Column graphs can also be used for making comparisons amongst different items – for example, comparing the relative importance of different revenue sources. Columns should be arranged so that the oldest data is on the left and the most recent data is on the right. When using a column graph to make comparisons where the data is not in temporal order, the smallest quantity should be on the left and the largest on the right. This allows the reader to more easily distinguish between the larger and smaller bars, especially where the underlying quantities are very similar.

Stacked and grouped column graphs can be used to help the audience make comparisons amongst a large number of variables. A stacked column displays multiple variables in a single column. For example, the entire column might be used to show total revenue for a given year, where the column is composed of shorter columns, with each shorter column representing a specific revenue source's share of total revenue. Grouped column graphs cluster multiple columns side by side. Columns within the cluster can be more easily compared to each other and to other clusters on the same graph. For example, columns representing the percent of total revenues comprising an individual revenue source might be clustered together by year.

The stacked column chart will often be preferred when the total of the component parts is important. The grouped column chart might be better where it is more important for the audience to compare the lengths of the columns within and amongst clusters, but the grand total of the quantities represented is not so important. For instance, in our example where we represent each individual revenue source's percent-of-total, if the total of all of the sources shown for a given year was always 100 percent, then it would not be very useful to represent the total on the graph. When presenting either a stacked or grouped column graph, the forecaster should limit the number of component columns shown. Too many can easily overwhelm the reader.

Exhibit 12.5 illustrates a stacked column graph that divides total general fund revenues into property taxes, sales taxes, hotel taxes, and other revenues. In this case, the story the forecaster wants to get across is the continued recovery of total revenues and the role of rapidly expanding hotel taxes, in particular, in the recovery. The stacked column graph communicates the total revenues, and the caption at the top confirms that the segments do, in fact, add up to the total, in case the reader is not sure. The individual segments allow the audience to easily compare the relative size of one revenue source to another. Placing hotel taxes on the bottom allows the audience to more easily observe its rate of growth. The other notable feature of this presentation is that the default legend produced by Excel has been eliminated in favor of color-coded captions that serve the dual purpose of identifying each segment and communicating points of interest.

Exhibit 12.5 – Example of a Stacked Column Chart

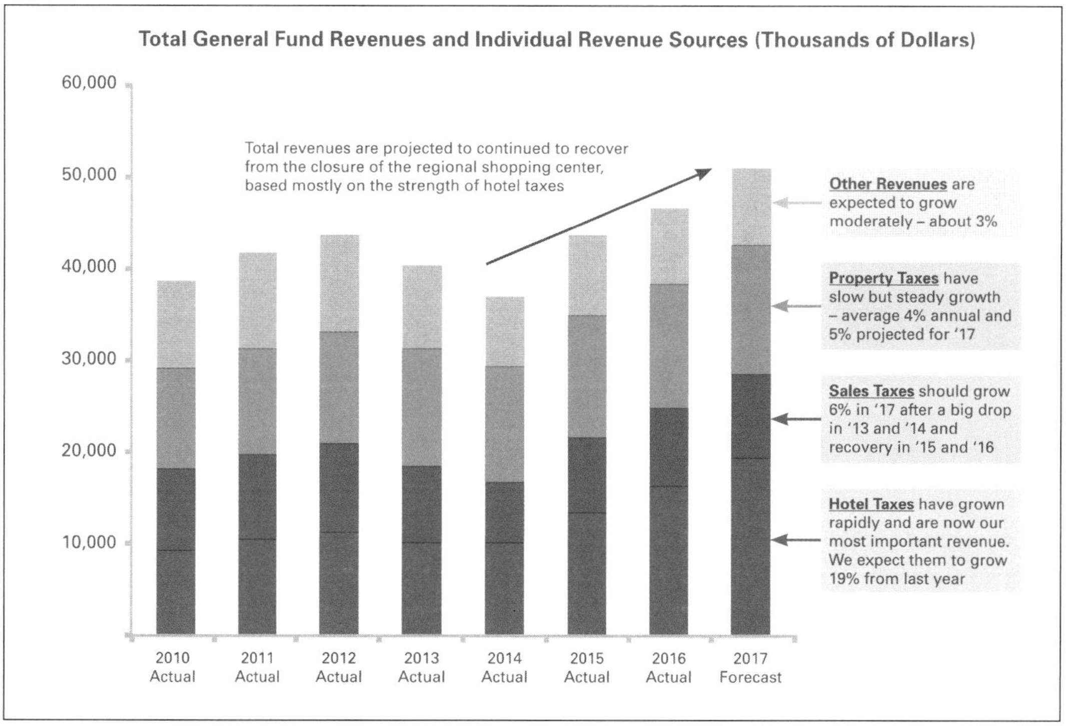
Total General Fund Revenues and Individual Revenue Sources (Thousands of Dollars)
60,000
50,000
40,000
30,000
20,000
10,000
Total revenues are projected to continued to recover from the closure of the regional shopping center, based mostly on the strength of hotel taxes
Other Revenues are expected to grow moderately – about 3%
Property Taxes have slow but steady growth – average 4% annual and 5% projected for '17
Sales Taxes should grow 6% in '17 after a big drop in '13 and '14 and recovery in '15 and '16
Hotel Taxes have grown rapidly and are now our most important revenue. We expect them to grow 19% from last year
2010 Actual
2011 Actual
2012 Actual
2013 Actual
2014 Actual
2015 Actual
2016 Actual
2017 Forecast

Line

Line graphs connect data points with lines, and are used primarily to show longer, continuous time series and to emphasize longer-term patterns or trends. They are a workhorse graphic for revenue forecasters. As with a column graph, the oldest data points should be plotted on the left-hand side, with the most recent data on the right. Different conventions can be used to distinguish amongst data series that are plotted on the same graph, such as colors, dotted and dashed lines, and unique shapes placed directly on the data points (e.g., triangles, crosses, and squares). However, placing too many series can cause the reader to struggle to distinguish one series from another – for example, the colors used to distinguish one line from another may become too similar, or the lines may overlap one another too much.

Exhibit 12.6 shows a line graph of actual and forecasted revenues. In this example, the forecasters want to demonstrate how a long-term trend of high revenue growth was interrupted by the Great Recession and the associated housing bust, but is projected to resume in the future. The graph shows the sharply escalating line of historical revenues along with a caption pointing out a 7 percent annual growth rate during this period. It then shows revenue growth stopping because of the bursting of the housing bubble in 2007 and beginning to pick up again as the local economy recovers, including pointing out the time lag between when ground is broken on new development and when the impact is seen in government revenues. The presentation of the forecast makes it clear that resumed revenue growth is expected, albeit at a lower rate than the period from 1994 to 2007, and includes a 90 percent prediction interval. The forecasters should supplement the graph with supporting information from the Community Development department to demonstrate that there are new building projects at sufficient stages of progress to justify the forecast.

Exhibit 12.6 – Example of a Line Graph

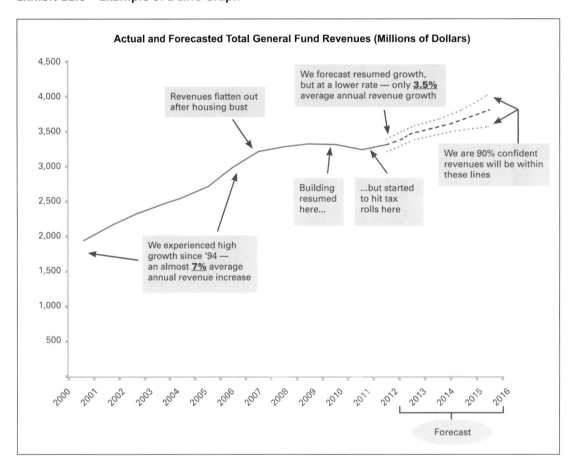

Pie

The pie chart is a circle with radii connecting the center to the edge. A slice is formed between adjacent radii, and each slice represents data value that is proportionate to the angle between the radii. Pie charts are commonly used to show proportional relationships amongst items within a group – like each revenue source's share of total revenues, for example.

Pie charts are subject to a surprising level of vitriol from some data graphic experts. Detractors of pie charts point out that it is difficult to distinguish between the relative sizes of the slices, especially where there are not great differences between the quantities and where there are many data points represented. Readers would be better able to distinguish between the lengths of bars on a bar chart than they would to distinguish between the size of the radials on a pie chart, for example. Further, for pie charts with many slices, many different colors or patterns would need to be used to distinguish the slices, perhaps introducing additional accessibility or interpretation problems.

Therefore, pie charts should be limited to applications where there are relatively few data points that need to be compared, and where precise differences are not important or where the differences are so big that they are obvious. For example, perhaps a forecaster wishes to make the point that revenue from sales taxes and property taxes together exceed all of the government's other revenue sources – here, a pie chart could make a helpful visual. For cases where there are a larger number of categories that need to be compared and/or the precise difference between them are important, consider a column or bar chart as an alternative to a pie chart.

Exhibit 12.7 – Example of a Pie Chart

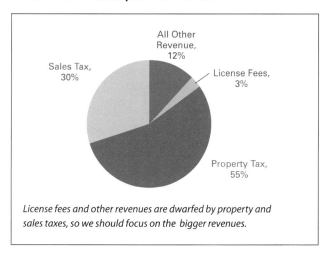

License fees and other revenues are dwarfed by property and sales taxes, so we should focus on the bigger revenues.

Exhibit 12.7 shows a pie chart where the forecaster wants to illustrate how unimportant other revenues are compared to property taxes and sales taxes. Perhaps the forecaster is providing justification for why so much more time is spent on forecasting property or sales taxes, or maybe the audience is preoccupied with an issue that could impact license fee revenues, but the forecaster wants to show that anything but the largest of changes in license fees would be inconsequential to the government's financial position. Other revenues and license fees are shown in the upper right corner because they are the focus of the message the forecaster is trying to get across; the eye tends to be drawn to slices at that position first.[28]

Bar

Exhibit 12.8 shows an example of a bar chart for comparing the amount of sales taxes generated by different categories of commercial activity. The bar chart makes it easy to see the descending order of importance, even among categories that are very close in size.

The bar chart is similar to the column graph except that the rectangles stem from the y-axis and the quantity is measured horizontally. A bar chart can be used to show the relationship amongst items that do not have a natural order, such as different categories of revenues or tax producers. A bar chart, then, is a good alternative to pie charts. A bar chart should not be used for time-series data like annual revenues because it would violate the convention of showing the oldest data to the left. Other than its inapplicability for time-ordered data, bar charts can follow the same conventions described for column graphs, including stacked bar charts.

Exhibit 12.8 – Example of a Bar Chart

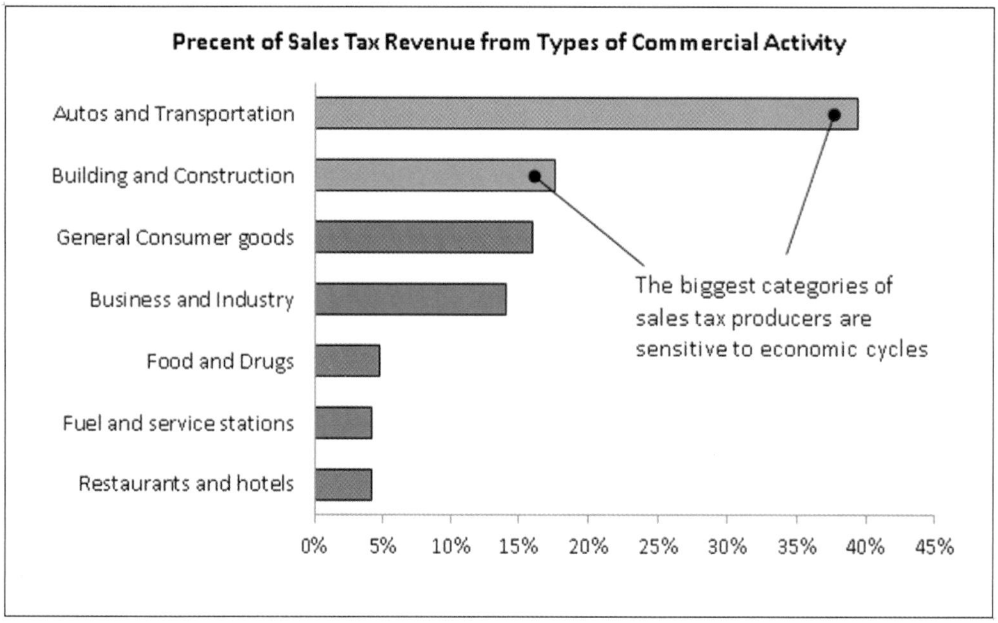

Area

Area charts can be understood as stacked line graphs, where each line represents an increment on the way up to the total, which is the uppermost line. The space between lines is filled with a color. An area chart can show how various component pieces add up to a total over a long time period. For example, you might use an area graph to show how the government's three major revenue sources and their total varied over a ten-year period. Like a stacked column chart, the forecaster should limit the number of dimensions displayed or the graph can become cluttered. Exhibit 12.1 provided an example of an area chart for the story of the City of Redmond's "price of government" forecast presentation.

Combination

Combination graphs use more than one type of graph in the same presentation. For a single data series, a column and a line graph might be used together where the line emphasizes the trend across the data series and the columns emphasize the relative differences amongst data points.

Combination graphs might make it easier to distinguish different data series where the points are very close together. For example, instead of showing two line graphs that intersect and overlap a great deal, one line graph and one column graph could be shown. Though intersection and overlap will exist, it should be easier to distinguish the data series. (Exhibit 15.3 in Chapter 15 shows an example of this type of combination graph.)

A combination graph can also show two variables that are measured on two different scales. This might be useful if the forecaster wants the audience to be able to compare the visual patterns or trends produced by two different data series, even if the data series have different units of measurement. Exhibit 12.9 shows a combination graphic that places equalized assessed valuation (EAV) on the same plot as property tax revenues for a county government. The challenge is that EAV is measured in billions of dollars and property taxes are measured in millions of dollars, so they would not fit well together on one graphical scale. The solution is to present them on two different graphical scales. In Exhibit 12.9, the EAV figures were divided by one hundred million and the property tax revenues were divided by one million to get figures for both that would display between "0" and "900" on the vertical axis.

Exhibit 12.9 – Example of a Combination Graphic with One Vertical Axis

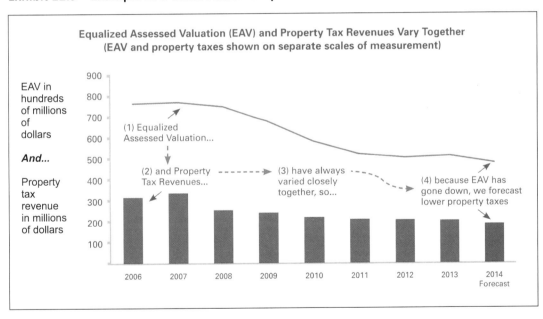

A combination graph could also work for variables with two totally different units of measurement. For instance, perhaps the causal variable the forecaster wants to show is not measured in dollars, like sales tax revenue and square feet of retail space in the community. Exhibit 12.10 provides another possibility. It combines line graphs of revenues and expenditures with a column and stacked column chart of reserves measured as a percent of annual expenditures. Because we have two totally different units of measurement (dollars and percent), we cannot put them on the same axis, like we did in Exhibit 12.9. Instead, we put dollars on the usual vertical axis on the left side of the graph, and add a second vertical axis to the far right-hand side of the graph to show the measurement scale for the other variable (percentage points, in our example). As in Exhibit 12.9, the horizontal axis serves as the time periods for both data series, and we plot the data so that all data series occupy the space above the horizontal axis. The difference is that the audience would need to consult the new axis on the right-hand side of the graph and read to the left in order to interpret the height of the columns, because the left-hand vertical axis is only relevant to the line graphs.

Exhibit 12.10 – Example of a Combination Graphic with Two Vertical Axes

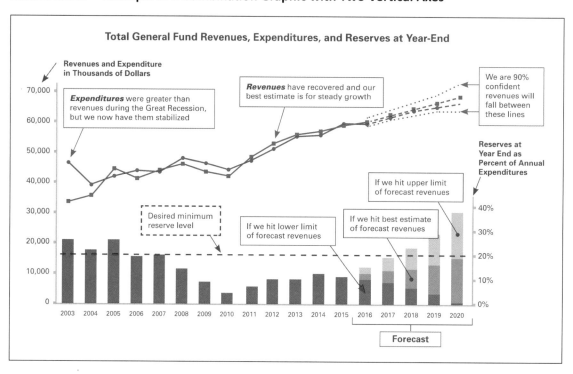

As the two examples show, combination graphs with multiple scales can be useful for comparing patterns in two multiple variables. However, combination graphs can create interpretation problems since multiple meanings have been assigned to the vertical dimension of the graph. For this reason, the forecaster must take extra care in designing multi-scale combination graphs, making use of labels and explanatory notes to help the audience understand it.

Even with the forecaster's best efforts, multi-scale combination graphs have an inherent complexity that is difficult to overcome. With so many variables plotted at once, the potential for confusion is higher. For instance, in Exhibit 12.10, it would not be unreasonable on the part of the reader to interpret the value for the first column on the left as about $20,000, rather than about 25 percent. One solution would be to erase the left-hand vertical axis below $30,000, much like the right-hand vertical axis has been erased above 40 percent. Another solution would be to remove the labels for $20,000 and $10,000, so that the eye isn't drawn to them when looking at the first column.

Table

A table places descriptors in the first column and in the column headings and data values in the body of the table. Tables are especially useful, first, when there are a small number of values to communicate such that it is not worth the forecaster's effort to develop a graphic or the audience's effort to read it. Second, when the precise data values are important, tables provide specificity that is not available from graphs. Tables can also be used in conjunction with graphs. For example, a number of the graphs presented in this chapter included forecasts. It is possible that at least some members of the audience would be interested in specific figures, so a small table could be placed below the graph to show the historical and forecasted figures.

Some of the same basic design guidelines apply to tables and graphs: avoid less readable fonts sizes and types, non-standard orientations of the text, and too much color coding, where it becomes difficult to distinguish between colors. Call attention to headers and important values with boldface and italics. Tables should be viewable on a single page and should be in the same orientation as the rest of the document. If tables are broken up over multiple pages or require the reader to reorient the document, the reader is likely to become frustrated or skip the table altogether.

Conclusion

We close this chapter with a real-life presentation from the City of Tempe, Arizona. In 2009, the City of Tempe had a policy to maintain unassigned fund balanced equal to 25 percent of general fund revenues. However, the City had been maintaining fund balances above 30 percent, which was causing some to question why the City was not in alignment with the policy and if the City had too much fund balance. The Council and staff agreed to change the policy to set a goal for unassigned fund balance between 20 percent and 30 percent of revenues. This range would provide more management discretion. The Council and staff also agreed to bring the amount of fund balance the City was holding into this new target range. In order to ensure everyone that an orderly transition would be made to the new policy, it was agreed that the new targets and fund balance level would be phased in over multiple years.

The staff developed a presentation of the City's revenue forecast in the context of this new arrangement and called it the "Golden Cone of Prosperity." Exhibit 12.11 shows the presentation, with the yellow cone representing the range of desired fund balance widens over the forecast horizon. The black line representing the actual fund balance gradually enters the cone.

Exhibit 12.11 – The City of Tempe's Golden Cone of Prosperity

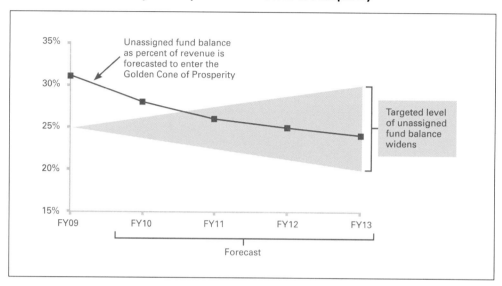

The City's Golden Cone of Prosperity presentation exemplifies many presentation strategies and guidelines for effective data graphics described in this chapter. It focuses on what the audience wants to know: Are fund balance levels coming into line with the City's new policy? It uses the fund balance policy, which the audience is interested in, as the point of reference for making the forecast more concrete and understandable. The name "Golden Cone of Prosperity" provides an unexpected and memorable character to the presentation, while the graphic representation of the cone is visually interesting and also functional. The proof of the presentation's ability to get the message across lies in the fact that the City still uses it as of this writing, over five years later, and has updated it to include other features, such as interactive what-if analyses. Tempe's experience also illustrates that forecasters don't necessarily need to implement every single guideline in this chapter to create an effective presentation; they just need to find a combination of techniques that will be effective given the situation.

Appendix – The Essentials of Expenditure Forecasting

Expenditure forecasts use different techniques than revenue forecasting. Also, because expenditures are often under the direct control of the government or are at least governed by explicit or known rules (e.g., a contract), expenditure forecasting is usually more straightforward. However, expenditure forecasts still have their own distinct set of challenges. This section touches upon some of the most essential points for solid expenditure forecasting. The endnotes point to resources that provide further guidance on expenditure forecasting.

First, let's address how to develop expenditure forecasts for a budget.

Salary and fringe benefit costs are often the largest single cost item for a government. These costs are difficult to reduce because layoffs, furloughs, and other cost-cutting actions are usually not easy to accomplish, politically. Therefore, the bulk of the forecaster's effort, in many cases, should be spent on projecting personnel costs. Many governments build detailed mathematical models to forecast spending on salaries, where the model includes salary detail for individual employees or the salary steps and grades that employees fall into.[29] Building a model at this level of detail allows for greater accuracy than using the average of employees across different salary levels. To estimate the cost of pay increases, a labor contract can be referenced, if one exists. If not, executive management or the human resources department will need to provide guidance on the assumptions to use for pay increases. Finally, the model should take account of special payments that employees might receive above their regular salaries (e.g., overtime, longevity pay, special duty pay for police, extracurricular activity pay for teachers), as well as any contractually obligated step increases.

The cost of fringe benefits should be taken from a contract governing the cost of the benefits, where one exists (e.g., a contract with a health insurance provider). Actuarial estimates are the next best option. For example, retirement systems often provide actuarial estimates of future contribution rates to their members. If neither of these sources are available, the forecast should rely on regional or national forecasts for cost increases. For example, both private research institutes and government agencies publish forecasts of future health-care cost increases.[30] Some agencies might also contract with consultants to provide cost estimates, especially for more important cost items.

In most organizations, it is likely that some budgeted positions will not be filled for at least some portion of the year. Hence, the entire cost of those positions will not be incurred. The forecast can account for these "vacancy savings," but it is important to make the forecast's assumption about the expected prevalence of position vacancies clear.

For the contractual services or commodities for which the government budgets, the ideal source of information is a long-term contract or schedule of costs. Examples include a multiyear contract with a technology services firm or a debt repayment schedule. The next best option is to use a cost-inflator that is suited to the particular type of expenditure being forecasted. The consumer price index is the most well-known inflation index, but is based on the basket of goods and services used by the typical consumer, which may not have much relevance to goods and services used by a government. Fortunately, a number of other sources of inflationary data exist that are more relevant to the work of a local government.[31] It might also be possible to engage specialists to provide insight on specific categories of expenditure, such as an insurance broker for insurance costs.

Capital asset acquisition costs might be a large expense for some governments. The annual capital budget should be closely tied to and flow from a detailed, long-range capital improvement plan.[32]

Finally, the forecaster should be clear about the role of carried-over balances from the prior year in balancing the subsequent year's revenues and expenditures. Ideally, a budget policy will define what happens to these balances each year, and the forecast presentation can be designed in accordance with the policy.

Expenditure forecasts for an annual budget will, of course, match the policy preferences of decision-makers. However, for longer-term forecasts, it is impossible to anticipate how policies might change or the consequences of these changes for the government's expenditures. Therefore, longer-term expenditure forecasts should project what the government would have to spend to maintain its existing portfolio of services in its current form. This serves to frame choices for decision-makers: if the existing portfolio is unaffordable compared to expected revenues, then decision-makers need to find a way to close the gap.

Long-term expenditure forecasts are not as detailed as a budget forecast, so a forecaster would typically use a more generalized set of assumptions to build the forecast. For example, the forecaster would not project future salary costs for individuals or narrow classifications of employees, but might use a more general inflation factor that is consistent with past experience and what is known about future costs through contracts, actuarial studies, etc. If the community will be experiencing significant growth, it might also be prudent to develop an assumption for the per-person cost of providing service in order to show how population growth might impact expenditure growth. The forecast might also account for reasonable expectations for changes in the demand for a service or known and planned changes in service levels that have been unambiguously defined in a policy or document that the audience of the forecast recognizes as valid. For example, if a long-term capital improvement plan that has been approved by the board calls for acquiring certain assets,[33] then the forecast should show the cost to acquire, operate, and maintain those assets.[34] Finally, the forecast should include any other changes in expenditure levels that have been previously agreed to by decision-makers or are otherwise widely recognized as valid. A leading example would be changes in debt service payments from year to year as set forth in a long-term debt repayment schedule. It is important that the forecaster not offer personal speculation on future service levels in the forecast.

Just as with revenue forecasts, all the key assumptions behind expenditure forecasts should be documented and made transparent to the audience.

Chapter 13

Step 6c – Use Forecasts: Monitor & Update

After the budget has been adopted, the forecaster switches from making forecasts to monitoring financial position to helping the organization make tactical adjustments during the year and maybe even changing its original budget plan when necessary. This chapter covers the use of short-term forecasts and leading indicators to monitor financial position as well as updating the original budget forecast.

Monitoring Financial Condition with Short-Term Forecasts

Short-term forecasts, those made monthly or quarterly, provide advance warning of when actual conditions might be diverging from what the budget forecast projected. Also, conducting short-term forecasts reinforces the need to be alert and adaptable to changing conditions. GFOA found that governments that have highly effective forecasting practices rigorously monitor their actual revenues against short-term projections. Most of these governments do this each month, while others do this each quarter. They then typically share these "short-term forecast versus actual results" comparisons with the governing board and use them to conduct formal reviews of financial positions with the executive management staff.

Some governments use simple algorithms to transform their annual forecast into a series of short-term projections. They determine the percent of annual revenues that are typically generated in each month and then apply that percent to the annual forecast. For example, if the forecaster knows that they typically receive 20 percent of total sales taxes for the year in January and their annual sales tax forecast is $100 million, then the forecast for January is $20 million. This approach can work well when revenue has very consistent annual patterns. For example, Fairfax County, Virginia, knows that it nearly always collects almost exactly two-thirds of its sales taxes for the year by March. Hence, if in March the actual revenues are materially above or below two-thirds of what was forecasted for the year, Fairfax County knows that the annual total will likely differ materially from what was forecasted.

A non-mathematical approach is the best way to set a short-term forecast if there are explicit legal arrangements governing when revenues will be received. For example, perhaps certain revenue is to be received according to the terms of a contractual agreement. Here, it is best to forecast the revenue to be received during the months contemplated in the agreement.

In cases where the expected revenue incomes at various point of the year are not so clear cut as the examples above, the forecaster may be better served by a statistical approach. If the forecaster has used deseasonalized monthly data to make the forecast, then total revenue for the next budget year has been forecasted by extrapolating forward deseasonalized data for the year. The annual forecast would consist of the forecast for the 12 months of the year added together. This would be sufficient for an annual budget total, but the individual monthly forecasted numbers would not be useful for monitoring revenue yields during the year to see if the government was on track to hit the forecast. For instance, many jurisdictions experience their highest sales tax income around the holiday season. A deseasonalized monthly forecast would not show a large spike in these months. Thus, it could be useful to reseasonalize data in order to produce more meaningful monthly revenue estimates.

If the forecaster used multiplicative classical decomposition (described in Chapter 4), forecasts can be reseasonalized by reversing the deseasonalization process. The formula is below:

$$F_s = F * S_d$$

This reads that seasonalized forecast for a given month is equal to the deseasonalized forecast for that same month times the damped seasonal factor.

The reseasonalization approach is similar for additive classical decomposition:

$$F_s = F + S_d$$

If the forecaster used annual data to make the forecast, but has access to at least a few years' worth of monthly data, he or she can compute seasonal factors using the method of classical decomposition described in Chapter 4. The forecasters should carry forward this method up to obtaining the damped seasonal factors (see column 9 in the classical decomposition exhibits in Chapter 4). This provides seasonal factors for each month. However, we cannot just multiply a simple monthly average (i.e., the forecast divided by 12) by the seasonal factors because the trend component is still needed.

We can find the trend component by taking the following steps:

1. Take the annual revenues for the year you are forecasting and the year before.
2. Subtract the monthly average of the first year from the monthly average of the second year and divide the results by 12 to get the monthly value of the slope for the trend.
3. If there is an even number of periods (e.g., 12 months, 4 quarters), then the middle of the year (and hence where our average value is technically located) is at some fractional

period (e.g., 6.5 months, 2.5 quarters). Therefore, to get the value for month 6, we would take half of the slope of the trend and subtract that from the monthly average for the year to get the month 6 value that includes trend.

4. The full slope would be subtracted from month 6 to get month 5, and subtracted again from month 5 to get month 4 and so on until values for month 5 through month 1 have been obtained. We would simply add the slope going the other direction to get values for months 7 through 12.

5. The damped seasonal factors can now be applied to the trended values or each month to get a monthly forecast that includes trend and seasonality.

A computation example of the foregoing steps is available at *www.gfoa.org/forecastbook.*

Finally, it could be that the forecaster only has access to annual data. In this case, seasonal impacts are unknown. However, we still could arrive at a monthly estimate of the trend using steps one through four as described above. This would show us the gradual increase or decrease throughout the year that ultimately takes us from the first month to the expected total annual revenue in 12 months. For revenues with significant seasonality effects, this estimate will be rather inaccurate, however.

Monitoring Leading Indicators

A common challenge with monitoring revenues during the year is that there is often a significant lag between the economic activity that generates the revenues and when the tax revenue is recorded by the local government. For example, property taxes, sales taxes, and income taxes are commonly collected by one level of government on behalf of another and then eventually distributed back to the rightful recipient (e.g., a state government collects sales taxes and then gives each local government its share). Though this process reduces the aggregate cost of administering the tax, it does result in a delay in the revenue making it to local government – sometimes as long as six months or more from when the tax money comes out of pocket of the citizen to reaching the local government's coffers. If the local government waits until it sees change in its actual revenue receipts to recognize that a change in the economy has happened, it could lose valuable time for accommodating itself to that change.

Therefore, forecasters should identify leading indicators that foreshadow change in actual revenues. To illustrate, the City of Tempe, Arizona, monitors the indicators below, which it obtains from University of Arizona each quarter:

- Inflation for the western United States
- Total disposable income
- Total retail sales
- Total restaurant sales

- Construction employment
- Hospitality employment

Each measure pertains to the Phoenix metropolitan area, except for inflation, which covers all urban areas in the Western United States. Retail sales, restaurant sales, construction employment, and hospitality employment foreshadow the performance of the associated specific segments of sales tax producers. Disposable income and inflation provide insight into future revenue performance more generally.

Leading indicators can be identified by careful study of the government's most important revenues and the fiscal and economic environment. Leading indicators could come from local or regional data, like the ones compiled by local universities, consulting firms, and state or federal agencies.

To be useful, a leading indicator must be able to be updated multiple times per year with current data and the time lag between a change in the indicator and a change in the associated revenue must be conducive to better decision-making. Too short a lag and the indicator doesn't provide any real foresight. Too long a lag and the indicator doesn't provide tactical, short-term value (though maybe it is useful for long-term planning).

Forecasters should think creatively about what might be used as leading indicators. For example, former Federal Reserve Chairman Alan Greenspan used the production of cardboard boxes as a leading indicator for the direction of the U.S. national economy, reasoning that most things produced by the economy use a cardboard box at some point in their lifecycle. As a result, more cardboard boxes being produced meant that demand for other items was heating up.[1] To illustrate how this line of thought might apply to a local government, one academic researcher found that because the City of Seattle is closely associated with the music industry, changes in the fortunes of the music industry, on a national scale, could be used to predict changes in sales and other consumption taxes in Seattle.[2]

The City of Irvine, California, took a creative approach to finding a leading indicator for sales taxes, its most important revenue. Due to the way sales taxes are administered in California, it takes as long as six months for the City to receive actual tax income after a merchant has made a sale. This means it takes a while for the impact of current economic conditions to be felt in the City's sales tax revenues. However, the City found that its hotel tax revenues are driven by the same basic underlying economic forces so that both taxes tend to vary together. The hotel tax revenues are received much more rapidly by the City, often within 60 days after the customer pays their hotel bill.

However, Irving had to exercise a bit of ingenuity to turn hotel taxes into an indicator of future sales taxes. The accounting data for hotel tax revenue included various adjustments and accruals such that the accounting numbers did not represent what the tax base was producing each month (though they represented what the City of Irvine was receiving). Irvine, therefore, had to use different sources of data and also perform some other permutations of the data in order to get numbers that were predictive of future sales taxes. The specifics are further described in Chapter 15, which provides a detailed case study about how Irvine used short-term forecasts and leading indicators as part of larger financial forecasting and planning strategy to work through the Great Recession.

Updating the Annual Forecast

During certain points of the year, the forecaster might wish to update the total revenue predicted by the annual forecast to reflect new information. Choosing if and when update the forecast requires careful consideration. On one hand, updating the forecast too frequently could confuse the audience and reduce the credibility of the forecaster. On the other hand, decision-makers need to stay abreast of important changes in revenues and to remain aware of the government's revenue outlook, even if there haven't been major changes recently.

The research on how frequently forecasts should be updated offers some conflicting evidence. GFOA's research found that governments with highly effective forecasting update their forecast a minimum of two times per year and as many as four times. However, other research has found that, among local governments generally, more frequent forecast updates are correlated with lower effectiveness of forecasting as a policy tool.[4] How do we reconcile this apparent contradiction? The answer may be that when the forecast is part of an effective system for using the forecast in decision-making and when it provides highly useful information, updates to the forecast will be welcome. If the forecast does not make a significant positive contribution to decision-making, updates to the forecast will not be valued. Put another way, in organizations that use forecasts effectively for making decisions, updates to the forecast may form a virtuous circle of improved decision-making and increased prestige for the forecast. For organizations that do not use forecasts effectively, updates within the year may cause a vicious cycle of confusion and stagnant or decreasing prestige for the forecast.

Forecast Updates and Accuracy

Research shows that forecasters that update their forecasts more frequently are more accurate because these forecasters do a better job of reflecting the full value of new information in their forecasts.[3] The implication for government revenue forecasters is that it might be advisable to make more frequent informal updates to the forecast, even if not all of those updates are shared with decision-makers.

Consequently, governments that have successfully implemented the guidelines for effective use of forecasts in decision-making and presenting forecasts, discussed in Chapters 11 and 12, should consider how they can integrate formal forecast updates into their financial planning and budgeting process. For example, among such governments, GFOA found it was common to have a forecast presented when the organization was starting to develop its budget and again as part of a mid-year update. Further updates might be provided throughout the year as circumstances suggest are necessary. For example, a significant development in the economy might call for a revised forecast, or the forecast might be revised as the organization works its way through the budget process in order to provide better information on the level of expenditures the organization can afford. Long-term forecasts were sometimes updated at the same time as the annual forecasts, as well.

To illustrate how an approach to more frequent forecast updating can work, let's examine the City of Bellevue, Washington. Bellevue calls their process a "rolling forecast" because the forecast is updated at least three times per year as part of a biennial budget process (the City's fiscal year is the same as the calendar year). All updates go to the City Council as well as a management team and include long-term forecasts. The three standard updates are:

- **March.** Long-term forecasts give the City an early look at what revenues are expected to do for the next few years.

- **July.** This is when cost-of-living adjustment information becomes available to the City from the U.S. Bureau of Labor Statistics. Cost-of-living adjustments have important implications for the City's labor costs. When providing frequent forecast updates, it is wise to plan the update schedule around the release of highly relevant economic data.

- **September.** This update covers any special changes in policy or conditions that may have occurred at the City and is used to inform the final deliberations on the budget.

Governments still working towards the guidelines described in Chapters 11 and 12 might be well advised to limit the number of updates they provide to decision-makers, perhaps presenting a forecast to frame budgeting discussions and presenting an update during the year to the extent that major changes in the financial environment require a significant adjustment in financial plans.

Conclusion

Using short-term forecasts and leading indicators are important for keeping decision-makers abreast of a government's financial position and giving them advance warning of conditions that might require them to change spending plans. The budget forecast might also be updated, especially if it becomes apparent during the course of the year that the actual revenues that will be received will differ substantially from the original forecast.

All governments should conduct these activities on a staff level, but the decision on how much and how often to share with policymakers is not a straightforward one. If the government has effective forecasts where forecasts are valued inputs to decision-making, then sharing updates more frequently should be beneficial. However, if forecasts are ineffective, then more frequent updates may not be beneficial. In this latter case, the forecasters should still perform updating and monitoring in order to improve their own forecasting knowledge and skill, but should take steps to improve forecast effectiveness before sharing the updates more widely.

Chapter 14

Step 7 – Evaluate Forecasts

"Experience is the teacher of all things."

–Julius Caesar, statesman of the Roman Empire, first century BCE

Once the forecaster has gone through the forecasting process, he or she should take time to learn from the experience. It is essential to evaluate how the forecast has performed so that the approach can be adjusted for the next time. Otherwise, the same deficiencies that afflicted the last forecast will be carried over into future forecasts. Furthermore, research has shown that the strongest predictor of improved forecaster performance is a deliberate, committed practice of self-improvement and updating one's assumptions.[1]

Therefore, the seventh and final step of the forecasting process is dedicated to evaluating how well forecasts have worked in terms of accuracy and effectiveness in impacting decision-making, and then using the experience to improve.

Evaluating Accuracy

The foremost requirement in evaluating accuracy is to retain the results from prior forecasts and the actual revenues for making a comparison. This includes not just original budget forecasts, but also updates that may have been made to the forecast, as well as long-term forecasts. In short, the final version of any forecast that is used to support decision-making in the government should be retained so that it can be later checked for the value of the information that it provided. Also, in Chapter 10 we discussed how errors or residuals can be used to express the level of uncertainty around the forecast. Therefore, retaining the errors doesn't help just to improve the forecast, but also allows you to express the uncertainty around it.

In addition to the forecast numbers themselves, the government should retain any background material necessary to understanding how the forecast was made. Foremost is an explanation of the quantitative method used to calculate the forecast. This is necessary to understand how the forecast was created.

Develop a Forecast Database!

We strongly recommend developing a dedicated database (it could be as simple as a Microsoft Excel file) that, as its dedicated function, stores historical forecast data. Computerized forecasting models often overwrite the old forecast in the output fields when new parameters are entered. Consequently, historical forecast results can easily be lost unless there is an active program of forecast retention. Although the computerized financial accounting systems used by almost all local governments do track some elements of the forecast, we believe a separate database is essential because:

- **It captures all of the relevant data elements.** Accounting systems often do not track all the information needed to evaluate forecasts. For example, they usually don't track underlying assumptions or multiyear forecasts.

- **Accounting systems often are not good at providing access to historical data.** Accounting systems are designed to process transactions. Getting data out of the system can often be a challenge. In some cases, historical data beyond a few years may not even be available. In fact, when we were collecting historical forecast data for this book, we encountered a number of governments that couldn't participate in our research for this reason.

- **Forecasting data isn't always the same as accounting data.** The government's accounting data may need to be adjusted to maximize its predictive power. There would be obvious problems with changing the data in a government's accounting system of record, so it should be kept in a separate database.

Forecasters should also retain critical assumptions or judgments made or other quantities used in the calculation of the forecast, and check their accuracy. If the assumptions were accurate, but the forecast accuracy was still unsatisfactory, the problem is likely in the selection or execution of the forecasting technique. If the assumptions are inaccurate, then the forecasters will need to first improve their basic knowledge of the financial and economic environment. Otherwise, any forecasting technique will likely produce unsatisfactory results.

Third, documentation and explanation of any adjustments made to the output of the quantitative model should be retained. This serves two purposes. First, it allows the forecasters to determine if the adjustments are adding to or detracting from forecast accuracy (research suggests it is sometimes the latter). Second, it is important to understand what adjustments were made and why in order to understand the complete story of where the forecast originates. If you don't understand it, you can't improve it.

Finally, forecast record-keeping should include policy changes made after the forecast was produced that have the potential to impact the accuracy of the forecast. Sometimes, after forecasts are made, and maybe because of the information provided by the forecast, decision-makers make policy choices intended to impact the actual revenue the government receives. For example, they might change tax or fee rates, expand or contract the tax base, or modify the technical rules for a tax or fee computation.

These kinds of situations and the revenue implications of the policy change need to be documented. It is also important to record which forecasts were made before the change, and where the time horizon of the forecast extends past the point in time at which the policy change becomes effective. The goal is to allow the organization to perform a more accurate evaluation of the original forecast. In fact, forecasters can even adjust for the policy change that the forecasters didn't know about when the forecast was predicted. This retroactively adjusted forecast can then be compared to actual revenues to get a better sense of forecast accuracy. The general formulas for accomplishing this are:

$$F_{Adj.} = F + P$$

$$e_{evaluation} = (A - F_{Adj.}) / F_{Adj.}$$

In the first formula, $F_{Adj.}$ is the adjusted forecast, F is the Forecast, P is the sum of positive and negative deliberate policy changes. P would need to be calculated by the forecasters using whatever methods are appropriate to the nature of the change.

The second formula is similar to the forecast error formula that we have been using throughout this book. A remains the actual revenue, but the original forecast is replaced with the adjusted forecast ($F_{Adj.}$) which produces a more accurate error statistic for the evaluation of the forecast ($e_{evaluation}$). The resulting error statistic is a ratio that should be represented as a percentage, which can be accomplished with a percent format in a spreadsheet, or by multiplying by 100. The error statistic can be used as part of monthly or quarterly monitoring, as well as for an annual evaluation of the forecast. This error statistic can also be used to calculate MAPE, RMSE, or any other forecast accuracy measurements.

With the proper data available, the forecaster is well positioned to conduct a thorough and formal evaluation of the forecast. Because the ability of the government to annually budget expenditures in line with available revenues is going to be of primary concern to most stakeholders, the annual forecast for budgeting purposes should be the focus of the evaluation. The forecast should be evaluated in aggregate (i.e., all general fund revenues) as well as disaggregated (i.e., the separate revenue sources that are forecasted forward to reach an aggregate forecast). The aggregate forecast error is important, because that is the forecast that is of greatest importance for budgeting decisions. However, in many cases, the aggregate forecast will, on average, tend to be more accurate than any single individual forecast because of the diversified revenues that comprise it (and the consequent opportunity for a negative forecast error in one to cancel out a positive forecast error in another). Therefore, it is also important to examine forecast accuracy for individual revenue sources to get a complete picture of how the forecast is performing. For example, individual forecasts that all produce relatively small errors are much more reassuring than individual forecasts that produce relatively large, but offsetting, errors.

In addition to evaluating annual forecasts, governments should strongly consider evaluating multiyear, long-range forecasts in a similar way. Although long-range forecasts are necessarily less accurate than annual budget forecasts, and although they usually don't have direct implications for how expenditure budgets are appropriated, long-range forecasts are still used to provide guidelines for financial planning, so it is good to know the available precision in these guidelines. To save time, long-range forecasts can be evaluated in the aggregate and for the most important subtotals (e.g., the government's most important source(s) of tax revenue).

Move Over Las Vegas: Revenue Forecasting and Office Betting Pools

A few of the governments in our research held informal office betting pools on the accuracy of their forecasts. This is more than a way to make forecasting more fun – some research suggests that this could be a powerful learning tool.[2] The participants get accurate and unambiguous feedback about how well they are doing: they either win or they lose the bet. (Research shows that learning occurs even if there is no real money being wagered.) Feedback is most effective when it happens within a short time after the estimate is made, which suggests that, ideally, participants should place bets for what revenue will be every month.

For either annual or multiyear forecasts, the error statistics can be compared to forecasts developed by the government in prior years. Is the error increasing, decreasing, or staying the same? It may also be worth noting whether forecast errors are consistently positive (actual revenues are greater than the forecast) or negative (actual revenues are less). You might also consider comparing the results to the forecasting accuracy benchmarks provided in Chapter 9.

The tone of the evaluation is as important as the data collected and the indicators examined. The evaluation should be a post-mortem to discover how errors can be corrected and successes duplicated. In order to be a productive learning experience, the evaluation should not take on the character of an inquisition, where participants seek to assign blame or make excuses.

When considering the results of the evaluation, if the forecaster finds that forecasts are doing well overall, but there have not been further increases in accuracy lately, it could be that the forecaster has achieved a good balance between the time and effort put into forecasting and the accuracy he or she is getting out of it. Remember there is a cost to achieving greater accuracy. Perhaps "improving" the forecast means streamlining the more cumbersome aspects of the process and better documenting how the forecast is produced, including key assumptions and forecast data for the benefit of future forecasters.

If a forecast's accuracy is unsatisfactory, the forecaster should investigate reasons for the errors. Were the forecaster's basic assumptions not met? Has the data been inadequately scrubbed and adjusted prior to use for forecasting, resulting in too much "noise" in the data? Does the quantitative forecasting technique provide a poor fit to the data? Are the quantitative forecasts being under- or overadjusted by the forecaster? Have policy changes after the forecast was made had an unanticipated effect on actual revenues?

The answers to these questions will suggest the path to improving forecast accuracy. Not often, though, will that path include the adoption of more sophisticated and complex forecasting techniques. As we have shown elsewhere in this book, more complex techniques do not necessarily create more accurate forecasts than simpler techniques. While each government will need to find its own answers, the following list, summarizing key points from previous chapters, might provide good starting points:

- **Improve your understanding of the financial and economic environment.** Good forecasting requires committing the time and energy to gain a thorough understanding of what makes the revenue tick. Don't just examine economic data though – talk to people closest to the economic activity that generates the revenue. Document an explicit model of the environment, like an influence diagram, so that it can be shared with others. Get feedback.

- **Polish up historical data.** The old information technology maxim "garbage in, garbage out" applies to forecasting. Invest the effort in cleaning up historical data to maximize its predictive power.

- **Get more perspectives.** Bring additional vantage points into the forecast. Ideally, this means using more than one quantitative technique so that the results can be averaged together. It could also mean getting different kinds of expert judgment by widening the circle of people who contribute perspectives to include people outside of the finance and budget office. For example, organizations with successful forecasts usually consult their community development staff on land-use trends to forecast property taxes and sales taxes.

- **Make things as simple as possible, but not simpler.** First, make sure that forecast model in use now is not too complex. For example, perhaps a forecaster has inherited a model that they don't understand or maybe the forecaster has just overreached when building their current model. Chapter 15 demonstrates how the City of Irvine made substantial gains in accuracy by going to a less complex model. That said, there are limits to how much a forecast can be simplified. At minimum, the forecast model should conform to the basic features of the forecasting techniques described in this book.

In any event, the effort put into investigation and refining the forecast for a given revenue should be commensurate with the relative importance of that revenue to the jurisdiction's total revenue.

Evaluating Effectiveness

Even the most accurate forecast is worthless if it does not impact real decisions. Therefore, an evaluation of the forecast must include an assessment of whether the message of the forecast is getting across and meeting the needs of decision-makers. Consider the fact that research shows that forecasters and decision-makers often have substantially different perceptions of each other's roles and responsibilities in the forecasting process.[3] We see the results in a diagram adapted from a study by Makridakis, et al[4]. The Venn diagram in Exhibit 14.1 shows that decision-maker and forecaster each perceive themselves to have a more limited role than the other party perceives them to have, resulting in certain responsibilities falling in the gap. For example, whose responsibility is to identify the most important issues

Exhibit 14.1 – Decision-Makers' and Forecasters' Perceptions of Mutual Responsibilities

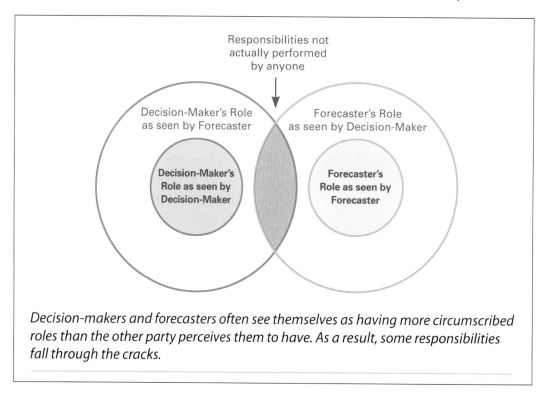

Decision-makers and forecasters often see themselves as having more circumscribed roles than the other party perceives them to have. As a result, some responsibilities fall through the cracks.

Source: Spyros Makridakis, Steven C. Wheelwright, and Rob J. Hyndman. *Forecasting: Methods and Applications*, 3rd Edition. (John Wiley and Sons). 1998.

impacting the decision-making process? Should the forecaster proactively find out what issues or concerns the decision-makers want modeled, or is it incumbent on the decision-makers to tell the forecaster what they want modeled? This research illustrates that there is a high potential for miscommunication between decision-makers and the forecaster.

This can lead to a) decision-makers becoming dissatisfied with the forecast because they think the forecaster isn't doing everything they should be doing; and b) the forecaster overestimating the perceived value of the work they are performing because they think they are meeting expectations when, in fact, they are not.

The forecaster's own observation and judgment is usually going to be the most practical way to determine how effective the forecast is in influencing decisions. Exhibit 14.2 provides some rules of thumb for making a judgment on whether or not the forecast is seen as valuable by others.

Exhibit 14.2 – You Know Your Forecast Is Valuable If…

> ✓ The financial forecasting staff is brought into decisions with important financial implications, like labor negotiations and land-use planning, to consult on the likely future financial impact *before* the decision is made.
> ✓ Decision-makers *request* a forecast, rather than the forecaster pushing forecast information onto decision-makers.
> ✓ Officials *ask questions* about the forecast that have clear implications for overall, long-term financial health, such as changes in one-time versus ongoing revenues and how that relates to expenditure plans.
> ✓ Officials *support* recommendations from staff that are aligned with the forecast.
> ✓ Officials *change* their positions on issues because of information provided by the forecast.
> ✓ When there is not enough money in the budget to do everything officials would like, they talk about *reprioritizing and restructuring* expenditures to find the resources rather than changing the forecast estimate.
> ✓ Departments *change* their budget requests in response to forecast information. For example, if revenues are projected to be down, departments take the initiative to withdraw, reduce, or defer budget requests.
> ✓ Departments *offer information* to help refine the forecast.

If the forecast does not seem to have the impact it should, consider reviewing the guidelines in Chapters 11 and 12 about how to use forecasts in decision-making and how to present the forecast. The points below summarize some of the critical elements of the forecast that contribute to good decision-making:

- **The decision-making system supports the use of forecasting.** Financial policies that emphasize the fundamental principles of financial health, such as minimum reserve levels and appropriate use of one-time revenues, set the tone for using forecasts in decisions. A budgeting process that emphasizes planning for the future, rather than just control of expenditure line items, will encourage the use of forecasts.

- **The forecast and the forecaster are seen as credible.** Foremost is for the forecaster to demonstrate deep knowledge of the financial and economic environment. When the audience perceives the forecaster to have command of the relevant facts, they will have much greater confidence in the forecast. The forecaster should use their knowledge of the environment to develop and present a set of coherent, logical assumptions that describe a causal relationship between the environment and the forecast.

- **The forecast is relevant to decision-makers' interests.** The forecaster should make sure to present the forecast in the context of decision-makers' service goals. Revenues are means to an end, so the forecast should show if those ends will be possible given the revenues available. A related point is that forecasters sometimes avoid modeling messy, controversial issues in the forecast in order to avoid making the forecast too speculative. However, it is precisely these kinds of issues that are often of greatest interest to decision-makers. Consider using scenarios to show the impact of these issues outside of the baseline forecast.

- **Information is presented so that it is accessible.** The forecaster presents a clear core message, embedded in a narrative about the situation the government faces and what it means for the future. The graphical presentation techniques reinforce the core message, including use of interactive "what-if" analyses.

Conclusion

We opened this chapter with a quote from Caesar about learning from your experiences. We close with a quote from another statesman, this time from 19th century Germany, Otto von Bismarck: "Fools learn from experience. A wise man learns from the experience of others."[5]

It is in the spirit of Bismarck's contrarian view on improvement and learning that we offer the following checklist of key features of accurate and effective forecasting, drafted from the hard-won experiences of public finance managers and forecasting science researchers.

To get the most accurate forecasts...

✓ **Know the details of how your revenues work.** Thoroughly investigate the financial and economic environment and understand the forces that impact revenue yield.

✓ **Have good data.** Clean and calibrate data to maximize its predictive power. Gather enough data to power good quantitative forecasting, but also to inform forecaster judgment by providing analogues and historical precedents.

✓ **Focus your efforts.** The biggest and most volatile revenues have the biggest potential impact on forecast accuracy.

✓ **Use multiple methods.** To rely on just one forecasting method is to place all of your eggs in one basket. Use multiple methods rooted in different sources of information on revenue performance, and use the combined results to reach a forecast.

✓ **Accept uncertainty.** Don't become fixated on a single forecast number. Accept that forecasts are uncertain and assess the level of uncertainty that you face.

✓ **Think like a fox.** A good forecaster seeks out new information and ideas, critically re-examines their forecast methods, and changes them as the circumstances suggest is necessary.

✓ **Collaborate with others.** Actively recruit experts with diverse viewpoints to contribute to the forecasting process, such as in land-use planning, economic development, or any other discipline that can provide relevant information to how a revenue might perform.

✓ **Monitor the performance of your annual forecast and conduct short-term forecasts.** Monitoring the forecast helps you learn from past mistakes. Regularly conducting short-term forecasts makes good forecasting practices a year-round habit rather than a once-a-year event.

To get the most effective forecasts...

✓ **Demonstrate a command of the details of how your revenues work.** When the forecaster can demonstrate a substantive command of the issues that impact revenue yield, the audience will be more confident in the forecast and more willing to use it to make decisions.

✓ **Have a clear and compelling set of forecast assumptions.** Knowing details about the revenues allows the forecaster to develop a set of assumptions that tell a clear story about the forecaster's expectations about the future of the financial and economic environments and, hence, the future of the revenues.

✓ **Make it clear that the assumptions will be wrong.** The future behavior of the financial and economic environments cannot be known with certainty. This means that actual revenues will inevitably be at least somewhat different from what was predicted. Helping decision-makers accept the uncertainty that is inherent in forecasting is the first step towards developing a financial plan and budget that is resilient under changing conditions.

✓ **Use a budget process that emphasizes planning and strategic thinking.** Governments whose budgets incorporate a planning orientation, factor in program performance when allocating resources, and weigh the potential use of resources against one another using an explicit structured approach are more likely to get value out of revenue forecasts.

✓ **Adopt governing principles and policies that support forecasting.** Policies that call for a structurally balanced budget and for the government to hold a specified amount of reserves and to refrain from using non-recurring revenue to fund recurring expenditures help create an environment where forecasts are needed to conduct governance.

✓ **Conduct long-term planning.** Long-term planning encourages the long-term and strategic thinking that make long-term forecasts valuable. Also, at their best, long-term plans create a shared vision for the future of the organization that includes long-term financial health. Forecasts are needed to achieve that vision.

✓ **Make a compelling presentation.** The presentation of the forecast should be clear about not only what the forecast is, but also its implications for the financial health of the organization and its service objectives.

✓ **Simulate the future.** Use techniques to help the audience put themselves in the future that is being forecasted. These techniques can include interactive what-if analyses, simulation, or scenario analyses.

Chapter 15

The City of Irvine Forecasts a Path through the Great Recession

Very few people saw it coming. Though the recession started in December 2007, most economists did not forecast a recession in the United States even as late as the fourth quarter of that same year.[1] In fact, as late as April 2008, the Federal Reserve Bank of New York gave only a 5 percent chance for a recession as deep as the one that ultimately happened. By November, they had increased that probability to just 15 percent.[2] It is not uncommon for people to miss the start of a recession, even when it is actually happening. For example, 95 percent of American economists said there would not be a recession in a survey conducted in March 2001, even though the 2001 recession had, in fact, started that month.[3]

Ken Brown, then the Strategic Business Plan Administrator for the City of Irvine, California, had, like other municipal budget officers, been following the economic news. In 2007, he was concerned by the frothy housing market and the inversion of the yield curve, where long-term interest rates dipped below short-term rates. This is a phenomenon that often precedes an economic recession. Later, he knew that the economy had slowed, but it only became fully apparent to him that this was no ordinary recession on September 15, 2008 – the day that the Wall Street Journal landed on his doorstep with news of Lehman Brothers declaring bankruptcy.

The City had experienced some slowdown in revenue receipts prior to the newspaper heralding what would come to be known as the Great Recession. However, in the fall of 2008 it was not just Lehman Brothers' catastrophe that portended greater difficulties ahead. We see in Exhibit 15.1 that the City's real (inflation-adjusted) per capita general fund recurring revenue, including sales taxes (the City's most important single revenue source), was already trending downward at the official start of the Great Recession at the end of 2007, and that by the fall of 2008, this trend had picked up momentum.

Exhibit 15.1 – Per Capita, Real (2005 Dollars) General Fund Revenues*

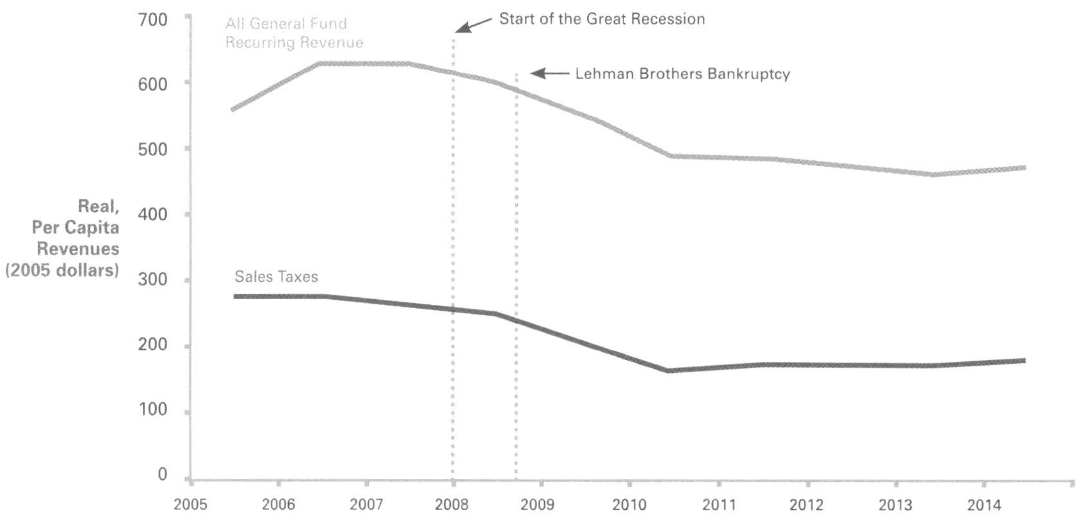

The City's revenues had started to slow by the time the Great Recession officially began. The rate of decline had become worse by the time of Lehman Brothers' bankruptcy.

*The graph shows general fund recurring revenues, which removes non-recurring revenues from the general fund total. The City had received some sizeable one-time revenues during the period shown, but they were not available to fund regular general fund operations because they were designated for other purposes.

Lehman Brothers and other seemingly cataclysmic events, like the federal government bailing out insurance giant AIG, also in September, and the Dow Jones Industrial Average suffering its worst weekly loss in history in the first week of October, spurred the City into action. Irvine's City Manager, Sean Joyce, called together a team to develop a plan to guide the City through the recession and to prepare for all possible contingencies. This team, reporting to him, included Assistant City Manager Wally Kreutzen, Director of Administrative Services Rick Paikoff, Manager of Budget and Business Planning, Dave Tungate, and Strategic Business Plan Administrator, Ken Brown.

Irvine's team had the advantage of the City's history of strategic financial planning: the City had begun long-term financial planning as a response to the 1994 recession, which had hit Irvine and the rest of Orange County hard, and the City Council and the staff considered these plans to be successful. Further, modern Irvine itself had its genesis in a 1959 master plan for a city of 50,000 surrounding the, then new, University of California at Irvine. The plan called for a full spectrum of residential, commercial, industrial, and recreation land uses and came to fruition in the 1960s and 1970s. This history imparted an identity to the City Council and staff: an organization and people who develop long-term, strategic plans and follow them to make the community a better place.

A Challenge with the Forecast

A forecast is the lynchpin of a long-term, strategic financial plan. However, Irvine's forecasting model underestimated the magnitude of the decline in revenues at the start of the recession. The problem had its roots in Irvine's history as a high-growth city. In the 1970s, the City experienced about 20 percent annual growth, and during the 1980s population increased at about 8 percent per year. While growth had come down from these stratospheric levels by the 1990s, it was still averaging about 4 percent average per year, which translated into about a 70 percent increase in total population between 1990 and 2007 – an additional 81,000 people. As a result, the City had developed a forecast model that emphasized the role of new development in the City's revenue income. However, with the bursting of the housing market bubble, the impact of the economy on the City's existing tax base became more important to future revenues than development growth, yet the City's quantitative, linear regression forecast model was heavily dependent on growth-driven variables.

What's more, though the City staff had come to realize this was no ordinary recession, they were still too optimistic regarding how well the City's revenues would perform. Staff thinking about revenues was influenced not only by their own assumptions about growth variables, but also by other economic forecasts from third-party institutions for variables such as home prices, taxable sales, gross domestic product, and the price of oil, each of which later proved over-optimistic. The fact that the City's largest revenue, sales tax, is strongly pro-cyclical exacerbated the problem; forecasts overestimated sales tax revenues by as much as 20 percent and overall revenues by as much as 8 percent, and then predicted a quicker and more rapid recovery than actually occurred. Exhibit 15.2 shows a history of revenue forecasts versus actuals for the years during and around the Great Recession.

Further complicating the situation was that after a shopper purchased a vehicle at Irvine Auto Center or had lunch at a local restaurant, it would take as long as six months for the taxes from the purchase to hit the City's books. This meant that the initial forecasts were based on sales tax data that did not yet include the up-to-date impact of the recession, so there was no direct and timely quantitative feedback to the City on how sales tax revenues were behaving.

Long-Term Planning Rewarded

Irvine has long emphasized the importance of education and public safety in its plans. The City has consistently provided direct financial support to its public schools; emphasized excellence in police hiring, leadership and community relations; worked to maintain open sightlines in the layout of new public, business, and residential spaces; promoted youth programs; and sought to prevent graffiti and other visible signs of deterioration. As a result, the City of Irvine, now over 240,000 residents, has recorded the lowest violent crime rate of any City with over 100,000 residents each year since 2004.

Exhibit 15.2 – Forecast Errors in General Fund Recurring Revenue and Sales Taxes

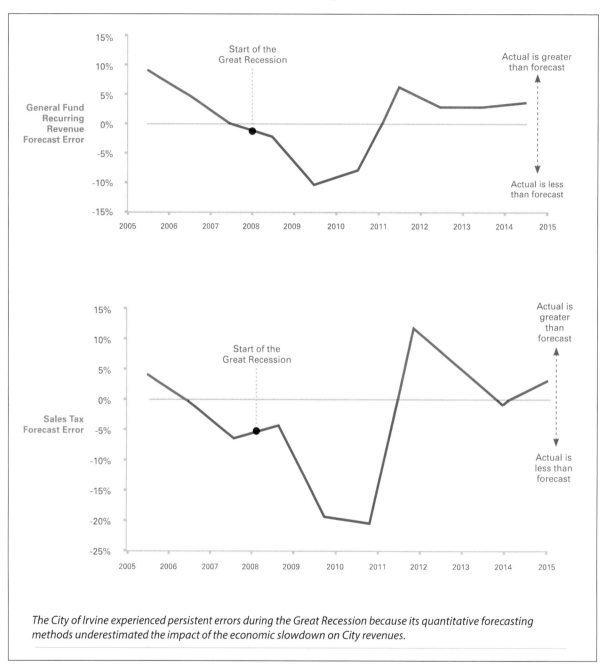

The City of Irvine experienced persistent errors during the Great Recession because its quantitative forecasting methods underestimated the impact of the economic slowdown on City revenues.

Finally, as one might expect during a major slowdown in revenues and growth, there was some disquiet among elected officials and staff. Fortunately, the City's finance team had built up a reservoir of good will with previous long-term financial plans, but it was still important for the City staff to find a way to help the City cope with its current predicament, maintain credibility of the planning process, and, ultimately, navigate through the Great Recession.

Bridging the Gap

A combination of expenditure reductions and reserves was to serve the City as a bridge across the budget gap created by the Great Recession. This "Three-Year Bridge Plan" had four central elements:

1. No tax increases

2. No layoffs

3. No pay raises

4. No material reductions to core services

Elements one, three, and four gave elected officials and the public confidence that that the City's budget wouldn't be balanced at the expense of the public's interest. The second element gave reassurance to staff that they would be able to keep their job while the City contended with the financial challenge. Further, the Plan only committed to use reserves as a bridge for a three-year period, after which the City's budget would have to balance without reserves and, if possible, start replenishing the reserves that had been used. It was thought that this should provide the City enough time for the City to restructure its services, but not such a long period that the City's reserves would be depleted to unacceptably low levels. Finally, though the plan did provide precise numerical targets for expenditure reduction and use of reserves over three years, the City staff were sure to emphasize that the plan was a guideline and that the City would need to be willing to adapt to changing circumstances.

The City Manager, Sean Joyce, and the City's finance team were able to secure acceptance of the Bridge Plan because of the balanced commitments made by the plan, and because the City Council and staff understood that the proverbial "rainy day" had arrived, so it was time to use the reserves it had saved up over the years. However, once the idea had been accepted, the staff had to make sure the City was able to arrive at a structurally balanced budget within three years. Good forecasting would be an important part of this, and staff knew that their existing forecast models were not as reliable as they had once been.

Ken Brown worked under the leadership of Sean Joyce to refine the City's five-year forecasting model. The forecasting method would transition away from a regression that emphasized growth and development variables to a method that placed greater emphasis on forecaster judgment and algorithms that mathematically modeled the causal factors behind the City's revenue income. Good shorter-term forecasts would be needed for balancing the budget each year and a long-term forecast would be important for meeting the goals of the Three-Year Bridge Plan and achieving financial sustainability beyond. Ken's strategy was to emphasize the state of the economy more heavily in the annual budget and shorter-term forecasts for periods of approximately one to five years, but to assume that new development would still be the most dominant force behind the City's long-term revenue performance.

Long-term forecasts, six years ahead and beyond, were to be used to make sure that the City's financial trajectory was sustainable. Anchoring these forecasts was a series of algorithms designed to capture key features of the tax base. For example, historical sales tax data for the previous five or more years was converted to revenue per square foot of retail space for each major type of retail establishment in Irvine (e.g., commercial serving local markets, commercial serving regional markets, auto dealerships). The 5-plus years of data included both recessionary and economically robust years, and each year was adjusted for inflation. This reflected an assumption that, over the long-term, the City should expect a "neutral" impact from the economy as the recessionary periods and growth periods would balance each other. Sales tax revenue for the City was then projected in the future, using the average, inflation-adjusted amount of revenue received per square foot of retail development, accounting for both the current amount of retail in Irvine and new retail space expected to be developed in the future. The timing of expected development was provided by the City's Community Development department from a survey of local developers.

To develop the annual budget forecast, the City contracted with a consultant to provide a baseline projection using more detailed algorithms than those used for the long-term forecast. To illustrate, the forecast for sales tax took into account the timing of the State's payment of sales taxes to the City (the State collected the tax on behalf of the City), changes in the number of retailers in different categories of sales tax producers, and other specific changes to the City's tax base that might impact revenues that year. With this baseline forecast in hand, the City examined projections of local taxable sales growth from forecast institutions such as Chapman University, University of California at Los Angeles, and California State University at Fullerton State. If these institutions projected growth significantly in excess of that presumed by the baseline forecast, the forecast might be adjusted. A final ingredient was the City staff's own knowledge about local events that might impact the year's sales tax revenues. For example, a significant renovation at a regional shopping center could disrupt sales in the short term, but have positive long-term impacts.

This annual budget forecast was then combined with the long-term forecast to arrive at a forecast for revenues two to five years in the future. To do this, the City assumed that revenues from the annual forecast would trend toward the revenue amount projected six years in the future in a continuous fashion. (The City did not try to simulate economic cycles.) To illustrate using highly simplified numbers, if the annual budget forecast was $100 million and the six-year-ahead forecast was $120 million, the two-year-ahead forecast would be approximately $104 million, three-years-ahead $108 million, and so on, though the exact estimates would be adjusted for specific events and conditions in the tax base that City staff knew would affect revenues.

The result was a forecast method that offered a number of advantages over the old one. Foremost was improved accuracy. As Exhibit 15.2 shows, from fiscal years 2012 through 2014, the new forecasting model produced an average error of just over 3 percent. Importantly, the errors were errors of underestimation, which helped the City remain on stable footing. In addition to the new forecasting method proving more accurate at the time, the City could be confident that it would be more reliable over time. This is because there were more perspectives brought to bear, so any bias inherent in any one source of information was more likely to be balanced out by another source. Also, the old regression equation required the City to obtain forecasts of the independent variables from third-party institutions. Forecasting items like GDP growth and oil prices is notoriously difficult, bringing a potentially large source of error into the City's forecasts. As a point of comparison, a major variable impacting sales tax projections under the new method was the volume of retail space in Irvine, measured in square feet – this was a much more easily predicted quantity. Finally, the new method was easier to communicate to other people. The algorithms were easier to understand than a regression equation. The additional expertise that the budgeting team brought into the forecast, including consultants, regional universities, and other City staff such as the Community Development department, bolstered the credibility of the process.

Even with these improvements to the City's forecasting, there was still a great deal of uncertainty surrounding preparation of the FY 2010-11 budget. To help the City Council feel better prepared to deal with these conditions, the staff, at a councilmember's request, presented two scenarios before the City Council got into the details of budgeting. The first scenario described a deepening recession, and the second addressed a recovery. These two alternative futures helped the Council better appreciate that the City needed to be prepared for conditions other than what the adopted budget projected, and gave the Council confidence that the City had considered an appropriately wide range of possibilities when formulating its budget.

In addition to improving the techniques used to develop its long-term financial forecast, the City's budget team worked with a consultant, Chris Swanson, to enhance its existing monthly forecasting model. Short-term forecasts would help the City make tactical adjustments within the fiscal year, and the short-term forecasts would serve as a conspicuous symbol of the need to be adaptable to changing conditions. While the City had previously modeled monthly revenues and expenditures based on historical experience at a department and budget category level (e.g., an all-encompassing "sales taxes"), the new Excel model tracked this City's budgetary data down to the object code level (e.g., all of the individual codes that comprise "sales taxes"). This made the model more adaptable to changing conditions because the object codes could be rearranged into different categories, if needed.

The model transformed the annual budget forecast for revenues and expenditures into a short-term forecast by applying one of a number of predefined algorithms. The most commonly used algorithms for developing monthly revenue estimates were:[4]

- **3-year average of monthly revenues.** The model looks back across the most recent three years to determine what percent of total revenue is typically received in a given month. For Irvine, that percentage was then applied to the current annual budget to get a budget for that month. For example, the City received an average of 9 percent of its sales tax revenues by the end of the first quarter in 2009, 2008, and 2007, so the monthly sales tax estimate for the first quarter of 2010 was also 9 percent of the annual budget. This City used this method for the majority of its revenues, but it was especially important for revenues following strong seasonal patterns.

- **Straight-line.** The annual budget is simply divided by 12 and that amount becomes the budget for each month. This method was used for revenues where there were not important seasonal patterns and where there was no better basis for developing a monthly budget.

- **Prior-year.** This is an alternative to the three-year average, where the pattern that occurs in the prior year is applied to the current year. This was used for revenue sources where there was reason to expect a similar pattern to the previous year's revenue income, but where a longer term historical pattern was not expected to be as helpful.

- **Manual.** For cases where none of the above methods were appropriate, the City distributed the annual forecast across the 12 months manually. Revenues from contractual services provided by the City, for example, could be modeled using this approach when the timing of a service and the resulting income was known.

This short-term forecast would then be compared to the City's actual revenues each month. Exhibit 15.3 shows some of the visualizations that the model produced. The monthly revenue chart was useful for revealing seasonal patterns. For example, the graph demonstrated that Irvine should always expect to receive much higher sales taxes in June than other points in the year (because that's when the City would receive revenue from sales made during the holiday season). The monthly forecast and budget graph (titled "monthly") shows how the budget compared to the actual in each month. Here we can see that, in 2011 when Irvine was recovering from the worst impacts of the recession, the actual revenues exceeded both the budget and previous year's actual in two months. The graph titled "cumulative" shows the individual monthly budgets and actuals aggregated, where the amount shown in June would be the total for the entire year (the fiscal year ends in June). Here, we can see that the two above-budget months translated into sales taxes being consistently above budget for the year through January, the last month for which data had been collected at this point. The model produced similar analysis for expenditures, allowing staff to monitor both sides of the budget.

As we saw earlier, an impediment to monitoring the accuracy of sales tax forecasts was the length of time it took—as long as six months—for the City to receive actual tax receipts

Exhibit 15.3 – Data Graphics from the City's Monthly Model

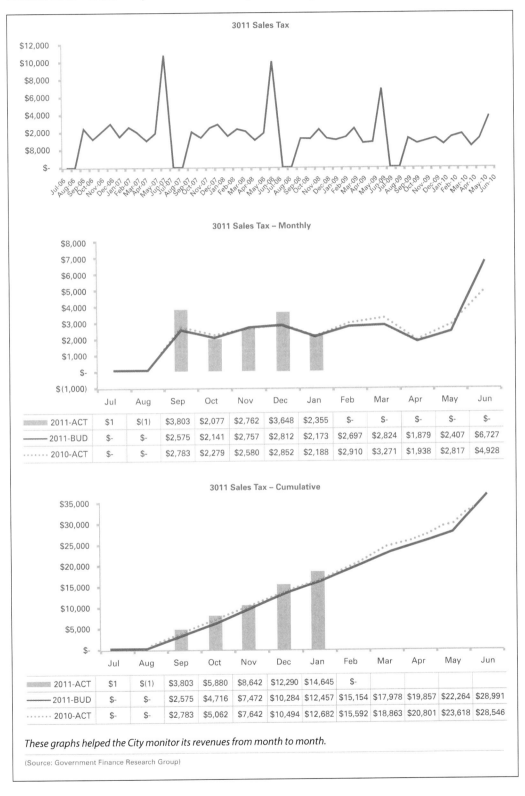

	Jul	Aug	Sep	Oct	Nov	Dec	Jan	Feb	Mar	Apr	May	Jun
2011-ACT	$1	$(1)	$3,803	$2,077	$2,762	$3,648	$2,355	$-	$-	$-	$-	$-
2011-BUD	$-	$-	$2,575	$2,141	$2,757	$2,812	$2,173	$2,697	$2,824	$1,879	$2,407	$6,727
2010-ACT	$-	$-	$2,783	$2,279	$2,580	$2,852	$2,188	$2,910	$3,271	$1,938	$2,817	$4,928

3011 Sales Tax – Cumulative

	Jul	Aug	Sep	Oct	Nov	Dec	Jan	Feb	Mar	Apr	May	Jun
2011-ACT	$1	$(1)	$3,803	$5,880	$8,642	$12,290	$14,645	$-				
2011-BUD	$-	$-	$2,575	$4,716	$7,472	$10,284	$12,457	$15,154	$17,978	$19,857	$22,264	$28,991
2010-ACT	$-	$-	$2,783	$5,062	$7,642	$10,494	$12,682	$15,592	$18,863	$20,801	$23,618	$28,546

These graphs helped the City monitor its revenues from month to month.

(Source: Government Finance Research Group)

after a consumer had made a purchase. This made it difficult for the City to estimate the effect that immediate economic conditions were having on sales tax revenue. However, there was a potential indirect indicator: the City's hotel tax. Like the sales tax, the hotel tax was highly sensitive to economic conditions. Thus, if the hotel tax decreased, there was a very good chance that the sales tax would too. Critically, the City would receive hotel tax money within 60 days or less from the time a guest visited a hotel in Irvine.

Unfortunately, however, turning hotel taxes into a leading indicator was not as easy as running a report from the City's computerized accounting system. Because the accounting data included various adjustments and accruals, it was an imperfect representation of the amount of revenue produced by the tax base in each period. The chief example was the monthly advances on sales tax revenues provided to Irvine by the State of California. These advances were provided by the State to help cities avoid cash flow problems in between quarterly payments, so they were not a helpful representation of how the sales tax base was actually performing. Each quarter, the State would then adjust its payments to cities to reflect how each city's local tax base had actually performed, but, at the same time, the State would also include another advance payment for the upcoming month. In fact, the graph of monthly revenues in Exhibit 15.3 shows four "peaks" in sales tax revenues each year, which is where adjustments occur.* Hence, the revenue recorded in the City's ledger was only a partial reflection of the actual performance of the City's tax base.

To overcome this problem, Ken Brown and the finance team used reports on the tax money actually paid by retailers and hotels and took a three-month moving average to smooth out some of the variation within quarters and better reveal the trends. The result they achieved is shown in Exhibit 15.4. We can see that the sales tax curve follows along closely with the direction of hotel taxes. In this particular example, hotel taxes have experienced significant year-over-year growth at the end of the analysis period, suggesting that sales taxes will follow.

Both monthly forecasts and the hotel tax bellwether were studied at regular meetings of the special team formed to respond to the recession. These meetings helped the City's management team understand trends in the City's revenues, review operational strategies to reduce costs while maintaining service levels, and develop and implement contingency plans. By monitoring the trend in hotel revenue receipts, for example, the management team was able to rapidly identify the point at which the local economy turned the corner and began to improve, providing reassurance that the worst was over.

Under the leadership of Sean Joyce, and supported by the forecasting tools developed by Ken and Chris, the City's department heads and management team worked together to reduce costs and adapt to the recessionary conditions.

Exhibit 15.4 –Using Hotel Taxes as Leading Indicator of Sales Tax Revenues

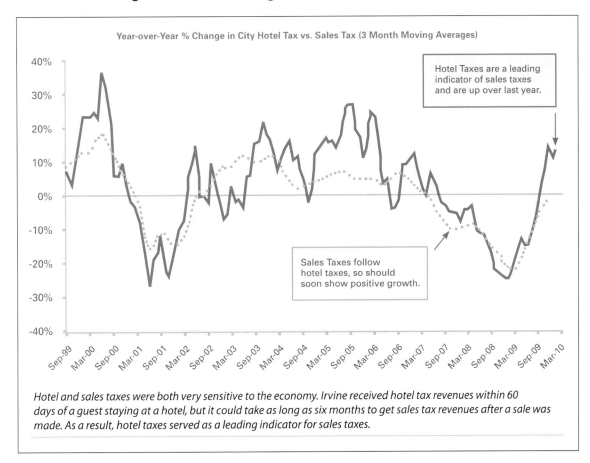

Year-over-Year % Change in City Hotel Tax vs. Sales Tax (3 Month Moving Averages)

Hotel Taxes are a leading indicator of sales taxes and are up over last year.

Sales Taxes follow hotel taxes, so should soon show positive growth.

Hotel and sales taxes were both very sensitive to the economy. Irvine received hotel tax revenues within 60 days of a guest staying at a hotel, but it could take as long as six months to get sales tax revenues after a sale was made. As a result, hotel taxes served as a leading indicator for sales taxes.

Arriving at the Other Side

The City was able to fulfill the four promises of the Three-Year Bridge Plan by eliminating over 70 full-time equivalent positions through attrition, consolidating duplicative activities across departments, deferring selected non-operating expenditures, re-evaluating interfund cost-sharing arrangements, and economizing on activities not core to the City's mission. Some of these activities were big and some were small. Among the measures adopted by the City to reduce costs, for example, was delivery of the City's "Art Beat" and "Shelter Scoop" in electronic format rather than paper, for $84,000 in annual savings. The City furthermore consolidated programs split between departments, including environmental program administration, traffic review and analysis, water quality, concrete repair, and advanced plan-

---

*The adjustment is almost always to provide cities with additional sales tax money produced by their tax base beyond what the state had advanced (so the quarters show as peaks rather than valleys).

ning. The City also reduced conference, training, and professional development budgets, re-negotiated federal lobbyist services, and consolidated after-school and camp programs. The City eliminated contract services for shrub fertilization in parks and began using volunteers to staff open studio time at the Fine Arts Center.

These and other reductions resulted in savings of more than $12 million, or 8 percent, from its general fund adopted budget from fiscal year 2008-09 to fiscal year 2010-11. In fact, while the City's forecast entering the recession proved too optimistic, it was correspondingly too pessimistic in projecting cost reductions that could be made without significant impact to the City's core services. For instance, the 2008 forecast projected operating costs at $144 million, but actual costs were only $141 million. This made it possible to return $3.2 million to the City's Contingency Reserve Fund. The agility shown by the City staff's response to falling revenues enhanced the credibility of the Bridge Plan and emphasized the need to be adaptable.

By the end of the Bridge Plan period, the City of Irvine was able to successfully present a balanced budget without the use of reserves or other one-time measures. It did so despite the fact that its most important revenue source, sales tax, was budgeted 3 percent lower than the peak it reached six years before. By outperforming its expenditure projections during the Bridge Plan years, the City was also able to replenish its Contingency Reserve Fund to a balance of over $20 million by the close of fiscal year 2011-12, or just under 15 percent of the City's budgeted appropriations. The City was even able to increase its support of local public schools at that time.

Under the direction of its City Council, the City is now working to prepare for the next recession by increasing its contingency reserve funding to a level of 20 percent of budgeted appropriations. The City uses the same monthly forecasting and monitoring system shown in Exhibit 15.3 to see if it is on track to meet its financial goals.

These financial accomplishments did not come at the expense of the City's core services: a 2013 resident satisfaction survey indicated that 92 percent of the residents surveyed were satisfied with the City's overall performance in providing municipal services, a satisfaction measure virtually unchanged from 2006, the last time the study was conducted before the beginning of the recession.

Finally, the City's new forecast model continues to perform well. Exhibit 15.5 shows the forecast versus actual results for the City's five-year forecasts for sales taxes and total general fund revenues. The table includes the forecasts made in late 2008 and early 2009, before the new model was fully in place, and compares those to the forecasts made in late 2009 and early 2010, using the new model. As you can see, Irvine's long-term forecasts made with the new model are a huge improvement over the old model and produce a level of accuracy that would prove enviable even for a one-year ahead forecast. The mean absolute percentage error (MAPE) using old forecast model in 2009 was 17 percent for sales taxes and 10 percent for total general fund revenues. The MAPE for the 2010 forecast, using the new model, was about 2 percent for both sales taxes and general fund total revenues.

Exhibit 15.5 – Forecast versus Actuals for Irvine's Five-Year General Fund Forecasts (Thousands of Dollars)

	2009-10	2010-11	2011-12	2012-13	2013-14	2014-15
Actual Revenues						
Sales Tax	39,735	45,788	49,226	51,065	55,580	58,767
Total Revenues	118,874	127,972	134,745	138,066	147,868	160,240
Forecasts Made in 2009 (old model)						
Sales Tax	49,421	53,040	56,342	60,397	63,589	N/A
Total Revenues	129,576	136,830	145,820	155,388	164,641	N/A
Sales Tax Error	-24.4%	-15.8%	-14.5%	-18.3%	-14.4%	N/A
Total Revenues Error	-9.0%	-6.9%	-8.2%	-12.5%	-11.3%	N/A
Forecasts Made in 2010 (new model)						
Sales Tax	N/A	44,763	47,987	50,565	53,685	56,830
Total Revenues	N/A	124,048	130,105	137,887	146,461	157,848
Sales Tax Error	N/A	2.2%	2.5%	1.0%	3.4%	3%
Total Revenues Error	N/A	3.1%	3.4%	0.1%	1.0%	2%

Lessons from Irvine's Experience

Simple is often better than complex. Earlier in this book, we cited experimental research that showed that simple methods often outperform complex ones, and Irvine's experience provides real-life confirmation. The algorithms that replaced the regression equation were mathematically simpler and relied on data that was easier to obtain. This is not to say that non-statistical algorithms will be better than regression in all cases, but, rather, that forecasters should err on the side of simplicity, while heeding Einstein's dictum: make things as simple as possible, but not simpler.

Bring in multiple perspectives. A critical feature of Irvine's new forecasting model was that it brought to bear many different perspectives on the forecast in addition to that provided by the budget and finance staff, such as those provided by outside consultants, regional economic experts, and staff from the City's Community Development department. Multiple sources of information help balance out biases that might be present in any one source, and one source may contribute information that covers a blind spot of another source.

Get feedback. Irvine was successful in navigating its challenges because it was adaptable. However, in order to adapt, you need to know that change is necessary. Feedback provides that knowledge. The Irvine budget and finance team sought many forms of feedback, including staying abreast of changes in the larger economic environment, using hotel tax revenues as a predictor for change in sales tax revenues and developing a refined short-term forecast model. For forecasters generally, the broader lesson is to remain keenly aware of changes in the local environment and to stay on top of differences between the forecast and actual revenues so that financial plans and budgets can change, and also so that forecast models can be changed when needed.

Accept uncertainty. The midst of the Great Recession was a very stressful time. Under such circumstances, it would be tempting to reassure stakeholders that the staff has everything completely under control. However, under conditions of extreme uncertainty, there is a high probability that such assurances would prove hollow. Thus, Irvine's staff took a different tact. They provided a broad outline for navigating the troubled times in the form of the Three-Year Bridge Plan, but emphasized that the City would need to be flexible in the details of its implementation. The short-term forecasts and monthly operational review meetings were tangible symbols of the acknowledgement of uncertainty. The scenario planning exercise the City conducted helped to assess the level of uncertainty of the City's future. In retrospect, one thing the City could also have done is to increase its expectations for volatility in its primary revenue forecast. Chapter 10 of this book provides evidence that human beings systematically and routinely underestimate the amount of uncertainty they face, and describes methods for managing uncertainty in forecasts.

Integrate reserves into the forecast presentation. Reserves are the closest thing local governments have to the financial bottom line. When a local government has a strong reserve policy that establishes why reserves are needed and how much the government will strive to keep on hand, the forecaster can reach the audience by describing the potential effect of the forecast on reserve levels. Irvine's Three-Year Bridge Plan was premised on the idea of using reserves as the "bridge," and the staff's subsequent forecast presentations always addressed the direction reserves were headed in.

Put the forecast in a compelling context. The Three-Year Bridge Plan and working through the greatest economic downturn in modern history clearly provided an overarching storyline for the forecast. Hopefully, you will not have a context to work within that is "compelling" in the same way as Irvine's during the Great Recession, but you still can link the forecast to an overarching storyline that will interest the audience. For example, in 2013, the Irvine City Council adopted a plan to aggressively pay down its unfunded pension liability within the next ten years. The plan has centered on a long-term forecast of the City's pension liability and, similar to the Bridge Plan, staff provides the City Council with regular progress reports so that policymakers can make course adjustments along the way, as necessary, to meet the pay-down target. The storyline does not necessarily have to be financial, though. Government services are ultimately dependent on adequate revenues, so the forecast could be presented in the context of the government's ability to achieve a high-profile service goal.

Find and appeal to an identity. Irvine used its identity as a highly successful master-planned community as inspiration to develop and follow a long-term plan to successfully traverse the Great Recession. An identity that supports long-term, strategic financial decision-making is not just an idiosyncratic characteristic of a few local governments. Rather, most, if not all, organizations probably have some something in their inventory of experiences that can be pulled forward to evoke an identity that is adaptive to current challenges.

Chapter 16

Turning around the City of Baltimore with Long-Term Forecasting and Scenario Analysis

Stephanie Rawlings-Blake became the 49th mayor of the City of Baltimore under less than ideal conditions. Formerly the City Council President, she became mayor in the middle of the budget process when Mayor Sheila Dixon resigned her position and, by City statute, the Council President assumed the vacant office. And this was no ordinary budget process. The City was facing a record budget shortfall in fiscal year 2011: $120 million in the general fund operating budget plus a $65 million pension shortfall. This deficit totaled about 9 percent of the City's budgeted 2010 expenditures of $1.35 billion. The challenge was even graver than these numbers suggest because just under half of the budget was already consumed by "fixed" costs like debt service, pension payments, and state-mandated levels of financial support for the Baltimore public schools. This meant the City had to take drastic measures to surmount a shortfall equal to about 17 percent of its discretionary resources.

The resulting "scorched earth" budget, as it was described by many, called for severe cuts to spending. To prevent the worst of the cuts, $50 million in revenue increases were approved, including: increasing the income tax to state limit; increasing hotel, energy, and telecom taxes; reinstituting a defunct beverage container tax; increasing parking taxes and meter rates and fines; and negotiating a payment in lieu of taxes with local non-profit hospitals and universities. Among the expenditure reductions still carried out were: employee furloughs; abolishment of 240 positions, including 100 layoffs; significant reductions to pay-as-you-go contributions to capital projects; cuts to tree maintenance, building maintenance, and bridge repair; reduced financial support for the arts museum and symphony; and ending transport subsidies for school students.

The 2011 budget gap was not an aberration – it was the culmination of many years of urban decline in Baltimore. Baltimore's population had dropped from a peak of about 950,000 people in 1950 to 620,000 in 2010, and, though the housing bubble had provided some temporary fiscal reprieve for the City, Baltimore's delicate post-industrial economy was now suffering the aftershocks of the Great Recession. One year later, these fundamental conditions had not changed and, accordingly, the fiscal year 2012 budget process was not much easier. The City closed a $60 million budget gap without raising any taxes, but made cuts to popular services such as graffiti removal, animal services, and youth sports. The City also continued employee furloughs, froze pay for all employees, and rotated fire company closures.

Mayor Rawlings-Blake knew that there had to be a better way to manage the City's finances.

Enter the Long-Term Financial Plan

The City's Budget Director, Andrew Kleine, was ready with a solution to the annual cycle of reactive spending cuts in the face of a declining tax base and increasing liabilities: a long-term, strategic financial plan. Using such a process, the City would define the root causes of its financial challenges, take a multiyear look at the City's resource needs and the revenues projected to be available to pay for them, and commit to a long-term strategy to grow the City's economy. A long-term forecast and plan addressed the concerns that the Mayor had articulated about the City's finances: that balancing the budget one year at a time was resulting in decisions that were not in the City's long-term best interest and that many of the steps taken to balance the Fiscal 2010-12 budgets were unsustainable.

Hence, the Mayor initiated and led, with the support of the City's Finance department, a comprehensive long-term financial planning process christened "Change to Grow" – based on the Mayor's goal of adding 10,000 new families to Baltimore in 10 years. The objective of the plan was to develop a fiscally responsible approach to funding core services, rebalancing employee compensation to make wages more competitive and benefits more comparable to those found in neighboring jurisdictions and peer cities, improving tax competitiveness, investing in infrastructure, and reducing long-term liabilities, thereby allowing Baltimore to grow and thrive.

When municipalities develop a long-term financial plan, they often focus on a three-year or five-year time horizon. However, the Mayor and the finance team knew that the City's biggest challenges, like declining population, a stagnating tax base, deteriorating capital infrastructure, and growing liabilities for employee pensions could not be adequately addressed over a five-year window. They thought that a ten-year time horizon was needed to effect meaningful change. Further, a longer-time horizon would allow the City to better assess the potential of strategies that might not make a big difference within a few years, but could have major positive impacts down the road. A ten-year window would also deemphasize the long-term plan as a response to the City's recent severe financial crises and emphasize the plan as a means of long-term transformation of the City's fiscal fortunes.

In order to gain support for the far-reaching strategies that would be needed to put Baltimore's finances on the right track, Change to Grow was a highly collaborative endeavor. The City Council, dozens of City department and division managers and professionals, and members of the public were all engaged. At the center of this engagement strategy were three "Guidance Committees," two of which were charged with providing policy direction on two of the City's most important challenges, the cost of employee health benefits and pensions. The third committee provided direction on the ten-year plan as a whole.

However, large, inclusive strategic planning processes in governments often have a tendency towards compromise and, as a result, middling strategies that would be insufficient to overcome challenges of the scale faced by Baltimore. The Mayor and Andrew needed a way to communicate financial information that could help the diverse set of participants in Change to Grow understand the magnitude of their task and create a sense of urgency for far-reaching reforms.

Scenario Analysis: A Different Perspective on the Future

An argument sometimes made against long-term financial planning is that long-term forecasts are not reliable, so to develop strategies that depend on the forecast number is a futile exercise. Because the uncertainty inherent in a forecast necessarily increases as the forecast looks further into the future, developing strategies based on a 10-year forecast could elicit strong reservations from some people. Andrew Kleine and the budget team recognized that a single 10-year forecast was bound to be wrong; still, the City's planning and analysis for Change to Grow had to be based on some set of financial figures.

Therefore, Andrew and his colleagues chose to develop three different forecast scenarios. Each scenario would vary the values of the key assumptions underpinning the forecast. This way, the finance and budget staff would acknowledge the economic sensitivity of some of the forecast assumptions and the resulting uncertainty inherent in long-term forecasting – yet, at the same time, provide financial figures to ground the plan. Critically, the scenarios were not used as a compromise on the economic assumptions in order to allay criticisms of the plan. Rather, it was a way to make the Change to Grow plan even more robust by helping the City to prepare for a future that differed from the forecasters' best estimates.

The City engaged a consultant to help develop the long-term forecast and scenarios. However, the baseline long-term forecast was developed using the City's existing forecasting techniques. For example, the City used an algorithm to forecast property taxes, including variables representing a rotating three-year assessment cycle, underlying growth rates, and the impact of accumulated homestead credits. The forecast also used econometric regression to forecast income taxes, used expert judgment from the city's lobbyist and other relevant city officials to forecast state-shared revenues, and used simple extrapolation and judgment for minor revenues.

To develop three scenarios, the consultant used the output of these methods and combined them with information from third-party entities that specialize in economic research, such as regional academic economists, agencies of the State of Maryland, and agencies of the federal government. The scenarios are described below, and Exhibit 16.1 summarizes some of the key variables under each scenario:

- **Baseline.** The baseline projection assumed a steady, but modestly paced, recovery. It was based on the consensus best estimate of the sources of economic information that the City consulted. The baseline scenario did not assume that the City benefited from population growth or positive changes in economic conditions resulting from City policy.

- **Pessimistic.** The pessimistic scenario assumed another near-term recession, with contraction of the gross domestic product (GDP) and delayed recovery. The pessimistic scenario was not a "worst case" scenario. In fact, the assumptions made for this scenario were considerably less severe than what the City had actually experienced during the Great Recession. These assumptions were chosen to ground the scenario in the City's recent experience of the Great Recession, while still maintaining greater plausibility than if the scenario imagined a repeat of the Great Recession or something worse.

- **Optimistic.** The optimistic scenario assumed a more rapid economic recovery compared to the baseline scenario. This was not an extreme "best case" scenario, but assumptions that were at the upper end of the spectrum of what were considered realistic expectations for the economy by the experts that the City consulted.

Exhibit 16.1 – Average Annual Change in Some Key Assumptions in the 10-Year Forecast Scenarios*

Assumption	Pessimistic	Baseline	Optimistic
Population	– 0.8%	+ 0.1%	+ 0.3%
Housing Prices	+ 1.9%	+ 3.6%	+ 4.0%
Pension Costs**	+ 5.2% / + 6.2%	+ 3.3% / + 3.4%	+ 0.9% / + 1.4%
Baltimore GDP	+ 1.0%	+ 1.5%	+ 2.4%
Health-Care Cost Inflation	+ 7.1%	+ 5.8%	+ 4.6%

*Baltimore had different percentage changes for each year of the forecast. This table summarizes the 10-year average.
**Figures shown for: employee retirement system / fire and police retirement system.

The three scenarios allowed Andrew and the budget team to show what different, yet plausible, versions of the future might look like and encouraged the participants in Change to Grow to ask questions like: If the economy improves, will our problems solve themselves? If another recession occurs, will the City be able to withstand it?

Also, in the past, the City budget staff had been accused of being overly fiscally conservative in their forecasts during labor negotiations and budgeting. The scenarios changed the conversation because there was not much value in arguing over whether the assumptions underpinning the baseline forecast were too conservative (or otherwise), because anyone who did not like the approach taken in the baseline forecast could avail themselves of the optimistic or pessimistic scenario and observe the impact on the City's financial position.

Having a consultant involved in the development of the long-term forecasts and scenarios also helped bolster credibility and prevent accusations that the forecasts or scenarios were not objective.

Armed with the scenarios, Andrew, the budget and finance team, and the consultants set out to inform the participants in Change to Grow and the City's other stakeholders of the situation Baltimore was in, using a graphic like Exhibit 16.2. The graphic showed that the baseline scenario was dire, that even the "optimistic" scenario was no panacea, and that the pessimistic scenario was disastrous. Something clearly needed to be done.

The Reaction: A Sense of Urgency

The long-term forecasts and scenario analysis were sobering to many of those who saw them. Most people were already aware of the problems underlying the City's financial challenges, like pension costs, health-care costs, and a declining tax base – but this was the first time they saw how these problems played out over a multiple-year period and under different possible economic conditions. For many people who were not closely involved in the City's financial analysis, this was a moment of insight when they became resolved that they would need to make some tough choices to change the City's trajectory.

The long-term forecast and scenarios gained a lot more attention when they were released to the public: the lead sentence of one news story read "The Baltimore city government is

Exhibit 16.2 – Baltimore's Scenario Analysis 10-Year Forecasts

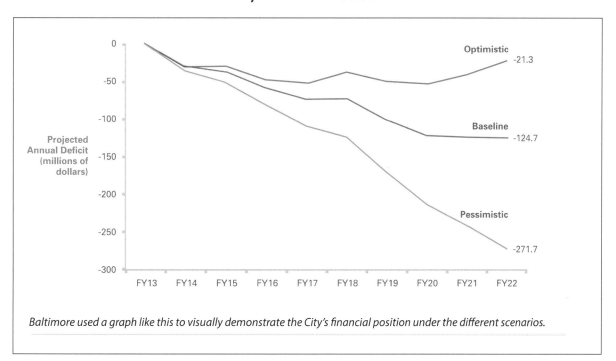

Baltimore used a graph like this to visually demonstrate the City's financial position under the different scenarios.

on a path to financial ruin and must enact major reforms to stave off bankruptcy, according to [its] 10-year forecast."[1] The media coverage worked to the advantage of the Mayor and Change to Grow. It captured the attention of many people in City government, especially those who weren't already involved in the long-term financial planning process, and helped galvanize the City to take action. It also provided the Mayor with a unique opportunity to articulate her vision to a public that now was much more interested in the City's financial condition, and to prepare people for the strategies that Change to Grow would recommend. She said:

> When you have budget after budget and you know that there are systemic problems, I felt an obligation to do more than what we have done in the past. The forecast shows that the city needs to address its financial challenges before it's too late, and somebody is coming in and making these choices for us.[2]

The sense of urgency fostered by the long-term forecasts and scenario analysis led the participants in Change to Grow to propose bolder actions to secure the City's financial future. For example, the cost of employee and retiree health benefits was a serious concern for the City because of both its overall size and its high rate of growth. The City's previous efforts to contain these costs mostly involved making marginal changes to cost-sharing ratios with plan participants, and most of these changes affected only retirees, such as dividing potential pharmaceutical purchases into pricing tiers in order to steer participants towards generic and preferred brands. After the scenario analysis, the participants in Change to Grow were willing to consider changes that affected active employees and that required negotiations with employee unions due to the scale of the change proposed. For instance, a 20 percent co-pay for drugs was proposed for all plan participants – a doubling of the copay for retirees, and an entirely new cost for active employees.

The sense of urgency and support for bolder strategies was not a consensus opinion among all stakeholders. However, there was at least enough support to move forward. The long-term forecasts and scenarios provided ready talking points for the Mayor and other elected officials who supported Change to Grow as they sought to make the case for change to the public. The scenarios also helped deflect attacks against the financial strategies suggested by Change to Grow, such as the changes to employee benefits, because the scenarios highlighted that a robust plan was needed under multiple possible futures.

The Results

In February 2013 the Mayor unveiled Change to Grow to the public. As the chief executive, the Mayor's substantive command of the financial issues facing the City and her ability to provide clear and decisive feedback to the planners and forecasters was essential to the success of the planning process. The scenario analysis helped provide the Mayor with insights into the financial future of the City that allowed her to successfully lead the financial planning process. Change to Grow marked the first time that the City of Baltimore had discussed financial strategy in this depth, and the Mayor received a lot of credit for her fiscal stewardship of the City as a result – as illustrated by the excerpt from the *Baltimore Sun* shown at right.

Critically, Baltimore's success with financial planning did not end with publishing the document. The sense of urgency created by the scenario analysis led to the implementation of the plan. Over the years since the plan has been adopted, the City has completed a number of strategies proposed by Change to Grow, some of which are shown in Exhibit 16.3.

Excerpt from a *Baltimore Sun* Editorial on Change to Grow[3]

[The Mayor's] proposals reflect a clear-eyed view of Baltimore's assets and liabilities and a remarkable willingness to take on politically unpopular causes. ... The answer is not higher tax rates, it's cutting costs and expanding the tax base, and that is what Ms. Rawlings-Blake's reforms are designed to do. ... Ms. Rawlings-Blake is taking a major political risk. But if she succeeds, she will accomplish what none of her immediate predecessors have managed: Change a vicious cycle of exodus and disinvestment into a virtuous one of growth and redevelopment.

Exhibit 16.3 – Some of the Strategies Implemented Since the Adoption of Change to Grow

Structural Budget Balance	Tax Competitiveness
• Change the fire shift schedule to reduce staffing requirements while maintaining coverage. • Implement higher cost-sharing for employee benefits.	• Reduce the property tax rate by 6% for homeowners, on track for a 10% reduction by 2020. • Diversify revenue base with new revenue sources.
Infrastructure Investment	**Long-Term Liabilities**
• More than double pay-as-you-go capital investment. • Invest in whole block demolition and relocation, street resurfacing, recreation centers, IT modernization, and more.	• Increase civilian employee contributions to the pension plan and replace defined benefit plan with hybrid defined contribution plan. • Change leave policies to reduce paid time-off accrual liabilities.

As a result of these and other initiatives from Change to Grow that have been implemented as of the fiscal year 2016 budget, the City projects it will save $255 million over a 10-year period. This will allow the City to reduce the cumulative size of all of the annual budget deficits shown in the baseline scenario (Exhibit 16.2) by 53 percent. These savings are net of the costs the City has incurred to provide tax relief, invest more in capital infrastructure, make City workers' pay more competitive, and other strategies designed to improve the quality of service the City provides. The City's efforts were recognized by a bond upgrade in 2014 from Standard & Poor's from AA- to AA, who cited the City's long-term financial plan as one of the factors underlying Baltimore's "very strong management conditions."[4] The City anticipates implementing other strategies from Change to Grow in the future in order to close the financial deficit the rest of the way.

However, large urban areas, especially those that have experienced de-industrialization, have challenges besides financial ones, as the civil disturbances of April 2015 in Baltimore starkly illustrated. Therefore, there is still work ahead to fully realize the City's goal of changing Baltimore to a growing, thriving community. The City's long-term financial plan, underpinned by long-term forecasting and scenario analysis, provides a cornerstone for what Baltimore is trying to build.[5]

Lessons from the Baltimore Experience

Lift the curse of knowledge. Because they are immersed in financial analysis, budget and finance professionals often gain an almost instinctive knowledge of the scale and scope of financial challenges their organization faces. A problem arises when communicating the gravity of financial issues to others. Though the audience may be generally aware of the issues, the communicator often unconsciously assumes that the audience has access to the same set of detailed facts and experiences as the communicator. As we saw in Baltimore, the City was beset by serious pension, health care, and tax base challenges, and this was not new information to most people. However, they still didn't have a good understanding of how big the challenges really were and the effects over time. The long-term forecasts and scenario analysis helped put the abstract financial challenges that were fully known by budget staff into more concrete terms that could also be appreciated by everyone else.

Explicitly acknowledge uncertainty and recognize risk. Uncertainty is inherent to forecasting, especially long-term forecasting. Rather than obscuring uncertainty by presenting a single forecast, which might have reduced the credibility of the long-term plan, Baltimore acknowledged it by presenting scenarios that showed different possible futures based on different assumptions about future economic performance. These assumptions were grounded in objective analysis, including historical experiences, but were not limited to a single view of what the future might hold.

Get the message across without coming across as alarmist. Forecasters are often challenged to make their audience aware of difficult issues – issues that many in the audience might prefer to ignore. One solution is to create a single forecast that is so dire that it can't be ignored, but that runs the risk of the audience perceiving the forecaster as dishonest or manipulative. Another approach is to let the numbers speak for themselves by framing them in a way that they can't be ignored. Baltimore did this by using scenarios that could be compared to the City's experience during the Great Recession, a reality that every audience member could appreciate. Hence, when the baseline scenario looked bad, some audience members might have chosen to dismiss it as the overly cautious analysis of the City finance and budget team. But when it is compared to a considerably worse pessimistic scenario that is based on assumptions about economic performance that are not as bad as what the City actually experienced during the Great Recession, the numbers become much more difficult to ignore.

Connect long-term forecasts to a long-term decision-making system. A common complaint of public-sector forecasters is that long-term forecasts don't impact decision-making. Baltimore's experience shows that long-term forecasts can greatly impact decision-making if they are presented properly and if they are an integral part of a collaborative long-term financial planning process.

Engage the leadership in the forecast. In Baltimore, the Mayor was not involved in the technical development of the forecast, but she was very engaged in using the forecast as a tool to realize her goal of improving Baltimore's vitality. Forecasters can help leadership become more engaged with the forecast by making the forecast more accessible using techniques such as scenario analysis or interactive simulation.

Use consultants wisely. Baltimore used consultants to help develop and present the long-term forecasts and scenarios. This provided some additional technical expertise and lent greater credibility to the process. However, the forecasts were still based on the same techniques that City staff had been using for forecasting, and the City staff were full partners with the consultants in making presentations. This meant that City staff was completely able to update the forecasts and maintain the long-term financial plan after the consulting engagement ended.

If you have a compelling presentation, be ready to handle success. Baltimore's presentation was successful in getting people's attention – so successful, in fact, that it generated a lot more public (and media) interest than long-term forecasts normally do. Baltimore was able to use this attention to increase the momentum behind Change to Grow. The lesson for other forecasters is that if you use techniques like scenario analysis, interactive simulation, or any of the other attention-getting techniques described in this book, then be prepared for them to work. This preparation includes making sure that leadership is engaged and that there is a strong decision-making system in place where this attention and energy can be positively directed. In Baltimore, this was the long-term financial planning process, but a budget process or financial policy development could also be outlets.

Better government through better financial management is a journey. Baltimore did not have an easy road during the financial forecasting and planning process. The additional public attention was not always positive or welcome. For example, in the immediate aftermath of the media stories about the City's impending "bankruptcy," the City had to take steps to reassure bond rating agencies that the City's debt would remain a good investment into the future. The City's bond rating was later upgraded, but having to explain to rating agencies that the City would not default on its debt was not a pleasant experience. Also, support for the financial strategies coming out of Change to Grow was not universal. Some felt they unfairly weighed on public employees. Baltimore did not enjoy an unbroken string of successes after the plan was adopted either. However, it has had many successes and has maintained focus on the plan by regularly updating the long-term forecast to show the impact of financial strategies that have been implemented. The lesson here is to recognize when planning and forecasting has worked and to demonstrate to decision-makers, other stakeholders, and the finance and budget staff themselves, that better forecasting and financial planning does make a difference to the community.

Chapter 17

Building and Maintaining Solid Infrastructure in the Town of Gilbert

Words like "crisis" and "crumbling" have been widely used in the media to describe the state of local infrastructure in the United States with good reason: one out of every nine bridges in the United States is considered deficient, and almost one-third of the major roads in the U.S. are in poor condition.[1] The worst examples, like bridge collapses and sink holes, make national news and even claim lives. In other instances, infrastructure failures create large, unplanned expenditures, disrupt the local economy, and reduce citizens' trust in government.

For many people, the issue of deteriorating infrastructure might evoke images of aging, post-industrial cities. However, preserving the investment the community has made in its capital assets is a concern for all local governments. In the Town of Gilbert, Arizona, the scenes of catastrophic infrastructure failure replaying in many American cities were not lost on Gilbert's leadership. Though Gilbert was not an aging community, it had its own challenge that stemmed from its history of explosive growth. From 1980 to 2010, its population grew by just over 3,500 percent, as shown in Exhibit 17.1. Since 2010, Gilbert has continued to grow rapidly – it has, for instance, routinely issued more building permits each year than the City of Phoenix, a city of over 1.5 million people. Gilbert expects to grow one-third larger than its current size to reach build out, so growth will continue to be a feature of life in Gilbert for years to come.

Because Gilbert experienced so much growth in a short time, a lot of infrastructure was built in a short time. Just over a quarter of Gilbert's entire infrastructure was built between 1990 and 1999 and just over half was built between 2000 and 2009. So, whereas a municipality that has experienced growth at a slower pace would have a smaller portion of its infrastructure reaching the stage of its lifecycle where significant maintenance and replacement outlays are required, Gilbert faced the prospect of a glut of repair and replacement bills coming due at once, all without the new revenues that accompanied the initial growth, such as impact fees, to pay for it. Further complicating the situation was that Gilbert was still growing, so the Town also had to determine how new growth would pay for itself and how existing infrastructure could support itself, without one subsidizing the other.

Exhibit 17.1 – Population Growth in the Town of Gilbert

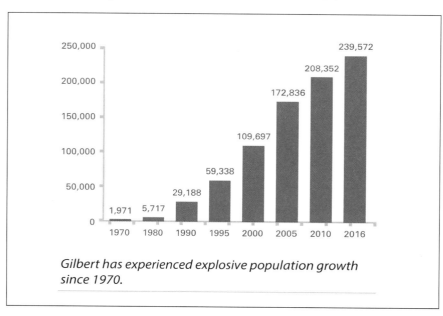

Gilbert has experienced explosive population growth since 1970.

Council and management knew that this was a challenge that could only be met through careful planning and forecasting. To that end, in 2011, "Long- and Short-Term Balanced Financial Plans" and "Proactively Address Infrastructure Needs" were included as two of only six strategic initiatives adopted by the Council. While work on these initiatives and the development of a long-range infrastructure plan (LRIP) was underway, in January 2013 an 8-inch potable water main broke in Gilbert's Heritage District, an area of upscale restaurants, entertainment, and shopping. A broken 8-inch water main moves enough water to fill a typical backyard in-ground swimming pool in less than 15 minutes. Gilbert Road, the main thoroughfare of the Heritage District, was closed and remained closed for 24 hours. Crews worked around the clock to repair the break and secure the site mostly in very poor weather conditions that included a lengthy and heavy rain storm. The water main break was near train tracks, so representatives from Union Pacific Railroad participated to ensure the integrity of the tracks was maintained as well as the safety of the public, and that all scheduled rail traffic continued during the Town's response actions.

The Heritage District water main break accentuated the urgency of long-term planning and infrastructure maintenance, and Gilbert's vision to be "the best-in-class, all lines of service" meant that well-maintained infrastructure was an imperative.

A cross-departmental team composed of representatives from the Manager's Office, Office of Management and Budget, Information Technology, Parks and Recreation, and Public Works led the analysis and development of a strategy.[2] In addition to the other elements of a long-term plan, revenue forecasting became an important part of the team's work for two reasons. First, much of Gilbert's infrastructure was built using revenues from impact fees – one-time charges paid by new development to cover the costs to the Town of creating

Exhibit 17.2 – Scenes from the Water Main Break in the Heritage District

The Heritage District water main break accentuated the urgency of long-term planning and infrastructure maintenance, and Gilbert's vision to be "the best-in-class, all lines of service" meant that well-maintained infrastructure was an imperative.

the capacity for new police, fire protection, parks and recreation, traffic signals, and utility systems needed to serve the new residents and businesses. As Gilbert reaches build out, between 2030 and 2040, there will be far less of this revenue available. However, at the same time, Gilbert's sales tax revenues have increased and are expected to increase into the future due to the economic activity created by new residents and business. Consequently, the forecasts and financial strategy would need to be mindful of this changing composition of the Gilbert's revenue portfolio and its implications for infrastructure financing.

Second, the citizens of Gilbert have consistently demonstrated a desire to keep taxes low, while balancing the provision of high-quality services. As a result of the state tax structure, Gilbert and many other communities in Arizona are heavily reliant on local sales tax revenues. The volume of transactions subject to sales tax in Gilbert has been sufficient enough to maintain a low rate of 1.5 percent, and the Town has not yet demonstrated a need for a primary property tax. In fact, Gilbert is one of the few larger cities in the United States without a general purpose property tax.[3] The organization's allocation of staff is also conservative, as demonstrated by the number of full-time equivalent employees (FTE) per 1,000 residents. In this and other metrics, like the average annual tax and fee burden per household, Gilbert consistently offers the lowest cost of any of the more sizeable municipalities in the Phoenix metropolitan region.[4] Therefore, accurate and effective forecasts are paramount in order to make the most of current and future revenues available, before proposing rate increases or new funding mechanisms.

Gilbert's Planning Process

The first step in Gilbert's planning process was for the public works and parks and recreation departments to develop an asset inventory, including an assessment of asset condition, in order to determine which assets were most in need of repair and when. The asset inventory helped the budget staff produce a useful revenue forecast in three important ways.

First and foremost, the inventory helped Gilbert fully understand the long-term maintenance costs it would need to cover. As a result, Gilbert's revenue forecasts were far more meaningful when they could be compared to the expenditures necessary to maintain the assets, thereby revealing the precise resource gaps that the Town would need to address.

Second, the detailed asset inventory provided an opportunity to start a conversation about the cost of infrastructure compared to the value of infrastructure. "Cost" only refers to the expenditures made for infrastructure, while "value" refers to both the cost of the infrastructure and the benefit provided. For example, when considering just cost, one would favor an infrastructure investment with a lower total cost over higher total cost, even if the low-cost asset also had a disproportionately shorter useful life. When considering value, one would favor the asset that provided the most service to the public for the expenditure required to acquire and maintain the asset. When the Council and management could talk about value, rather than just cost, they could have an informed conversation about how expenses and revenues together can maximize the useful life of Gilbert's infrastructure. If value were not taken into account, the conversation would be focused on how to minimize the cost of infrastructure.

Finally, the details about infrastructure that were provided by the asset inventory helped the budget staff learn about how operating departments approach infrastructure, and gave budget staff a better understanding of how infrastructure ages and the conditions that contribute to longer or shorter useful lives for assets. This new knowledge gave the budgeting team additional credibility when talking about infrastructure planning. For example, the team learned why different assets in the water treatment facility needed to be replaced on a given schedule, and why failing to replace one asset could have deleterious effects on other assets involved in producing potable water. This knowledge helped the budget staff and public works develop regular schedules for funding maintenance and replacement that would keep the assets in good working order while also preventing big spikes in repair costs in some years.

With the asset inventory in hand, the second step in the planning process was to hold a conversation about the level of service Gilbert would find acceptable for its assets. For example, a "variable frequency drive" starts, stops, and regulates the speed of a water pump, which results in more efficient use of energy and a longer asset life for the pump. Variable frequency drives at Gilbert's North Water Treatment Plant have a 15-year industry standard useful life. After examining the condition of the drives and evaluating how the assets were performing in Gilbert, it was discovered that the variable frequency drives typically last for 17 to 20 years. However, the rate of failure was found to be much higher after 15 years. After a discussion, Gilbert placed the drives on a 15-year replacement cycle due to the risk of failure and the criticality of the drives to plant operations. The level of service for other asset classes was determined in a similar fashion, taking into account factors like historical levels of service, anticipated levels of service based on growth projections, population, various master plans, etc.

The decisions about the desired level of service for its assets prepared Gilbert for the third step in the planning process: Determine the revenues available to fund asset upkeep at the desired level of service. To make this determination, Gilbert's departments compared the maintenance requirements to their current labor capacity and funding. If existing resources were not sufficient, then the departments would request additional resources, and the Budget Office would verify that revenues could support the request in the next year, and for five to ten years into the future, depending on the fund. For example, the revenues for funding asset maintenance in the Streets Fund and General Funds were largely composed of state-shared revenues. Since state-shared revenues can be volatile, a five-year outlook made sense. Enterprise funds have revenues that are under the direct control of the Town, so a ten-year time horizon worked well.

Enterprise funds account for many of Gilbert's assets and provide a good illustration of how Gilbert used revenue forecasting to support its decisions about asset maintenance planning. In the enterprise funds, the paramount concern was the ability of user-fee revenues to fund operations, meet debt obligations, and support Gilbert's minimum desired reserve levels. Gilbert's forecast model[5] used algorithms that included variables to represent the total number of utility accounts the Town would service, potential changes in water rates, expected changes in usage patterns, and other factors that impact water sales. The model also disaggregated revenues to a level of detail necessary to distinguish between revenues from existing rate payers and revenues from anticipated new accounts. It was important to know not just what system development charges were forecasted to be as a result of new customers coming on to the Gilbert's utility system, but also how water usage fees would be affected

by new growth. This is because as Gilbert's rate of growth declines, the Office of Management and Budget must be able to distinguish between (1) revenue growth caused by the addition of new accounts and (2) the amount of revenue growth that occurs within the existing customer base from rate adjustments or other factors. This way, Gilbert can develop more realistic projections of reve-

Exhibit 17.3 – Gilbert's Algorithm for Long-Term Water Rate Revenue Forecasts	
	Base rate revenue from existing customers
+	Additional rate revenue from growth
=	Subtotal of rate revenue
X	Proposed water rate percentage increase
=	Annual rate revenue, including increase
-	Adjustment for elasticity of demand*
=	Total revenue from water usage
* Reduction in demand caused by increasing rates.	

nue as the rate of growth in new accounts begins to slow down. Exhibit 17.3 shows how the Town's forecast model projected revenue from just water sales, as an example.

Gilbert also used "what-if" analyses to help analyze resource requests. For example, the wastewater division requested approximately $400,000 to migrate to magnetic meters that would no longer require costly annual recalibration and that would have a longer useful life. The enterprise fund rate model was used to compare the one-time expense of purchasing and installing the new meters to existing revenues. Exhibit 17.4 shows a representation of the type of analysis the staff performed. The graph shows the fund's reserve levels, in dollars, if Gilbert were to continue with its existing meters compared to replacing the meters with the new model. Both scenarios are then compared to Gilbert's desired mini-

Exhibit 17.4 – Example of Analysis of Impact on Reserves of Different Asset Management Strategies[6]

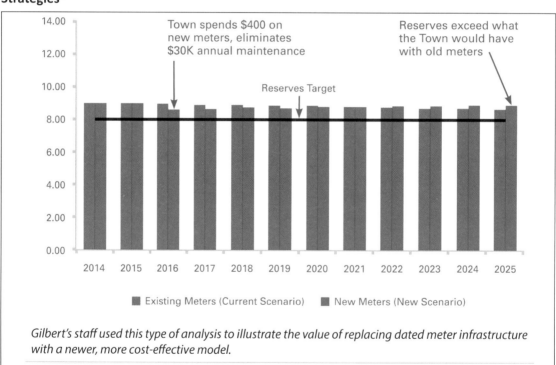

Gilbert's staff used this type of analysis to illustrate the value of replacing dated meter infrastructure with a newer, more cost-effective model.

mum reserve level, and revenue forecasts were a critical ingredient to determining what the future reserve levels would be under each scenario. The graph shows that investing in the new meters would cause a short-term drop in reserves as Gilbert uses accumulated reserves to purchase the meters, but the reserves slowly build back up, due to the reduced operating and maintenance costs, and exceed what the reserves would be if the Town were to remain with the existing meters. Staff found that this method of analysis was particularly effective when it was conducted live with members of the Council in one-on-one meetings. This allowed interested Council members to ask about changes to key variables and observe the results immediately. For example, what might the graph look like if the purchase of the meters was deferred for two years, or if the purchase was phased in over multiple years? The answers to these questions helped the Council gain a better understanding of the sensitivity of different planning and funding decisions, which then better prepared them to explain the Town's course of action to a public that expects the highest value at the lowest possible cost.

The revenue forecasts allowed Gilbert to move to the next step in the planning process, which was to weigh proposals for spending on infrastructure against other potential uses via annual budget deliberations. Gilbert used a zero-base budgeting process, where every three years departments were required to re-justify all of the expenditures that comprised the baseline level of services that they provide to the public. In other words, the budget had to be rebuilt from a base of zero, as a way to critically re-examine what Gilbert was spending money on and to avoid reauthorizing obsolete expenditures. The departments also had to provide detailed spending plans for any programs or services they proposed that went above and beyond baseline spending. Gilbert's budget analysts and executive management team then conducted a detailed review of all of the requests. Under this system of budgeting, the Council could weigh new maintenance programs against other possible use of funds, and existing maintenance programs could be re-examined to see if the level of service was still what was necessary. In many cases, the Council decided to approve the new spending for infrastructure maintenance because the presentation of the asset maintenance needs, forecasts of revenues, and Gilbert's budgeting method created an environment that supported decision-making with foresight. In the words of then-Councilperson Ben Cooper, the Council came to the realization that "an investment in infrastructure is an investment in a community's future. Cities and towns that make the effort to understand the assets they own are much smarter about how they maintain and replace them."

The Impact of Planning

The most fundamental impact of Gilbert's planning process was to establish a better link between asset maintenance and replacement needs and its forecasted revenues, so that the Town could better compare its infrastructure needs to the available funding. For example, each year, Gilbert had spent between $2 million and $4 million on preventative street maintenance in neighborhoods around the community. After the inventory and condition-based assessment, it was determined that in order to maintain the assets at the acceptable level of service, the annual funding required would rise to approximately $7 million. Gilbert's financial projection models were updated to see if the supporting revenue stream (Highway User Revenue Fund and Vehicle License Tax) would be able to accommodate the significant increase in maintenance. This was essential to determining the long-term sustainability of the fund source as well as the infrastructure assets.

The information provided by forecasts and planning led to better decisions about how to use resources. Many local governments operate infrastructure until failure and then replace it. This is a more costly and less predictable strategy than effective planning of maintenance, rehabilitation, repair, and scheduled replacement. The challenge is that effective planning requires making investments in maintenance and repair before replacement becomes necessary – and making those investments consistently over time. Gilbert's forecasting and planning helped the Office of Management and Budget align the resources necessary for a timely and consistent infrastructure maintenance strategy. For instance, a policy was established to direct non-recurring revenues, like spikes in sales tax revenues, towards funding non-recurring expenditures, like replacing assets. According to then-Councilperson Ben Cooper, the realization that the Town needed to make sustained and smart investments in its infrastructure in order for Gilbert to continue to be a great place to live and do business was one of the most important outcomes of the forecasts and plans.

The planning process also helped create teamwork between the departments to support this vision for sustained investment infrastructure. For example, the forecast information shared by budget staff helped departments better understand all of the variables involved in funding a long-range infrastructure plan. This was part of creating a more open dialogue and greater trust between budget and public works staff about infrastructure needs. The Public Works Director felt that working closely with budget staff helped him get a better understanding of where the revenues to pay for infrastructure come from, how much revenue Gilbert expects to have in the future to pay for infrastructure, and, therefore, how Gilbert might be able to pay for all of the infrastructure work that needs to be done. The Public Works Director found that having budget staff engaged from the beginning of the infrastructure planning process resulted in a plan that balanced the infrastructure needs of the community with the fiscal realities faced by the Gilbert municipal government.

Lessons from Gilbert's Experience

Identify a clear problem that the forecast (and planning process) will help solve. A forecast, especially a long-term one, will be much more successful if there is a clear challenge or issue the government is facing that the forecast is intended to help resolve. In Gilbert, all of the revenue analysis and forecasting was performed in support of the objective of finding a sustainable infrastructure maintenance and replacement strategy. This meant that the forecast was not just an intellectual exercise, but had immediate practical value to decision-makers.

Understand the details of the issue or problem the forecast (and planning) are designed to help solve. The budget team in Gilbert dove into the details of the asset inventory and condition assessment. This helped them communicate more effectively with the Public Works department and allowed them to build more accurate financial models, and their ability to cite and be conversant about the details of the inventory increased their credibility.

Put the forecast in context. In Gilbert, the budget staff did not present revenue numbers in isolation. The revenue numbers were placed in the context of the expenditures the Town would need to make to provide service to the public. For example, the graph shown in Exhibit 17.4 does not have any element that represents just revenues. Rather, it uses reserves as a kind of bottom-line indicator of financial health, where the revenue forecast is one component of the forecast of reserves. This context made the revenue forecast much more meaningful to its audience.

Help non-financial leaders understand the forecast and analysis. One of the dangers of becoming immersed in the details of a planning and forecasting issue is that the forecaster can forget what it was like to be a novice. When once arcane details become second nature, the forecaster may unconsciously come to assume a level of knowledge on the audience's part that they do not possess. This does not mean that the forecaster needs to explain all of these details to the audience, but he or she does need to find a way to impart to the audience an almost intuitive understanding of what the forecaster knows. One very powerful method, and one that Gilbert used, is simulation through interactive forecast models. When decision-makers can see how changes in decision parameters change the Town's financial condition graphically and right in front of their eyes, it helps them get some of the same intuitive understanding of the forecast that the forecaster has. Gilbert also gave its elected officials the opportunity to work with the interactive model in one-on-one meetings with budget staff, which provided a more immersive experience than if the model were shown to all officials at once at a Council meeting, for example.

Work closely with operational departments. Especially when the issue the forecast is meant to address is one that involves an operating department, the forecaster should work closely with the operating department to develop the forecast. In Gilbert, the Public Works department helped the budget team learn the details of asset maintenance, and the Public Works department learned more about the funding streams available to support asset maintenance from the budget team. Hence, both groups benefited from working together and produced a more rigorous and credible forecast and plan as a result.

Integrate the forecast into a decision-making process. A large part of Gilbert's success is attributable to the decision-making system it had in place. It started with establishing a broader vision for Gilbert to "best in-class, all lines of service." This vision created an identity among Gilbert's decision-makers that led them to see well-maintained infrastructure as a necessity. Gilbert also had limited number of more specific long-term strategic initiatives, including "Long- and Short-Term Balanced Financial Plans" and "Proactively Address Infrastructure Needs." Finally, Gilbert's zero-base budgeting process provided a means to compare investments in infrastructure maintenance to other possible uses of Gilbert's available revenues. The forecast was a natural and necessary part of the decision-making process that elected officials and executive management used.

Build the forecast model to suit the purpose of planning. Gilbert's forecast model disaggregated growth revenues from regular ongoing revenues. This included separating water sales from new accounts and sales from existing accounts, not just separating water sales from impact fees. This design was essential to finding out if Gilbert would later be able to maintain the infrastructure it was building. A less detailed model would not have made these distinctions in water sales revenues, making it much harder to accomplish the goal of the planning process.

Be open to arriving at new conclusions. For instance, one of the conclusions the Gilbert team arrived at early on was that many of the items staff had long viewed as "one-time" investments could be considered ongoing maintenance costs. Though the specific purchases and parts for maintenance may vary from year to year, an approximate ongoing baseline can be established, from which any spikes or true one-time expenditures may be forecast. In essence, embarking on a multifaceted, multiyear effort to inventory all Town-owned infrastructure while forecasting future needs may evolve into other discussions. Deviance from the original plan should not be viewed as an obstacle, but rather one of the beneficial outcomes of the research and resources dedicated to forecasting and planning.

Chapter 18

The City of Boulder Forecasts under Extreme Uncertainty

On November 6, 2012, voters in the State of Colorado passed Colorado Amendment 64, addressing personal use and regulation of marijuana, including commercial cultivation, manufacture, and sale, thereby regulating marijuana in ways similar to alcohol.[1] Since Colorado is a strong home rule state, the state and local taxing jurisdictions could set their own tax rates on this new business. Similar to alcohol, each city and county in Colorado had to determine whether it would allow retail, wholesale, and/or manufacturing operations within in its borders and, if so, create local regulations, including local tax rates. The City Council of Boulder decided to authorize the full range of cannabis businesses, thereby requiring the City to come to grips with an assortment of issues that were without precedent in the United States[2] and, in fact, the rest of the world.[3] In addition to the public safety and licensing issues that would need to be addressed, the City would need to estimate the financial impact of marijuana regulation, including revenue from the new taxes on recreational marijuana (RMJ). The RMJ taxes would be composed of three elements: 1) the City's local, home rule retail sales and use taxes collected on RMJ sales; 2) an excise tax based on the value of product from operations where marijuana would be grown; and 3) a proportional share of the sales taxes collected by the State, with the proportion equal to the portion Boulder composed of the total sales in the State.

Why Study the Case of Boulder?

While taxes on recreational marijuana are only levied by a small number of local governments, the experience of Boulder has relevance to all forecasters because:

- Uncertainty bedevils many forecasts. Boulder overcame extreme uncertainty.
- A lack of historical data occurs with any new revenue, and existing revenues when records are poor.
- Boulder used many of the techniques described in this book.
- Boulder shows how an uncertain forecast can be integrated into a risk-aware decision-making process.
- Boulder shows how all of the above can be accomplished when the forecast takes place in a charged political environment.

Forecasting a New Revenue Wasn't the Only Challenge

While estimating the financial impact of totally new revenue would be difficult enough on its own, Boulder faced a couple of additional complications. First was the fanfare surrounding legalization and the wide range of opinions on its impact, including the financial impact. For example, third-party estimates on what the State of Colorado would receive were numerous and ranged from $32 million[4] to $130 million[5] in new revenues for the State's budget (with estimates in between as well). The City of Boulder received a similarly wide range of opinions from community members on the new revenues Boulder would realize, and particularly from enthusiasts for legalization who foresaw a groundswell of demand for recreational marijuana (RMJ) and suggested that the City should plan to increase its budget accordingly.

The second complication was the financial stress that the City had been experiencing since 2001. The 2001 "dot.bomb" recession hit the City particularly hard. During this time, a regional shopping mall that was located in Boulder closed its doors and, on top of that, a number of new retailers opened in nearby communities, drawing shoppers away from Boulder. Also, the technology sector of the economy was well represented in Boulder, so employment and economic growth was hit especially hard, compared to other cities. The City experienced a general fund revenue decline of over 17 percent in the years 2001 through 2003 and had to lay off over 7 percent of its workforce during this period. The challenges inspired the City to begin the practice of long-term, strategic financial planning so that it would be better prepared for the next set of financial challenges. As a result, the City was better able to withstand the Great Recession by implementing a variety of revenue and expenditure strategies, such as eliminating earmarks on some major revenue streams that prevented the City from directing revenues to where they were most urgently needed and implementing budget practices that focused the City's limited resources on its core priorities. Regardless, there were still pressures on revenues, such that the City did not ultimately return, in real dollars, to the revenue it had in the year 2000 until 2011 (see Exhibit 18.1).

Accordingly, the City had been economizing its services for over a decade and many members of the community were eager to use the anticipated windfall from RMJ to restore services that had been cut, such as library hours, or to add entirely new services, like expanding safety inspections on rental units and implementing aspects of the City's master plans for parks and recreation, police and fire, and transportation.

During the course of its protracted period of budgetary austerity, the City had developed a strong set of financial policies and a long-term financial planning process. As a result, the City had closed a structural deficit and, in the process, developed a culture among the City Council and staff where financial resiliency was an extremely important goal. The City staff recognized that while services such as restored library hours or implementing the master plans were certainly desirable, predicating the budget for these services on revenues from RMJ was a risky proposition. Not only was the potential revenue from RMJ unknown, but

Exhibit 18.1 – City of Boulder General Fund Revenues from 1999 to 2013 in Real (Year 2000) Dollars

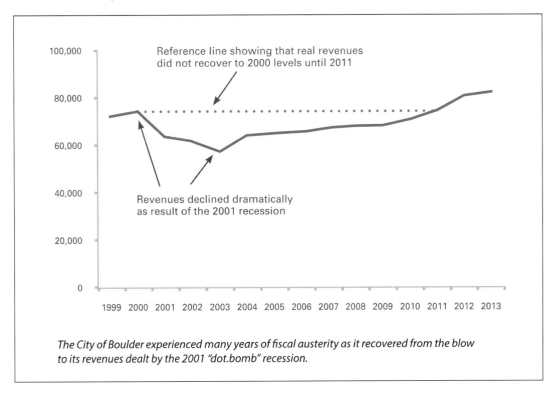

The City of Boulder experienced many years of fiscal austerity as it recovered from the blow to its revenues dealt by the 2001 "dot.bomb" recession.

the specter of federal override of Colorado's legal decision to authorize RMJ threatened to eliminate the revenue entirely. If revenues did not materialize as hoped, the City could find itself back in the structural deficit that it had worked very hard to escape from the past decade. Hence, the City Manager, Jane Brautigam, realized that a special process for budgeting this new revenue was needed – one that would produce a financially sustainable outcome for the first year and into the future. She asked Bob Eichem, CFO, to lead the development of this process. Along with his teammates, Budget Officer Peggy Bunzli and Senior Financial Analyst Elena Lazarevska, the path to projecting revenues for RMJ began.

Forecasting and Budgeting under Extreme Uncertainty

In addition to a complete lack of historical data on the activities that Boulder anticipated taxing, the team did not have knowledge of the economics underlying the RMJ industry. The first step, then, was to gather information about this new revenue source and develop a model for how it might behave. While there wasn't a shortage of opinions on the financial implications of legalization at the state and national level, the team needed information relevant to how this revenue would develop in Boulder. Fortunately, there was a local reference point that could be used: medical marijuana (MMJ). Like many states, Colorado had, since 2000, legalized the use of marijuana for medical purposes (see Exhibit 18.2 for a summary of all MMJ and RMJ taxes in Boulder). Boulder's first collections of taxes on MMJ occurred in late 2009. There were a number of MMJ dispensaries within the City limits and it was widely believed that a significant number of people were using MMJ as a substitute for the previously-illegal RMJ,[6] such that: a) the demand for MMJ might serve as a sort of bellwether of the demand for legal RMJ; and b) rather than going through the process of obtaining the special authorization necessary to purchase MMJ, many consumers might opt to simply purchase RMJ over the counter.

Exhibit 18.2 – All MMJ and RMJ Taxes in Boulder (Including Local, State, and Overlapping Jurisdictions)

Medical	Recreational	Grow Operations (Crops)
3.56% city's general sales tax 2.9% state general sales tax 1.9% overlapping govt's sales tax	3.56% city's general sales tax 3.5% city's RMJ sales tax 2.9% state general sales tax 10% state RMJ sales tax 1.9% overlapping govt's sales tax	5% city's excise tax* 15% state excise tax* *Based on value of plants grown, standard plant value set by State
8.4% total tax	**21.86% total tax**	**20% total tax**

Bob Eichem and his team engaged the City's manager of licensing for MMJ dispensaries, Mishawn Cook, in the research on the forecasting problem. First, she was able to provide him with basic information on how the local medical marijuana businesses worked. Second, she was considered a subject matter expert on medical marijuana by many people in Colorado. Since she was included in the State of Colorado's deliberations on how to regulate recreational marijuana, she was able to provide insight on how the RMJ market might form. She could also help project the portion of revenue that would be attributable to the City's share of the sales tax revenue collected by the State (where the City's share was based on its proportional share of total overall sales of RMJ in the State). Third and critical to final projections, it was assumed that a significant number of the MMJ dispensaries would want to expand or convert to RMJ sales. Mishawn was able to connect Bob with the savviest of the MMJ entrepreneurs in the community. Drawing on his own previous professional experience in the restaurant industry, Bob knew that although many people can open a restaurant and many more can offer an opinion on the trends in cuisine, only a very small portion of people are astute enough to fully understand the dynamics of the restaurant industry and have a business model that will allow them to stay in business for a long time. The emerging RMJ market was similar in this respect, so Bob needed to tap the knowledge of the few critical entrepreneurs who would be closest to the birth of a new market and could provide the keenest insights on how it might develop, answering questions, such as:

- **What is the propensity of current businesses to switch from MMJ to RMJ?** As Exhibit 18.2 shows, the tax rates on RMJ were significantly higher than MMJ. Therefore, it was important to know if current MMJ retailers would convert to selling RMJ and if their customers would make the switch as well. While the greater accessibility of RMJ would be attractive to many, the higher tax rate might discourage people from converting.

- **What is the extent to which RMJ will be an "export" business versus serving the local community?** This question was important because if the market for local RMJ businesses was essentially limited to Boulder residents, then the City's revenues would be less than if these businesses also served a significant customer base outside of Boulder. There were two facets to consider. First, grow operations, those businesses that grow the plants, were expected to produce more product than would be used in Boulder, and that the excess would be exported to other cities and counties in Colorado (e.g., those that permitted RMJ retailers, but not grow operations). Second, the RMJ retailers themselves could draw customers from outside Boulder (e.g., tourists), but if they served only local demand then new dispensaries would only further divide a fixed customer base and there would not be an increase in overall revenue that could be expected from new retailers.

- **What drives production of marijuana plants?** The City's excise tax was based on the number of plants grown. Therefore, it was necessary to have a basic understanding of what led to success in how marijuana is grown.

- **What is the long-term growth potential of this industry?** It was important to know if RMJ taxes would be a revenue that grew continuously over time or one where growth levels off quickly.

- **What amount of production would be generated by the new category of marijuana usage called marijuana-induced products?** This includes all products that have marijuana included in their production, such as oils and baked goods.

- **Would the higher tax rate on RMJ reduce or radically slow the sales of RMJ?** Two economic aspects were in play for this item. The first is price elasticity: What impact would the higher taxes have on migration from medical to recreational marijuana? The second was supply and demand: If supply was increased substantially would prices drop precipitously and greatly reduce taxes collected on RMJ?

To help organize the voluminous amount of input they were receiving into a model that could inform a forecast, Bob, Peggy, and Elena built upon the City's experience using influence diagrams to model its general sales tax revenues. The reader can refer to Chapter 3 for a discussion of influence diagrams and an example of Boulder's diagram for its general sales tax, but, to summarize, an influence diagram graphically maps out the factors thought to impact a revenue, and shows how each factor has a positive, increasing (+) influence or negative, decreasing (-) influence on other factors, and, ultimately, the revenue in question.

Exhibit 18.3 shows the influence diagram for RMJ sales tax. The finance team hypothesized that RMJ sales tax revenues would be driven by three primary factors: the number of legal purchases made (box 1), the tax rate on those purchases (box 2), and the ability of the City to collect the taxes it was owed on those purchases (box 3).

Exhibit 18.3 – City of Boulder's Influence Diagram for RMJ Sales Tax

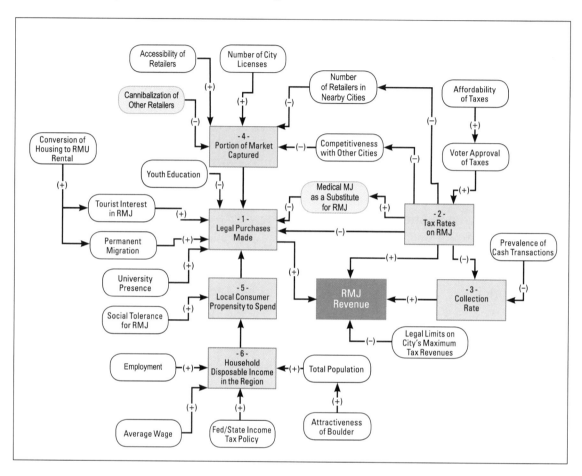

Legal purchases made were a product mainly of the portion of the RMJ market captured within the City's borders (box 4), local consumer propensity to spend (box 5), and tax rates (box 2). There were also some minor influencers, such as the potential for tourism and in-migration due to the new laws, the probable greater demand for RMJ from the City's university population, and the potential to reduce demand for RMJ by way of youth educational campaigns that the City was planning.

The factors influencing local consumerism (box 5) were much like a general sales tax, with the exception that increasing social acceptability of RMJ use could raise local propensity to spend on RMJ. However, things began to get more interesting as Bob investigated the portion of the market captured (box 4) and tax rates on RMJ (box 2). As Exhibit 18.2 showed, the combined state and local tax rates on RMJ would be considerably greater than that for MMJ. This had two principal impacts. First, it might incentivize people to use MMJ as a substitute for RMJ, thereby reducing the purchases of RMJ. Second, some people might elect to continue to purchase RMJ from the black market and avoid the tax altogether. Based on this research, Bob, Peggy, and Elena saw these potential effects of the tax rates as the key determinants of how RMJ revenues would develop.

The diagram also shows that the size of the tax rates on RMJ could impact the portion of the RMJ market captured within the City of Boulder. If the tax rates were too high, it could make Boulder retailers less competitive vis-à-vis other Colorado cities. However, because local RMJ tax rates were a relatively small portion of the total (only 3.5 percentage points of the 21.86 percent total rate), tax rate differences between Boulder and other cities were not the most important factor in play for the portion of the market captured. The most important factors were the extent to which: 1) RMJ retailers would be competing with each other for the limited demand within the City of Boulder versus attracting additional consumers from outside the City; and 2) the rate at which MMJ retailers would convert to RMJ, hence potentially contributing to intra-city RMJ retailer competition and effecting the migration of MMJ to RMJ. Ultimately, after discussion and review of the findings, the finance team concluded that the difference in the total tax rate between RMJ and MMJ meant that there would not be a major migration from MMJ to RMJ. Instead, most of the growth in RMJ would come from buyers who would prefer to purchase in the legal market instead of the illegal market.

Finally, the City needed to gauge its ability to collect the taxes it was rightfully owed (box 3). Banks were hesitant to work with MMJ or RMJ retailers because of the federal government's opposition to legalization of marijuana.[7] This meant that retailers could not process credit cards, so conducted all transactions in cash, making financial records more difficult to track. When this was combined with the considerable tax rate on RMJ, retailers potentially had the motive and opportunity to evade the tax. From the City's experience with collecting taxes and performing tax audits on MMJ dispensaries, it was evident that RMJ would also be an all-cash business, with the attendant difficulties of accurately tracking and reporting tax liabilities. However, the City's experience had also shown that most MMJ businesses wanted to be known as reputable and upstanding members of the business community. It was felt this would carry over into the RMJ businesses, especially since many of the same MMJ entrepreneurs would be entering the RMJ market. Thus, while the potential challenge to City's ability to collect the taxes it was owed was acknowledged, Boulder's forecast team did not conclude that it would have an outsized impact on how much revenue the City would collect.

Once a model for how the new taxes would work was in place, Bob was ready to work with his team in the finance department to develop a forecast and a process to use the forecast in budget decision-making. The starting point for deriving a forecast number was the existing gross sales of MMJ, since it was thought that some of these sales would migrate to RMJ. Furthermore, it was thought that MMJ sales could also be an indicator of the demand for RMJ that was currently being met by the black market. Bob's research led the finance team to conclude that between 10 percent and 20 percent of MMJ sales would migrate to RMJ and that new sales of RMJ would represent between 80 percent and 90 percent beyond current gross sales of MMJ. This level of sales would not happen immediately, but would phase in over time, as the market formed, so the team took into account the expected rate of conversion of MMJ retailers to RMJ and the extent to which new RMJ retailers would increase the total RMJ business in the City. This allowed the team to come up with a predicted interval of potential revenues and suggest a recommended estimate, which fell between the low-side and high-side estimates shown in Exhibit 18.4. The final forecast aggregated the separate forecasts for the individual marijuana taxes shown in Exhibit 18.2. This was important because an aggregate forecast will generally be more accurate because, assuming that each component forecast has an equal chance of being over or under, the errors in each individual forecast tend to cancel each other out, at least to some extent.

With these numbers in hand, it was now time to use them in the decision-making process. Because of the high level of public interest in this issue, the process had to be designed carefully in order to produce good decisions. First, Bob decided to make this process part of a special, supplemental appropriation to the budget and not part of the regular budget process. Even under the budget office's best-case estimate, marijuana-related revenues would only comprise a small portion (less than 2 percent) of the City's general fund budget. However, these revenues were commanding a disproportionate amount of attention, so if they were made a part of the regular budget process, the City risked marijuana revenues distracting from much larger and, ultimately, more important policy issues and community goals. Further, a special supplemental process would give the public the opportunity that it wanted to be heard at each meeting.

Second, Bob presented to the City Council and public the range of all potential marijuana-related revenues, from $1.7 to $2.5 million, along with the staff's recommended budget estimate of $2 million. Bob presented the forecast as an aggregate number. As well as mitigating the error of each individual forecast, the aggregate number helped prevent the discussion from getting bogged down in the details of those individual forecasts and to keep the conversation focused on the big picture. He established the historical sales of MMJ as a reference point and anchor for the audience. This helped ground the audience in a reality that they could all agree was relevant to the City's future marijuana-related revenues. He then proceeded to outline conditions under which the assumptions underlying the forecast would lead to the staff's high estimate and those that would lead to the low estimate. For example, a much higher portion of MMJ users would need to migrate to RMJ than was expected in order to reach the high-side estimate. Establishing MMJ as a reference point and showing how a very favorable performance in the forecast assumptions was needed to reach the high end of the range helped to moderate the expectations of the most optimistic participants or at least inform them that City staff had taken a deliberate and thorough approach to reaching its estimate. The influence diagram supplemented the presentation by providing transparency on all the factors that were considered when developing the forecast.

Exhibit 18.4 – Boulder's Presentation of High and Low Revenue Interval Estimates

	Based on Current MMJ Sales	50% Increase over Current MMJ Sales
City's Local RMJ Tax		
Projected RMJ Sales	$24,000,000	$36,000,000
Sales and Use Tax at 3.5% (applied to MMJ)	**$840,000**	**$1,260,000**
City of Boulder Excise Tax Rates		
Wholesale cost as % of retail cost (modeled at 40%)	40%	40%
Wholesale cost	$9,600,000	$14,400,000
Estimated City Excise Tax Collected (Excise Tax at 5%)	**$480,000**	**$720,000**
Projected Recreational Marijuana Sales		
Estimated recreational sales	$24,000,000	$36,000,000
New state sales tax rate on recreational RMJ	10.00%	10.00%
City share back from state	15%	15%
Total sales tax received by the city from state share back	**$360,000**	**$540,000**
Estimated Total Taxes if Assumptions are Met	$1,680,000	$2,520,000
	Low-Side Estimate	High-Side Estimate

Finally, although the City had to settle on a single number for the purposes of making a budgetary estimate, it still needed to recognize that there was substantial risk associated with the forecast – both in that the forecast could be wrong by a significant margin and that the federal government could attempt to put an end to RMJ sales in Colorado. Here, the City was able to draw on its history of strategic, long-term financial planning and financial resiliency – recognizing risks and being prepared to bounce back from the unexpected was part of the City's identity. Further, the City staff had been able to establish personal credibility through this history and thereby effectively lead the participants through decisions that needed to be made as part of the supplemental budget process.

Given the high level of uncertainty around the budgetary estimate of the revenue and its potential continuity into the future, the City staff recognized that it would have been imprudent to direct the revenue towards ongoing current operating or new operating expenditures. Consistent with the City's policy for non-recurring / highly volatile revenues, the budgetary revenue estimate of $2 million was divided into the following tranches:

1. The first $513,000 in revenue the City would receive was to be set aside for covering the City's estimated new costs for implementing Colorado Amendment 64 (the law that addresses personal use and regulation of marijuana), such as licensing, police services, collections, etc.

2. The next $250,000 received would go for an educational campaign to be designed to inform the community's youth about the risks of marijuana use.

3. The next $400,000 would go into a special contingency managed directly by the City Manager, to be used for covering additional costs for implementing Amendment 64 that were not known or accounted for in the City's original estimates.

4. The final $836,000 and anything additional would go into an unallocated contingency. The intent was to reassess how the new taxes were performing and then decide how to use these funds in the subsequent year's budget.

Describing the revenue estimate tranches in terms of expenditures (e.g., licensing, policing, youth education campaign), helped participants in the process better understand the forecast and its role in helping the City make financially resilient decisions.

The Aftermath: How the Forecast and Decision Worked Out

The City budgeted $2 million for marijuana tax revenues, and its final revenues were just under $2.04 million, for an error of about 1.7 percent.[8] While the forecast proved remarkably accurate, the City's risk-aware approach to forecasting and budgeting has proved prudent as well. The legal environment around marijuana sales has remained highly uncertain: as of this writing, the State of Colorado is reconsidering the amount of money it will share with local governments and the possibility remains open that the federal government could try to preempt Colorado legislation. Hence, the City will continue to treat these revenues as if they might not be available in future budgets.

The biggest unanticipated expense arose from the RMJ tax payments being made almost totally in cash. The City had to remodel a space in the finance department conducive to counting large amounts of cash, go from a bicycle to armored car service to take cash to the bank, and purchase a larger safe. These costs were relatively minor, and the City was able to fund them easily with the RMJ tax income.

The City made some of its planned expenditures, but deferred others because the anticipated need for the service did not materialize within the expected time period. For example, the City did go forward with increases in staffing to process licenses for RMJ and to administer the various other regulations associated with RMJ. Also, the City bought a new police vehicle and additional breathing masks for officers for use during any necessary confiscations.

An example of a planned expenditure that was rolled over into the following year's budget was the youth education campaign. This was deferred because more data was needed on how youth view legalization so that communications could be designed for the best effect. For the youth educational campaign and services that might yet need to be provided, the budget rollover preserves the flexibility to act when the need materializes. Bob and the City expect that future expenditures will continue to be budgeted under the assumption that revenue streams are not necessarily permanent. This practice is essential to ensuring that Boulder can continue to provide core services that are not dependent on potentially unstable revenues.

Lessons from the Boulder Experience

The experience of the City of Boulder points to a number of lessons that are generalizable to forecasting other revenues, especially when forecasting under conditions of high uncertainty:

Find a reference case or analogue, especially when there is no historical data. Boulder used MMJ as the reference case for RMJ, thereby providing a starting point for what RMJ revenues might look like. In addition to the technical benefits for forecasting, a reference case or analogue helps to ground the audience for the forecast in something tangible. In Boulder, using MMJ as a reference case helped temper expectations for RMJ revenues when the forecast was presented.

The value of an analogue is not limited to totally new revenue sources. For example, imagine that a small city has a local income tax and is dependent on a few large manufacturing plants for much of its revenue. It needs to forecast the impact of a plant closing. The ripple effects of such a closing would be difficult to predict in isolation, so the city could use the experiences of another smaller town that lost a plant as an analogue to begin to estimate the effects.

Engage subject matter experts in the forecast. Boulder engaged not only the City staff that work directly with the MMJ retailers, but sought the views of the MMJ retailers themselves to gain insight into what would determine the City's revenues. Getting the experiences of the people closest to the economic activities that generate the revenue is often invaluable.

Organize information into a model. An explicit model, like an influence diagram, forces the forecaster to clarify his or her own thinking about the revenue and allows the forecaster to share the model with others, thereby facilitating communication and feedback.

Disaggregate the analysis; aggregate the forecast. Rather than trying to estimate the sum total of all marijuana taxes for the City, Boulder examined each tax separately. Dividing the forecasting task into chunks (i.e., the City's local retail sales and use tax, excise tax, and the City's share of the State's taxes) made it easier to digest. However, for the purposes of presentation and decision-making, the individual forecasts were aggregated. This helps reduce variability in the forecast-versus-actual results and focuses the decision-makers' attention on the big picture.

Acknowledge the uncertainty in the forecast presentation. Boulder used a prediction interval to demonstrate uncertainty, but any of the methods described in Chapter 10 could accomplish the same ends. The key is to demonstrate to the audience that there is significant potential variance in the actual revenue, to describe how changes in important, real-world, tangible variables (e.g., conversion from MMJ to RMJ) can contribute to revenues coming in either high or low, and to highlight the risks that need to be mitigated through the government's budget decisions.

Design the public forum appropriately. The forum in which the forecast will be presented and decisions made must be designed to suit the situation. In Boulder's case, the high level of public interest in the revenue suggested the need for a totally separate process from the regular budget so as to not distract from larger issues in the primary budget process and to give the parties who were intensely interested in RMJ revenues a chance to be fully heard. Hence, the quality of the City's larger budget decisions was preserved and the City maintained its credibility in the eyes of the public.

Establish an environment for good decisions. Key to Boulder's success is that this is not the first time the City has successfully identified, defined, and mitigated risky situations in its financial planning. Previous successes built the credibility of the City's lead finance staff—Bob Eichem, Peggy Bunzli, and Elena Lazarevska—to lead the City through the forecasting and decision-making process. Also, it established an identity among other staff and the Council, where making strategic financial decisions is seen as a part of being a financially sustainable and resilient city.

The lesson for other local governments is twofold. First, begin to create a supportive environment for good forecasting and decision-making before those forecasts and decisions need to be made. For instance, establishing financial policies puts in place baseline "rules of the game" for making financial decisions, much as Boulder's non-recurring/volatile revenue policy did for marijuana taxes. Second, when it is time to confront difficult choices, make the link back to positive past practices. Frame the situation not as striking out in a bold new direction, but as a continuation or extension of an earlier success due to good decisions made by using strong practices in financial management and long-range fiscal planning.

Chapter 19

Conclusion

As a conclusion, we will review all of the key ideas in this this book in the form of a step-by-step checklist. It is our hope that this will help you better put the ideas into practice.

Step 1 – Problem Definition

✓ Determine your most important revenue sources in terms of total size and volatility. You will want to focus your forecasting efforts on these.

✓ Land-use patterns are a key determinant of local government revenues and land-use issues often have a high public profile. Think about the important land-use trends in your community and the implications for making an accurate forecast that speaks to the concerns of the audience.

✓ Identify any other high-profile issues that the audience will want to see addressed in the forecast presentation. It is important not to ignore issues that are highly uncertain or speculative if the audience is very interested in them. At the same time, this does not mean the issue's presumed impacts should be included in budgeted revenue. The forecaster can look for other ways to satisfy the audience's curiosity about the issue.

Step 2 – Gather Information

✓ Thoroughly investigate how your revenues work in order to develop a mental model of the forces that impact revenue yield. Having a firm understanding of how revenues work is essential to forecast accuracy and the forecast's effectiveness in impacting decisions.

✓ Gather information from a variety of sources. Other departments, other governments, academic institutions, private firms, and other entities may have different and valuable perspectives to share.

✓ Document your mental model in a format that allows you to get feedback from others. We have suggested the influence diagram format, but even a less elaborate format, like a checklist, would be useful.

✓ Make an effort to understand both general, persistent factors impacting revenue yield and special, unusual events that can cause a disruption in the environment and in prevailing trends.

✓ Forecasters should compile revenue data for as many years back as is practical. Historical data is important for using statistical forecasting techniques. It can also provide an analogue for anticipated, future events that have a historical precedent.

✓ Ideally, the data will provide information about revenues for each month or, if that is not available, each quarter. However, this may not be necessary in all cases (e.g., when revenues are very small or infrequently received).

✓ Historical data will need to be scrubbed and adjusted to maximize its predictive power. This includes: establishing uniform accounting rules so that data is recorded consistently in the accounting system of record; summarizing data into larger categories to make forecasting more efficient; finding and adjusting outliers; adjusting for one-time revenues; and making other adjustments that might be necessary to optimize predictive power.

Step 3 – Exploratory Analysis

✓ Exploring the data that the forecaster gathered in Step 2 improves the quality of the forecast by giving the forecaster insight into the quantitative forecasting techniques that are most appropriate. It also improves the forecaster's sense and feel of the data.

✓ Graphing the data is the most fundamental tool of exploratory analysis. This helps the forecaster visualize data in a way that would be much more difficult with just an inspection of the numbers.

✓ Statistics like the mean, median, and range of the data set are traditional ways to describe a data set. Histograms might be the most informative and understandable alternative in many cases.

✓ Forecasters should also look for the impacts of business cycles in the data. This will give the forecaster a better idea how revenue might behave the next time there is a downturn or upswing in the economy.

✓ Disaggregate complex forecasting problems into smaller, more manageable questions. For example, it might be easier to forecast the behavior or discrete segments of the tax base than to forecast the behavior of the entire tax base.

✓ The forecaster should look for seasonality effects in the data. If there are seasonality effects, that data can be adjusted to remove them. Some forecasting research shows that removing seasonality can reduce the size of forecast errors by up to 25 percent in some cases.

✓ Correlation analysis is a statistical method to see how changes in some variable, typically an economic or demographic one, might correspond with changes in revenue yield. If there is a correlation, the variable might be useful as a leading indicator of revenue performance.

Step 4 – Select Forecasting Methods

Judgmental Forecasting

✓ Judgmental forecasting is most appropriate when the forecaster has access to information that would not be reflected in the results from a statistical model; the expert has a history of making similar forecasts and the environment is relatively stable; or there is little or no good historical data.

✓ When judgment is used to construct a forecast, whenever possible, develop even a simple algorithm to guide the forecast. Non-statistical algorithms (also known as mathematical models) can be quite accurate, if developed with care.

✓ When using judgment, get several independent judgments rather than relying on just one.

✓ Whenever possible, find analogues or reference cases in historical experiences or the experiences of other jurisdictions. Use these to inform the judgmental forecast.

✓ Be aware that the human mind is affected by a number of cognitive biases that work against good forecasting. Take steps to help mitigate their worst effects. For example, develop a habit of actively questioning your forecast assumptions. The forecast assumptions are usually where cognitive biases are most dangerous.

✓ Recruit "fox" thinkers into the forecasting process. Fox thinkers are those that take a multidisciplinary approach to forecasting, using many ideas and changing approaches as circumstances change.

✓ Be careful with how groups are used in forecasting. Simply gathering a number of people around a table to discuss the forecast will often result in a lower quality decision. However, many heads are in fact better than one, so design the group forecasting process to mitigate the disadvantages of group forecasting while accentuating the benefits.

Extrapolation Forecasting

✓ Extrapolation techniques are a fundamental statistical forecasting technique, so they are a good option to consider for all forecasters. Most extrapolation techniques are not statistically complex and should be within the ability of most forecasters to perform. The results of our forecasting competition can be used to guide which technique might be best, given the characteristics of the data set that will be forecasted.

✓ Forecasters should use error and bias statistics like root of the mean squared error, mean absolute percent error, and mean error to measure accuracy and bias of the forecast.

✓ Extrapolation techniques may account for just the "level" of the data, while others may account for both the level and the "trend." Trend refers to an underlying tendency for the revenue to increase (or decrease) over time. If the data has a trend, it is important to pick an extrapolation technique that takes account of the trend.

✓ Extrapolation techniques that account for the trend will usually be more appropriate for long-term forecasting because the effect of a trend will be more noticeable over the long-term.

Regression Forecasting

✓ Regression forecasting is a more advanced technique. Statistical novices should stick to extrapolation.

✓ Even where the forecaster does have sufficient expertise to use regression, it will usually be best to use regression in conjunction with other techniques. Regression methods can often be very accurate, but also are more prone to making severe errors. Using regression with other methods can help balance these errors out.

✓ The most effective use of regression is to use causal forces to forecast. This requires information about the causal forces.

✓ Time-indexed regression is not a good substitute for extrapolation methods.

Step 5 – Implement Forecasting Methods

✓ Forecasts should be tested before they are used to make decisions. Out-of-sample testing, comparison to the naïve forecast, and comparison to GFOA's forecast accuracy benchmarks can all be used to test a forecast.

✓ When multiple forecasts are made using substantially different techniques, the forecaster should average the results to get a final forecast. This applies to both quantitative techniques and judgmental techniques. Research has shown that averaging forecasts improves accuracy.

✓ Making adjustments to the results produced by quantitative forecasting methods can provide a substantial increase in accuracy. However, forecasters often over-adjust forecasts. Therefore, forecasters should be selective about when they adjust a forecast, limiting adjustments to instances when the forecaster has access to important information that is not reflected in the model or when the model has weak predictive power. Adjustments should be agreed upon before the quantitative forecast results are known.

✓ Forecasters should take steps to communicate uncertainty in the forecast, such as with prediction intervals, by using a normal distribution (bell curve) to estimate uncertainty, or through Monte Carlo simulation. A common feature of these methods is to express uncertainty in clear, probabilistic terms (e.g., I am 90 percent confident that next year's revenue will be at least $20 million).

✓ Forecasters should consider scenario analyses to communicate uncertainty and expand decision-makers' thinking about how issues in the financial and economic environment could impact the government's financial health.

✓ In addition to acknowledging uncertainty in the forecast, the forecaster should help decision-makers think about strategies to mitigate the downside risk in the forecast. These strategies include reserves, short-term forecasting to give advance warning of significant variations from budgeted revenues, and budgetary contingency plans.

Step 6 – Use Forecasts

✓ The foundation to the effective use of forecasts is to create an environment that supports them. Key features of such an environment are: clear financial principles and policies; a budget process that incorporates a planning orientation, takes program performance into account when allocating resources, and takes an explicit, structured approach to weighing competing potential uses of resources against each other; and strategic, long-term financial planning.

✓ The credibility of the forecaster is essential for a forecast to influence decision-making. Credibility is a product of perceived production of valuable work, honesty, and dependability. Forecasters should take steps to increase their credibility because people routinely overestimate how credible others perceive them to be.

✓ With the above two foundational components in place, the forecaster needs to develop a presentation of the forecast that answers the questions that most interest the audience and that makes the forecast numbers understandable and relatable.

✓ Data graphics are an important part of a forecast presentation. A high-quality data graphic can enhance a presentation, but too many or low-quality graphics can clutter the presentation and impede understanding.

✓ After the forecast has been adopted, the forecaster should monitor the government's financial condition using short-term monthly or quarterly forecasts.

✓ Forecasters should develop leading indicators of revenue income to provide advance warning of downturns.

✓ The forecaster will occasionally need to update the total revenue predicted by the annual forecast. The recommended frequency of updates depends on the effectiveness of the forecast. Decision-makers will welcome more frequent updates of an effective forecast.

Step 7 – Evaluate Forecasts

✓ Learning from feedback is essential to better forecasting. Evaluating how the forecast worked and then adjusting the forecast approach should take place as an explicit step of the forecasting process. Evaluation should be honest and unflinching, but focused on learning and improvement, not on assigning blame or making excuses.

✓ The forecaster should evaluate the accuracy of the forecast. This starts by retaining a rich set of data, including the forecasts themselves, assumptions made, and judgmental adjustments made to the output of quantitative models.

✓ If the accuracy of the forecast needs to be improved, adopting more complex forecasting methods will rarely be the answer. Improving the analysis of the forecast environment, scrubbing historical data, or bringing more perspectives into the forecast (so they can be averaged) will usually be more helpful.

✓ The forecaster should evaluate the effectiveness of the forecast. The forecasters' own observation and judgment is usually going to be the most practical diagnostic of decision-makers' satisfaction with the information provided and how well the forecast is influencing decisions. The keys to improving forecast effectiveness are creating a decision-making system that supports the use of forecasting, increases forecaster credibility, and answers the questions that are of most concern to decision-makers.

Endnotes

Chapter 1

1. According to a survey conducted by GFOA and Holly Sun, a PhD candidate in Public Policy and Public Administration at George Washington University. A summary of the survey results was published in: Holly Sun. "Improving the Effectiveness of Multi-Year Fiscal Planning." *Government Finance Review*. February 2014.

2. Quote taken from: Spyros Makridakis and Michele Hibon, "The M-3 Competition: Results, Conclusions, and Implications." *International Journal of Forecasting* 16 (2000) 451–476. The "M Competitions" were a series of three forecasting accuracy tests conducted over nearly two decades by Makridakis and various colleagues. The results have been widely studied, replicated, and cited.

3. Forecasting science expert J. Scott Armstrong describes "strong empirical evidence" in favor of using quantitative over qualitative methods as a general principle of forecasting. See: J. Scott Armstrong, ed. *Principles of Forecasting*. (Kluwer Academic Publishers: Boston, MA). 2001.

4. These factors are amalgamated from a number of researchers. See for example: Robert Fildes, Paul Goodwin, Michael Lawrence, Konstantinos Nikolopoulos. "Effective Forecasting and Judgmental Adjustments: An Empirical Evaluation and Strategies for Improvement in Supply-Chain Planning" *International Journal of Forecasting*. January-March 2009.

5. Material for this excerpt adapted from: Donald N. McClosky. "The Art of Forecasting: From Ancient to Modern Times." *Cato Journal*, Vol 12., No. 1 (Spring/Summer 1992).

6. "Leading" practitioners are defined as participants in GFOA's Distinguished Budget Presentation Award program. GFOA used sampling procedures and did not survey every single participant.

7. The survey was conducted by Holly Sun, a PhD candidate at George Washington University. See the first endnote in this chapter for a full citation. This survey was conducted from a sample of governments, so it did not necessarily include all local governments. As a result, there was not necessarily a high degree of overlap in the specific agencies that participated in the accuracy and effectiveness surveys.

Chapter 2

1. We would like to acknowledge Rebecca M. Hendrick, author of *Managing the Fiscal Metropolis*, for her contribution to this section.

2. Based on estimates compiled by Paul R. Harris, Ronald D. Berkebile, and Julia M. Martin, budget/finance staff from the City of Virginia Beach in a working paper entitled "Economic Development Projects: Distinguishing between New Revenues and Spending Transfers within a Community."

3. Rebecca M. Hendrick. *Managing the Fiscal Metropolis*. (Georgetown University Press: Washington, D.C.). 2011.

4. Spyros Makridakis, Steven C. Wheelwright, and Rob J. Hyndman. *Forecasting: Methods and Applications*, 3rd ed. (John Wiley and Sons). 1998.

Chapter 3

1. Based on personal interviews with those governments that scored the highest in GFOA's survey of forecast accuracy.

2. Based on personal interviews with those governments that scored the highest in GFOA's survey of forecast accuracy.

3. In their book *Wiser*, Sunstein and Hastie cite a large body of evidence that shows that statistical groups of experts (e.g., taking the average of many experts) regularly outperform single experts in making forecasts, even when comparing the single best expert (as measured by performance in prior forecasts) to the average of all experts. See: Cass R. Sunstein and Reid Hastie. *Wiser: Getting Beyond Groupthink to Make Groups Smarter*. (Harvard Business Review Press.) 2014.

4. The "influence diagram" is a tool taken from the field of systems theory, though the approach here is highly simplified compared to the version that is typically recommended by systems theory.

5. This quote is commonly attributed to Keynes, though there is some controversy over the exact wording and if he actually said it.

6. The characteristics in this paragraph adapted from the advice of trendspotter Rohit Bhargava in: Rohit Bhargava. *Non-Obvious: How to Think Different, Curate Ideas, and Predict the Future*. (Ideaspress Publishing.) 2015.

7. The first two strategies are from: J. Scott Armstrong in "Extrapolation for Time-Series and Cross-Sectional Data." 2001.

8. Forester found that forecasts are more highly valued by the governing board when the departments' inputs into the forecast are valued by the forecaster. See: John P. Forester. "Budgetary Constraints and Municipal Revenue Forecasting." *Policy Sciences*. 24: 333-356. 1991.

9. Armstrong, J. S. *Long-Range Forecasting: From Crystal Ball to Computer*. (Wiley: New York, New York). 1978.

Chapter 4

1. Spyros Makridakis, et al. *Forecasting Methods and Applications*, 3rd ed (Hoboken, New Jersey: John Wiley and Sons). 1998.

2. Note that the table uses 2006 data that is not predicted to calculate a rate of change for 2007.

3. The term "flaw of averages" originated by Sam Savage in *The Flaw of Averages*. Wiley. 2012.

4. Histogram provided courtesy of Sam Savage author of *The Flaw of Averages*. Wiley. 2012.

5. Histogram provided courtesy of Sam Savage author of *The Flaw of Averages*. Wiley. 2012.

6. These percentages are commonly accepted measures of standard deviation derived using statistical techniques that are beyond the scope of this chapter.

7. As of the writing of this book, Excel offers multiple STDEV functions. Forecasters should Use STDEV.P if all observations are available or STDEV.S when the data are a sample. When in doubt, use STDEV.S.

8. Note that the table uses 2006 data that is not predicted to calculate a rate of change for 2007.

9. Definition from investopedia.com.

10. The calculation for a 12-month or 4-quarter moving average can be modified so that the average is centered exactly in the middle of the year – that is at 6.5 months or 2.5 quarters. In contrast, the simplified approach given in the main text places the center at 6 months or 2 quarters, which results in the average being slightly off center, but makes it easier to calculate. The loss of precision is inconsequential for the purposes of the exploratory analysis. When a moving average is being used to calculate numbers that will be used directly in forecasting, more precision is desirable.

11. J. Scott Armstrong in "Extrapolation for Time-Series and Cross-Sectional Data" in *Principles of Forecasting* (2001), discusses results obtained via the M-Competition, a study conducted by Spyros Makridakis, et al. "The accuracy of extrapolation (time series) methods: Results of a forecasting competition," *Journal of Forecasting*. 1982, pages 111-153.

12. New York State tax data are collected from numerous individual reports found at http://www.tax.ny.gov/research/collections/monthly_tax_collections.htm on July 24, 2013.

13. Very sophisticated statistical seasonality software may modestly adjust for December with these data, but simple techniques are unlikely to provide methods that improve a forecast.

14. Quantitative techniques exist to measure seasonality, but they are more complicated than what will be explained in this text.

15. Miller, D., Williams, D. (2003). "Shrinkage Estimators of Time Series Seasonal Factors And Their Effect On Forecasting Accuracy." *International Journal of Forecasting*, 19(4), pages 669-684.

16. The formula is somewhat simplified over full rigor deseasonalization in order to omit unnecessary complications.

17. As of this writing, the Excel command is "correl."

18. Mathematically astute readers may know that exponential relationships can be transformed into linear relationships (by taking the log, for example). However, most revenue forecasters will not ever need to use this technique.

19. Material from the description of FICO adapted from: Kaiser Fung. *Numbers Rule Your World*. (McGraw Hill: New York, New York). 2010.

Chapter 5

1. J. Scott Armstrong cites "strong empirical evidence" that quantitative methods generally are less biased and make more efficient use of data. See J. Scott Armstrong, "Standards and Practices for Forecasting" in J Scott Armstrong, Ed. *Principles of Forecasting*. Springer. 2006. See in particular principle 6.4 of Armstrong's chapter.

2. Phillip E. Tetlock. *Expert Political Judgment: How Good Is It? How Can We Know?* (Princeton University Press: Hoboken, New Jersey). 2005.

3. Louis Menand. "Everybody's an Expert." *The New Yorker*. December 5, 2005.

4. Nate Silver. *The Signal and the Noise: Why So Many Predications Fail – but Some Don't*. (The Penguin Press: New York, New York). 2012.

5. Robert Fildes, Paul Goodwin, Michael Lawrence, Konstantinos Nikolopoulos."Effective Forecasting and Judgmental Adjustments: An Empirical Evaluation and Strategies for Improvement in Supply-Chain Planning." *International Journal of Forecasting*. Volume 25, Issue 1, January–March 2009. Pages 3-23.

6. Michael Lawrence, Paul Goodwin, Marcus O'Connor, Dilek Onkal. "Judgmental Forecasting: A Review of Progress Over the Last 25 Years." *International Journal of Forecasting*. Vol 22. 2006. Pages 493-518.

7. Material for this section adapted from the work of Tali Sharot. See primarily Tali Sharot. *The Optimism Bias: A Tour of the Irrationally Positive Brain.* (Random House: New York). 2011.

8. Spyros Makridakis, et al. *Forecasting Methods and Applications, 3rd ed.* (Hoboken, New Jersey: John Wiley and Sons). 1998.

9. Table adapted from: Spyros Makridakis, et al. *Forecasting Methods and Applications, 3rd ed.* (Hoboken, New Jersey: John Wiley and Sons). 1998. GFOA reviewed the Makridakis' list with a group of public managers and against other sources to select the biases to highlight in this book.

10. Daniel Kahneman. *Thinking Fast and Slow.* (Farrar, Straus, and Giroux: New York). 2011.

11. Most notably, Phillip Tetlock and Dan Gardner discuss how techniques based on the ideas pioneered by Kahneman can be applied to forecasting. See: Phillip Tetlock and Dan Gardner. *Superforecasting: The Art and Science of Prediction.* Crown Publishing. 2015.

12. Nigel Harvey. "Improving Judgment in Forecasting" in J. Scott Armstrong, *Principles of Forecasting.* Springer. 2001.

13. Lawrence, et al. "Judgmental Forecasting" in *International Journal of Forecasting*, Vol 22, 2006.

14. Daniel Kahneman. *Thinking Fast and Slow.* (Farrar, Straus, and Giroux: New York). 2011.

15. Lawrence, et al. "Judgmental Forecasting." 2006.

16. The pre-mortem concept was originated by psychologist Gary Klein.

17. The improvement is almost as great as getting a second estimate from another person, according to: Phillip Tetlock and Dan Gardner. *Superforecasting: The Art and Science of Prediction.* (Crown Publishing). 2015.

18. Thomas R. Stewart. "Improving Reliability of Judgmental Forecasts" in J. Scott Armstrong, *Principles of Forecasting.* 2006.

19. Tetlock originally borrowed the basic construct from Isaiah Berlin.

20. Silver is best known for his high level of accuracy in predicting the outcomes of elections. For example, in 2012, he correctly predicted the presidential winner of all 50 states and the District of Columbia. Silver's predictions of U.S. Senate races in 2012 were correct in 31 of 33 states.

21. Adapted from: Nate Silver. *The Signal and the Noise.* (The Penguin Press: New York, New York). 2012.

22. The test has been put into an Excel spreadsheet by GFOA, using guidance from the "overcoming bias" website run by George Mason University professor of economics Robin Hanson. See: www.overcomingbias.com blog post contributed by Hal Finney, dated November 21, 2006.

23. Author of the best-selling books *Good to Great* and *Built to Last.*

24. Jim Collins. *Good to Great: Why Some Companies Make the Leap and Others Don't.* (Harper Collins: New York: New York). 2001.

25. Cass R. Sunstein and Reid Hastie. *Wiser: Getting Beyond Groupthink to Make Groups Smarter.* (Harvard Business Review Press). 2014.

26. Ibid.

27. These psychological experiments were conducted by Solomon Asch in the 1950s.

28. Cass R. Sunstein and Reid Hastie. *Wiser: Getting Beyond Groupthink to Make Groups Smarter.*

29. Ibid.

30. Chip Heath and Rich Gonzalez, "Interaction with Others Increases Decision Confidence but Not Decision Quality: Evidence Against Information Collection Views of Interactive Decision Making," *Organizational Behavior and Human Decision Processes* 61 (1995): Pages 305-326.

31. The Delphi technique was originally designed in the 1950s, but the information on the Delphi technique in this chapter is supported by Gene Rowe and George Wright in "Expert Opinions in Forecasting: The Role of the Delphi Technique" in J.S. Armstrong, *Principles of Forecasting.* 2001.

32. Gene Rowe and George Wright. "Expert Opin-

ions in Forecasting: The Role of the Delphi Technique" in J.S. Armstrong, *Principles of Forecasting.* 2001.

33. Cass R. Sunstein and Reid Hastie. *Wiser: Getting Beyond Groupthink to Make Groups Smarter.* Harvard Business Review Press. 2014.

34. The figures shown in this chapter are for teams of regular forecasters. The study also examined teams of "super-forecasters," who achieved even better results. "Super-forecasters" was the term used by the study to describe individuals who achieved superior results by following a series of specific forecasting practices. These practices are consistent with what is described in this chapter and other parts of the book concerning forecaster judgment and preparation. The study results are fully described in: Phillip Tetlock and Dan Gardner. *Superforecasting: The Art and Science of Prediction.* (Crown Publishing). 2015.

35. Modeling principles derived from two main sources. First, the work of: Frits Willem Vaandrager, Principal Investigator, Institute for Computing and Information Sciences, Department of Model-Based System Development, Radboud University Nijmegen, Netherlands. Second: Sam L. Savage. *Decision-Making with Insight.* (Thomson Learning, Belmont, California). 2003.

36. Suggestion provided by Chris Swanson, professional Excel modeler, via e-mail.

37. Sam Savage references Donald Knuth, a Stanford computer scientist.

Chapter 6

1. For the most recent M-Competition, see: Spyros Makridakis and Michele Hibon. "The M3-Competition: Results, Conclusions, and Implications." *International Journal of Forecasting.* Vol 16. 2000.

2. Spyros Makridakis, Robin M. Hogarth and Anil Gaba, "Why Forecasts Fail. What to Do Instead," *MIT Sloan Management Review*, Winter 2010.

3. The source for these and all state government tax data used in these chapters, except certain more detailed New York State data, is http://www.census.gov/govs/statetax/.

4. As of this writing, for Excel there is an Analysis Took Pak add-in for producing a moving average, but the columnar location that the add-in prefers is neither the correct "centered" location, nor the correct location for forecasting purposes. A moving average is so simple that it is easier to compute by hand.

5. Before making the forecast, the income tax data are converted to constant 2012 dollars using CPI on the assumption that income closely follows consumer prices. The forecast made from this model must be adjusted by increasing it by the expected change in CPI from 2012. Typically, CPI forecasts are obtainable from a variety of sources.

6. Note that the error statistics have been calculated to be compatible across the various examples that appear in this chapter by using only error statistics available to each calculation.

7. The Excel Analysis Tool Pak formula for SES will compute the correct result; however, it does not use common terminology. The "dampen factor" is not related to damping as discussed in this chapter. It is in fact the value 1-" as discussed in this standard expression of SES.

8. Note that in the author's experience, Excel-based methods to automate the optimization of these constants is vulnerable to returning substantially suboptimal results.

9. See: Gardner, E. S., Jr. (1999). Rule-Based Forecasting vs. Damped-Trend Exponential Smoothing. M*anagement Science, 45*(8), 1169-1176. doi: 10.2307/2634814 and Gardner, E. S., & McKenzie, E. (1985). Forecasting trends in time series. *Management Science, 31*(10), 1237-1246.

10. Phi can be optimized, but the mathematics to do so are more complex than the level of skill we want to assume our readers can access. Readers interested in Phi optimization methods can consult work by E.S. Gardner Jr. (see references in this book).

Chapter 7

1. P. Geoffrey Allen, "Econometric Forecasting" in J. Scott Armstrong, Ed. *Principles of Forecasting* (London: Kluwer Academic Publishers). 2001.

2. P. Geoffrey Allen refers to work by J. Scott Armstrong.

3. In Chapter 4 we discussed correlation analysis as a way to explore historical data and noted that correlated, but not causal, relationships are often used to successfully forecast. However, these relationships may not be stable over time, so a forecast model based on such relationships may be prone to creating significant unexpected errors.

4. The personal income tax data is the same as the time series variable for West Virginia personal income tax revenue in Chapter 6.There we had rounded it to thousands for convenience of

demonstration; here we restored its full size.

5. Data used here are from various sources: Population data http://www.be.wvu.edu/demographics/populationestimates.html, http://www.census.gov/popest/data/intercensal/st-co/index.html, http://www.census.gov/popest/data/historical/index.html; Per capita income http://bber.unm.edu/econ/us-pci.html; CPI from http://research.stlouisfed.org/fred2/

6. Any two trending variables will be highly correlated without any actual relationship.

7. The reader may recall that in Chapter 4, in the correlation analysis section, we showed how the correlation coefficient does not fully valuate a non-linear relationship. The basic concept is the same for linear regression: a linear regression equation will not adequately reflect a non-linear relationship.

8. It is similar to the number "pi" in this way: it is a repeating irrational number that has special value for mathematical applications.

9. Note that Excel has multiple logarithm functions for multiple types of logarithms (e.g., natural, common). For example, as of this writing, the function for the natural logarithm is "LN".

10. In Exhibit 7.8, we have made refinements to the default scatterplots produced by Excel, including hand-drawing the dotted line to illustrate the "n" shape.

11. Or an alternative index.

Chapter 8

1. The most widely cited forecasting competitions were held by Spyros Mikridakis and his associates. See for example: Makridakis, S., Andersen, A., Carbone, R., Fildes, R., Hibon, M., Lewandowski, R., Winkler, R. (1982). "The Accuracy of Extrapolation (Time Series) Methods: Results of a Forecasting Competition." *Journal of Forecasting*, 1(2). Pages 111-153.

2. The data sets were provided to GFOA by the local governments in response to a survey request. The governments were given a template to complete or were given the option to provide the data in a format outputted by their computerized financial systems.

3. For an in-depth explanation of the competition see: Daniel Williams and Shayne Kavanagh. "Local Government Revenue Forecast Methods: Competition/Comparison." *Journal of Public Budgeting, Accounting & Financial Management*. In press, scheduled for September 2016.

4. Put another way, the governments only provided raw data and we did all of the rest of the work to produce a forecast in order to ensure that the forecast for each government was produced in a consistent manner.

5. We invited Autobox and ForecastPro to participate in the competition based on their reputations in the forecasting software industry, generally, and their interest in local government as a potential market for their software, specifically. These packages automate the technical forecasting process almost entirely, which makes them accessible to moderately skilled forecasters, an important criteria for our competition. However, it was not our objective to perform a complete analysis of the forecasting software tools a local government might use. Rather, the objective was to find out if automatic forecasting software could provide an appreciably greater level of accuracy than using just Microsoft Excel.

6. The vendors were required to note any data preparation they performed outside of their automated forecasting functionality. Neither vendor performed any significant preparation outside of the software.

7. In the competition, we tried different variations on damped trend and Holt exponential smoothing, but these variations were minor. Readers interested in the details can consult the full article in the *Journal of Public Budgeting, Accounting & Financial Management*, cited earlier.

8. In addition to collecting data from the vendors, we received a live demonstration of ForecastPro in order to verify how the software worked and that manual intervention was not responsible for the accurate forecasts.

9. The competition used some variations on damped trend exponential smoothing that we did not describe in this book. Damped trend exponential smoothing performed well, generally, in the competition, so the explanation of damped trend exponential smoothing that is provided in this book should be sufficient for most readers. Those readers interested in learning more about the variations of exponential smoothing that were tested can consult: Williams and Kavanagh. "Local Government Revenue Forecast Methods." *Journal of Public Budgeting, Accounting & Financial Management*. In press, scheduled for September 2016.

Chapter 9

1. Story of Maine's experience adapted from: "Managing Volatile Tax Collections in State Revenue Forecasts," a research report published by the Nelson A. Rockefeller Institute of Government and the Pew Charitable Trusts in March 2015.

2. For an overview of research on forecast averaging see: J. Scott Armstrong, "Combining Forecasts," in J. Scott Armstrong, ed. *Principles of Forecasting.* (Kluwer Academic Publishers: Boston, Massachusets). 2001.

3. Spyros Makridakis and Robert L. Winkler. "Averages of Forecasts: Some Empirical Results." *Management Science.* Vol. 29, No. 9. September 1983. Pages 987-996.

4. Spyros Makridakis, Robin Hogarth, and Anil Gaba. *Dance with Chance: Making Luck Work for You.* (Oneworld Publications: Oxford, England). 2009.

5. Robert T. Clemen. "Combining Forecasts: A Review and Annotated Bibliography." *International Journal of Forecasting.* Vol 5. 1989. Pages 559-583.

6. Robert Fildes, Paul Goodwin, Michael Lawrence, Konstantinos Nikolopoulos."Effective Forecasting and Judgmental Adjustments: An Empirical Evaluation and Strategies for Improvement in Supply-Chain Planning." *International Journal of Forecasting.* Volume 25, Issue 1, January–March 2009. Pages 3-23.

7. Nada R. Sanders and Larry P. Ritzman. "Judgment Adjustment of Statistical Forecasts" in J. Scott Armstrong, Ed. *Principles of Forecasting.* 2006.

8. Michael Lawrence, Paul Goodwin, Marcus O'Connor, Dilek Onkal. "Judgmental Forecasting: A Review of Progress Over the Last 25 Years." *International Journal of Forecasting.* Vol 22. 2006. Pages 493-518.

9. Guidelines adapted from forecasting researchers. See primarily: Nada R. Sanders and Larry P. Ritzman. "Judgment Adjustment of Statistical Forecasts" in J. Scott Armstrong, Ed. *Principles of Forecasting.* 2006.

10. Williams, D. W., & Miller, D. (1999). Level-Adjusted Exponential Smoothing for Modeling Planned Discontinuities. *International Journal of Forecasting*, 15(3). pages 273-289.

11. Cass R. Sunstein and Reid Hastie. *Wiser: Getting Beyond Groupthink to Make Groups Smarter.* (Harvard Business Review Press). 2014.

12. Donald J. Boyd and Lucy Dadayan. "State Tax Revenue Forecasting Accuracy." A technical report published by the Nelson A. Rockefeller Institute of Government. September 2014.

13. In the report, Boyd and Dadayan present medians rather than the means to express their findings. We obtained Boyd and Dadayan's data and calculated the MAPE for this book. Hence, readers who consult Boyd and Dadayan's report will not find MAPE data in the format that is presented in this chapter.

Chapter 10

1. In their book *Decisive*, Chip Heath and Dan Heath cite the work of Nobel prize-winning behavioral psychologist, Daniel Kahneman. See: Chip Heath and Dan Heath. *Decisive: How to Make Better Choices in Life and in Work.* (Crown Business: New York, New York). 2013.

2. This is the conclusion reached by Chip and Dan Heath in *Decisive*.

3. This quote is usually attributed to Helmuth Karl Bernhard Graf von Moltke, a Prussian general from the late 1800s, but is actually a pithier adaption of his original statement to the same effect.

4. Nassim Nicholas Taleb. *Antifragile: Things That Gain from Disorder.* (Random House). 2014.

5. The concept of two types of risk was adapted from: Makridakis, et al. *Dance With Chance.* Oneworld Publications. 2009.

6. In reference to a judgmental forecasting competition: Phillip Tetlock and Dan Gardner. *Superforecasting: The Art and Science of Prediction.* (Crown Publishing). 2015.

7. A prediction interval is very similar to another statistical concept the reader may be familiar with: a confidence interval. The term "confidence interval" is typically used to describe the more general practice of estimating the mean of a population by defining an interval that the true mean is likely to fall within. As such, the formula for a *confidence interval* uses more general statistical terms and symbols, which we haven't covered in this book. A prediction interval is a variation on confidence intervals that uses a number of terms that we have already covered in this book.

8. Note that the z-scores shown in Exhibit 10.3 are for what is known as "two-tailed distribution," which accounts for the possibility of actual revenue falling on either side of the interval. The z-scores provided by generic, standard catalogues of z-scores are often for "one-tailed distributions," which means that it only accounts for the

possibility of actual revenue falling on one side of the interval. One-tailed z-scores can easily be converted into two-tailed scores though. For example, a 95 percent confident z-score for a one-tailed distribution is the same as a 90 percent confident z-score for a two-tailed distribution: instead of just accounting for a 5 percent chance of being outside the interval on one side, we account for a 5 percent chance of being outside of the interval on <u>both</u> sides, or 10 percent in total, or 90 percent confident.

9. Jack Soll and Joshua Klayman (2004), "Overconfidence in Interval Estimates," *Journal of Experimental Psychology: Learning, Memory, and Cognition* 30, pages 299-314.

10. "Overconfidence" does not necessarily mean that the forecaster has an inflated sense of his or her abilities. It simply means that the forecaster underestimates variability.

11. Technique taken from: Chip Heath and Dan Heath. *Decisive: How to Make Better Choices in Life and in Work.* (Crown Business: New York, New York). 2013.

12. Jack B. Soll and Joshua Klayman. "Overconfidence in Interval Estimates." *Journal of Experimental Psychology: Learning, Memory, and Cognition.* (2004), 30. Pages 299-314.

13. Ibid.

14. Prospective hindsight concept is taken from: Deborah J. Mitchell, J. Edward Russo, and Nancy Pennington (1989), "Back to the Future: Temporal Perspective in the Explanation of Facts," *Journal of Behavioral Decision-Making* 2. Pages 25-38. Ideas on how to integrate perspective hindsight with prediction intervals is taken from: Chip Heath and Dan Heath. *Decisive: How to Make Better Choices in Life and in Work.* (Crown Business: New York, New York). 2013.

15. Makridakis, et al. *Dance With Chance.* Oneworld Publications. 2009.

16. Colorado Springs was one of the first municipalities to take an explicitly risk-based approach to determining how much money to hold in its general fund reserve. See: Shayne C. Kavanagh. "A Risk-Based Analysis of General Fund Reserve Requirements." (Government Finance Officers Association). 2013.

17. Elizabeth Fu. "Implementing a Risk-Based Reserve Strategy in Colorado Springs." *Government Finance Review.* June 2015.

18. Example of normally distributed phenomena taken from: Charles Wheelan. *Naked Statistics:*

Stripping the Dread from Data. (W.W. Norton & Company: New York, New York). 2013.

19. Robin M. Hogarth and Emre Soyer. Using Simulated Experience to Make Sense of Big Data. *Special Collection of MIT Sloan Management Review: Making Better Decisions.* Winter 2015.

20. Ibid.

21. Sam L. Savage. *The Flaw of Averages: Why We Underestimate Risk in the Face of Uncertainty.* (John Wiley & Sons, Inc.: Hoboken, New Jersey). 2012.

22. "Probability Management in Financial Planning," Sam L. Savage and Shayne Kavanagh. *Government Finance Review.* February 2014.

23. "Probability Management 2.0," by Sam Savage and Melissa Kirmse, an overview of the 2nd generation of Probability Management, *ORMS Today*, October 2014.

24. Hogarth and Soyer. "Using Simulated Experience to Make Sense of Big Data." 2015.

25. The authors would like to acknowledge Thomas J. Chermack, author of *Scenario Planning in Organizations: How to Create, Use, and Assess Scenarios* for his advice on this section.

26. Shayne C. Kavanagh. "A Risk-Based Analysis of General Fund Reserve Requirements." (Government Finance Officers Association). 2013.

27. Elizabeth Fu. "Implementing a Risk-Based Reserve Strategy in Colorado Springs." *Government Finance Review.* June 2015.

Chapter 11

1. According to a survey conducted by GFOA and Holly Sun, a PhD candidate in Public Policy and Public Administration at George Washington University. A summary of the survey results were published in: Holly Sun. "Improving the Effectiveness of Multi-Year Fiscal Planning." *Government Finance Review.* February 2014.

2. These governments were identified by first surveying a random sample of winners of the GFOA's Distinguished Budget Presentation Award to find those governments that self-identify as being highly effective in using forecasts in decision-making. We then personally interviewed the finance/budget staff primarily responsible for forecasting to verify that their practices were generally consistent with what secondary research says contributes to highly effective forecasting. The sample used for this survey and the sample used to find our most accurate governments were not the same sample.

3. In their book *Switch*, Chip and Dan Heath describe an experiment originally described in: Brian Wansink. *Mindless Eating.* (New York, New York: Bantam Dell). 2006. The description that appears in this book is adapted from their description. Chip and Dan Heath. *Switch: How to Change Things when Change is Hard.* (Broadway Books: New York). 2010.

4. Deming is also considered the most influential outsider in Japan's economic resurgence in the 1950s and '60s. In fact, "The Deming Prize" has been Japan's national quality award for industry since 1951.

5. Also referenced in *Switch*. See: Lee Ross. "The Intuitive Psychologist and His Shortcomings: Distortions in the Attribution Process" in L. Berkowitz, ed. *Advances in Experimental Social Psychology*, volume 10. (New York, New York: Academic Press). 1977.

6. GFOA has been researching the potential principles since the 2012 GFOA publication *Financial Policies*. Since then, experiences from multiple government agencies and the experiences of other researches (Particularly Chip Heath and Dan Heath in *Decisive*) suggests that principles are potentially very powerful.

7. Reno's principle describes a number of specific contingent liabilities it will pay down and the order it will pay them down. This detail has been omitted to make it easier for the reader of this book to grasp the underlying intent.

8. Concept inspired by: Simon Sinek. *Start with Why: How Great Leaders Inspire Everyone to Take Action.* (Portfolio Trade; Reprint edition). 2011.

9. John P. Forester. "Budgetary Constraints and Municipal Revenue Forecasting." *Policy Sciences.* 24: Pages 333-356. 1991.

10. Wording is paraphrased from: Forester. "Budgetary Constraints and Municipal Revenue Forecasting." 1991.

11. You can also learn more about this concept in: Shayne C. Kavanagh, Jon Johnson, and Chris Fabian. "Anatomy of a Priority Driven Budget Process." (Government Finance Officers Association). 2011.

12. Descriptions of target-based budgeting and priority budgeting adapted from: Shayne Kavanagh. "Zero-Base Budgeting: Modern Experiences and Current Perspectives." (Government Finance Officers Association: Chicago, Illinois). 2011.

13. Based on a survey conducted by the author in: Shayne Kavanagh, "Zero-Base Budgeting," 2011.

For the seminal article on TBB, see: Irene S. Rubin. "Budgeting for Our Times: Target Base Budgeting." *Public Budgeting and Finance.* Fall 1991. Pages 5-14.

14. See: Robert L. Bland and Irene S. Rubin. *Budgeting: A Guide for Local Governments.* (International City/County Management Association). 1997. Page 14.

15. Based on a survey conducted by the author in: Shayne Kavanagh, "Zero-Base Budgeting," 2011. The survey was addressed to winners of the GFOA's Distinguished Budget Presentation Award, a group that is presumably more favorably predisposed to towards progressive budget reforms than local governments on average.

16. Priority-based budgeting was first discussed under the name "Budgeting for Outcomes" in *The Price of Government* by David Osborne and Peter Hutchinson (Basic Books, 2006). The concept has evolved since then. For a discussion of the variety of priority-based budgeting methods in use by local government practitioners, see: Shayne C. Kavanagh, Jon Johnson, and Chris Fabian. "Anatomy of a Priority Driven Budget Process." (Government Finance Officers Association). 2011.

17. Based on a survey conducted by the author in: Shayne Kavanagh, "Zero-Base Budgeting," 2011.

18. Daniel Kahneman. *Thinking Fast and Slow.* (Farrar, Straus, and Giroux. New York). 2001.

19. See the GFOA publication *Financing the Future: Long-Term Financial Planning for Local Governments.*

20. The survey, was developed and performed by Holly Sun in collaboration with one of the authors. It was sent to 1,341 governments in March 2013. Survey questions were primarily focused on multiyear planning practices in the general fund. The response rate was 41.5 percent, with 559 responses. GFOA Distinguished Budget Presentation Award winners made up the sampling groups. Survey responses came from 44 U.S. states and several Canadian provinces, representing a variety of local governments including municipalities, counties, special taxing districts, and two state governments. Most survey respondents were directors or senior managers who oversee budget or finance. Because these findings are not from a random sample of all local governments, readers should not make generalizations of all local governments based on the results. The survey results that are presented in this chapter are taken from: Holly Sun. "Improving the Effectiveness of Multi-Year Financial Planning." *Government Finance*

Review. February 2014.

21. James March. *A Primer on Decision-Making: How Decisions Happen.* (New York: Free Press). 1994.

22. Example adapted from: Chip Heath and Dan Heath. *Switch: How to Change Things When Change is Hard.* (New York: Broadway Books). 2010.

23. Chip Heath and Dan Heath. *Made to Stick: Why Some Ideas Survive and Others Die.* (Random House). 2007.

24. Roderick M. Kramer, "Rethinking Trust," *Harvard Business Review*, June 2009.

25. Ulrich Boser. *The Leap: The Science of Trust and Why it Matters.* (Amazon Publishing: New York, New York). 2014.

26. We would like to acknowledge Gerald T. Gabris, Distinguished Teaching Professor, Division of Public Administration, Northern Illinois University, for his contribution to this exhibit.

27. From personal interview with finance staff from this government. Names have been withheld in this case due to the sensitivity of the information.

28. Consensus forecasting has been recommended to state officials by: The Nelson A. Rockefeller Institute of Government; The Pew Charitable Trusts; The Volcker Alliance; and the Center on Budget and Policy Priorities, among others. See: "Managing Volatile Tax Collections in State Revenue Forecasts." *The Nelson A. Rockefeller Institute of Government and the Pew Charitable Trusts.* March 2015. "Truth and Integrity in State Budgeting." *The Volcker Alliance.* 2015. "Budgeting for the Future." *Center on Budget and Policy Priorities.* February 2014.

Chapter 12

1. Description of the Stanford experiment adapted from *Made to Stick*. Chip Heath and Dan Heath. *Made to Stick: Why Some Ideas Survive and Others Die.* (Random House). 2007.

2. Chip and Dan Heath point out that effective messages make abstract concepts more concrete. Chip Heath and Dan Heath. *Made to Stick: Why Some Ideas Survive and Others Die.* (Random House). 2007.

3. This method was originated by: David Osborne and Peter Hutchinson. *The Price of Government: Getting the Results We Need in an Age of Permanent Fiscal Crisis.* (Basic Books). 2006.

4. Total personal income for the community is calculated by multiplying Redmond's per capita income from the U.S. Census Bureau's "American Community Survey" by the total population of Redmond. While this does not capture income from Redmond's commercial sector, the City still finds it a useful proxy.

5. David Spiegelhalter, Mike Pearson, and Ian Short. "Visualizing Uncertainty About the Future" *Science* Vol. 333. Page 9. September 2011.

6. Chip and Dan Heath posit that when messages present something that is unexpected to the audience, it gets their attention: Chip Heath and Dan Heath. *Made to Stick: Why Some Ideas Survive and Others Die.* (Random House). 2007.

7. This story is from the consulting experiences of one of the authors of this book.

8. Chip and Dan Heath advocate for including an emotional component to messages. Chip Heath and Dan Heath. *Made to Stick: Why Some Ideas Survive and Others Die.* (Random House). 2007.

9. Heath and Heath. *Made to Stick.* 2007.

10. Christopher Chabris and Daniel Simons. *The Invisible Gorilla: And Other Ways our Intuitions Deceive Us.* (Crown Publishers: New York). 2010.

11. Chip and Dan Heath point out that stories are important for helping audiences absorb a message. Chip Heath and Dan Heath. *Made to Stick: Why Some Ideas Survive and Others Die.* (Random House). 2007.

12. Edward R. Tufte. *Visual Explanations: Images and Quantities, Evidence and Narrative.* (Graphics Press). 1997.

13. Ibid.

14. Ibid.

15. Ibid.

16. Jerry Cleaver. *Immediate Fiction: A Complete Writing Course.* (New York, New York: St. Martin's Griffin). 2005.

17. Tufte. *Visual Explanations.* 1997

18. Estimates are that about 8 percent of men in the Western world are affected by color blindness and about 0.5 percent of women. Figures are based on one of the author's review of a number of support and advocacy websites for the color blind.

19. Noah Iliinsky. "Choosing Visual Properties for Successful Visualizations." (IBM Corporation). 2013.

20. These lines are called the "Müller-Lyer illusion" and were devised by Franz Carol Müller-Lyer, a German sociologist, in 1889. Müller-Lyer, FC (1889), "Optische Urteilstäuschungen"; *Archiv für*

Physiologie Suppl. Pages 263-270.

21. Research shows that where you were born and raised can affect how susceptible you are to the Müller-Lyer illusion. North Americans and Europeans are around 90 percent susceptible. People outside these categories are about 80 percent susceptible. See: Marshall H. Segall, Donald T. Campbell, Melville J. Herskovits. "Cultural Differences in the Perception of Geometric Illusions." *Science*. New Series, Vol. 139, No. 3556 (February 22, 1963). Pages 769-777.

22. Richard L. Gregory, *Eye and Brain*, McGraw Hill, 1966.

23. This pie chart was developed by one of the authors. The quantities represented by the slices adds up to 100, where: A = 30; B = 12.5; C = 25; D = 20; and E = 12.5. The chart was inspired by a blog post on www.businessinsider.com date June 17, 2013, by Walter Hickey called "The Worst Chart In The World."

24. Based on an average of annual US inflation data from the US Bureau of Labor Statistics for 1983 through 2014, plus and minus one standard deviation and rounded to the nearest half percent.

25. For a discussion of the various types of price indices that a government might use and other considerations in applying price indices to expenditures, see: "GFOA Best Practice: Inflationary Indices in Budgeting." (Government Finance Officers Association). 2010. www.gfoa.org.

26. Tufte. *Visual Explanations*. 1997.

27. Colin Wheildon. *Type and Layout: How Typography and Design Can Get your Message Across - Or Get in the Way*. (Berkeley, California: Strathmoor Press). 1995.

28. While we did not find rigorous evidence to support this point, it appears to be a widely held belief among graphic designers.

29. For more information on budgeting salaries and wages, see: "GFOA Best Practice: Effective Budgeting of Salary and Wages." March 2010. www.gfoa.org.

30. See, for example, the forecasts produced by US Department of Health and Human Services, Centers for Medicare & Medicaid Services or the PwC's Health Research Institute.

31. For a list of indices and other strategies to calculate inflation for government services, see: "GFOA Best Practice: Inflationary Indices in Budgeting." March 2010. www.gfoa.org.

32. For more information on linking the capital budget to a capital improvement plan, see: "GFOA Best Practice: Incorporating a Capital Project Budget in the Budget Process." January 2007. www.gfoa.org.

33. For the structure of a long-term capital improvement plan see: "GFOA Best Practice: Multi-Year Capital Planning." February 2006. www.gfoa.org.

34. For considerations in evaluating the cost of different types of capital projects, see: Joseph P. Casey and Michael J. Mucha, eds. *Capital Project Planning and Evaluation: Expanding the Role of the Finance Officer*. (Government Finance Officers Association: Chicago, Illinois). 2007.

Chapter 13

1. Story of Greenspan's use of cardboard boxes as a leading indicator taken from: Bruce D. McDonald, III. "A 'Dirty' Approach to Efficient Revenue Forecasting." *Journal of Public and Nonprofit Affairs*. March 2015.

2. The predictive power of the fortunes of the music industry on the City of Seattle's revenue was demonstrated in: McDonald. "A 'Dirty' Approach to Efficient Revenue Forecasting." March 2015.

3. Phillip Tetlock and Dan Gardner. *Superforecasting: The Art and Science of Prediction*. (Crown Publishing). 2015.

4. John P. Forrester. "Budgetary Constraints and Municipal Revenue Forecasting." *Policy Sciences*. November 1991, 24 (4). Pages 333-356.

Chapter 14

1. Phillip Tetlock and Dan Gardner. *Superforecasting: The Art and Science of Prediction*. (Crown Publishing). 2015.

2. Based on a personal conversation between one of the authors and Doug Hubbard, author of: *How to Measure Anything: Finding the Value of Intangibles in Business, 3rd Ed.* (Wiley). 2014.

3. Steven C. Wheelwright and Darral G. Clark. "Corporate Forecasting: Promise and Reality." *Harvard Business Review*. November-December 1976.

4. Spyros Makridakis, Steven C. Wheelwright, and Rob J. Hyndman. *Forecasting: Methods and Applications, 3rd Edition*. (John Wiley and Sons). 1998.

5. Bismarck's quote has been translated in various forms. For the record, we do not necessarily totally agree with his sentiments!

Chapter 15

1. "America's Vulnerable Economy." *The Economist.* November 15, 2007.

2. From: Simon Potter, "The Failure to Forecast the Great Recession" in *Liberty Street Economics*, a blog produced by Federal Reserve Bank of New York. http://libertystreeteconomics.newyorkfed.org.

3. "America's Vulnerable Economy." *The Economist.* November 15, 2007.

4. Note that the model used additional distribution methods for monthly expenditure forecasts.

Chapter 16

1. "City of Baltimore Is on a Path to Financial Ruin, Report Says." www.foxnnews.com. February 6, 2013.

2. From a statement made by the Mayor to the Associated Press. The last part of the statement makes reference to the fact that Baltimore is not among those older industrial cities that have experienced default or receivership.

3. "The Mayor Goes Out on a Limb." *The Baltimore Sun*. February 11, 2013.

4. "Summary: Baltimore Mayor & City Council, Maryland; Appropriations; General Obligation; Joint Criteria" Standard & Poor's. July 22, 2014.

5. In an editorial that was critical of the Mayor's handling of the civil unrest, the *Baltimore Sun* did acknowledge the work the Mayor had done to put the City on firmer financial footing. See: "Rawlings-Blake gets defensive." *Baltimore Sun*. May 13, 2015.

Chapter 17

1. Steve Kroft. "Falling Apart: America's Neglected Infrastructure." CBS News. November 23, 2014.

2. GFOA would like to thank the following staff from the Town of Gilbert for their assistance and involvement: Patrick Banger, Town Manager; Marc Skocypec, Assistant Town Manager; Rod Buchanan, Parks and Recreation Department Director; Dawn Marie Buckland, former Budget Director; Amber Costa, Budget Administrator; Gabriel Engeland, former Assistant to the Town Manager; Andrew Jackson, Water Distribution Superintendent; Laura Lorenzen, Management and Budget Analyst; Rick Kilborn, Utility Supervisor; Mark Kramer, Information Technology Director; Kenneth C. Morgan, Public Works Department Director; Cris Parisot, Management and Budget Analyst; Kelly Pfost, Budget Director; and Mary Vinzant, Assistant to the Town Manager.

3. Gilbert does have a property tax that is used exclusively to pay down debt that the Town has issued.

4. The sources for this information are the budget offices of the Town of Gilbert and the City of Tempe. Both offices develop comparisons of the eight larger cities in the region: Gilbert, Chandler, Scottsdale, Tempe, Phoenix, Glendale, Peoria, and Mesa.

5. The Town's customized forecasting models for each of its enterprise funds were created as part of a comprehensive utility rate study by Burton & Associates, Inc., a financial management consulting firm.

6. The example graphic does not use actual figures from Gilbert's budget. Approximations are used to more clearly illustrate what Gilbert found.

Chapter 18

1. From www.regulatemarijuna.org, a website advocating for Amendment 64 on the basis of its similarity to alcohol regulation.

2. The voters of the State of Washington also passed a comparable marijuana reform initiative, Washington Initiative 502, on November 6, 2012, but the implementation of the legislation took place on a slower schedule than Colorado.

3. While decriminalization of marijuana possession and personal use has occurred in a number of developed countries, never before has complete regulation of retail, wholesale, and manufacture of marijuana occurred on the scale authorized by the Colorado legislation.

4. "Amendment 64 Would Produce $60 Million in New Revenue and Savings for Colorado." Colorado Center on Law and Policy. August 16, 2012.

5. Estimate pertained to fiscal year 2014/15. "The Fiscal Impact of Amendment 64 on State Revenues." Colorado Futures Center, Colorado State University. April 24, 2013.

6. John Hudak of the Brooking Institution is quoted as saying that it was an "open secret" in Colorado that many MMJ users were really recreational users and that a legal RMJ market could draw those users into legitimate RMJ. See: Christopher Ingraham. "Colorado Marijuana Tax Revenues Surge as Recreational Sales Surpass Medical." *Washington Post*, September 11, 2014.

7. Banks were concerned that transacting with MMJ/RMJ retailers would put them at risk of prosecution under existing federal drug and money laundering statutes.

8. The error of 1.7 percent uses precise actual revenue figures, not the rounded value of $2.04 million.

Index

Benefits of GFOA Membership

For over a century, government finance professionals have relied upon the Government Finance Officers Association (GFOA) to provide timely information, practical educational opportunities, high-quality professional publications, and the latest information on best practices.

In doing so, the GFOA offers public-sector finance professionals an unparalleled opportunity to:

- obtain "how-to" instruction on a wide range of financial topics,
- enhance their technical skills,
- broaden their knowledge and deepen their expertise,
- achieve professional recognition,
- coordinate efforts with colleagues,
- develop leadership skills, and
- network with peers.

Members receive the latest information on developments in all aspects of public finance. They also enjoy many opportunities to participate in continuing professional education training that fosters their professional growth and career advancement. Naturally, members receive special discounts on GFOA products and services.

For information on how you can become a GFOA member, please visit *www.gfoa.org*, or e-mail the GFOA at *membership@gfoa.org*.